PREVENTIVE NEGOTIATION

PREVENTIVE NEGOTIATION
Avoiding Conflict Escalation

I. William Zartman

CARNEGIE COMMISSION ON PREVENTING DEADLY CONFLICT

CARNEGIE CORPORATION OF NEW YORK

ROWMAN & LITTLEFIELD PUBLISHERS, INC.

Lanham • Boulder • New York • Oxford

ROWMAN & LITTLEFIELD PUBLISHERS, INC.

Published in the United States of America
by Rowman & Littlefield Publishers, Inc.
4720 Boston Way, Lanham, Maryland 20706
www.rowmanlittlefield.com

12 Hid's Copse Road
Cumnor Hill, Oxford OX2 9JJ, England

British Library Cataloguing in Publication Information Available

Library of Congress Cataloging-in-Publication Data

Preventive negotiation : avoiding conflict escalation / edited by I. William Zartman.
    p. cm.—(Carnegie Commission on Preventing Deadly Conflict series)
    Includes bibliographical references and index.
    ISBN 0-8476-9894-7 (cloth : alk. paper)—ISBN 0-8476-9895-5 (paper : alk. paper)
    1. Diplomacy. 2. Negotiation. 3. Conflict management. 4. International relations. I.
Zartman, I. William. II. Series

JZ1305 .P74 2000
327.1'7—dc21

99-087905

Printed in the United States of America

⊗™ The paper used in this publication meets the minimum requirements of American
National Standard for Information Sciences—Permanence of Paper for Printed Library
Materials, ANSI/NISO Z39.48-1992.

This book is dedicated to
The PIN Group
Rudolf, Franz, Victor, Olivier, Paul, Gunnar, and Ulrike,
an extraordinary venture in international intellectual collaboration
in its twelfth year
and to
Dr. David Hamburg,
a tireless physician to an ailing world,
in his seventy-fifth year.

ABOUT THE
Carnegie Commission on Preventing Deadly Conflict Series

Carnegie Corporation of New York established the Carnegie Commission on Preventing Deadly Conflict in May 1994 to address the threats to world peace of intergroup violence and to advance new ideas for the prevention and resolution of deadly conflict. The Commission is examining the principal causes of deadly ethnic, nationalist, and religious conflicts within and between states and the circumstances that foster or deter their outbreak. Taking a long-term, worldwide view of violent conflicts that are likely to emerge, it seeks to determine the functional requirements of an effective system for preventing mass violence and to identify the ways in which such a system could be implemented. The Commission is also looking at the strengths and weaknesses of various international entities in conflict prevention and considering ways in which international organizations might contribute toward developing an effective international system of nonviolent problem solving. The series grew out of the research that the Commission has sponsored to answer the three fundamental questions that have guided its work: What are the problems posed by deadly conflict, and why is outside help often necessary to deal with these problems? What approaches, tasks, and strategies appear most promising for preventing deadly conflict? What are the responsibilities and capacities of states, international organizations, and private and nongovernmental organizations for undertaking preventive action? The Commission issued its final report in December 1997.

The books are published as a service to scholars, students, practitioners, and the interested public. While they have undergone peer review and have been approved for publication, the views that they express are those of the author or authors, and Commission publication does not imply that those views are shared by the Commission as a whole or by individual Commissioners.

ABOUT THE
Processes of International Negotiation (PIN) Program of the
International Institute of Applied Systems Analysis (IIASA)

Since 1988, the PIN Program at IIASA in Laxenburg, Austria, has been conducted by an international Steering Committee of scholars, meeting triannually to develop and propagate new knowledge about the processes of negotiation. The Committee conducts an annual workshop devoted to the current collective publication project and involving scholars from a wide spectrum of countries, in order to tap a broad range of international expertise and to support scholarship on aspects of negotiation. It also offers mini-conferences on international negotiations in order to disseminate and encourage research on the subject. Such "road shows" have been held at the Argentine Council for International Relations, Beijing University, the Center for Conflict Resolution In Haifa, the Center for the Study of Contemporary Japanese Culture, the Netherlands Institute of International Relations-Clingendael, the Swedish Institute for International Relations, the University Hassan II in Casablanca, and the University of Helsinki. The Program publishes a semiannual newsletter, PINPoints, and sponsors a network of over 4,000 researchers and practitioners in negotiation. The Program is supported by the Hewlitt Foundation and this current project has been supported by the Carnegie Commission. Contact: neudeck@iiasa.ac.at.

The Carnegie Commission Series

Published in the series:

For orders and information, please address the publisher:
Rowman & Littlefield Publishers, Inc.
4720 Boston Way
Lanham, MD 20706
1-800-462-6420
Visit our website at www.rowmanlittlefield.com

Selected Reports Available from the Commission

John Stremlau with Helen Zille, *A House No Longer Divided: Progress and Prospects for Democratic Peace in South Africa*, July 1997.

Nik Gowing, *Media Coverage: Help or Hindrance in Conflict Prevention*, September 1997.

Cyrus R. Vance and David A. Hamburg, *Pathfinders for Peace: A Report to the UN Secretary-General on the Role of Special Representatives and Personal Envoys*, September 1997.

Preventing Deadly Conflict: Executive Summary of the Final Report, December 1997.

Gail W. Lapidus with Svetlana Tsalik, eds., *Preventing Deadly Conflict: Strategies and Institutions*, Proceedings of a Conference in Moscow, Russian Federation, April 1998.

Scott Feil, *Preventing Genocide: How the Early Use of Force Might Have Succeeded in Rwanda*, April 1998.

Douglas Lute, *Improving National Capacity to Respond to Complex Emergencies: The U.S. Experience*, April 1998.

John Stremlau, *People in Peril: Human Rights, Humanitarian Action, and Preventing Deadly Conflict*, June 1998.

Tom Gjelten, *Professionalism in War Reporting: A Correspondent's View*, June 1998.

John Stremlau and Francisco R. Sagasti, *Preventing Deadly Conflict: Does the World Bank Have a Role?* June 1998.

Edward J. Laurance, *Light Weapons and Intrastate Conflict: Early Warning Factors and Preventive Action*, July 1998.

Donald Kennedy, *Environmental Quality and Regional Conflict*, December 1998.

George A. Joulwan and Christopher C. Shoemaker, *Civilian-Military Cooperation in the Prevention of Deadly Conflict: Implementing Agreements in Bosnia and Beyond*, December 1998.

Essays on Leadership (by Boutros Boutros-Ghali, George Bush, Jimmy Carter, Mikhail Gorbachev, and Desmond Tutu), December 1998.

M. James Wilkinson, *Moving Beyond Conflict Prevention to Reconciliation: Tackling Greek-Turkish Hostility*, June 1999.

Graham T. Allison and Hisashi Owada, *The Responsibilities of Democracies in Preventing Deadly Conflict: Reflections and Recommendations*, March 1999.

To order *Power Sharing and International Mediation in Ethnic Conflicts* by Timothy Sisk, co-published by the Commission and the United States Institute of Peace, please contact USIP Press, P.O. Box 605, Herndon, VA 22070, USA; phone (800) 868-8064 or (703) 661-1590.

Full text or summaries of these reports are available on the Commission's web site: http://www.ccpdc.org

To order a report or to be added to the Commission's mailing list, contact:
Carnegie Commission on Preventing Deadly Conflict
1779 Massachusetts Avenue, NW, Suite 715
Washington, DC 20036-2103
Phone: (202) 332-7900 Fax: (202) 332-1919

Members of the PIN Steering Committee

The PIN Series of Publications

Victor Kremenyuk, ed., *International Negotiation: Analysis, Approaches, Issues* (Jossey-Bass 1991).

Gunnar Sjöstedt, ed., *International Environmental Negotiations* (Sage 1993).

G. O. Faure and Jeffrey Z. Rubin, eds., *Culture and Negotiation: The Resolution of Water Disputes* (Sage 1993; UNESCO, Chinese edition).

Bertram I. Spector, Gunnar Sjöstedt, and I. William Zartman, eds., *Negotiating International Regimes: Lessons Learned from UNCED* (Nijhoff 1994).

I. William Zartman, ed., *International Multilateral Negotiations: Approaches to the Management of Complexity* (Jossey-Bass 1994; Keio University Press, Japanese edition).

Gunnar Sjöstedt and Victor Kremenyuk, eds., *International Economic Negotiations* (Elgar 2000).

I. William Zartman and Jeffrey Z. Rubin, eds., *Power and Negotiation* (University of Michigan Press 2000).

I. William Zartman, ed., *Preventive Negotiation: Avoiding Conflict Escalation* (Rowman & Littlefield 2001).

Rudolf Avenhaus, Victor Kremenyuk, and Gunnar Sjöstedt, eds., *Containing the Atom: International Negotiations on Nuclear Security and Safety* (in press).

Gunnar Sjöstedt and Winfried Lang, eds., *Professional Cultures: Negotiating among Negotiators* (in press).

Guy Olivier Faure, ed., *How People Negotiate* (in press).

Contents

Acknowledgments

We are grateful to the Hewlitt Foundation for support of the PIN Program, to the Carnegie Commission for support for the Preventive Negotiation Project, and to the Swedish Institute of International Relations for hosting the project workshop on June 8–9, 1997. Thanks are given to Ulrike Neudect for her administrative skills, and to Linda Carlson, the world's best research librarian, for her help in extremis in final sourcing.

1

Preventive Diplomacy: Setting the Stage

I. William Zartman

W ere it not for the frequent practice of preventive diplomacy on many levels, this conflicted world would be a much more hostile place than it is. In the current interest on the prevention of conflict, most authoritatively articulated in the seminal work of former UN Secretary-General Boutros Boutros-Ghali (1992, 1995), the search has turned to new ways of blocking conflict escalation and managing violence. But much can also be learned from the many ways in which these goals have been accomplished in the past, particularly through the effective exercise of negotiation to handle issues before they became problems and problems before they became violent conflicts. Because conditions and characteristics of this activity differ by issue, it is hard to begin with broad generalizations that cover all the types of conflict in which preventive diplomacy may be practiced. But by examining practices with a focus on the particular methods associated with particular problems, insights from one issue area can be made available for use elsewhere.

Thus, unlike most studies of preventive diplomacy, this book will focus on preventive diplomacy by negotiation as practiced in different issue areas, in the belief that only if the differences as well as similarities among issues are recognized can these efforts benefit from each other. Also, unlike most studies of preventive diplomacy, this analysis emphasizes process, not simply outcomes or even tools but the way in which tools are and can be used to achieve outcomes, for it is no use identifying the Promised Land if one does not know how to get there. This introduction will examine prevention, negotiation, and issues, in turn.

Prevention

The most authoritative and comprehensive definition of preventive diplomacy is offered by Secretary-General Boutros Boutros-Ghali (1995, 45): "Preventive diplomacy is action to prevent disputes from arising between parties, to prevent existing disputes from escalating into [violent] conflicts and to limit the spread of the latter when they occur."

The element of violence has been added to his words to make explicit a characteristic that is inherent in the rest of the UN secretary-general's Agenda for Peace. So defined, the subject is still very broad. A more restricted version of the definition is necessary in order to have a subject focused enough to analyze. Preventing disputes—here called conflicts—from arising is a tall order and goes back so far into the nature of relations among parties on any given issue that it becomes analytically, if not practically, unmanageable. But if attention can be focused successfully on the middle element, escalation, then there is no need to be concerned about the spread of conflicts. So it is escalation and violence that become the principal targets of preventive action as discussed here.

Although some preach "provention," it is unlikely that conflict can be eliminated from human interaction. Conflict "provention" or transformation is a worthy goal in the long run but one that is necessarily subsequent to and dependent on conflict management—the demotion of conflict from the level of violence to that of politics. Conflict prevention alone, in the sense of reducing escalation and violence, is such a daunting challenge that it deserves concentrated effort and all the attention of this study. The 1998 Ecuador-Peru boundary settlement, for example, may not in itself have created a new conflict-transforming relationship between the two neighbors, but it was a necessary prelude—a necessary if not sufficient condition—to doing so (Nordquist, in this volume). This is not to say that conflict transformation is a meaningless goal, unworthy of effort. To the contrary, conflict once managed cannot stay so unless further attention is devoted to its gradual resolution and eventual transformation into a positive relationship. Thus, dealing with conflict does not end with prevention and management, but it does start there.

Two different types of conflict are the subjects of prevention. One is the more commonly referred conflict between parties, also known as distribution or collaboration conflict, in which incompatible positions or demands send the parties searching for the means to prevail over each other. As long as incompatibilities are unpursued or unescalated, parties can hold different positions without impinging on each other. But if each party's position blocks the other's and achievement of their goals is important to them, the participants turn to muster the means of pursuit, first political and then violent. For example, cultural differences can exist side by side within the same state, but when they carry implications of sovereignty, they invoke an escalation of means to achieve a new expression of the goal (Ayissi, in this volume). The early challenge is to keep the parties satisfied in the expression of their cultural differences without impinging on each other; the challenge in the next phase becomes one of devising ways to achieve as much of the goals as possible— using the various means of concession, compensation, and reframing that are the subject of negotiation analysis—before the search for the means to prevail overcomes the possibility of a common agreement (Hopmann 1996; Pruitt and Carnevale 1993; Zartman and Berman 1982; Walton and McKersie 1965). Here, the urgency of prevention depends on the cost of escalation as compared to the cost of compromise (Young 1975, 135, 263).

In the second type of conflict—conflict against nature—the parties face a common external threat. Such conflicts generally involve public goods or bads (externalities). Basically, the parties should cooperate against the danger, but their degree of cooperation will depend on the degree of threat and benefit to each and the degree of cooperation required (Taylor 1987). Thus, conflicts against nature can also entail conflicts among parties, but the two differ in regard to the position of the adversary within the conflict. By the same token, conflicts among parties can also involve conflicts against nature, as parties get caught up in the dynamics of escalation that are seemingly beyond their control (sometimes known as "intransitive escalation") (Smoke 1977; Zartman and Faure 2000). In this case, the parties have the same common interest in bringing these dynamics under control as they do when faced with an external threat, such as global warming. The threat that a peace process will be derailed or the threat of natural disasters or security escalations can make opponents allies, even though they may have different degrees of interest in combating the external threat (Sisk, Lang, Goodby, and Kremenyuk, in this volume). In such a situation, the urgency of prevention depends on the distant costs of the danger as compared to the present costs (and benefits) of prevention.

Conflict is not like a house fire, an unmitigated evil, and preventive diplomacy is not like fire fighting, an unquestioned social good. There are a number of problems and ambiguities in the practice of preventing violent conflict. To begin with, conflict is a universal condition, inevitable, often necessary, and sometimes beneficial. It cannot be exorcised from human relations, and it is present wherever there are incompatibilities that prevent both parties' demands from being met at the same time (Deng et al. 1997). Establishing priorities, allocating resources, setting standards, creating institutions, and providing for orderly methods of making choices are basic means of handling conflict. Only when such methods are not firmly in place and carefully followed does conflict get out of hand and turn violent. And it is the violent expression of conflict that is most properly the focus of preventive diplomacy. If nonviolent means of handling conflicts are not available or if such means are available but are not employed, negotiations are needed to prevent the conflict from turning to violent means. As this introductory discussion has already shown, negotiation, which is designed to prevent escalation and violence, also and often depends on the very threat of escalation and violence to make the parties realize that heightened conflict would be more expensive than reducing or restructuring goals.

Thus, paradoxically, intensity may be a prerequisite for prevention, whether the conflict is between parties or against nature. Ripeness theory indicates that conflicts are managed best (and, it appears, only) when they are at the level of a mutually hurting stalemate (Zartman 1983, 1989, 2000; Touval and Zartman 1985). Although such mutual perceptions of pain can come at any level in a conflict, they are generally associated with relatively intense conflictual behavior. Trade wars carry normally peaceful commercial competition into pressure tactics to make others hurt (Conybeare 1987; Sjöstedt, in this volume); cooperation to control environmental effects comes about when the parties finally become aware of the impending pain of their conflict with nature (and not before) (Porter and Brown 1996; Chasek 2000). Mutually hurting stalemate occurs when the parties perceive that they are suffering in their current deadlock: They realize they cannot ignore the conflict and cannot escalate their way unilaterally to victory at an acceptable cost. Consequently, high levels of conflict would seem to be required before preventive diplomacy can take hold.

Happily, experience seems to indicate the contrary, somewhat by default and largely unrecorded. In fact, many conflicts never reach a high intensity level but are managed at a lower level, before much power and commitment are invested in them. The lessons of that reality are not very clear, however. Is resolution reached because a mutually hurting stalemate is perceived at a lower level of investment or because preventive diplomacy is able to work under such conditions even before a deadlock is perceived? Because most of the work on preventive diplomacy focuses on cases of high intensity (Jentleson 2000), it is not yet possible to answer that question.

The link, however, seems to lie in escalation, the second defining element to be prevented in conflicts. Even where violence is not the impending characteristic, the prospect of a worsening or damaging cycle of conflict provides the occasion—and potentially the motivation—for negotiations to manage, de-escalate, reduce, and possibly resolve the conflict. Therefore, preventive diplomacy works to prevent escalation of a conflict to levels that threaten damage and call for further retaliation and costly countermeasures. This common characteristic ties together the two types of conflict—both between parties and against nature—in regard to prevention.

Thus, the question "Prevent what?" shades into the further question "Prevent when?" By definition, negotiations to accomplish preventive diplomacy as defined here need to take place before a conflict has entered its violent phase, and by practice, they must begin before the resource and process commitment engendered by escalation has developed its own momentum; otherwise, negotiations are no longer preventive diplomacy but crisis management or something else. It is easy to tell when a conflict has gone beyond the limits of preventive diplomacy, that is, when it has entered the phase of violence or uncontrolled escalation (or worsening of another sort), but these are the very signs that mark a conflict as serious enough to warrant intervention or at least attention. If preventive diplomacy means "negotiate early," how does one know when to begin?

In many ways, this is a puzzling question. Growing attention has been devoted to the question of early warning, in a search for new ways of identifying potentially serious conflicts before they escalate into view and out of control (George and Holl 1997; Baker and Weller 1998; Davies and Gurr 1999; Rupesinghe and Kuroda 1992; FEWER 1998; Verstegen 1999). But early warning suffers from some very contradictory problems. One is overabundance, because intelligence, news, and research generate quantities of data that are readily available to those who need them. The other problem is the absence of early awareness of these warnings and early action on them. Policymakers are reluctant to make the necessary responses, for many reasons. At one extreme lies the ambiguity of a clear warning wherein advance signals stand out as the necessary and sufficient preludes to crisis. There is a high correlation between violence or danger and their preconditions but a low correlation between early warnings and subsequent violence or catastrophe. At the other extreme lies bureaucratic inertia—the safety in doing nothing in the midst of uncertainty; until the danger of violence or catastrophe becomes certain, it is deemed wisest simply to hold the course. In the absence of unambiguously clear and early warnings, bureaucratic inertia becomes rational.

Yet some warning must have been compelling in the many cases in which early prevention was practiced. Furthermore, in many issue areas, the conflict is obvious (either specifically or from the type of situation involved), and the question is whether to pursue it toward a unilateral victory or toward a cooperative solution. Undelimited or demarcated boundaries, unordered arms races, peace processes without a potential mediator of last resort, commercial competition without a dispute settlement mechanism, transboundary environmental problems without a responsibility norm, and other identifiable situations are problems calling for prevention, constituting their own early warnings. More specific conflicts have their own profiles, which may be generic to their types of subject. A deeper examination of this question of early warning by issue area is needed to bring useful distinctions and lessons to light.

This still leaves the other "when" question: When is it best, in the early life of a conflict, to turn to preventive negotiations? Preventing conflict is impossible, but preventing its expression in escalation and violence is a desirable goal. This, in turn, entails either settling the conflict by producing a decision that is accepted as legitimate and final by the parties (such as the series of decisions that led to German unification) or channeling the conflict into political expressions until a settlement can be found (such as the series of decisions that led to the less conclusive process of Yemeni unification). Preventing escalation is also desirable, although escalation may be necessary to convince the other party of the need for serious attention or a just solution. The "orderly armament" agreements that punctuated the Cold War were often preceded by "shots across the bow" to induce a preventive course by threatening a unilateral advantage. Determining when negotiations can take hold in the previolence and preescalation phases is an important tactical consideration.

Negotiation

The reference to "action" in Boutros-Ghali's definition of preventive diplomacy is also limited in the present discussion to refer to negotiation, direct or mediated. The Agenda for Peace lists many ways of preventing escalation and violence (Boutros-Ghali 1995, 46–50) and other studies fill an entire toolbox (Lund 1996, 142–63; Lund et al. 1997, III; Bauwens and Reychler 1994), but this study will focus on the one most encompassing method. Negotiation lies at the core of preventive diplomacy, and to the extent that it moves the conflict toward resolution, preventive diplomacy almost always operates through negotiation.

Negotiation can be carried out directly by the parties themselves, by a third party through mediated negotiation, or, in multilateral settings, by a mixture of the two, with some of the parties serving as mediators among the others. Parties conduct their own preventive diplomacy when they become aware of the need to resolve their conflict by other means than coercion. In that case, they will negotiate directly with their opponents to defuse the conflict and seek either a solution or a mechanism for continuing the conflict by political (nonviolent) means.

Mediation is simply a form of negotiation in which a third-party catalyst is needed to produce negotiations that the parties are unable to perform unaided (Touval and Zartman 1985; Kressel and Pruitt 1989). In the end, mediated outcomes are negotiated by the parties themselves, but the mediator's presence has been important in getting the negotiations started and even in keeping them going. Mediators play one of three roles, depending both on the type of blockage that keeps the parties from negotiating directly and on the effort needed to overcome that blockage (Zartman and Touval 1996). The mediator as communicator carries messages, breaking the communications barrier and acting in the true sense of a catalyst, with no input of its own. The mediator as a formulator brings in its own ideas, overcoming the parties' inability to see solutions to the conflict and making a nontangible input into the search for a solution. The mediator as a manipulator makes a contribution to the outcome itself; overcoming the lack of attraction to a solution provided by insufficient payoffs to the parties, it either sweetens the pot or imposes sanctions for noncooperation. Thus, a variety of levels of engagement may be required to conduct preventive mediation effectively.

Whether the parties themselves see the need for preventive diplomacy and carry out negotiations directly or whether a third party is needed to sensitize them and to mediate the conflict, three elements are involved in moving the contestants away from violence and escalation: stakes, attitudes, and tactics. These elements have no special sequence; indeed, all are involved at the same time. Nor do they as yet carry many well-defined effects or even hypotheses to guide investigation or practice. Therefore, the study of preventive diplomacy as negotiation moves into new analytic territory as the examination of various issue areas identifies propositions and characteristics of the issue areas on the basis of components of the process. The emphasis in this examination is on process, defined as the way in which stakes and attitudes are changed and tactics are used to achieve preventive results.

Stakes are the ostensibly "objective" elements in the conflict, although, in fact, like all objects, they are the subject of perceptions. Stakes are those things that matter to the parties—the costs and benefits that each faces as the particular issue is handled early rather than later. In preventive diplomacy, negotiators must change the stakes or the parties' perception of stakes, moving the issue from a negative- or zero-sum to a positive-sum situation. Stakes must be presented in such a way as to no longer pose an "I pay, what do I get?" or "You win, I lose" type of situation; each of the parties must be seen to gain something out of an agreement, overcoming, to some degree, the incompatibility (conflict) inherent in both or multiple parties' holding on to their positions. These positions tend to be positive wants or absolute gains: When parties want the same things or at least things whose attainment is blocked by the other party's wants, prevention of collision, escalation, and violence requires raising the resources or scaling down the demands.

Stakes can be changed from negative- or zero-sum to positive-sum in only one of three ways (Pruitt and Olczak 1995, 67): (1) by differentially evaluating the items so as to permit trade-offs between items differently valued by the respective parties (Homans 1961, 62; Nash 1950); (2) by reframing the issue so as to permit competing solutions and joint payoffs (Walton and McKersie 1965; Raiffa 1982); or (3) by providing side payments or new benefits in order to enlarge the outcome and allow for additional trade-offs or different goals. Trading economic for political payoffs in the unification of Germany and Yemen, redefining the Peru-Ecuador boundary conflict as a joint development issue, and providing economic incentives for Russia in German reunification are examples of each of these approaches. Conflicts arise because there is not enough of an item or items to go around to the satisfaction of the claimant parties, and conflicts can be prevented by either providing more items or by changing the parties' perception of those items that are available. Given the host of other examples, many of which are cited in the following issue studies, it is sometimes surprising to see the lack of inventiveness employed in those conflicts that escalate past obvious solutions.

However, positions may also be negative or relative when what one party wants is not something in and of itself but simply the denial of what the other party wants. Conflicts stemming from such positions are much more difficult to handle because, in the terms they are posed, the addition of new or perceivedly new stakes does nothing to address the underlying problem. The only thing to do, other than inducing a change of heart on its merits (similar to reframing, as mentioned earlier), is to use new stakes to buy the opponents off of their positions (similar to the aforementioned side payments). But both reframing and bribing require a change in attitude on the part of the opponent, beyond mere perceptions. Much current international relations theory focuses on demands for relative gains as the basis of conflict and emphasizes the importance of maintaining relationships among the parties, even in conflict, as a counterweight to demands of denial (Stein and Pauly 1993).

As indicated, parties may be able to deal with issues of stakes directly. If they cannot do so, they will be dependent on the efforts of third-party mediators. Making differential or additional trade-offs and reframing of stakes may well be within the power of the parties themselves; side payments for additional trade-offs depend on available resources, but differential trade-offs and reframing involve perceptions of existing stakes rather than the introduction of new stakes. If the willingness to reframe or to trade is not present within the parties, it needs to be generated by the mediator, acting, above all, as a formulator to propose new ways of viewing the stakes in the conflict. If the stakes are insufficient to provide acceptable outcomes to both parties at the same time, even with new perceptions of those stakes, then the mediator is required to act as a manipulator, providing side payments of its own along with other positive and negative incentives to head off the conflict. In this situation, relations with the mediator often provide the material for reconciliation and conflict prevention, more so than relations between the parties directly. When the preventive effort is multilateral, some of the parties themselves tend to play this mediating role.

Attitudes are the subjective element in conflict, coloring the black-and-white portrayals of stakes. Two very different attitudinal problems are involved in preventive negotiations, depending on whether the conflict is among parties or against nature, but these different problems are nonetheless closely connected. Preventive diplomacy in interparty conflict involves the alteration of parties' attitudes from conflictual to accommodative, in regard both to the opponent and to the conflict itself. Conflictual attitudes portray the opponent as the enemy, an evil adversary to be beaten; both zero-sum perceptions and denial of benefits to the enemy are involved. Such attitudes are the motor of escalation and violence and the major barrier to the prevention of escalation and violence in conflicts among parties.

Accommodative attitudes regard the problem as the enemy and the opponent as an ally in overcoming it; positive-sum perceptions and legitimate demands are involved. In fact, accommodation means a shift from conflict among parties to conflict against nature, as parties unite to prevent the impending threat from being realized. Here, a different—indeed, a contrary—attitudinal problem is posed, the problem of raising consciousness or creating awareness concerning the threat, and the attitudinal difficulty is not demonizing but complacency. Both demonizing and complacency hinder cooperation to prevent escalation and violence.

These extremes are presented as stereotypes and caricatures with important caveats. Conflictual attitudes may not be as strongly hostile as described, particularly when relationships hold the parties together despite their dispute. In fact, the importance of relationships is reinforced beyond their objective existence by their effect in overcoming demonizing or overly adversarial attitudes. Nonetheless, such extreme attitudes too easily take over in the heat of the interaction, and they do so in both directions. Border, territorial, and ethnic disputes quickly move from objective geographic stakes to subjective enemy perceptions; even in conflicts against nature, although awareness is the challenge, parties aware of the dangers of global warming, ethnic explosion, arms races, or offensive alliances can quickly begin demonizing those who drag their feet (doubtless for personal benefit!) against collective measures. As is well noted (Rubin, Pruitt and Kim 1994), demonizing is a natural tendency, but it makes conflict prevention more difficult; complacency is an inertial state that makes conflict prevention impossible.

Thus, new stakes may be piled on as incentives and trade-offs, but if attitudes toward the problem or conflict and toward the other parties are not changed, the objective elements will simply not be seen. As long as accommodation is regarded as surrender, the opponent is seen as unworthy and untrustworthy, the opposing demands are deemed illegitimate and ill intentioned, and the danger of escalating costs and violence is believed to be ill founded and exaggerated, preventive diplomacy is bound to fail, whatever the objective compatibility of demands over stakes may be. Preventive diplomacy was successful in South Africa because of a change in the attitudes of the South African government and the opposition toward each other and the collision course of their policies; it succeeded in Yemen because of the changed attitudes of the two Yemeni half-states toward each other; it worked because of changes in the attitudes of the former Cold War protagonists toward the definition of the North Atlantic Treaty Organization (NATO); and it was successful because of the changed attitudes of the world community toward the dangers of global warming. And if the preceding examples are less than perfect in their results, that, too, illustrates the effect of incomplete changes in attitudes on the chances of cooperation. Left alone in their conflict, opposing parties may not be able to see a way out; unconvinced of the unclear and distant danger, they will not be motivated to cooperate. Such situations often require the ministrations of a mediator to enable the parties to respond to efforts to communicate and formulate solutions. Attitude change becomes a separate target for efforts and a separate element for analysis, as a condition for successful negotiation. It is clear from the following issue-area examinations that changes in stakes alone will not provide the basis for preventive negotiations; attitudinal change is necessary.

Attitude change involves several dimensions of sequencing (Walton and McKersie 1965, chapters 6 and 8). It can occur either separately from discussions on stakes (as a precondition to a positive-sum consideration of outcomes) or concomitantly with the consideration of stakes (so that consideration of outcomes becomes a vehicle and an illustration for changes in attitudes). The latter scenario is probably both more likely and more difficult. As a result, attitude change can occur unequally among the parties, with one party adopting a problem-solving attitude (first) and then working to convince the other party to drop its complacent or confrontational attitudes and come to the same problem-solving approach. Such disjointed change is likely to occur whether preventive diplomacy is practiced bilaterally or through mediation, and it poses all the problems of the Toughness or Negotiator's Dilemma that are inherent in any negotiation (Zartman 1978; Lax and Sebenius 1986). It is important not to assume that the Toughness Dilemma only occurs in preventing the escalation of confrontational conflicts among parties, as seen, for example, in the negotiations over divided states examined by Sukyong Choi in this volume. Even when the attitudinal problem is one of complacency about preventing conflicts against nature, those who want action face the same negotiating problem in dealing with the complacency of those who oppose action, as seen, for example, in the negotiations over state disintegration or global warming that will be analyzed by P. Terrence Hopmann and Winfried Lang in later chapters.

Tactics are the third component of preventive diplomacy negotiations, as involved in any negotiations facing the Toughness Dilemma. Despite the crucial importance of tactics in negotiation, too little systematic attention has been paid to the subject and particularly to an identification of its basic parameters; concern with tactics dominates most business treatments of negotiation but without any unifying conceptual dimensions (Karrass 1970; Nierenberg 1973). Essentially, tactics involve three elements: timing, terms, and toughness (Lax and Sebenius 1986). Tactics can be defined as doing the right thing at the right time, and therefore, they are concerned with the art of persuasion and induced attitude change that is so important to negotiation. In preventive diplomacy, persuasive arguments for the reconsideration of stakes and for changing attitudes must be presented at a time and in a manner that will capture attention and alter behavior.

Persuasion can be expressed in a number of ways: in relation to altered goals or to altered means of achieving the same goals, in relation to higher values or to the narrow outcomes of the conflict, in relation to costs or to benefits, or in relation to one's own goals or to the opponent's goals, among others (Petty and Cacioppo 1981; Clavel 1991). Doubtless, the choice of the terms of persuasion is situation-dependent, defined in regard to issue or, again, timing. A better understanding of effective tactics seen as timing and terms of persuasion and of the situational determinants of that effectiveness will enable a better practice of preventive diplomacy.

Although many of the artifices of presentation and persuasion are matters of packaging, the essentials of the "right thing" involve the basic dilemma in negotiations over when to be tough and when to be soft—that is, when to hold firm, thus increasing the chances of achieving one's demands but decreasing the chances of reaching agreement, and when to make concessions, thus increasing the chances of reaching an agreement but decreasing the chances of achieving one's demands (Lax and Sebenius 1986; Bartos 1987). Again, there are a number of ways of analyzing the Toughness Dilemma, which remains a dilemma—in other words, is unresolvable—in the absence of intervening variables (Zartman 1998). One set of intervening variables is situational. The decision to be tough or soft can be analyzed as depending on whether a party sees itself in a symmetrical or asymmetrical situation of power (Zartman 1997) or in a Prisoner's Dilemma Game (PDG) or a Chicken Dilemma Game (CDG) (Snyder and Diesing 1977) or inside or outside a bargaining range, among others; much more analysis is required in all cases.

Another set of intervening variables is processual. Analyses of turning points in negotiation indicate that parties make concessions in the process of approaching an agreement until they reach a point where serious stakes are uncovered and an evaluation of the cost of further concessions compared with the value of an impending agreement needs to be considered; such a moment of crisis involves a toughness decision, resulting in either rupture or a return to negotiations (Druckman 1986). Because these questions are applicable to any negotiation, negotiation for preventive diplomacy joins questions still unanswered in theory or in practice about the normal and normative conduct of reconciliation.

But in that case, how does negotiation as preventive diplomacy differ from any other type of negotiation? Part of the answer is that all types of negotiation have similar characteristics, as noted, and that prevention is merely the subject: Preventive diplomacy can learn from everything that is being discovered in the deeper study of negotiation (Hopmann 1996). And by the same token, all negotiation (or diplomacy) is preventive, forestalling worse outcomes and presenting an alternative to violence, whether prospective or occurring. These similarities should be built upon, not dismissed.

But beyond that, there is a crucial difference. Preventive negotiation is pitched forward, anticipating not only its own consequences but also its own necessity. Most negotiations occur under the pressure of crisis or opportunity, when "it can't go on like this" or "a window just opened up" (Zartman and

Berman 1982, 45–68). Why should parties turn to negotiations or let a mediator in if they do not "need" to? Preventive negotiations have no hurting stalemate behind them and no sharply defined window of opportunity in front of them. They need to justify their outlays of time and effort by some very uncertain opportunity costs; they are neither fire brigades nor fire insurance but merely the timely housecleaning of firetraps when there are a million other more pressing things to do, amid a myriad of fires to put out. Preventive negotiation must create its own opportunities, its own justification, and its own pressures because the absence of these elements as preconditions does not mean that they are dispensable; it only means that they have to be created, along with appropriate outcomes.

The less frequently studied occasions for negotiation not under crisis become more salient. These occasions include situations where new multilateral solutions have to be invented to replace ones that are no longer acceptable or are outmoded, situations where a new outcome or exchange of outcomes is needed that can only be created jointly, and situations where new orders or regimes must be created for the routinized handling of problems or where old orders or regimes need to be reaffirmed (Zartman and Berman 1982, 42–86). Negotiations in such situations are generally problem-solving exercises, "cold" diplomacy as opposed to Henry Kissinger's dictum to treat crises only when they are hot, and therefore, the parties and mediators have a greater control of the timetable.

Nonetheless, at one end of the process, this consideration returns the problem to that of seeking entry points and justifications and, in the normal situations of power asymmetry, to questions of who initiates preventive negotiations—the stronger party to dominate or the weaker to avoid domination (Keohane and Nye 1989; Zartman and Rubin 2000)? At the other end, this consideration also poses the problem of closure because no crisis dogs the proceedings. As John Cross (1969, 13) has written, "If it did not matter *when* the parties agreed, it would not matter whether or not they agreed at all." Preventive diplomacy has its own characteristic challenges that much negotiation theory does not yet address.

Issues

The consideration of these three components—stakes, attitudes, and tactics—allows an analysis and evaluation of the practice of preventive diplomacy through negotiation along its basic dimensions, but it leaves a large terrain of experience to be covered. Rather than treat the playing field as flat and featureless, this project divides it into issue areas, following the notion that preventive diplomacy may be practiced differently according to subject matter. Eleven issue areas will be treated: boundary problems, territorial claims, ethnic conflict management processes, divided state unification, state disintegration, cooperation disputes, trade wars, transboundary environmental disputes, global natural disasters, global security disasters (armaments and alliances), and, for contrast, labor disputes from which lessons in internal relations can be transferred to the international field. Through comparisons, cross-fertilizing results can be uncovered, resulting in better analysis and an improved practice of preventive diplomacy.

To set the stage for the deeper analyses in the chapters that follow, the stakes and prevention goals in each issue area need to be identified. Boundary conflicts concern the location of lines separating states, in dispute either because they are imprecisely located (undelimited or undemarcated) or because their location is contested. Such disputes can be settled by careful negotiations involving guiding principles and specific trade-offs, but left untended, they have a conflict-generating potential that can lead to hostile relations, even to the point of war between neighbors. Beyond the location of lines, territorial disputes involve larger parts of states claimed by neighbors for reasons of security, identity, or prosperity. Negotiations involve shifting the nature of the claim from territorial possession to some lesser form of concern (such as cultural preservation or political autonomy), but again, if left unshifted, claims can permanently sour relations, provide occasions for escalation, and eventually lead to war.

Divided state unification concerns restoration of the integrity of a state artificially separated, usually for external powers' purposes, through restoration of the overarching national identity that both parts claim and through renunciation of the ideological justifications for their separate existences. Unless one half physically conquers the other, that unification must be negotiated in order to provide the conditions for reintegration of the two territories and populations and to prevent the necessarily hostile relations from turning, by design or by accident, into hostilities. The reverse process, the disintegration of formerly united (generally compound) states, can be accomplished gently, by negotiating the terms of separation and the distribution of assets, or violently, by war over the same items, which negotiations would prevent.

Peacemaking processes and cooperative conflicts provide two limiting extremes to preventive diplomacy. Peacemaking processes dealing with ethnic conflicts that have not been prevented entail a situation where continuation and even escalation of the violence are the alternatives to a negotiated settlement. Here, a revival of conflict escalation and violence is to be prevented. Peacemaking efforts seek to achieve the same goal by providing a transition to a new permanent regime through the management or settlement agreement. Such efforts come at the very end of the preventive spectrum but have characteristics quite similar to efforts at the beginning. In cooperative conflicts, the regime for handling relations and problems already exists, but conflicts arise to test its effectiveness and strength. Such conflicts among friends can escalate to strain and destroy friendly relations (an escalation that timely negotiations would prevent), even though violence is usually not likely. Similar to cooperative disputes are trade wars, where a trade regime between countries is disrupted by a dispute over the flow of goods covered by the regime. Negotiations restore the regime, in original or altered state, to prevent an escalation of retaliatory measures that threaten to damage relations and even destroy the regime.

Transboundary disputes and global natural disasters generally involve environmental problems of pollution, resource scarcities, and accidents, either on a bilateral or global scale. Allocation disputes over sources, responsibilities, effects, and payments may involve regime building and may be simply punctual, but their effects, if unmanaged, can escalate into serious damage to the environment, the parties, and their relations, which negotiation would seek to prevent.

Global security conflicts are a prime subject for preventive diplomacy involving regimes. In such conflicts, runaway competition in arms races and alliance races has often led to crisis and catastrophe. A major category of security relations involves arms-control negotiations, which are designed to prevent the much discussed escalatory effects of arms races and their propensity to end in war. "Orderly armament," more than disarmament, is negotiated in order to obviate the results of disorderly armament. Alliances are also regimes covering each of the sides in global security relations, but alliances are also well known for their propensity to escalate and cause violent conflict. Negotiations provide for "orderly alliance interaction," creating regimes among regimes, lest expansion of alliances or frictions where they rub together cause heat and explosions.

In all this, there is much to learn from labor negotiations, where collective bargaining and conflict management regimes usually already exist but where negotiations are frequently needed to prevent conflict from escalating into costly strikes and violence. But labor relations are also involved in conflicts over domestic allocation systems and in the establishment of new sets of internal rules and relationships, created to prevent incidental conflicts from arising or to facilitate within-system conflict management.

At this stage, some preliminary characteristics of preventive diplomacy through negotiation are already noticeable. First, preventive diplomacy requires proactive initiatives rather than simply putting out fires. In familiar terms of negotiation analysis, this means a sustained effort in diagnosing the issue area to identify problems before they become conflicts and to come up with solutions in the form of formulas for negotiation. The description of this activity is banal, but it is so far from the usual approach to foreign policy situations that it is striking. Many issue areas are strewn with conflicts waiting to happen, situations in which some preemptive attention to potential causes—unmarked boundaries, ethnic discrimination, impermeable separations and constraining unifications, unchecked pollution, dumping and tariff initiatives, new arms technologies, and changes of government in exposed allies, among other destabilizing conditions—can catch "precancerous conditions" before they turn into cancers. Some of these are ongoing conditions, which continue unnoticed until aggravated; others are new destabilizing changes that call for a reaction and set escalatory cycles into motion. Each is its own early warning, one by its existence and the other by its occurrence. Issue area studies can tell us more about the nature and effects of each.

Second, preventive diplomacy generally requires either the creation or the maintenance of regimes—routinized or institutionalized ways of dealing with a particular type of problem (Hasenclever, Mayer and Rittberger 1997). It is important to note that the focus of preventive diplomacy is not regimes per se but the process of creating, using, and repairing them through negotiation, akin to Mark Anstey's systems change and systems management. To say that regimes are the solution to conflict is merely to pose the problem, which is how to use regimes to handle challenges or exceptions to them and how to establish the solution when it does not exist. If a regime does not exist (yet), it is either because the problem has not yet become endemic enough to require an institutionalized response or because the conflicts of interest engendered by the problem have prevented an institutionalized response from crystallizing. If a regime already exists, either the conflict needs to be brought in under it (or one chosen among competing regimes) or it has to be revised to deal with the conflict—the problem has to fit the regime or the regime has to be changed to fit the problem. How preventive negotiations are carried out depends first on identifying which of these four types of situation exists.

Third, the key to the initiation and success of preventive negotiations is the mutual perception that the costs of early action are outweighed by the averted costs of future conflict. There are four elements to this calculation: an initial awareness that there is a calculation to be made, a sense of the costs of present action, an estimation of future costs of a continued and worsening (escalating) conflict, and the creation of immediate benefits of present action. The second element is continually present (even, paradoxically, without the first). Efforts to promote preventive diplomacy therefore need to concentrate on the first and last two elements, the need and opportunity for an initiative, the costs of inaction, and the provision of action payoffs now, not later.

The first element is an awareness problem, requiring an identification of the types of opportunities that exist and the easiest ways to exploit them. The third element involves a more complicated calculation because it pits current real costs against future discounted estimates, with an unending horizon that stretches beyond the term of the current incumbents. In addition to a discount factor, there is also a probability factor, for continuation, worsening, and escalation are not certain (Kahneman, Slovic, and Tversky 1982). Until there is a better sense of that probability, which can only be developed by a comparative study of preventive diplomacy by issue areas, it will be impossible to break the face-off between opponents of a preemptive démarche who claim a worsening eventuality is unlikely against proponents who feel it is likely. The last element involves the creation of immediate opportunities, to buy a constituency into the preventive action. Identifying these ingredients is the ultimate challenge of this study.

References

Baker, Pauline, and A. Weller. 1998. *An Analytical Model of Internal Conflict and State Collapse.* Washington, D.C.: Fund for Peace.

Bartos, Otomar. 1987. "How Predictable Are Negotiations?" In *The 50% Solution,* ed. I. William Zartman. New Haven: Yale University Press.

Bauwens, W., and L. Reychler, eds. 1994. *The Art of Conflict Prevention.* London: Brassey's.

Bazerman, Max, and M. Neale. 1992. *Negotiating Rationally.* New York: Free Press.

Boutros-Ghali, Boutros. 1992. *An Agenda for Peace.* New York: United Nations.

———. 1995. *An Agenda for Peace,* rev. ed. New York: United Nations.

Brams, Steven, Ann Dougherty, and Matthew Weidner. 1994. "Game Theory." In *International Multilateral Negotiation,* ed. I. William Zartman. San Francisco: Jossey-Bass.

Chasek, Pamela. 2000. *Environmental Negotiations.* Boulder: Westview.

Clavel, Jean-Janiel. 1991. *De la négociation multilatérale.* Brussels: Bruylant.

Conybeare, J. 1987. *Trade Wars.* New York: Columbia University Press.

Cross, John. 1969. *The Economics of Bargaining.* New York: Basic.

Davies, John, and Ted Gurr, eds. 1999. *Preventive Measures: Building Risk Assessment and Early Warning Systems.* Boulder: Westview.

Deng, Francis, et al. 1997. *Sovereignty as Responsibility.* Washington, D.C.: Brookings.

Druckman, Daniel. 1986. "Stages, Turning Points and Crises." *Journal of Conflict Resolution* 30, no. 2: 327–60.

Dupont, Christophe. 1994. "Coalition Theory." In *International Multilateral Negotiation,* ed. I. William Zartman. San Francisco: Jossey-Bass.

FEWER (Forum on Early Warning and Early Response). 1998. *Early Warning Resource: Manual for Early Warning and Early Response.* London: FEWER.

George, Alexander, and Jane Holl. 1997. *The Warning-Response Problem and Missed Opportunities in Preventive Diplomacy.* New York: Carnegie Commission on Preventing Conflict.

Gurr, Ted, et al. 1994. "Special Issue on State Collapse and Early Warning." *Journal of Ethno-Development* 4, no. 1.

Hasenclever, Claus, Peter Mayer, and Volker Rittberger. 1997. *International Regimes.* New York: Cambridge University Press.

Homans, G. C. 1961. *Social Behavior.* New York: Harcourt, Brace and World.

Hopmann, P. Terrence. 1996. *The Negotiation Process and the Resolution of International Conflicts.* Columbia: University of South Carolina Press.

Jentleson, Bruce. 2000. *Opportunities Seized, Opportunities Missed.* Lanham, Md.: Rowman & Littlefield.

Kahneman, Daniel, and Amos Tversky. 1979. "Prospect Theory: An Analysis of Decisions Under Risk." *Econometrics* 47, no. 2: 263–91.

———. 1995. "Conflict Resolution: Cognitive Perspective." In *Barriers to Conflict Resolution,* ed. Robert Mnookian and Kenneth Arrow. New York: Norton.

Kahneman, Daniel, Paul Slovic, and Amos Tversky, eds. 1982. *Judgment Under Uncertainty.* New York: Cambridge University Press.

Karrass, Chester. 1970. *The Negotiating Game.* New York: World.

Keohane, Robert, and Joseph Nye. 1989. *Interdependence and International Politics.* Boston: Little, Brown.

Kressel, Kenneth, and Dean G. Pruitt, eds. 1989. *Mediation Research.* San Francisco: Jossey-Bass.

Lax, David, and James Sebenius. 1986. *The Manager as Negotiator.* New York: Free Press.

Lund, Michael. 1996. *Preventing Violent Conflicts.* Washington, D.C.: U.S. Institute of Peace.

Lund, Michael, et al. 1997. *Managing and Mitigating Violent Conflicts.* Washington, D.C.: Creative Associates International.

Nash, John. 1950. "The Bargaining Problem." *Econometrica* 18, no. 1: 155–62.

Nierenberg, Gerard. 1973. *Fundamentals of Negotiating.* New York: Hawthorne.

Petty, R. E., and J. T. Cacioppo. 1981. *Attitudes and Persuasion.* Dubuque, Iowa: Brown.

Porter, Gareth, and Janet Brown. 1996. *Global Environmental Politics.* Boulder: Westview.

Pruitt, Dean G., and Peter J. Carnevale. 1993. *Negotiation in Social Conflict.* Pacific Grove, Calif.: Brooks/Cole.

Pruitt, Dean G., and Paul Olczak. 1995. "Beyond Hope: Approaches to Resolving Seemingly Intractable Conflict." In *Conflict, Cooperation and Justice,* ed. Barbara Bunker and Jeffrey Rubin. San Francisco: Jossey-Bass.

Raiffa, Howard. 1968. *Decision Analysis.* Reading, Mass.: Addison-Wesley.

———. 1982. *The Art and Science of Negotiation.* Cambridge, Mass.: Harvard University Press.

Riker, William. 1962. *The Theory of Political Coalitions.* New Haven: Yale University Press.

Rubin, Jeffrey Z., Dean G. Pruitt, and Sunghee Kim. 1994. *Social Conflict.* New York: McGraw-Hill.

Rupesinghe, Jumar, and M. Kuroda, eds. 1992. *Early Warning and Conflict Resolution.* New York: St. Martin's.

Sfez, Lucien. 1973. *Critique de la décision.* Paris: Colin.

Smoke, Paul. 1977. *War.* Cambridge, Mass.: Harvard University Press.

Snyder, Glenn, and Paul Diesing. 1977. *Conflict Among Nations.* Princeton: Princeton University Press.

Spector, Bertram I. 1994. "Decision Analysis." In *International Multilateral Negotiations,* ed. I. William Zartman. San Francisco: Jossey-Bass.

Spector, Bertram, Gunnar Sjöstedt, and I. William Zartman, eds. In press. *Negotiating Regimes.*

Stein, Janice, and Louis Pauly, eds. 1993. *Choosing to Cooperate.* Baltimore: Johns Hopkins University Press.

Taylor, Michael. 1987. *The Possibility of Cooperation.* New York: Cambridge University Press.

Touval, Saadia, and I. William Zartman, eds. 1985. *International Mediation in Theory and Practice.* Boulder: Westview.

Tversky, Amos, and Daniel Kahneman. 1981. "The Framing of Decisions and the Rationality of Choice." *Science* 211: 453–58.

Verstegen, Suzanne. 1999. *Conflict Prognostication.* The Hague: Netherlands Institute for International Relations Clingendael.

Victor, David, Kal Rautiala, and Eugene Skolnikoff, eds. 1998. *The Implementation and Effectiveness of International Environmental Commitments.* Cambridge, Mass.: MIT Press.

Walton, Richard, and Robert McKersie. 1965. *A Behavioral Theory of Labor Negotiations.* New York: McGraw-Hill.

Young, Oran, ed. 1975. *Bargaining.* Urbana: University of Illinois Press.

Zartman, I. William. 1983. "The Strategy of Preventive Diplomacy in Third World Conflicts." In *Managing US-Soviet Rivalry,* ed. Alexander George. Boulder: Westview.

——. 1989. *Ripe for Resolution.* New York: Oxford University Press.

——. 1995. "Negotiating the South African Conflict." In *Elusive Peace: Negotiating an End to Civil Wars,* ed. I. William Zartman. Washington, D.C.: Brookings.

——. 1997. "The Structuralist Dilemma in Negotiation." In *Research on Negotiation in Organizations,* vol. 6, ed. Roy Lewicki et al. Greenwich, Conn.: JAI Press.

——. 1998. "The Toughness Dilemma." Report to the International Studies Association annual meeting.

——. 2000. "Ripeness Revisited." In *International Conflict Resolution After the Cold War,* ed. Paul Stern and Daniel Druckman. Washington, D.C.: National Academy of Sciences.

Zartman, I. William, and Maureen Berman. 1982. *The Practical Negotiator.* New Haven: Yale University Press.

Zartman, I. William, and Saadia Touval. 1996. "International Mediation in the Post–Cold War Era." In *Managing Global Chaos,* ed. Chester Crocker, Fen Hampson, and Pamela Aall. Washington, D.C.: U.S. Institute of Peace.

Zartman, I. William, ed. 1978. *The Negotiation Process.* Newbury Park, Calif.: Sage.

Zartman, I. William, and Guy Olivier Faure, eds. 2000. *Escalation and Negotiation.* Laxenburg, Austria: International Institute for Applied Systems Analysis.

Zartman, I. William, and Jeffrey Z. Rubin, eds. 2000. *Power and Negotiation.* Ann Arbor: University of Michigan Press.

2

Boundary Conflicts: Drawing the Line

Kjell-Åke Nordquist

Several international conventions formulated during this century, from the UN Charter to regional international documents, directly or indirectly stipulate that changes of interstate boundaries are acceptable only when made through peaceful means. But crisis situations in which boundaries or boundary-related issues are at stake are frequent in the international system. Some boundary problems are settled before they escalate into serious crises. Others seem irreconcilable and involve frequent military exchanges. Regulated or not, boundary and border relations will remain a potential source of conflict in the international system of states for the foreseeable future. New states have been established, the Cold War has kept many unsatisfactory solutions alive, and the penetration of states into neighboring border areas, not the least for economic purposes, has increased. Such developments put boundaries on the agenda in international relations.

Boundaries are interesting phenomena. They bring states together whether they want it or not. States with a common boundary share at least a minimum degree of relation and cannot totally ignore each other. In fact, boundaries create a prima facie hostile situation because "my neighbor is my enemy" (Kautilya 1960, 293). Boundaries are, by definition, shared. They define a state territorially and thereby provide a condition for state sovereignty, yet their relational nature is an infringement upon that sovereignty. Thus, a boundary can be a mirror of internal disputes as well as a root of an interstate dispute in itself. Another aspect that adds to the intricacy of boundary relations is the fact that they are based on both internal and international legislation: A boundary agreement is an international legal document, even if its making and ratification involves exclusively internal political processes.

Together with the characteristics just mentioned, a boundary crisis almost necessarily constitutes a complicated mix of interests, actors, and actions—a mix that will be analyzed here from the perspective of conflict prevention. This chapter draws conclusions from experiences of preventive diplomatic measures undertaken at various levels of boundary conflicts. Such measures can work in two ways: They can prevent disputes from arising or they can prevent existing disputes from escalating. The first effort involves standard practices of delimitation, demarcation, and monitoring and the establishment of border regimes. It is the second effort, the prevention of the escalation, that is the main problem here. When and how do preventive diplomatic measures through negotiation make boundary conflicts de-escalate?

Defining Boundary Conflict

The term *boundary* is used here in reference to the line separating two states, irrespective of its degree of implementation (i.e., delimitation or definition on paper, and demarcation or marking on the ground). *Border* refers to the area surrounding a boundary, and a *frontier* is the area where two states meet in interests and penetration, not necessarily with an agreed territorial limit for their aspirations.

A boundary conflict involves a line that, at a minimum, is defined or in the process of being defined by the parties, whether by implicit consent or explicit agreement. This statement implies that the stakes and issues leading to disputes and armed conflicts are related to existing and somehow agreed upon boundaries. This definition therefore excludes conflicts over frontiers, territorial claims, or border areas, which are discussed in the following chapter. Boundary conflicts include minor problems and disputes as well as major armed confrontations. A list of boundary conflicts covering the period from 1947 to 1996 will be used as the empirical basis for the analysis (Nordquist 1992 updated). Some cases in this list are presented in greater depth to provide further insights for the concluding analysis.

Interstate boundary conflicts de-escalate in at least two ways: formally, through a negotiated agreement that regulates behavior or issues at stake, or informally, through a gradual reduction in the importance of the matter in dispute on its own, transforming it into an issue that the opposing parties no longer consider politically relevant. Boundary conflicts can also become "historic residuals," as might happen following the restructuring or disappearance of the state. Examples of this are the formally divided Germany and Yemen, the former Soviet Union and Yugoslavia (examined in the subsequent chapters by Sukyong Choi and P. Terrence Hopmann, respectively), and Ethiopia. Frequently, however, such processes give rise to new boundary problems, as occurred in the last three cases.

In this chapter, the term *preventive diplomacy* refers to processes of de-escalation through negotiation, employed in situations in which escalation on any level is thwarted before it can develop into violence. It may be neither possible nor desirable to prevent all kinds of conflicts, but escalation toward organized violence between the opposing parties should, in principle, be the target for preventive negotiations.

Boundary Conflicts Are Post–Cold War Conflicts

It is commonly held that the post–Cold War period has involved a large number of ethnic conflicts, some of them escalating into civil and even interstate war. In line with this view is the argument that boundaries have become more fluid, more often challenged, and generally more prominent bones of contention than they were during the Cold War. If this assertion is true, that reality has not, thus far, been reflected at the level of major armed conflicts (defined as involving more than one thousand battle-related deaths since the conflict began). In 1996, there were thirty-six major armed conflicts active in twenty-nine countries, but only fifteen of them dealt with territory, and only one of these (between India and Pakistan) involved boundaries (see table 2.1). So far, the international system has been able to keep boundary conflicts at a level far below many other types of conflicts.

At a lower level of casualties than that used in table 2.1—a minimum of twenty-five casualties in one year—the post–Cold War period between 1989 and 1996 witnessed three additional interstate conflicts that were boundary-related: the Mauritania-Senegal conflict (1989–90), the Ecuador-Peru conflict (1995–98) and the Nigeria-Cameroon conflict (1996). Potentially serious situations abound. Africa, for instance, is filled with potential boundary conflicts, notably between states with the same previous colonizer where demarcated boundaries were not deemed necessary. A recent case is the war that broke out in 1998 between Ethiopia and Eritrea, where no dispute had ever been indicated. In Latin America alone, at least eight boundary situations can be identified as potential threats to regional stability (Aravena 1997), plus cases of litigation and other foreseeable problems (such as the status of Guantanamo or the Panama Canal) can be included. Thus, there is more than enough subject matter for prevention efforts to address.

On the higher end of casualties, the second Gulf War between Iraq and Kuwait (1991) was not a conflict over the boundary line but a state-formation conflict. Iraq regarded Kuwait as its nineteenth province and was determined that the smaller nation would disappear as a sovereign state. After the restoration of Kuwaiti sovereignty and through the UN-led Iraq-Kuwait boundary-making process, the conflict did become a boundary conflict in its final stages.

Table 2.1. Major Armed Conflicts over Territory, Active in 2000

Parties	Year Formed/Joined*
Europe	
United Kingdom versus Provisional Irish Republican Army (IRA)	1969/1969
Russia versus Republic of Chechnya	1991/1994
Middle East	
Iran versus Kurdish Democratic Party of Iran	1972/1979
Iraq versus Patriotic Union of Kurdistan	1977/1980
Israel versus Palestinians	1947/1964
Turkey versus Partiya Karkeren Kurdistan	1974/1984
Asia	
Bangladesh versus Jana Samhati Samiti/Shanti Bahini	1971/1982
India versus Kashmir insurgents	1947/1989
India versus Bodo Security Force	† /1992
India versus United Liberation Front of Assam	1982/1988
India versus Pakistan	1947/1996
Indonesia versus Fretilin (East Timor)	1975/1975
Myanmar (Burma) versus Karen National Union	1948/1948
Sri Lanka versus Liberation Tigers of Tamil Eelam	1976/1983
Africa	
Sudan versus Sudanese People's Liberation Army	1980/1983

Source: Wallensteen and Sollenberg 1997, updated.
*Formed indicates the year of stated incompatibility; *joined* indicates the year in which the use of armed force was begun or recommenced.
†This conflict has no defined beginning date.

The De-escalation of Boundary Conflicts

The division between formal and informal de-escalation processes can be used to categorize the thirty boundary conflicts active at some point between 1947 and 1979 and then to study their fate up to the year 2000, whether they had reached agreement in this period or not. Each conflict is identified with one of four different outcomes:

1. escalation into a major war and/or being an active conflict in 2000
2. termination through a durable agreement or an international legal decision
3. evaporation into nonexistence or insignificance as a political issue
4. transformation by a new state's formation, which either removed or activated conflict

To provide information about the stakes for the parties, each conflict can also be described with respect to four causal issue categories:

1. transboundary minorities in the disputed area
2. transboundary resources in the disputed area
3. an unclear frontier as a result of a colonial situation
4. implementation problems of an earlier agreement between the parties

Taken together, these characteristics yield a list of thirty-four boundary conflicts (table 2.2), some of which have more than one agreement. In three cases, there has been a restructured context, making them irrelevant for comparison purposes, but one restructuring actually gave rise to a new boundary dispute. Eight cases continue to be active, some having reached the level of major armed conflict, including the China-India, Cameroon-Nigeria, India-Pakistan, Iran-Iraq, and Ethiopia-Somalia conflicts.

The remaining twenty-three cases have all de-escalated, formally or informally. Thus, two-thirds of all boundary conflicts after World War II have been brought to a settled or nonactive situation, largely through negotiation. This represents, in itself, a major process of conflict de-escalation. In all of the nineteen formal de-escalation cases, there has been a negotiatory component in the process, and we find negotiating initiatives in the informal solutions as well. The formal and informal de-escalation categories are interesting to compare, prompting several questions: Are stakes managed differently? What role does preventive negotiation play in conflict de-escalation? Are the informal de-escalation processes examples of effective preventive negotiations or not? Before turning to these questions, a few more observations should be made about the content of table 2.2.

The number of major issues in the conflicts that were maintained (A) or formally de-escalated (B) is significantly higher than for the informally de-escalated group (C). Although conflicts in the C group have, on average, 1.3 issues per conflict, those in the B group have 2.4 and those in the A group have 2.5. Thus, the informally de-escalated conflicts have fewer issues to manage. But this does not necessarily mean that they are easier to manage. It may well be that the opposite is true: Because the pie is smaller in terms of the number of pieces, there is less to share. Also, the fact that a given conflict has few issues cannot, in itself, be seen as a sign of less intensity: Not the number but the character of stakes sets the intensity. The relatively low number of issues in the informal de-escalation processes can be interpreted as involving conflicts in which issues were relatively unimportant to the parties and were therefore "left to their own fate" among other conflicts competing for management. Even if a conflict had an important issue at its heart, the smaller number of issues allows an input of external resources that can make the pie larger and thus easier to regulate than complex situations.

Another observation is that among the informally de-escalated conflicts, four out of six (the last four cases in that category) were settled through the acceptance of a preindependence colonial agreement. For these cases, all of

Table 2.2. Boundary Conflicts after World War II and Status as of 2000

| Parties (Period) | Issues | | | | Status in 2000 |
	Minorities	Resources	Dispute	Implementation	
A. Maintained conflict					
1. China-USSR/Russia (1963–88)	–	+	–	+	Inactive
2. China-India (1954)	–	–	–	+	Active
3. India-Pakistan (1947–)	+	–	+	–	Active
4. Guyana-Suriname (1967–68)	–	–	+	–	Active
5. Guyana-Venezuela (1962–)	–	+	–	+	Active
6. Iran-Iraq I/II (1937/1969–75)	+/+	+/+	+/–	+/+	1975 agreement restored 1990
7. Somalia-Ethiopia (1960–63, 1964–67, 1977–78)	+	+	+	+	Managed 1964, 1967, 1988
8. Cameroon-Nigeria (1963–67, 1995–98)	+	+	+	+	Agreement 1967/ active
9. Guinea-Bissau-Senegal (1974–)	+	+	–	–	ICJ award 1993/ refused, active
B. Formal de-escalation (negotiated agreement or International Court of Justice award)					
1. Algeria-Tunisia (1961–70)	–	+	+	–	Agreement 1970
2. Algeria-Morocco (1962–70)	+	+	+	–	Agreement 1970
3. Argentina-Chile I/II (1881/ 1958–84)	–/–	–/+	+/–	–/+	Agreement 1984, Active
					(continued)

Table 2.2. Boundary Conflicts after World War II and Status as of 2000 (*continued*)

Parties (Period)	Issues				Status in 2000
	Minorities	Resources	Dispute	Implementation	
4. Argentina-Uruguay (1969–73)	–	+	–	–	Agreement 1973
5. Ecuador-Peru I/II/III (1829/1942/1998)	–/–/–	–/+/+	+/–/–	+/+/+	Agreement 1942, 1998
6. Honduras-Nicaragua (1957–61)	+	+	–	+	ICJ 1961
7. Belgium-Netherlands (1957–59)	–	–	–	+	Agreement 1959/ICJ
8. Burma-China I/II (1941/1960)	+/+	+/+	+/+	–/–	Agreement 1960
9. Cambodia-Thailand (1953)	–	–	+	–	ICJ 1962
10. China-Nepal (1959–61)	–	–	+	–	Agreement 1961
11. Ethiopia-Kenya I/II (1947–70)	+/+	–/+	+/+	–/–	Agreement 1963, 1970
12. Mali-Mauritania (1960–63)	+	+	–	+	Agreement 1963
13. Chad-Libya (1935–90)	+	+	+	–	ICJ 1994
14. Dahomey (Benin)–Niger (1963–65)	+	–	+	–	Agreement 1965
15. Kenya-Somalia (1962–84)	+	–	+	–	Agreement 1984
16. Mali–Burkina Faso (1963, 1975, 1985)	+	+	+	+	ICJ 1986
C. Informal de-escalation—inactive					
1. Afghanistan-Pakistan (1947–63)	+	–	+	–	No agreement
2. Cambodia-Thailand (1961–)	–	–	+	–	No agreement

(continued)

Table 2.2. Boundary Conflicts after World War II and Status as of 2000 (*continued*)

Parties (Period)	Issues					Status in 2000
	Minorities	Resources	Dispute	Implementation		
3. Malawi–Tanzania (1967–)	–	–	–	+		No agreement
4. Ghana–Burkina Faso (1964–66)	–	–	?**	–		No agreement
5. Equatorial Guinea–Gabon (1972)	–	+	–	+		Colonial agreement accepted
6. Ivory Coast–Liberia (1958–60) Yemen* (1948–63)	+	–	+	–		Colonial agreement accepted
D. Restructured conflict context						
1. Aden/United Kingdom–North	–	–	+	+		New state, inactive
2. Italy–Yugoslavia (1947–54)	–	–	–	+		Changed state, inactive
3. Ethiopia–Eritrea (1998–2000)	–	+	+	+		New states

Sources: Butterworth 1976, 1980, updated.

Notes: – indicates no conflict issues

+ indicates conflict issue.

I/II indicates two agreements and years; I/II/III indicates three agreements and years.

ICJ = International Court of Justice.

*See chapter 5 in this volume, by Sukyong Choi, on divided states.

†One major issue remains from the 1984 agreement (Southern Ice Field/Patagonia Glaciers).

**Issue unclear. Toural (1972) suggests the boundary was a mirror of internal antagonisms between the two countries.

which are African, this meant an application of the Organization of African Unity (OAU) principle of respect for territorial integrity and boundaries inherited at independence.

Managing Stakes in Formal De-escalation

The formally de-escalating cases described earlier involve the regulation of major issues. In most cases, there is one agreement, but in some cases, there are two or even three (i.e., at least two escalation and de-escalation processes). They often involve conflict management—that is, the reduction of tensions and the removal of violence but not the resolution of the issues at stake. And management without subsequent resolution promises renewed conflict. Five different ways of creating trade-offs, through a substantial reshaping of the stakes, are used in the boundary agreements:

- compensation
- partition
- sharing
- accommodation (practical adjustments, mostly on ethnic grounds)
- consolidation (overcoming the conflict by joining forces for or against a higher cause, such as a common economic gain or a common external enemy)

The purpose of mutual trade-offs is, of course, to create durable boundary agreements. Table 2.3 shows that trade-offs are connected to durable agreements in all but two of the twenty cases. This indicates a clear relationship between a substantial restructuring of stakes and agreement durability.

The two cases that had trade-offs in the agreement but were not durable were the Burma-China I conflict and the Ethiopia-Kenya I conflict, both of which included a change of status for one of the parties after the agreement from a colonial administration to independence. In both cases, this was a most important factor behind the decision to conclude a second agreement.

If compensation, sharing, partition, accommodation, and consolidation are the mechanisms behind a durable agreement, how do changes come about? Two types of changes are possible: (1) changes in the structure of the conflict system (e.g., in the composition of actors, the availability of resource, and the number of stakes), or (2) changes in a party's positions in an otherwise unchanged conflict system.

Changes in both structures and positions can be targeted by preventive diplomatic initiatives. In some cases, one of the two types of change seems to be a sufficient explanation; in others, both types can be (and usually are) combined. Effecting the second type of change is mainly the task of an indi-

Table 2.3. Durable ("Yes") and Not Durable ("No") Negotiated Boundary
Agreements (excluding most International Court of Justice awards) Following
Post–World War II Conflicts

Conflict	Durable?	Trade-Off	Conflict	Durable?
Mali-Mauritania 1963	Yes	Accommodation	Ecuador-Peru II 1942	No
Algeria-Morocco 1970	Yes	Accommodation	Iran-Iraq I 1937	No
Burma-China II 1960	Yes	Accommodation	Burma-China I 1941	No
Argentina-Uruguay 1973	Yes	Consolidation	Iran-Iraq II 1975	No
Argentina-Chile 1984	Yes	Partition	Ecuador-Peru I 1829	No
Ecuador-Peru III 1998	Presumably	Consolidation	Ethiopia-Kenya I 1947	No
China-Nepal 1961	Yes	Accommodation	Argentina-Chile I 1881	No
Ethiopia-Kenya II 1970	Yes	Consolidation	Cameroon-Nigeria 1976	No
Algeria-Tunisia 1970	Yes	Consolidation		
Dahomey-Niger 1965	Yes	Sharing		
Mali–Burkina Faso 1986	Yes	Partition		
Kenya-Somalia 1984	Yes	Consolidation		

Source: Nordquist 1992, updated.
Note: Mutual trade-offs indicated by italics.

vidual party. In the first type, however, the parties themselves are not always
capable of influencing change. Third parties, especially powerful third parties,
may be required. In all of these cases, the need for good relations with a
neighbor outweighed the particular claims of one of the parties.

The Algeria-Tunisia conflict is a case of changes in the conflict system: Already in 1963, seven years before the boundary agreement, a number of
treaties concerning cultural relations, postal services, customs, commerce,
electric power, and other issues were signed between the two countries. In addition, oil was later discovered on both sides of the de facto boundary. Both
parties, then, had an interest in a final, positive solution. Tunisian president
Habib Bourguiba described the setting aside of territorial claims for greater
mutual benefits in other issues as a *dépassement* process (Zartman 1987). In
this case, the changing structural conditions in the years before the boundary
issue was regulated clearly paved the way for a peaceful conclusion.

The Ethiopia-Kenya conflict in 1970 involved the same type of changes. The negotiations of a boundary agreement started before Kenyan independence, but even if a text was agreed upon earlier, negotiations were not finalized until 1970 (Touval 1972, 249). The main problem of the conflict was the Gadaduma wells, which the British claimed from Ethiopia during their administration. For Kenya, it was more important to obtain a positive security relationship with Ethiopia, against Somalia, than to change certain aspects of the boundary. The changing conflict system for Kenya, going from British rule to independence (which made security concerns prominent for the then newly independent state), caused a shift in priorities vis-à-vis Ethiopia, which had newly independent and vocally irredentist Somalia as an enemy-neighbor, involving a much larger boundary (and territorial) dispute.

The Algeria-Morocco conflict is a final case in point in the first category. Morocco gradually abandoned its claims to the Algerian Sahara after a brief confrontation with Algeria in 1963, ending with the boundary agreement in 1970. Although the boundary matter, as such, was complicated and required several strong OAU interventions, the economic prospects for the Tindouf region and its potential for Morocco's southern economy were an important factor in the final settlement process (the Tlemcen meeting), as was Morocco's need to consolidate security relations with its neighbor in preparation for the decolonization of the Spanish Sahara.

If these cases are examples of conflict system changes, the Mali-Mauritania case is an example of changing positions. In this instance, the changes were made by an individual leader. In 1960, Mauritanian president Moctar Ould Daddah was critical toward Mali, straining the boundary relations between the two countries. He consciously developed a more conciliatory standpoint in the years that followed, and the boundary was altered to approximate traditional grazing patterns. It is debatable whether this change was primarily based on a reevaluation of the situation or on the effects of the historically based Moroccan pressure on Mauritania and the consequent need for Mauritania to develop good relations with at least one other neighbor, Mali (Touval 1972). The basic conditions were the same for Mauritania during those years of position change. A constructive approach, through the change in position, was taken in this way, and from the Treaty of Kayes in 1963 onward, no further serious boundary problems arose.

The Prevention of Boundary Conflict Escalation

From observations on the way stakes were managed in formal agreements, we now turn to the experiences of thwarting escalation before it turns into violence. The four cases selected for this analysis are found in table 2.2: the Kenya-Somalia conflict and the Ethiopia-Somalia conflict (the Somali conflicts), the Honduras-Nicaragua conflict, and the Ecuador-Peru conflict.

These cases represent four different types of situations, as depicted in table 2.2. One case was finalized through an international legal decision (the Honduras-Nicaragua conflict), one was the subject of three successive negotiated agreements (the Ecuador-Peru conflict), one has de-escalated without any formal agreement (the Kenya-Somalia conflict), and one was brought under control through a conflict-management arrangement without actual resolution (the Ethiopia-Somalia conflict). In each of the four cases, examples of the manipulation of stakes, the attitudes of the parties toward each other, and the tactics employed for reaching a particular goal will be given. Even though stakes, attitudes, and tactics are hardly separate in actual preventive processes, they will nonetheless be treated separately in the following discussion.

Managing Stakes

The Somali Conflicts

The conflict between Somalia and two of its neighbors, Ethiopia and Kenya, started with Somali independence in 1960. It can be traced to problems created by the lack of congruence between the inherited colonial boundaries, on the one hand, and ethnically homogenous areas, on the other hand. The idea of a Greater Somalia encompassing all Somali-speaking peoples was designed to rectify the situation created by the colonial powers on the Horn of Africa. But the Somali claims posed a threat to practically every African state because they all contain regions that would be affected by claims similar to those Somalia made upon its neighbors—the Pandora's Box effect.

The main issue for Somalia—bringing all Somalis under one nation-state—was not regulated either in the 1988 agreement with Ethiopia or in any treaty with Kenya. Consequently, the stakes Somalia brought into these conflicts—the idea of Greater Somalia—were only managed, not resolved, and have since been set aside in favor of other priorities. The period leading up to the 1988 agreement between Somalia and Ethiopia can be described as a mutually hurting stalemate following the Ogaden war in 1978 (Zartman 1989, chapter 3). Besides the lack of resolution of the Greater Somalia goal, there have also been processes of escalation (1961, 1963, 1977) and de-escalation (1964, 1967, 1978, 1986–88). In connection with these, a series of mediation efforts were taken by the OAU, as well as by individual heads of state and others (Touval 1972; Agbi 1986; Nweke 1980).

The Somali case shows that de-escalation through preventive negotiation and mediation is possible even when a major issue is left unregulated. In fact, in this case, "unregulation" was the key to progress in other areas. De-escalation in the Somali situation was a parallel process of influences and diplomatic efforts from an emerging regional organization (the OAU) and a subregional organization (the Inter-Governmental Agency on Drought and

Development, IGADD), combined with individual instances of mediation. In a way, the Somali challenge to African unity and territorial integrity helped the emerging organization of the newly independent African states, the OAU, to develop a position on territorial matters. A normative basis or regime for interstate relations in Africa was developed on a regional basis through these extraordinary measures, undertaken to avoid an escalation of Somali border relations problems. The Somali challenge also gave the subregional organization, the IGADD, a mission to develop that was later exercised in the Sudanese conflict as well.

The Honduras-Nicaragua Conflict

This conflict had two crises situations, both of which resulted in a particular management of the stakes involved. The Bonilla-Gomez boundary treaty was signed between Honduras and Nicaragua in 1894. A mixed commission was set up to solve problems involved in the implementation of the agreement, but it was not able to settle all of the issues. The outstanding issues were referred to arbitration by the king of Spain. His award, handed over in 1906, was well received in Honduras, but Nicaragua argued it was invalid because, to a large extent, it met Honduran claims. As one scholar has noted, "Although the award did not grant Honduras all that it had desired, the award can hardly be called a compromise" (Johnson 1964, 7). Efforts at negotiation throughout the interwar period were fruitless, and in 1957, Honduras created a local district, extending the government's penetration into the area disputed by Nicaragua. This caused an acute crisis. The Organization of American States (OAS) intervened and managed to get the parties to agree to place the matter before the International Court of Justice (ICJ), which, in 1960, ruled that the 1906 award was valid. One year later, the Inter-American Peace Committee (IAPC) of the OAS was forced to intervene in order to prevent the impending repetition of the 1957 military confrontation.

Honduras and Nicaragua tried to settle the matter through direct talks in 1960 and 1961, but the talks stalled in February 1961. And though Nicaragua agreed to abide by the judgment of the ICJ, Honduras wanted a more rapid execution of the decision than did Nicaragua. At that point, all the two states could agree on was that IAPC should take action to execute the ICJ decision. Following several drafts, a "basis of arrangement" was agreed upon, regulating the steps and stages of withdrawal and the insertion of new authorities. Both countries were asked to withdraw troops immediately from the areas concerned. Inhabitants could chose between staying and changing nationality or moving into Nicaragua proper. The arrangement also provided for demarcation procedures.

As a third party in the execution of the ICJ judgment, the IAPC was able to smooth the movement of goods and people, including the facilitation of cross-border farming. In all, some four thousand people moved into Nicaragua. The IAPC Mixed Commission executing the ICJ judgment acted effectively and with a view to practical solutions. Its social and boundary-making tasks were complementary because these two processes are closely related. As E. W. Johnson (1964, 163) concludes, "Without the available machinery of the Organization of American States in 1957 and in 1961 it is highly probable that the dispute would not have been solved or that increased violence would have occurred before a settlement was reached."

This situation was an ideal case of stake handling in the sense that it involved an agreed upon procedure at a higher level than the parties, limited to issues that the parties were not able to handle themselves. It also included a combination of conditions necessary for successfully preventing escalation: The conflict was not over a core issue, it was dealt with over a long time, several governments in the respective countries were part of the procedures, and preventive diplomacy was an official process, involving a long-standing commitment.

The direct preventive initiatives (that is, the referrals to ICJ and OAS) did not imply a complete assumption of the process by those organizations, and finalizing the agreement was left to the parties. The parties themselves took over the settlement process on a level where it could be managed peacefully, thus giving them a stake in maintaining what they achieved in the conclusion of the process. This is not always the case.

The Ecuador-Peru Conflict

Peru gained independence in 1821; the following year, Quito also gained independence from Spain but immediately joined the Gran Colombia Republic under Simon Bolivar. The Treaty of Guayaquil of 1829 between Peru and Gran Colombia, both independent, established a boundary through the work of a joint commission. The treaty was approved by the respective congresses, and instruments of ratification were exchanged. In 1830, Ecuador seceded from Colombia and became independent, but Peru did not accept the idea that the new Ecuadorian state had inherited any rights under the Guayaquil Treaty.

Several political, military, and diplomatic confrontations took place over the border issue in the following years. Negotiation efforts in the 1840s were fruitless, and in 1853, Ecuador passed a law addressing free navigation on disputed rivers. Peru broke relations with Ecuador in 1857. Thirty years later, after "perhaps half a dozen attempts" (*Area Handbook for Ecuador* 1966, 289) to settle the issue, both countries agreed, in the Espinosa-Bonifaz Treaty, to ask the king of Spain to arbitrate a division of the disputed Oriente region as a whole. However, both parties felt in advance that the award might turn out unfavorably, albeit for different reasons. When the Spanish king was again approached for arbitration in 1904, he accepted, and five years later, the Spanish

Council of State recommended a borderline to be adopted by the king in his award. However, because the proposed line became publicly known before being awarded, the king decided, in 1910, not to make any award in view of the tension between the two parties. At that point, "war between the two states seemed imminent" (Maier 1969, 42).

In this tense situation, the United States, Argentina, and Brazil offered mediation. However, Ecuador and Peru were not able to settle their differences through the services of the mediating powers. Following the establishment of the 1936 status quo line, both countries accused each other of frequent border incursions. In May 1941, the United States, Argentina, and Brazil again offered their friendly services to mediate in the conflict, an offer that Ecuador accepted but Peru did not; Chile was also made a mediator in the 1942 Rio de Janeiro conference.

In July 1941, fighting broke out in two border areas: the Zarumilla and the Oriente. About five hundred individuals were killed or wounded, at least two-thirds of whom were Peruvians (*Area Handbook for Ecuador* 1966, 296–97). Following a truce in October (the Talara Truce), by which a demilitarized zone controlled by neutral observers was established, the mediators tried to reach consensus on an agreement. After the Japanese attack on Pearl Harbor on December 7, the United States allowed Brazil to take the initiative on behalf of the mediating group. Brazilian Foreign Minister Oswaldo Aranha proposed a line, without total consensus in the mediating group, in order to reach an agreement during the Third Consultative Meeting of Foreign Ministers in Rio de Janeiro in January 1942. With two exceptions, the line is the same as that agreed on in the 1942 Protocol of Peace, Friendship and Boundaries, signed by Ecuador, Peru, and the four mediating powers (Argentina, Brazil, Chile, and the United States) and formally ratified by the congresses of Ecuador and Peru.

However, Ecuador was unhappy with the protocol from the beginning and did not accept the line, on various grounds (historical, moral, and legal); in 1960, it declared the protocol null and void. Peru appealed, and the guarantors declared the protocol valid, raising both legal and nonlegal arguments. One argument was that only 78 kilometers of the total boundary were uncompleted in 1960; another argument held that "it is a basic principle of international law that the unilateral will of one of the Parties is not sufficient to invalidate a boundary treaty nor to liberate it from the obligations imposed therein" (Whiteman 1964, 676–80, cited in Kaikobad 1988, 91). However, Ecuador did not accept the guarantors' decision and in 1965 again claimed the protocol was invalid because, among other reasons, it "was illegally secured by the employment of armed force, and by the occupation and retention of large portions of its territory" (Wood 1978, 219).

Military incidents in the border area took place in 1953, 1977–78, 1981, and 1995, with different levels of casualties. In September 1977, U.S. President

Jimmy Carter raised the border issue with the two parties on signing the Panama Canal treaties, but negotiations were again suspended in 1978. Hostilities also occurred in 1981, and the OAS became involved in preventing an escalation of the conflict. A cease-fire was agreed to after five days of fighting. A minor diplomatic controversy arose in 1991, when the issue was raised in the United Nations, following the first visit of a Peruvian president to Ecuador. In January 1995, severe confrontations took place in the Upper Cenepa region of the Oriente, where aerial surveys had discovered previously unknown topological features. The 1995 Declaration of Itamaraty provided the political basis of continued talks between the two countries. Finally, in 1998, the parties were able to conclude a comprehensive agreement, defining the boundary in the new disputed areas, creating a nature park along the border, allowing nonsovereign access for Ecuador to the upper tributaries of the Amazon, and providing for joint development of the isolated border area (Simmons 1999). In these negotiations, both parties saw that economic benefits in transborder cooperation outweighed a continued standoff. In the process, the stakes changed from a zero-sum territorial confrontation to a positive-sum trade and development agreement.

From the early phases of this conflict, the parties nurtured two different perspectives in understanding its eventual solution. Ecuador stressed the historical documents and their congruence with the basic national aspirations of the country—to be an Amazonian nation, combining effective contact with the Pacific as well as with the Amazon River. For Peru, by contrast, the Amazonian dimension was secondary to state building, to an effective presence in frontier regions, and to the use of diplomatic and military means to secure its interests. The differences between the two states in population, size, and economic capacity added to these political differences. Furthermore, Ecuador and Peru have had different stakes in the border regions. Ecuador has been idealistic, stressing the colonial heritage and historical and legal rights and trusting the inter-American system as a partner in dealing with an often superior neighbor. Meanwhile, Peru has nurtured materialistic stakes, stressing the evidence of physical presence, the unclear legal situation, and the need to increase its penetration into Upper Amazonas.

After the 1942 Rio Protocol, the stakes did not change, but their material basis did. Ecuador accepted the protocol as a foundation for a negotiated solution, and after 1995, so did Peru, which had long claimed that no substantial matters remained to be dealt with after 1942. The peace process after the 1995 incidents, based on the Itamaraty Declaration, initiated management of the stakes in a way that moved closer to a conclusion than in previous attempts. The key to the prevention of future conflict was the reformulation of stakes as the jointly profitable economic development of the region, impossible without an agreement, rather than zero-sum sovereignty. Nonsovereign access to the Amazon was also provided for Ecuador.

Attitudes and Tactics

The Somali Conflicts

Somalia changed its approach to the boundary problems it had with Kenya and Ethiopia in the space of a few months in 1967. Escalations in the conflict had occurred several times during the first half of the 1960s. In September 1967, however, the first steps were taken toward a new relationship between the three countries, beginning at a meeting in Kinshasa, after mediation by President Kenneth Kaunda of Zambia. The Somali leadership was overthrown two years later, and a new military junta took over. When the Ethiopian revolution of 1974 appeared to weaken Somali's neighbor and the conflict-management agreement of 1967 showed no promise of a boundary resolution, Somali president Mohammed Siad Barre saw an opportunity to contest the border, and in 1976, he began to plan the 1977–78 Ogaden war. His decisive defeat, a subsequent coup attempt, and pressure from Ethiopian-backed dissidents opened the parties to careful mediation by IGADD in 1986, leading to another conflict-management agreement two years later (Zartman 1989, chapter 3).

When substantial changes take place in the relations between parties, the situation is often described as a change in attitudes. Saadia Touval (1972, 233), for instance, wrote about the Somali cases after a series of agreements in 1968 and 1969: "These agreements, and the rapid change from hostility to conciliation, became possible because of a modification in the attitudes and positions of the disputants." The problem is, which is the chicken and which is the egg? It is crucial for this analysis to consider the extent to which both positions and attitudes are the primary movers of changes and why positions and attitudes have changed.

Tracing the process backward shows that the tactics employed by the Somali government, once it had decided upon its new approach to the boundary problems, were different from any previous attempts. Before the Kinshasa meeting, Somalia ceased hostile propaganda and guerrilla activities. It also approached Ethiopia and Kenya simultaneously (not one at a time, as in previous attempts), thereby making it difficult for either of those countries to hinder the other. In fact, a third party, France, also became involved at some point, when it and Somalia agreed to lessen tensions over the Territories of the Afar and Issa (French Somaliland), claimed by both Ethiopia and Somalia.

If the tactics employed are to be successful, what attitudes do they require? In the Somali case, the key was the view that the core value of Greater Somalia did not need to be realized immediately: Somalia could gain more from other values being strengthened while waiting for an opportunity to pursue the most important value. Such a position did not imply a compromise or abandonment of the core value as a main stake. Again, as in other preventive cases, Somalia considered it increasingly necessary to have good relations with the surrounding countries in the late 1960s and 1980s.

This change of attitudes, in its turn, required a core issue that could be managed. Unification, a principle affecting neighboring states, has been a demand in many constitutions (e.g., in Germany, Yemen, Korea, Ireland). This issue can be managed through postponement—a change of time perspective, not only space conditions. It should also be noted that the stable and peaceful relations that developed between Somalia and its surrounding states lasted only until 1969; after a new president, Siad Barre, seized power, the conflicts escalated again. The Ogaden war in 1978 was a major confrontation in that process, and its inconclusive results led to another conflict-management agreement in 1986–88 and then to the ultimate change—the collapse of the Somali state (Zartman 1989, chapter 3; Adam 1995).

The Honduras-Nicaragua Conflict

The long-standing Honduras-Nicaragua conflict, the product of diametrically different views among the parties over where to locate the boundary line, has been managed in spite of consistent and temporarily inflamed feelings among the parties. The opponents' weak interest in settling the conflict at all during the first part of the twentieth century caused a slow and inefficient management of the issue by both parties at critical moments. In its early stages, the problem was a remote and insignificant incompatibility over a territory whose characteristics were little known by the respective governments. Nicaraguan congratulations to Honduras after having lost to it a sizable piece of territory in the 1906 award is indicative: There was a need to show respect for "civilized means of settlement of disputes" (Johnson 1964, 15), and the territory in question was not the main concern. However, Nicaragua raised concerns in 1907 and 1912 over matters that remained part of the dispute throughout, including consideration by the ICJ, and that supported the animosities surrounding the matter. Also, the value of the disputed territory gradually became important for the two governments, particularly in connection with oil drillings in the area in the 1950s.

The many preventive measures advanced by the United States, the IAPC, Venezuela, and Costa Rica were all promoted while both parties insisted that their positions could not be changed (Johnson 1964, 17). This partly explains the dragging process. In fact, it is impossible to identify any significant change of attitudes relevant for the conflict process in the literature about this dispute. In retrospect, then, the most important lesson is that the process could be brought forward to a settlement and finally accepted in spite of the strong negative feelings. All ingredients for military confrontations were at hand: Only the preventive measures undertaken—at least ten separate initiatives between 1913 and 1961—can explain the low level of violence during the conflict period.

The Ecuador-Peru Conflict

The parties to this complex conflict, with all its escalation and de-escalation processes, have changed their outlook in recent years in regard to the emotional aspects of the conflict, in stark contrast to their postures over the dispute's long history (Wood 1978). This is not to say that the old patterns are not expressed in current popular and political views. However, the 1995 crisis and its diplomatic continuation continued to be dealt with by both parties in a way that confirmed a gradual evolution on both sides since 1981 toward a recognition of the existence of a problem (Peru) and the need to find a political solution based on the conditions created by the Rio Protocol (Ecuador). This attitudinal shift is due to generational changes among the military and diplomatic elites, as well as the gradual idiosyncratic appearance of the whole matter, in a region of modernization, integration, and globalization processes.

Conclusion

From this brief analysis of ongoing and regulated boundary conflicts, a set of observations about preventive diplomatic efforts in such situations can be made. It was shown that a large majority (two-thirds) of boundary conflicts de-escalated, through negotiation as well as in informal ways, during a twenty-year period. The more complex conflicts (in terms of issues at stake) needed formal regulation, which was not true for the simple (one-issue) cases. In the complex cases, recurrent conflict was prevented by managing the stakes in one of five ways: (1) compensation, (2) partition, (3) sharing, (4) accommodation, and (5) consolidation. Consolidation—overriding the boundary issue to foster joint development or face a common enemy—occurred most frequently, followed by accommodation—changes in the boundary to meet local population needs; compensation does not appear to have been used. Such measures were shown to be effective preventive measures in boundary conflict processes.

It is interesting that those conflicts that entailed few issues were the ones that faded away unregulated. The difference as compared to the more complex issues is significant. The most plausible reason for this is that, in these cases, the issues at stake were surpassed by other matters that made them fade away into a politically insignificant status—Bourguiba's notion of *dépassement*. This is, in addition, more likely to happen in cases with few issues as long as those issues are not major strategic concerns for one of the parties. Such issues are "indivisibles" and are less susceptible to bargaining than material stakes and so can only be worn out rather than traded off. This topic is well worth further attention, and it suggests that conflicts should be helped to disappear while they are simple, lest they gather other grievances and turn into tough cases to crack.

In the final analyses, examples were given from cases in which a series of preventive diplomatic efforts kept serious interstate boundary conflicts from escalating (Honduras-Nicaragua, the Somali cases) and consistently intransigent attitudes were overcome by a systematic application of internationally based third-party preventive initiatives. Like the general overview of issues and informal de-escalation, the case studies also indicate that differences in the nature of stakes can be an asset, not necessarily an obstacle, in the process of finding a durable basis for peaceful boundary relations.

References

Adam, Hussein. 1995. "Somalia: A Terrible Beauty Being Born?" In *Collapsed States: The Disintegration and Restoration of Legitimate Authority*, ed. I. William Zartman. Boulder: Lynne Rienner.

Agbi, S. O. 1986. *The Organization of African Unity and African Diplomacy, 1963–1979*. Ibadan: Impact.

Allcock, J., G. Arnold, A. Day, D. S. Lewis, L. Poultney, R. Rance, and D. J. Sagar. 1992. *Border and Territorial Disputes*, 3rd ed. London: Longmans.

al-Najjar, Mustafa, and Najdat Fathi Safwat. 1984. "Arab Sovereignty Over the Shatt al-Arab During the Kaíbide Period." In *The Iran-Iraq War: An Historical, Economic and Political Analysis*, ed. M. S. El Azhary. London: Croom Helm.

Amankwah, H. A. 1981. "International Law, Dispute Settlement and Regional Organizations in the African Setting." *Indian Journal of International Law*, vol. 21 (official organ of the Indian Society of International Law, Scindia House, Kasturba Gandhi Marg, New Delhi).

Aravena, Francisco Rojas. 1997. *Latin America: Alternatives and Mechanisms of Prevention in Situations Related to Territorial Sovereignty*. Santiago, Chile: Flacso.

Area Handbook for Ecuador, 1966. 1966. Washington, D.C.: United States Government Printing Office.

Brownlie, Ian. 1979. *African Boundaries: A Legal and Diplomatic Encyclopaedia*. London: C. Hurst.

Butterworth, Robert L. 1976. *Managing Interstate Conflict, 1945–74: Data with Synopses*. Pittsburgh, Pa.: University of Pittsburgh.

———. 1980. "Managing Interstate Conflict, 1975–79: Data with Synopses–Final Report." Mimeograph.

Calvert, Peter. 1983. *Boundary Disputes in Latin America*. London: Institute for the Study of Conflict.

Carrion Mena, Francisco. 1989. *Política exterior del Ecuador: Evolución, teoría, práctica*. Quito: Editorial Universitaria.

Chang, Luke T. 1982. *China's Boundary Treaties and Frontier Disputes*. London: Oceana.

de Kun, Nicolas. 1965. *The Mineral Resources of Africa*. Amsterdam: Elsevier.

Diehl, Paul F. 1998. *A Road Map to War: Territorial Dimensions of International Conflict*. Nashville, Tenn.: Vanderbilt University Press.

Diehl, P. F., and G. Goertz. 1988. "Territorial Changes and Militarized Conflict." *Journal of Conflict Resolution* 32, no. 1: 103–22.

Eduards, Maud. 1985. "Samarbete i Maghreb: On regionalt samarbete mellan Marocko, Algeriet, Tunisien och Libyen 1962–1984." *Stockholm Studies in Politics*, 27. Ph.D. diss., Stockholm University.

Fisher, Charles A. 1964. *South-East Asia: A Social, Economic and Political Geography*. London: Methuen.

Goertz, G., and Paul F. Diehl. 1992. *Territorial Change and International Conflict*. London: Routledge, Chapman and Hall.

Gurr, Ted Robert. 1990. *Polity II: Political Structures and Regime Change, 1800–1986*. Ann Arbor, Mich.: ICPSR.

Hertslet, E. 1967 [1907]. *The Map of Africa by Treaty*, vols. 1–3, reprint of 3rd ed. London: Frank Cass.

Huth, P. 1996. *Standing Your Ground: Territorial Disputes and International Conflict*. Ann Arbor: University of Michigan Press.

Jarring, Gunnar. 1983. *Rikets förhöllande till frömmande makt: Memoarer 1952-1964*. Stockholm: Albert Bonniers.

Johnson, Earl Wayne. 1964. "The Honduras-Nicaragua Boundary Dispute, 1957–1963: The Peaceful Settlement of an International Conflict." Ph.D. diss., University of Denver.

Kacowicz, A. 1994. *Peaceful Territorial Change*. Columbia: University of South Carolina Press.

Kaikobad, Kaiyan Homi. 1988. *The Shatt-al-Arab Boundary Question: A Legal Reappraisal*. Oxford: Clarendon Press.

Kautilya. 1960. *Arthasastra*, trans. R. Shamasastry. Mysore: Mysore Printing and Publishing House.

Khadduri, Majid. 1988. *The Gulf War: The Origins and Implications of the Iraq-Iran Conflict*. New York and Oxford: Oxford University Press.

Kocs, S. 1995. "Territorial Disputes and Interstate War, 1945–87." *Journal of Politics* 57, no. 1: 159–75.

Kratochwil, F., P. Rohrlich, and H. Mahajan. 1985. *Peace and Disputed Sovereignty: Reflections on Conflict over Territory*. Lanham, Md.: University Press of America.

Krieg, William L. 1980. *Ecuadorean-Peruvian Rivalry in the Upper Amazon*. Author's abstract published as *Peru-Ecuador Boundary*, International Boundary Study, Office of the Geographer, U.S. Department of State. Washington, D.C.: Bureau of Intelligence and Research.

———. 1986. *Ecuadorean-Peruvian Rivalry in the Upper Amazon: Second Edition Enlarged to Include the Paquisha Incident (1981)*. Washington, D.C.: Department of State External Research Program.

Maier, Georg. 1969. "The Boundary Dispute Between Ecuador and Peru." *American Journal of International Law* 63, no. 1: 28–46.

Morgan, W.T.W. 1973. *East Africa*. London: Longman Group.

Morris, Michael A. 1985. "The 1984 Argentine-Chilean Pact of Peace and Friendship." *Oceanus* 28, no. 2 (Summer).

Morris, Michael A., and Victor Millan, eds. 1983. *Controlling Latin American Conflicts: Ten Approaches*. Boulder: Westview.

Newman, D. 1999. *The Dynamics of Territorial Change*. Boulder: Westview.

Nordquist, Kjell-Åke. 1992. *Peace After War: On Conditions for Durable Inter-State Boundary Agreements*. Report 34, Department for Peace and Conflict Research, Uppsala University.

Nweke, Aforka G. 1980. *Harmonization of African Foreign Policies, 1955–1975: The Political Economy of African Diplomacy*. Boston: African Studies Center, Boston University.

Office of the Geographer, U.S. Department of State. 1963. *British Guiana-Venezuela Boundary.* International Boundary Study no. 21. Washington, D.C.: Bureau of Intelligence and Research.

——. 1963. *Mali-Mauritania Boundary.* International Boundary Study no. 23. Washington, D.C.: Bureau of Intelligence and Research.

——. Various years. *Boundary Series.* Washington, D.C.: U.S. Bureau of Intelligence and Research.

Pillar, Paul R. 1983. *Negotiating Peace: War Termination as a Bargaining Process.* Princeton: Princeton University Press.

Prescott, J.R.V. 1965. *The Geography of Frontiers and Boundaries.* London: Hutchinson University Library.

——. 1975. *Map of Mainland Asia by Treaty.* Melbourne: Melbourne University Press, in association with the Australian Institute of International Affairs.

——. 1987. *Political Frontiers and Boundaries.* London: Allen & Unwin.

Randle, Robert F. 1973. *The Origins of Peace: A Study of Peacemaking and the Structure of Peace Settlements.* New York: Free Press.

Roy, A. B. 1999. *Blood and Soil.* Columbia: University of South Carolina Press.

Schofield, Richard N. 1986. *Evolution of the Shatt Al-Arab Boundary Dispute.* Cambridgeshire, England: Middle East & North African Studies (Menas) Press.

Scott, Gary L. 1975. *Chinese Treaties: The Post-Revolutionary Restoration of International Law and Order.* New York and Leiden: Oceana Publications and A. W. Sijthoff.

Simmons, Beth. 1999. *Territorial Disputes and Their Resolution.* Washington, D.C.: U.S. Institute of Peace.

Starr, H., and B. A. Most. 1976. "The Substance and Study of Borders in International Relations Research." *International Studies Quarterly* 20 (December): 581–620.

Teran, Francisco. 1986. *Geografia del Ecuador.* Quito: Libresa.

Tinker, Hugh. 1956. "Burma's Northeast Borderland Problems." *Pacific Affairs* 29, no. 3 (September): 324–46.

——. 1967. *The Union of Burma: A Study of the First Years of Independence.* London: Oxford University Press.

Touval, Saadia. 1972. *The Boundary Politics of Independent Africa.* Cambridge, Mass.: Harvard University Press.

Trout, Frank E. 1969. *Morocco's Saharan Frontiers.* Geneva: Droz.

Vasquez, J. 1995. "Why Do Neighbors Fight? Proximity, Interaction, and Territoriality." *Journal of Peace Research* 32, no. 3: 277–93.

Wallensteen, Peter, and Margareta Sollenberg. 1997. *States in Armed Conflict.* Report no. 46, Uppsala Conflict Data Project, Department of Peace and Conflict Research, Uppsala University, Sweden.

Widmalm, Sten. 1997. "Democracy and Violent Separatism in India: Kashmir in a Comparative Perspective." Ph.D. diss., Department of Government, Uppsala University.

Wood, Bryce. 1978. *Aggression and History: The Case of Ecuador and Peru.* Ann Arbor, Mich.: University Microfilms International, and New York: Institute of Latin American Studies, Columbia University.

Zartman, I. William. 1987. *International Relations in the New Africa,* updated ed. Lanham, Md.: University Press of America.

——. 1989. *Ripe for Resolution: Conflict and Intervention on Africa,* updated ed. New York and Oxford: Oxford University Press.

3

Territorial Conflicts: Claiming the Land

Anatole Ayissi

Communal claims to territory are among the basic threats to peace in the post–Cold War world. With the universalization of liberal democracy, peoples have gained freedom of expression and found room to act, channels of political expression have been unblocked, means for political organization have increased, and opposition forces in antiregime struggles have been empowered (Auvinen and Kivimäki 1997, 7). In a world made up of many states that incorporate several nationalities, the territorialization of nations has every potential for becoming one of the most disruptive factors in the twenty-first century (Niebuhr 1932, 59). It is already a matter of concern that over two hundred ethnic and religious minorities and subordinate majorities throughout the world "are contesting the terms of their incorporation into the 'world order'" (Gurr 1993, IX). In this perilous climate, it is good to try to solve territorial claims once they burst into open confrontation; it is better still to prevent them from escalating into mass violence.

This chapter discusses negotiation practices and the conditions that must be met to ensure the effectiveness of initiatives aimed at preventing violence and violent escalation in areas where a communal group claims its own territory within a sovereign state. *Territorial claim* refers to a situation of conflict in which an organized group of people (the communal group) claims a right of ownership over a piece of land that is, or is supposed to be, an integral part of a sovereign state. The claim can be categorized as either mutually exclusive vis-à-vis the state's perceived right (leading to secession) or accommodatively inclusive (leading to autonomy, power sharing, or decentralization). Cases of boundary conflicts between two or more sovereignties—already discussed in the preceding chapter—are not considered here; instead, this chapter focuses on situations of contested decolonization (e.g., Western Sahara) or aborted incorporation within the international borders of a sovereign state (e.g., Eritrea, East Timor).

For preventive action to be effective, a sound knowledge of what exactly constitutes the problem in needed; that is, the stakes and attitudes in the confrontation must be clearly understood. Because "the transition from war to peace is essentially the reverse of the transition from peace to war, what causes nations to cease fighting one another must be relevant in explaining what causes nations to begin fighting one another" (Blainey 1973, VIII). Consequently, a thorough grasp of the explanatory factors of the claims (stakes) and, most important, of what makes those claims escalate into open forms of mass violence (attitudes) is vital in the search for the most productive ways and means (tactics) to prevent this escalation. Put another way, efforts to avert the outbreak of violence or to contain its escalation in a communal claim for territory "must be preceded by an understanding of the sources and patterns of that conflict" (Horowitz 1985, 564).

This approach implies that one should proceed beyond the methodological orientations imposed, for instance, by a case study context and begin with a rigorously elaborated taxonomy of stakes, attitudes, and tactics. What is a territorial claim? Why and how is territory claimed? What preventive tactics are most effective? What are the basic obstacles to negotiation or transactional practices and processes? These are important questions that demand rigorously framed general answers—not specific answers for each case of territorial contest but globalized responses that apply to territorial claims in general (despite the fact that each claim is unique and dependent on contextual and circumstantial factors and parameters).

Thus, this chapter seeks to put into perspective a taxonomy of the constant general situations and relationships favoring or hindering preventive initiatives in cases of territorial claims. This broad explanatory nomenclature should help to systematically establish commonalties for situations of violence escalation or de-escalation among such varied and specific cases of territorial claims as the Chiapas insurrection in Mexico, the Sahrawi rebellion in Western Sahara, the Ibo uprising in Nigeria, the Tamil fighting in Bangladesh, the Irish Republican Army (IRA) war in Northern Ireland, the Kashmiri unrest in India, the Basque and Corsican struggles for self-determination in Spain and France, respectively, the French-speaking Canadians' claims for a "free Quebec" in Canada, the German-speaking Italians' struggle for cultural exceptionality in South Tyrol, or the white South African extremists' battle for their own Volkstaat (national state) in South Africa. The classification will also help explain why and how preventive negotiation is successful in some cases but unsuccessful in others.

A scientific, issue-area study of the efficacy of preventive action in territorial conflicts requires "explanation[s] that will hold cross culturally, ... definition of basic principles by which to classify cases, [and] an understanding of patterns of conflicts" (Horowitz 1985, XI). On this basis, the first fundamental question is why territory is claimed by a communal group within a sovereign state.

Territory as a "Common Good" and Territory as a "Need"

A state's territory is normally a common good, an equally shared heritage for the citizens of the state. For that reason, territory is considered to be one of the three basic components—together with people and a government—endowing a state with a sovereign moral personality that is universally recognized by the law and the community of nations. As long as a state's territory is perceived as a patrimonial asset equally possessed and enjoyed by the whole assembly of citizens, there is no room for territorial claims. Such claims only occur when the national territory (or what the state's authorities suppose to be the national territory) is no longer perceived as a common good by a concerned group of citizens and instead becomes a "need" for this group. Territorial claims are about the desacralization of territorial absoluteness. They represent iconoclastic uprisings by politically active communal groups determined to question the absolutely sacred dogma of the state's territorial integrity. As a process of deconstruction and deinstitutionalization of the national state's order and boundaries, this clash of perceptions in regard to the stakes is a potential source of instability and violence.

But what, at a specific point in time, makes a group of people become heretics and openly question the sacred absoluteness of the national territory? Why do people rebel against the territorial order? For a politically assertive communal group (Gurr 1993, 1), how does the perception of the state's territory as a common good become transformed into a contradictory and desacralizing perception of the national territory as their basic human need? If we know the process leading from peace to violence in situations of territorial claims and if we thoroughly understand how territorial claims run from nonviolent enunciation to violent affirmation, by turning the available explanation on its head (Zartman 1995, 3) it will be possible to determine the most efficient tactics for violence prevention.

The conversion of a portion of a sovereign state's territory into a need for a given group of people is essentially a political issue. Because politics is a matter of who gets what, when, and how, this need for a national territory is fundamentally a need for a different and better governance, that is, a new and just power distribution in terms of goods, justice, well-being, symbols, and hopes. Yet politics is just the tree hiding the forest, for the real ultimate objectives, obscured by a thicket of politicized claims, involve the basic tangible and intangible human needs of the claiming group (that is, the host of deprivations, frustrations, dissatisfactions, humiliations, insecurities, ambitions, and aspirations as related to the enjoyment—or lack thereof—of a national territory). Hence, the question of why people rebel against a given territorial order within the context of a given sovereignty can find a first-degree answer in some central conclusions of human needs theories (Gillwald 1990, 118). People rebel against a given state's territorial order to satisfy at least three fundamental needs: security, identity, and prosperity.

Security

A politically assertive communal group rebels against a state's territorial order when the claiming party perceives the claimed territory as necessary for its security. In other words, members of the group (1) do not consider their security fully assured within the context of the existing national territorial order, and (2) believe that the only way to ensure their safety is to remake the territorial order by establishing a new sovereignty (secession) or reconfiguring authority (integration, decentralization, autonomy). This security obsession can be reciprocal. Given the communal group's claim on the territory as an asset for its security, the state frequently believes that the loss of the claimed territory will jeopardize its own security. The case of the Palestinians and the state of Israel is a prime example of this scenario. The reciprocal obsession for territorial security has shaped the highly complicated nature of the "territory for peace" solution in the Middle East. When the Israeli representative to the United Nations declared that "Israel's aim has always been to have the right to live in an area where peace and security prevail" (Yativ 1992, 1) or when former Israeli prime minister Yitzhak Shamir affirmed that "peace without security will be a disaster for Israel" (in Corm 1997, 118), they were expressing the obsession for security that animates both Israelis and Palestinians. In the same way, the Ibos' uprising for a separate state of Biafra in Nigeria during the 1960s was largely explained by the fact that they strongly felt their physical and economic security was no longer guaranteed in the non-Ibo regions of the country—precisely in the Northern part where massive and merciless anti-Ibo pogroms occurred and the wealth of the rich Ibo traders and businesspeople was ransacked (Balencie and De La Grange 1996, 1:318–19).

Identity

Describing territorial demands as "claims to preserve identity" (UNPREDEP 1996, 27) is a potentially explosive way of defining the stakes when the claimed piece of land is considered to be a constitutive part of the claiming group's identity, as Jerusalem is in the Middle East, Quebec is for the French-speaking Canadians, Corsica is for the Corsicans in France, and southern Sudan is for non-Muslim and non-Arab Sudanese.

In the former Soviet Union, the seductive appeal of national territories for those seeking to preserve national identities repeatedly led to escalating violence, as will be discussed by P. Terrence Hopmann in chapter 6. Ethnic identity has long played a strong role in the Caucasian region, where the notion of the "people's right of self-determination" was developed by Vladimir Lenin (in article 9 of the Communist Party program); seven decades later, the communist "good cause" against capitalist colonialism had become a determining factor in the disastrous dislocation of the communist dream. Today, merciless struggles for national identities and territories remind us that (in Leon Trotsky's words) the Soviet Union has never been a "national state" but just a "state of nationalities" (Trotski 1979; Goldenberg 1994; Frederick 1996).

In Western Cameroon, Quebec, South Tyrol, and Euskadi, linguistic groups consider a specific territory integral to their identity. Although Cameroon has two official languages, French and English, anglophone militants claim a separate status for their territory (Balencie and De La Grange 1996, 1:327). The case of English-speaking Cameroonians resembles that of French-speaking Canadians in Quebec, who have a strong sense of ethnic self-identity and little desire or opportunity for assimilation into the Anglo-Canadian majority (Gurr 1993, 159). German-speaking Italians in South Tyrol, another community with a strong sense of group identity, appeal for greater autonomy for their territory within Italy (Gurr 1993, 157). The Spanish Basques, who were briefly autonomous under the Spanish republic in the 1930s, were subordinated to a severely centralized and authoritarian state and denied all manifestations of cultural or political identity from 1939 until Francisco Franco's death in 1975. Consequently, a radical faction of the Basque independence movement, Euskadi Ta Askatasuna (ETA), is leading a terrorist campaign for the complete independence of the Basque nation, despite a reinstatement of autonomy since Franco (Gurr 1993, 154–55; Clark 1995).

Similar territorial claims for the sake of identity also play a role in the Casamance (Senegal), Brittany, and South Africa. The Volkstaat project is a separatist ambition aimed at preserving and protecting white identity in a pluralist South Africa through the creation of a specific political entity for "the only white indigenous tribe of Africa"—a "tenth white province" constituted of the regions where Afrikaners represent "an important proportion of the population" (Balencie and De La Grange 1996, 1:498–99). The opposite of the white state dream is found in the aspirations of the Inkatha Freedom Party (IFP) for a Kwazulu-Natal state within a federal republic of South Africa; to better preserve Zulu identity, the IFP wants to "give a land [to the] Zulu nation" (or keep the Zulu nation in its "fatherland") (Balencie and De La Grange 1996, 1:500). Similarly, the Bretons in France "have since 1898 given birth to a succession of regionalist movements. These movements are rooted [among other factors] in their distinct Celtic language and customs" (Gurr 1993, 155; also see Reece 1977). As Ted Gurr (1993, 155) noted, "A 1975 poll showed that half of all inhabitants of Brittany identified themselves as being as much Breton as French, and one-quarter felt more Breton than French." Similarly, the Diolas of Casamance feel more Casamançais than Senegalese, and for years, they have been fighting for the liberation of Casamance and the elimination of the "rampant cultural and linguistic assimilation" by the Dakar government (Balencie and De La Grange 1996, 1:264).

In the absence of a single ethnicity or language, territory itself can be the source of identity when "dissimilar groups voluntarily choose to live territorially separate within the same sovereign State" (Eide 1993, 25) or, for secessioned claims, in a different new sovereignty. In Chad, people from the southern region do not feel any common identity with the northerners who have been governing the country since 1975 when they overthrew the government of François Tomabalbaye, a southerner with whom they themselves had felt no common identity. Southern secessionist aspirations were nearly realized during the weak and anarchic regime of Goukouni Weddeye in 1980 (Balencie and De La Grange 1996, 1:224). In Sudan, the southern Sudanese rebelled against the Muslim government in Khartoum from 1955 to 1972 and again after 1983. Many southerners feel their communal identity is deeply threatened by Arabization and Islamization from the north and so claim a national territory in which their identity can be secured, although they are torn between aspirations for federal autonomy and full independence. And in northern Somalia (Somaliland), two areas of former colonization inhabited by different clans of the same ethnic group have failed to meld into one nation. In 1991, after the overthrow of the Somali dictator Mohammad Siad Barre, Somaliland proclaimed its "independence," which no one has recognized (Balencie and De La Grange 1996, 1:432). In all these cases, violent conflict has arisen from assertions of identity incarnated in territory.

Prosperity

There are two types of territorial claims for the sake of prosperity or material well-being: claims from poverty and claims from abundance. In the first type, the claiming group feels that it is unfavorably discriminated against in the allocation of the national wealth. For that reason, this group affirms its right to economic and social development and demands the establishment of a new and just territorial order. These words from a Chiapas (Mexico) peasant reveal much about unjust wealth distribution as an explanation for his group's claims for a new territorial order in Mexico: "Misery is everywhere ... we have nothing to eat, we have no money, we have nothing. . . . We work a lot, but we never benefit from our efforts." Consequently, the Chiapas people not only claim but violently fight for a new and just territorial order. As one of the Chiapas "freedom fighters" said about a "liberated" area of this region: "We have declared Huitiupan an autonomous area. We have named a [new] president, for the one who was there before was not constitutional: he was not elected by a popular vote" (in Lemoine 1996, 43). In the 1960s, the strong independence claims from separatists in Quebec were, in part, motivated by a perceived economic injustice in the province to the detriment of the Francophones (Balencie and De La Grange 1996, 1:183). Similarly, the historical poverty and isolation of Brittany compared with the rest of France gave impetus to regional political movements and separatist campaigns after World War II (Gurr 1993, 155).

In the second type of prosperity claims—claims from abundance—the claimed territory is endowed with rich resources that the claimants consider to be legitimately theirs. The heated demands of the anglophone secessionist militants in Western Cameroon are tied to the important oil resources located in the southwestern province (Balencie and De La Grange 1996, 1:328). In the former Zaire (today the Democratic Republic of Congo), a vast country regularly shaken by centrifugal dynamics, Katanga's secessionist crises in the early 1960s, together with the development of a Katangese identity discourse, is partly explained by the region's riches in precious minerals, the benefits of which the Katangans wanted to keep for themselves. The same is true for the Kasai region, which contains the main diamond mines of the Congo (Balencie and De La Grange 1996, 1:392, 406). In Angola, Cabindan nationalism among the 250,000 inhabitants arises from the fact that the tiny enclave of 7,270 square kilometers is so extravagantly rich in oil reserves that it is sometimes called the "African Kuwait"; the separatists hope that the "Cabindese nation" will one day fully enjoy the benefit of "its" oil (Balencie and De La Grange 1996, 1:522–23). Similarly, the tireless and merciless Chechens' struggle for independence is animated, among other factors, by the hope that the important oil resources of Chechnya can someday support an independent developmental process for the Chechen nation (Longuet-Marx 1996). In Papua New Guinea since 1988, Bougainville Island has been under attack from a separatist guerrilla group; the "Islanders are deeply unhappy with the modalities of exploitation of the important mining resources" on "their" island (Balencie and De La Grange 1996, 2:326). And in Chad, the prospects of the coming oil exploitation are already renewing separatist fever. Some southern rebellious movements, such as the Forces Armées de la République Fédérale (Armed Forces of the Federal Republic [FARF]), categorically refuse to allow their oil to benefit the "people from the north" (Balencie and De La Grange 1996, 1:227).

Far from being generated by an atavistic, aggregative basic instinct, many of these separatist struggles are the consequence of the state's hypercentralization and nation-building policies. Harsh and tactless policies to unify and homogenize the population create feelings of insecurity among communal groups and lead to the dislocation of national unity (Clastre 1974). As Donald Horowitz (1985, 567–68) rightly observed, "Several groups that underwent cultural revivals in order to thwart tendencies to assimilation also became strongly separatist, and conscious policies of assimilation have frequently provoked the same response." Consequently, one of the essential tasks of preventive diplomacy in such an uncertain and fearful environment is not only to reestablish trust and confidence but also to reconfigure the exercise of political power so that the decision-making processes become participatory, undertaken with the full involvement of all segments of society.

The factors stimulating territorial claims—security, identity, and prosperity—are not mutually exclusive; typically, they overlap one another. For instance, a feeling of communal solidarity through the recognition of a common identity may underpin a territorial claim for prosperity if the territory on which the politically active communal group lives is endowed with rich natural resources. Similarly, members of a communal group may feel their security is at stake because of their shared identity. Furthermore, members of the claiming group most often feel they are victims of a pervasive social discrimination due to their unique identity (Gurr 1993, 67); they would prefer to enjoy *positive* discrimination because of their position in a specific part of the national territory as a defined communal group, distinct from the other citizens.

In addition to being thoroughly informed about the basic reasons pushing people to rebel against a state's territorial order, anyone hoping to effectively undertake preventive action in a dispute should also be aware of the protagonists' perceptions of the conflict. Ultimately, perceptions determine the nature of the confrontational "game."

The Nature of the Game

The term *nature of the game* refers to the attitudes of the protagonists as they fight each other. Is the confrontational process pursued with a merciless, zero-sum logic of winner takes all and loser forfeits all? Is the possibility of mutually benefiting trade-offs or compromises entertained? Is an "indeterminate" situation of the Chicken Dilemma Game involved? Obviously, there are no clear-cut answers to these key questions concerning the nature of the game.

Beyond the basic needs for security or prosperity, many of the previously mentioned claims involve the glorification of the claiming group's identity (recognition and prestige). This appears to be a tough point for preventive negotiation. In the words of Donald Horowitz (1985, 566): "Since group prestige or well being is relative, many claims will be zero-sum and therefore not susceptible to a strategy of enhancing everyone's rewards." Moreover, when the issues at hand are recognition and prestige, the stakes are mainly "symbolic, [and] symbolic demands seem to be less compromisable than claims that can be quantified" (but cf. Gurr 1985, 3).

One of the central characteristics of territorial claims is that the object of the conflict is an asset with zero supply elasticity. That is, the claimed territory cannot be expanded or multiplied. In a secessionist claim, what is won by one side is automatically lost by the other. Compromise may be possible in regard to how the territorial pie is divided, but there is no way to enlarge the total sum represented by the territory in dispute. In such a situation, attitudes toward and perceptions of the stakes define the nature of the game. Consequently, a claim for territory can be either a hard zero-sum situation, a soft zero-sum situation, or a gray-zone situation, depending on each party's attitude or degree of determination to pay whatever price is required to reach its goal.

Hard Zero-Sum Situation

When the issue is security, the very survival of the claiming group is considered to be at stake. Consequently, the conflict tends to be perceived as a matter of life and death and as a hard zero-sum game. In such a situation, accommodation and compromise are very unlikely as long as the claiming party continues to perceive its incorporation within the state order as suicidal. The group has an "us-or-them" mentality, and the probability of escalation is high. A typical hard zero-sum scenario is the Israeli-Arab conflict, particularly as it was configured before the Oslo Accords. Palestinians believe that the claimed territories are their communal home and that possession of the disputed land is critical to their very survival—hence, their extremely hard attitude vis-à-vis Israel, the occupying foe. Egyptian president Gamal Abdel Nasser once said, in the name of the Arab nation, "Our basic aim will be to destroy Israel" (in Lindsey 1992, 61). The zero-sum nature of this game is doubly hardened when, in response to the extreme position of the claiming group, the Israeli government responds with an equally annihilative attitude. Because the stake—the disputed territory—cannot be multiplied or enlarged, the situation becomes one of a suicidal cohabitation between two equally determined protagonists engaged in a merciless and hard zero-sum struggle for security and, indeed, for life.

Soft Zero-Sum Situation

When the issue is a matter of prosperity, a soft zero-sum game results. At this level, possibilities for accommodation and compromise do exist, to the extent that a more or less constructive and mutually rewarding solution to the distributive problem can be found. In Cabinda, Brittany, South Tyrol, or even Quebec, the promotion of economic and social prosperity in the claimed regions has greatly softened the nature of the war game between the communal group and the state.

Gray-Zone Situation

Issues engaging group identity produce a gray-zone situation. The nature of the process is determined by the intensity of the claiming group's parochial feelings, the density of committed power and engagement, the strength of contextual factors such as external support, and the degree of overlap between the identity factor and the other two needs, security and prosperity. The fact, for instance, that the security and prosperity factors are quite intangible in the French-speaking Canadians' claims for a "free Quebec" or that the security factor is absent in the claims of the Bretons or South Tyroleans explains, in part, why these conflicts hardly escalate beyond the level of a constitutional confrontation; in these disputes, compromise and accommodation are the rule, and rough intolerance and a mutual lack of understanding are the exception.

Basic Characteristics of Territorial Claims

Once the reasons for the territorial claim and the nature of the conflictual process are understood, the third step on the road to preventive diplomacy is to determine the fundamental characteristics of the conflict itself.

Asymmetry

Claims for territory generally pit a state (the stronger protagonist) against a fraction of its citizens (the weaker protagonist); these conflicts are disputes "between a dominant center and a peripheral group" (Eide 1993, 9). For that reason and because they are internal conflicts, such disputes are marked by structural asymmetry. This provides a difficult terrain for preventive diplomacy because asymmetry is generally considered unconducive to negotiation. One may think that this flaw can be overcome by redressing the asymmetry and thereby balancing the situation. Unfortunately, case studies show that attempts to redress asymmetry only further complicate negotiation dynamics (Zartman 1995, 3–4). The dramatically asymmetrical nature of territorial conflicts pushes the weaker party to avoid a face-to-face confrontation in a conventional war with the stronger party and explains why most territorial contests are low-intensity wars without a front, undertaken with guerrilla strategy.

Fixed Stakes

A state's territory is a fixed asset: It does not vary. Consequently, an increase in the demand or claim for territory can never be met by an increase in the supply of the "goods." This makes territorial claims highly complicated issues for preventive action. Moreover, the fact that these disputes are civil conflicts make them more difficult to negotiate, for civil confrontations seem to have an inherent tendency to intractability. Less than one-third of modern civil wars (including anticolonial wars) have been influenced by negotiation (compared to one-half of modern interstate wars), and two-thirds of the internal conflicts have ended in the surrender or elimination of one of the parties (compared to fewer than one-quarter of the international conflicts). Because an internal conflict is so obdurately resistant to negotiations (Zartman 1995, 3; Pillar 1983; Stedman 1991), it becomes nearly insoluble if it also entails a claim for territory (Vasquez 1993; cf. Thompson 1995).

Stratification

Claims for territory are usually multilayered confrontations with both communal and regional dimensions. They also have a strong appeal for those who would intrude from the outside. In reality, few internal wars are purely internal, and many of them, although more or less autonomous and self-sufficient, have a substantial and often dominant international dimension. Internal rebellions over territory necessarily mirror regional conflicts because of transnational populations and interests. And when "the overarching state identity breaks down," as I. William Zartman (1995, 4) noted, "the component pieces draw in external support from their brothers in neighboring states." As a result, many claims for territory turn into proxy wars for distant powers. However, though they are "regionalized, exploded, proxied, and supported," these conflicts nonetheless remain internal in their cause and and at their core (Zartman 1995, 4).

Double Veto

It is not easy for one party in a territorial conflict to achieve a definitive military victory over the other, and if negotiations are held, each party has the power to block the resolution of the conflict. So, despite the asymmetrical nature of the conflict, the ultimate constructive solution usually depends on the goodwill of the warring parties. One might assume that these intractable conflicts could be effectively dealt with by favoring or supporting a military victory by one side and thereby crushing the rebellion. But in reality, military victory typically does not bring an end to the conflict. In fact, case studies show that "defeat of the rebellion often merely drives the cause underground, to emerge at a later time" (Zartman 1995, 3). The refusal to accept the double-veto reality makes the territorial claim a confrontation with "cyclical-sequence escalation" (Smoke 1977, 27).

Parochiality

Territorial claims usually stem from a sentiment of relative deprivation. Claimants feel frustrated or believe they have been poorly or unjustly treated by the national state, a perception that runs counter to their expectation that the state will not discriminate among its citizens Thus, claims for territory are parochial, mass-mobilizing contests. The claimants develop their fight for justice with a deep sense of group consciousness: The circumscribed destiny of a whole community is considered to be at stake in such a struggle. This parochial aspect is most often dramatized by the fact that the claimants usually are (or come to be) identified as an ethnocentric community. Furthermore, the high sense of injustice and the deep group consciousness accompanying claims for territory lead to egocentric behaviors. The group develops a ferocious, autonomous will to increase its well-being in terms of security, recognition, or prosperity, independent of the possible consequences for the rest of the state's population—or even the short-term cost to the group itself.

As parochial conflicts mainly concerned with issues of faith (identity), survival (security), and justice (prosperity), territorial claims also tend to involve very high levels of power and commitment and be laden with emotion. Indeed, the irrational bent of human beings is especially obvious in these types of disputes because they evoke irrational liberative or separatist behaviors. Many communal groups claiming territory suffer from cognitive dissonance—the extraordinary "ability to maintain belief in spite of continual, definite evidence to the contrary" (Zeigler 1990, 378; also see Festinger 1957). The fact that there may be a huge gap between claims and attainable expectations does not diminish the determination of the claiming party. This explains why ethnic groups attempt secession "even when it appears they would have much to gain by remaining in the undivided state and much to lose by leaving it" (Horowitz 1985, xii).

In such a situation—and for preventive negotiation in general—it can be dangerous and illusory to believe that a rational approach to the conflict will succeed. Indeed, it may be a catastrophic error to try to explain to a communal group that its separatist claims are irrational because the group can hardly survive as an independent state. Among a group suffering from cognitive dissonance syndrome, the peace broker, even if he or she is "logically" honest, will be accused of being partial and acting against the group's interest (in other words, *for* the state's interest).

The five broad characteristics of territorial claims are listed in table 3.1, together with their related effects. These characteristics should only be considered as general tendencies that are helpful in better understanding the nature of territorial-claim conflicts when examined independent of contexts and circumstances. Most but not necessarily all of these characteristics are generally operative in a given dispute.

Once the issue at stake, the nature of the conflictual process, and the characteristics of the conflict are known, it is easy to determine which conditions and contexts will promote or hinder preventive diplomacy.

Strength and Weakness of Tactics

What Tactics Work and Why They Succeed

Preventive negotiation is designed to transform conflict from violent to nonviolent expression. For territorial claims, three basic preventive tactics are available: exit, autonomy, and access (Gurr 1993, chapter 10). One piece of good news for

Table 3.1. Basic Characteristics of Territorial-Claim Conflicts and Their Related Effects

Characteristic	Key Feature(s) of the Conflict	Related Effects
Asymmetry	A stronger protagonist (the state) is pitted against a weaker one	Low-intensity disputes
Fixed stakes	The object of the conflict (the territory) cannot be increased	Often zero-sum, intractable situations
Stratification	The conflict is multilayered, with communal, regional, and/or international dimensions	Spillover, interference, power borrowing
Parochial	The conflict is communal, involving noninclusive (exclusive) group interests	Ethnocentricity, egocentricity, massmobilization, emotionality, irrationality, relativity, demonstrativeness
Double veto	Any sustainable solution requires both sides' approval	Recurrent and protracted disputes

those who practice preventive diplomacy is that "all [these options] are suscepti-ble to accommodation by means of transforming policies and new institutional arrangements" (Gurr 1993, 292).

The exit option implies a complete withdrawal and a total severance of ties be-tween the claiming communal group and the state, so once the exit choice becomes effective, the conflict—if it persists—ceases to fit into the operational definition used in this chapter. In other words, the issue stops being an internal problem and becomes an international one between two sovereign states. For that reason, only the last two options—access and autonomy—will be considered in this analysis.

Access means that minority peoples, individually and collectively, are guaran-teed the means to pursue their cultural, political, and material interests with the same rights (and restraints) that apply to other groups. Autonomy means that the claiming group "acquires a collective power base, usually a regional one, in a plu-ral society" (Gurr 1993, 292). Access is about sharing power within a centralized political-administrative system. Autonomy is about building a regime within a new context of decentralized political and administrative authority.

Autonomy preserves group identity, security, and prosperity, whereas access (though it, too, may preserve these goods) can also entail pressures to integrate citizens as individuals and thus destroy the group. To reach a constructive and sus-tainable accommodation, the elaborated preventive tactics must address the needs of both parties to the conflict. On the one hand, public officials have interests and obligations to protect, the most fundamental of which are (1) maintaining the state's integrity and authority, and (2) assuring the support and revenues needed to keep their positions and pursue their objectives. Officials' responses to com-munal demands are a function of these larger interests (Gurr 1993, 292). On the other hand, communal leaders also have interests and obligations to protect, and they must offer a Promised Land (or a better and brighter future) to their rela-tively deprived people. How these communal political entrepreneurs respond to the state offers and how they react to preventive diplomacy tactics is conditioned by these interests and obligations.

The First Tactic of Accommodation: Access

Accommodation through access is an application of the Laswellian definition of politics as "who gets what, when and how." Struggles for territory are rebellious uprisings over the enjoyment of tangible and intangible goods derived from the exercise of political power within a state. When managing territorial claims, com-munal elites are real political entrepreneurs interested not only in the well-being of their people but also in their personal political destiny (Zartman 2000). Con-sequently, access to the political system involves both the provision of guarantees and means for communal groups to pursue their cultural, political, and material interests with the same rights (and restraints) that apply to other groups and the integration of the communal group's leaders within the governing body of the state (in high and most often strategic or symbolic positions).

Access Through Elite Integration: Power Sharing   This tactic tacitly supposes that communal political leaders are also—and maybe most of all—political entrepreneurs. Their investment in the group's claims is justified by personal political ambition as well as more or less genuine nationalist sentiments. Thus, preventive diplomacy applies power-sharing tactics to defuse violence by dynamically integrating group leaders into the governing machine.

This tactic has at least two powerful therapeutic effects. First, it neutralizes the leaders' will to mobilize the integrated community, which is now happy enough to enjoy its "situational rent" within the state's governing body. Communal leaders have an enormous power to mobilize, influence, or orient the opinions and behaviors of their group members. Consequently, the use of this tactic supposes that if leaders are given a rent, they will appease their people. And if one of their own gains access to the political system, the communal group senses that it, too, "got the power" and really runs the state. This representative, symbolic satisfaction defuses the violence instinct.

Access tactics are an application of the grand coalition condition of the consociational model. As Arend Lijphart noted, "The primary characteristic of consociational democracy is that the political leaders of all significant segments of the plural society cooperate in a grand coalition to govern the country" (in Horowitz 1985, 574–75). Some theoreticians of consociationalism (e.g., Lijphart 1977) attribute the peaceful stability of heterogeneous societies such as Switzerland, Austria, Belgium, and the Netherlands to the establishment of a balanced power-sharing system via grand coalitions in which cooperation among the leaders of different groups transcends segmental and cultural cleavages (Horowitz 1985, 571). Consociationalism is essentially about balanced power sharing. Where communal identities and organizations are the main components of society and politics, power is exercised jointly by the constituent communities; the groups are proportionally represented in government, and they have mutual veto power. In Africa, for example, consociationalism has been an effective power-sharing tactic in Cameroon (albeit with no veto power for any of the governing factions).

The elite integration tactic was also successfully used in South Africa to moderate the Kwazulu-Natal claims for independence or autonomy. The Inkatha Freedom Party's leader, Chief Mangosuthu Buthelezi, used the group's leadership position and skills to maximize its "access" within the new democratic South African regime governed by its political archrival, the African National Congress (ANC). As a matter of fact, the IFP quit the Constitutive Assembly in 1995 and wrote a regional constitution for the Kwazulu-Natal that would provide special status for the group within a federal South Africa. This move was potentially disruptive for the peace process in the region. The stake was a high one for Buthelezi: With the end of both the Cold War and apartheid, he was about to lose his position as an influential political actor on the South African scene. Consequently, he needed to raise the stakes by blackmailing the Constitutive Assembly with his separatist ambition. To alleviate his frustrations, he was given a situational rent by being integrated into the new South African government as minister of the interior, a high-ranking post.

If the access tactic involving situational rent is to be fully effective, two conditions have to be met: The integrated elite must be truly representative, and group cohesion must exist (Laitin 1987).

In terms of the first condition, the leader needs to be a true daughter or son of the communal group and a person the group respects, honors, and even venerates. This was the case in 1961 in Cameroon. People in the two English-speaking parts of Cameroon (the northern and southern portions bordering on Nigeria) were given the choice, through a referendum, to join Nigeria or to remain with the Republic of Cameroon. Those in the northern part chose to join Nigeria, but the southerners decided to remain in Cameroon, following their paramount leader, John Ngu Foncha. After the vote, Cameroon became a bilingual federal republic with both a French-speaking and an English-speaking part. Foncha, as well as many other anglophone elites, were integrated into high positions in the Cameroonian federal government.

In regard to the second condition (which is a requirement for the first), the group should recognize itself in the ideals and ambitions of the leader, and the leader should be in phase with the aspirations of the group—if he or she does not actually inspire or create those aspirations.

When there is no recognition of the representativeness of the integrated elite and no comprehensive communion at the level of the ideals and ambitions of the claiming group, elite integration can only work if two further conditions obtain: (1) The veto power of the fighting faction within the communal group must be weak enough to oblige this faction to seek an agreement with the government, and (2) the fighting faction must be unimportant enough so that its tactical decision either to join the government or to continue fighting has no decisive impact on the attitude and perceptions of the communal group's leading (that is, nonfighting) faction.

This hypothesis can be better understood by analyzing the situation of the Inkatha Freedom Party and its leader, Buthelezi, within the South African scene during the transition from apartheid to democracy. There are about eight million Zulus in South Africa, comprising 22 percent of the population. Of these, the IFP claims two million members, or just 25 percent of the Zulu population (the real percentage is probably lower). This means that at least 75 percent of the Zulus do not share the ideals, interests, and ambitions of the IFP and its leader. Moreover, in the 1994 elections, the IFP obtained only 9.1 percent of the vote at the national level, and even in the Kwazulu-Natal, its traditional fief, it won only 50.32 percent of the vote. Nevertheless, Chief Buthelezi continues to be obeyed, respected, and venerated by the (small) fighting faction of the Zulu community. Given this situation, it would be easier to defuse violence by integrating Buthelezi into the government rather than having him remain a paramount warlord of all the Zulus of South Africa or letting his authority within the IFP be shaken by serious actions on the part of rebellious elements.

Access through elite integration can also be a collective matter. Instead of giving access to one dominant leader in the government, members of the claiming group can be recruited en masse. In Canada, for instance, following the recommendations of the Royal Commission on Bilingualism and Biculturalism (established in 1963), which aimed at equal partnership and institutional bilingualism, French-speaking Canadians were given wider representation within the higher levels of the bureaucracy (McRae 1990). The Quebecois have not been fully satisfied by the federal government's accommodation policies, but violence has been largely averted, and although the movement for a free Quebec is not dead, referenda on Quebecois sovereignty have never passed.

Access Through Norm Integration: Regime Building Another aspect of violence prevention involves negotiating constitutional arrangements that give the communal group guarantees that its identity, security, and prosperity will be fully and equally assured within a plural state. In postapartheid South Africa, the IFP sought both access to a government position for its leader and integration of specific norms into the South African constitution that would guarantee the preservation and promotion of Zulu identity and the freedom of its expression and peaceful affirmation. At the same time, the democratic character of the South African constitution enabled the Freedom Front and the Conservative Party (both of which were fighting for the South African "white tribe's" identity) to express their claims peacefully and legally in the context of a parliamentary regime (Balencie and De La Grange 1996, 1:502).

Because separatist aspirations are usually generated by the fear of being maltreated or oppressed due to one's communal identity, regime building through constitutional arrangements is a valid form of preventive action. A good constitution is an effective peace-building instrument if it recognizes and legally reaffirms the basic, self-evident truth that all human beings "are created equal [and] endowed by their Creator with certain unalienable Rights [among which] are Life, Liberty and the pursuit of Happiness" (as expressed in the U.S. Declaration of Independence). Constitutional recognition of plurality within a context of unity canalizes the physically violent expression of claims into peaceful verbal or rhetorical enunciation.

The tactic of norms integration also explains why territorial claims are less likely to degenerate into chaotic, merciless violence in a democracy. Moreover, even when there is an outbreak of violence, the situation can be rapidly mastered, as shown by the experience of the Quebecois, the Bretons, the South Tyroleans, the Berbers in Morocco, and others.

The Second Tactic of Accommodation: "Sweeteners" (Symbolic Autonomy)

A second tactic of accommodation consists of "being sweet" to the communal group within a territory. Two options are available in this regard: (1) recognizing or glorifying the communal group's identity, and (2) promoting the group's prosperity.

The Glorification of Identity Claims for the recognition or glorification of identity are intensely polarizing issues. Consequently, preventing violence through constructive manipulation of identity is a very delicate operation. The process should start with an answer to one fundamental question: What is the conflict all about (Saunders 1999)? This was the démarche adopted by the Canadian government when it established the Royal Commission on Bilingualism and Biculturalism (McRae 1990). Among the many measures elaborated by this commission were recommendations for equal partnership and institutional bilingualism. As a result, the federal government developed policies to improve the position of French speakers and the French language in its agencies. Bilingualism in public service improved, and Ottawa slowly began to take on the appearance of a bilingual national capital. This "glorification" of the French language greatly defused the tension between the Canadian government and its French-speaking citizens.

The same tactic was used by the French government vis-à-vis Brittany, where recognition and glorification of the national culture and identity of the Bretons was used preventively to contain or avert violence. The distinct Celtic language and customs of the Bretons had gradually eroded after French was made the language of public education in the 1880s. Ultimately, the Front for the Liberation of Brittany (FLB) carried out a sustained protest, including bombings of public property, from 1966 to 1979 (Gurr 1993, 156). But in the 1970s and 1980s, the French government began to promote the Breton language (Gurr 1993, 155–56), a move that contained and finally eradicated violence in the region.

In Sudan, the military government that took power in 1969 recognized the historical and cultural differences between the north and south segments of the country and proposed regional autonomy within a united Sudan. As a result, violence gradually dissipated, and negotiations produced the Addis Ababa Accord of February 1972, which granted autonomy to the south as a single region with substantial internal self-rule (Montville 1990). Similarly, the three hundred thousand German speakers of the northern region of Italy's South Tyrol were granted autonomy in 1948 in order to preserve their German cultural identity (Gurr 1993, 157). In both cases, violence was prevented as long as autonomy was respected.

Promotion of Prosperity Because relative deprivation is a defining element in the outbreak and escalation of violence in a territorial claim, economic measures designed to reduce the unjust situation are important. In Brittany, central government policies in the post–World War II period have promoted regional economic development, and as the economic gap between Brittany and the center closed by the early 1990s, the more extreme manifestations of Breton nationalism disappeared (Gurr 1993, 156). But in South Tyrol, the recognition of cultural identity was not followed by a correction of economically and politically unjust situations, and the Italian majority continued to dominate political and economic affairs in the larger Trentino–Alto Adige region, strengthened by continued Italian immigration into the territory (Gurr 1993, 158). In the 1950s, this situation led to the South Tyroleans' appeals for greater autonomy, which were followed by escalating violence and terrorism that persisted into the early 1960s. The Italian government reacted constructively with a revision of the 1948 statute and the institution of a new autonomy status in 1972, under which the German minority gained effective control of public administration, education, and cultural affairs. In fact, positive discrimination tactics have been so successful that South Tyrol has become one of the most prosperous regions of Italy (Gurr 1993, 158).

But how far can the government go in its politics of positive discrimination without provoking the ire of the other populations, communities, or regions? The situation in South Tyrol shows that such preventive initiatives should be carefully considered and thoroughly balanced in a context of limited state resources and unlimited human wants. Positive discrimination in South Tyrol may, in time, become a victim of its own success. One serious issue is the resentment felt by the region's Italian minority over the preferential treatment given to ethnic Germans, which is expressed in electoral support for a neofascist party in the region (Gurr 1993, 158).

The Third Tactic of Accommodation: Autonomy

Another way to prevent violence or contain its escalation in a conflict involving a territorial claim is to grant autonomy to the claiming party. Autonomy is a middle-ground solution, lying between exit and access or between integration and secession. The autonomy solution gives a parochial home to the communal group within the comprehensive universe of a pluralistic state. As a tactic to defuse violence, autonomy was used in Spain for the Basques in 1980, in Nicaragua for the Miskitas in 1990, in India for the Nagas and Tripuras in 1972, and in the Philippines for part of the Moros in 1990 (Gurr 1995, 8).

The basic challenge for an autonomous regime is to strike the proper balance between the comprehensive rights and prerogatives of the state and the political power and administrative competence devolved to the autonomous region. Issues of national defense, finance, and foreign affairs usually do not constitute subjects for controversy, but problems arise when it comes to defining competencies in the sphere of social and economic development. Usually, it takes more than one stroke of a pen to establish the right balance. In South Tyrol, for example, three autonomy pacts were crafted within a period of forty years (in 1948, 1972, and 1988), but Ein Tyrol separatists are still far from fully satisfied (Gurr 1993, 159). In Sudan, the 1972 agreement fell apart after eleven years of a profoundly uncertain equilibrium. And in the Basque region of Spain, violence continues despite the existence of an autonomous regime.

If tactics of accommodation are employed, why is preventive action effective in some cases of territorial claims but ineffective in others? There seems to be a close correlation between the democratic or nondemocratic nature of the regime and the outcome of the claim: Historical records tend to show that authoritarian regimes are not prone to accommodation. For these regimes, territorial claims, like any other type of civil insubordination, constitute a direct challenge to the personal authority of the head of state. In such a polarizing context, conflict management is reduced to the eradication (at any cost) of the opposition, and preventive diplomacy becomes nearly powerless. The Ibos were crushed in Nigeria in the 1960s, and the Bagandas met the same tragic fate in Uganda, as did the Kurds in Turkey, Iraq, and Iran, the Tamils in Sri Lanka, various nationalities in the former Soviet Union, and the East Timorese in Indonesia until 1999.

By contrast, most politically assertive communal minorities in Western democracies since the 1970s have received a positive response to their political demands, producing a substantial decline in political protest and violence. One general conclusion is that preventive negotiations leading to elite integration, norm integration, and regime building are employed more frequently in liberal democratic states with participatory and responsive governments than in monolithic authoritarian states (Gurr 1993, 137). This hypothesis is corroborated by the experience of the Bretons in France, the South Tyroleans in Italy, and the French-speaking Canadians in Canada.

Ripening Attitudes and Rhetoric

Although it is hard to define the precise moment when a conflict is ripe for resolution (Zartman 1989), it *is* possible to indicate the kind of rhetoric and attitudes that might lead conflict to the ripening point. A study of the discursive structures of conflict shows that as long as the protagonists remain trapped within abrasive and "rigidifying interpretations of the dispute" (Auvinen and Kivimäki 1997, 11), there is little hope that preventive diplomacy will be effective. However, a rhetoric of appeasement and détente moves the dispute into a ripening zone. In the conflict in the Middle East, the 1993 Oslo Accords were made possible by a rhetoric of appeasement, in part resulting from the pressure that Norway, a robust and honest peace broker, provided to give a chance to the negotiations. In Israel, the Palestine Liberation Organization (PLO) was officially recognized as an honorable partner and legitimate representative of the Palestinians (instead of being perceived as a terrorist organization). Before that, PLO chief Yasser Arafat wrote an unprecedentedly accommodating letter to the Israeli prime minister, expressing a number of ripening rhetorical propositions: Arafat stated (1) that the PLO officially recognized Israel's right to exist and live in peace and security, (2) that he himself supported peaceful negotiation of the conflict, (3) that he opposed terrorism and promised to use his authority to prevent the use of violence by Palestinians, and (4) that he officially declared null and void the articles of the Palestinian Charter denying Israel's right to exist (Corm 1997, 128–32). These reciprocal ripening attitudes and rhetoric were fundamental to the Oslo Accords.

Like rhetoric and attitudes, ripening circumstances and contexts facilitate preventive negotiation. In a situation of territorial claims, changes in the state's government or in the rebellion's leadership can blow a breath of hope into the conflict. This happened during the June 1992 legislative elections in Israel when the confrontationist hawks from the Likud were defeated by the much more accommodative doves from the Labor Party; the Oslo Accords were the outcome. In Sri Lanka, after the August 1994 legislative elections had brought the Popular Alliance to power and the leader of the party, Chandrika Kumaratunga, was elected president of the republic, a cease-fire agreement was signed within two months between the government and the rebellious Liberation Tigers for Tamil Eelam (LTTE) (Meyer 1996, 38), although it did not last.

Obstacles to Preventive Negotiations

Claims for territory give rise to notoriously complicated conflicts. In these double-vetoed disputes, negotiation appears to be the best option "not because it is such a good solution but because all the others are so bad" (Clark 1995, 62). Conflicts of this type contain all the pitfalls of civil wars and nearly none of their "better" qualities, at least as far as conflict negotiation and preventive diplomacy are concerned. They are highly intractable conflicts—lengthy and merciless wars without a front. Moreover, they are permeable to outside intervention. Because of this explosive combination of factors, these disputes are probably among the worst that preventive negotiators must confront. An examination of the main weaknesses of preventive negotiation in situations involving territorial claims illuminates the conditions required for effective violence prevention and containment.

The first fundamental obstacle is the *structural complexity* of the conflict—the perverse tendency of territorial claims to compound within single disputes more than one of the five characteristics and their connected effects described in table 3.1. Facing a structurally complex conflict, preventive negotiators will have to deal not only with each characteristic individually but also with any combination of them. Timing appears to be particularly important for any preventive tactics at this level: Early engagement in preventive diplomacy, when power and commitment are still at low levels and the complexifying process is just beginning, is the right way to do the right thing at the right time.

Many territorial conflicts are *stratified conflicts,* with more than one geopolitical dimension. Most often, the purely communal layer of the claim is compounded by one or two more layers related to a regional structural rivalry or a global struggle for power, as often occurred during the Cold War. The Western Saharan conflict is a typical instance of a stratified conflict with a defining regional dimension—the Algeria-Morocco rivalry. As noted by Zartman, "The Saharan conflict [is] deep-seated and multilayered. ... By the end of 1984, the Saharan conflict had lost its specific focus on a piece of land and had become a clash of alliances in the Maghrib" (Zartman 1989, 70 and 61). Consequently, efforts to prevent or contain violence in the conflict must take into consideration the regional structural rivalry opposing Algeria and Morocco and their respective allies (Mohsen-Finan 1997). The same observation is valid for Northern Ireland, where the effectiveness of any initiative to prevent violence is conditioned by the relationship between the United Kingdom and the Republic of Ireland, as negotiated in the Good Friday Agreement of 1998. In Sri Lanka, the separatist war of the

LTTE is reflected in the strained relations between India and Sri Lanka. (Meyer 1996, 38; Maitra 1995, 36–37). The civil war in Sudan attracted significant external involvement from neighboring African states, the parties in the Arab-Israeli conflict, European countries, and the superpowers.

It is therefore necessary to take into account each layer or dimension of the conflict, none of which should be neglected or subordinated in the search for constructive and sustainable solutions. It is an illusion to believe that violence at the communal level can be prevented or contained without considering the regional rivalry for power, the second layer of the conflict, or the international global confrontation for hegemony, the third. This reality was clearly addressed by President Bill Clinton when he identified the resumption of dialogue between the Irish and British governments as a critical precondition to establishing a lasting peace in Northern Ireland (O'Clery 1997, 48). Former Assistant Secretary of State Chester Crocker (1992) has indicated that it was necessary to resolve the Namibian and Angolan conflicts first on the superpower level and then on the regional level before the local dimensions of the disputes could be resolved; in other words, the allies and sources of power were moved away from the local contestants.

It is equally illusive to believe that violence can be prevented or contained only by ameliorating power relations at the regional or the international level, without considering the grassroots or communal level. Despite the decisive impact that the external sources of power have on the conflict outcome, the communal dimension retains a certain level of autonomy; the confrontation is not just a proxy war remotely controlled by external masters. For example, it is a fallacy to think that a gentlemen's agreement between Turkey and Greece alone will make for a lasting peace in Cyprus (although those two nations must, of course, be taken into consideration). In the 1950s and 1960s, peace initiatives failed to contain violence in Cyprus because they were insufficiently attentive to the intercommunal dimensions of the conflict and to each community's security interests. The first peace initiatives concentrated on finding a settlement acceptable to Greece and Turkey, even at the expense of the two Cypriot communities. The London-Zurich Accords and the subsequent Constitutional Accord failed because they were imposed on the two ethnic communities. Ironically, they solved the immediate problem—the matter of independence—without preventing the ensuing problem—the creation of a viable state. Efforts to prevent the outbreak and escalation of violence fell short, and worse still, they also contributed to the escalation of the conflict by failing to strike the right balance in the negotiations and subsequent settlement between regional and intercommunal interests in Cyprus (Hampson 1996, 48–49). Similarly, in Afghanistan, a 1989 settlement on the superpower and regional levels in the Geneva Accords left the Afghan factions free to continue fighting among themselves over the spoils of the state for the next decade (Bokhari 1995; Rubin 1995). Clearly, international settlements are necessary but insufficient conditions for local resolution.

Any peace process operates on two fronts: the fighting front, occupied by the conflicting protagonists, and the prevention front, where one or more peace brokers work (Corm 1997, 8 and 125). Effective violence prevention or containment requires that each of these fronts remain unified. An ideal situation for a peace initiative has only three agendas—the two fighting parties' agendas and the peace brokers' agenda. *Front dislocation* occurs when the fighting front stops being homogenous (e.g., when a guerrilla force splits into two or more rival branches) or when those in the peace-brokering front stop following a common path (e.g., when mediators compete with each other). If there are more than two fighting parties, with multiple and competing agendas, stakes, and commitments, or if the peace brokers' front falls apart, the task for preventive diplomacy becomes much more difficult.

Such a situation occurred at the beginning of the conflict in the former Yugoslavia and led to what Richard H. Ullman (1996, 109) called the "European fiasco" in the Yugoslavian crisis. The peace brokers' front became dislocated when "the problem of recognition" deeply divided the European mediators. Germany and Italy (as well as Austria, a candidate for membership in the European Community [EC]) argued for prompt recognition of Croatia and Slovenia, which were seen as exercising their right to self-determination, whereas the Dutch, French, and British, supported by the United States, the UN secretary-general, and his envoy, Cyrus Vance, were against immediate recognition (Ullman 1996, 105). As a result, preventive diplomacy could not succeed. Violence was not contained, and Yugoslavia was transformed into a huge nightmare for Europe and the international community. Later, the question of an arms embargo on Bosnia divided Europe and the United States for a long time.

The lessons are clear, if difficult to put into practice. Mediators and all who seek to prevent violence must coordinate their actions and work together rather than at cross-purposes. In pursuing prevention, they should seek out the strongest factions from the center of the impending conflict—neither the most moderate nor the most extreme—and further strengthen them to prevent escalation.

Conflict prevention often suffers from *spineless initiatives* that are advanced by weak intervenors or that stem from a lack of conviction. Unless the peace efforts are backed by a robust and honest peace broker, there is no hope for success. Another reason for the European fiasco in the former Yugoslavia, for instance, was that the Organization for Security and Cooperation in Europe (OSCE) was an unwieldy body as yet unsuited to be an effective negotiator or a collective security force; its members did not show enough commitment to its role to make it effective (Ullman 1996, 109; Hoffmann 1995). The OAU in the Western Saharan conflict, the United Nations in Cyprus, or even, after 1992, the United States in the Mideast (Stein and Lewis 1991) all were inadequately organized or committed to pursue preventive diplomacy. Again, the solution is easy enough to prescribe but requires a reversal of the factors of weakness: Preventive engagement must have the commitment and concentration of third parties, sometimes for long periods.

The way words are said, phrases are framed, and propositions are enunciated largely determines how the words are understood, how phrases are interpreted, and, ultimately, whether proposals are adopted or rejected. In the preventive diplomacy of conflict, the *tyranny of words* is considerable. Preventive negotiation is only indirectly about conflict resolution. Preventive diplomacy makes the bed for conflict resolution by containing the outbreak or escalation of violence, so that conflict can be managed and resolved in a safer, less tense, less polarized, and more politically enabling environment. The enlargement of the preventive diplomacy agenda beyond its legitimate "territorial" borders carries with it potentially explosive confusion. The tendency to slide from the language of prevention to a rhetoric of judgment can have dangerous effects in a situation of open conflict characterized by high levels of power and commitment and deep misunderstanding and distrust. Any sideslipping to judgmental rhetoric may cause at least one of the protagonists to consider itself betrayed and to withdraw from the preventive efforts, and the peace broker will automatically be discredited and delegitimized (Ould Abdallah 1996).

When the OAU voted to admit the Sahrawi Arab Democratic Republic as a member in 1982 instead of continuing the work of its Implementation Committee to prevent further escalation of the Western Sahara conflict, when the United States in 1992 withheld recognition of the PLO as one of the parties to the Madrid peace process to handle the Palestinian conflict, or when some European states recognized Croatia and Slovenia in 1991 instead of preventing Yugoslavia from tearing itself apart, they each took a side in a conflict and lost their preventive capacity.

Conclusion

A close examination of the stakes, attitudes, and tactics for preventive diplomacy in situations involving territorial claims makes it clear that these conflicts are highly complicated confrontations for which preventive action remains, in large part, unarmed. Even with apparent success stories such as Quebec, South Tyrol, or Belgium, a tireless, recurrent cycle of verbal or physical violence constantly reminds us that, in cases of territorial claims, nothing should be taken as a success in preventive diplomacy until, after much time has passed, the divisive power of parochial memory is defeated by the wisdom of objective reason.

References

Aguirre, Mariano. 1997. "Vers la fin du conflit du Sahara occidental." *Le Monde Diplomatique* (November): 6.

Auvinen, Juha, and Timo Kivimäki. 1997. "Towards More Effective Preventive Diplomacy: Lessons from Conflict Transformation in South Africa." Working papers 4, University of Lapland, Faculty of Social Sciences.

Balencie, Jean Marc, and Arnaud De La Grange. 1996. *Mondes rebelles: Acteurs, conflits et violences politiques.* 2 vols. Paris: Editions Michalon.

Blainey, Geoffrey. 1973. *The Causes of War.* New York: Free Press.

Bokhari, Imtiaz. 1995. "Internal Negotiation among Many Actors: Afghanistan." In *Elusive Peace: Negotiating an End to Civil Wars*, ed. I. William Zartman. Washington, D.C.: Brookings.

Burton, John. 1990. *Conflict: Human Needs Theory.* New York: St. Martin's.

Clark, Robert P. 1995. "Negotiations for Basque Self-Determination in Spain." In *Elusive Peace: Negotiating an End to Civil Wars*, ed. I. W. Zartman. Washington, D.C.: Brookings, pp. 59–76.

Clastre, Pierre. 1974. *La société contre l'Etat.* Paris: Les Editions de Minuit.

Corm, Georges. 1997. *Le Proche-Orient éclaté: Mirages de paix et blocages identitaires, 1990–1996.* Paris: Editions La Découverte.

Crocker, Chester A. 1992. *High Noon in Southern Africa.* New York: Norton.

Deutsch, Karl. 1965. "Introduction." In *A Study of War*, ed. Quincy Wright. Chicago: University of Chicago Press.

Eide, Asbjørn. 1993. *New Approaches to Minority Protection.* Report 93/4. Geneva: Minority Rights Group International.

Enderlin, Charles. 1997. *Paix ou guerres: Les Secrets des négociations israélo-arabes, 1917–1997.* Paris: Stock.

Festinger, Leon. 1957. *A Theory of Cognitive Dissonance.* Stanford, Calif.: Stanford University Press.

Frederick, Bernard. 1996. "Les Frontières incertaines de la Russie." *Conflits: Fin de Siècle.* Paris: Le Monde Diplomatique, Collection "Manière de voir" 29, pp. 21–25.

Gillwald, Katrin. 1990. "Conflict and Needs Research." In *Conflict: Human Needs Theory*, ed. John Burton. New York: St. Martin's, pp. 115–24.

Goldenberg, Suzanne. 1994. *Pride of Small Nations.* London: Zed.

Gurr, Ted. 1993. *Minorities at Risk: A Global View of Ethnopolitical Conflicts.* Washington, D.C.: United States Institute of Peace Press.

Hampson, Fen Osler. 1996. *Nurturing Peace: Why Peace Settlements Succeed or Fail.* Washington, D.C.: United States Institute of Peace Press.

Hoffmann, Stanley. 1995. "The Politics and Ethics of Military Intervention." *Survival* 37, no. 4 (Winter): 29–51.

Horowitz, Donald L. 1985. *Ethnic Groups in Conflict.* Berkeley: University of California Press.

Laitin, David. 1987. "South Africa: Violence, Myths, and Democratic Reform." *World Politics* 39, no. 2 (January): 258–80.

Lemoine, Maurice. 1996. "Ombres de guerre sur le Chiapas." *Conflits: Fin de Siècle.* Paris: Le Monde Diplomatique, Collection "Manière de voir" 29, pp. 42–46.

Lijphart, Arend. 1977. *Democracy in Plural Societies.* New Haven: Yale University Press.

Lindsey, Hal. 1992. *The Late Great Planet Earth.* New York: Harper Paperbacks.

Longuet-Marx, Frédérique. 1996. "Pride of Small Nations—Suzanne Goldenberg." *Conflits: Fin de Siècle.* Paris: Le Monde Diplomatique, Collection "Manière de voir" 29.

Maitra, Ramtanu. 1995. "Who Is Escalating Tension in Kashmir?" *EIR* 22, no. 25: 6–7.

Marcos, Sous-Commandant. 1994. *Ya Basta: Les Insurgés zapatistes racontent un an de révolte au Chiapas.* Paris: Dagorno.

McRae. Kenneth. 1990. "Canada: Reflections on Two Conflicts." In *Conflict and Peacemaking in Multiethnic Societies*, ed. Joseph Montville. Lexington: Heath.

Meyer, Eric. 1996. "Impasse au Sri Lanka." *Conflits: Fin de Siècle.* Paris: Le Monde Diplomatique, Collection "Manière de voir" 29, pp. 38–40.

Mohsen-Finan, Khadija. 1997. *Sahara occidental.* CNRS Editions.

Monod, Aurore. 1994. "Feu Maya: Le Soulèvement au Chiapas." *Ethnies* 9: 16–17.

Montville, Joseph, ed. 1990. *Conflict and Peacemaking in Multiethnic Societies.* Lexington: Heath.

Niebuhr, Reinhold. 1932. *Moral Man and Immoral Society.* New York: Scribner's.

O'Clery, Conor. 1997. *Daring Diplomacy: Clinton's Secret Search for Peace in Ireland.* Boulder: Roberts Rineharts.

Ould Abdallah, Ahmedou. 1996. *La Diplomatie pyromane.* Paris: Calmann-Lévy.

Peres, Shimon. 1993. *The New Middle East.* New York: Henry Holt.

Pillar, Paul R. 1983. *Negotiating Peace: War Termination as a Bargaining Process.* Princeton: Princeton University Press.

Prier, Pierre. 1997. "Cameroun: La Grogne des anglophones." *Le Figaro,* October 11–12.

Reece, Jack E. 1977. *The Bretons Against France.* Chapel Hill: University of North Carolina Press.

Rubin, Barnett, 1995. *The Search for Peace in Afghanistan.* New Haven: Yale University Press.

Rupesinghe, Kumar. 1995. *Conflict Transformation.* New York: St. Martin's.

Saunders, Harold. 1999. *A Public Peace Process.* New York: St. Martin's.

Smoke, Richard. 1977. *War.* Cambridge, Mass.: Harvard University Press.

Stedman, Stephen J. 1991. *Peacemaking in Civil War: Internal Mediation in Zimbabwe, 1974–1980.* Boulder: Lynne Rienner.

Stein, Kenneth W., and Samuel W. Lewis. 1991. *Making Peace Among Arabs and Israelis.* Washington, D.C.: United States Institute of Peace Press.

Thompson, William. 1995. "Principal Rivalries." *Journal of Conflict Resolution* 39, no. 2: 195–223.

Trotski, Léon. 1979. *Histoire de la révolution russe.* Paris: Le Seuil.

Ullman, Richard H. 1996. *The World and Yugoslavia's War.* New York: Council on Foreign Relations.

UNPREDEP (United Nations Preventive Deployment Force) and Open Society Institute— Macedonia. 1996. *Inter-Ethnicity: Turning Walls into Bridges.* Skopje, Macedonia: Open Society Institute.

Vasquez, John. 1993. *The War Puzzle.* New York: Cambridge University Press.

Yativ, Yehiel. 1992. "Statement by Ambassador Yehiel Yativ, Representative of Israel to the First Committee of the United Nations General Assembly." Forty-seventh Session.

Wright, Quincy. 1965. *A Study of War.* Chicago: University of Chicago Press.

Zartman, I. William. 1989. *Ripe for Resolution: Conflict and Intervention in Africa.* New York: Oxford University Press.

———. 2000. " The Art of Mediation." *Orbis* 40, no. 2: 255–66.

Zartman, I. William, ed. 1995. *Elusive Peace: Negotiating an End to Civil Wars.* Washington, D.C.: Brookings.

Zeigler, Harmon. 1990. *The Political Community.* New York: Longmans.

4

Peacemaking Processes: Forestalling Return to Ethnic Violence

Timothy Sisk

The brutal and deadly violence in several internal conflicts that broke out immediately after the Cold War—especially the anarchy and mass starvation in Somalia, the "ethnic cleansing" in the Balkans, and the premeditated genocide in Rwanda—spawned an intensive assessment in the international community of how identity-based, or ethnic, conflict can be prevented. What actions can be taken by third-party intervenors to pre-empt the escalation of conflict as tensions are spiraling toward violence, as in Somalia or the former Yugoslavia, or when a nascent peace process is threatened by renewed violence, as in Rwanda? How can essentialist—kill-or-be-killed—attitudes in multiethnic societies be moderated? How can the stakes of intergroup conflict be highlighted more clearly? Which tactics will be successful in preventing a slide into violence among ethnic groups sharing a common territory?

These burning questions have resonated across continents and capitals, with considerable attention being given to the causes of ethnic violence, the key variables that provide an early warning of impending violence, and the range of instruments and actions that can be used to channel conflict within peaceful, institutionalized boundaries. Some concentrated efforts to prevent the expected outbreak of ethnic violence have clearly been successful. The deployment of UN peacekeeping troops in Macedonia, for example, inhibited the spillover of the Balkan wars to that newly independent country, and deft diplomacy prevented tensions between ethnic Russians and ethnic Estonians from erupting in violence after the dissolution of the Soviet empire.

The analysis of preventive action in ethnic conflicts has rightfully focused on the initial escalation spiral. But because preventive action is frequently demanded, as I. William Zartman argues in chapter 1, attention needs to be paid to the equally critical issue of preventing the *recurrence* of violent ethnic conflict. Once a cease-fire is reached, can a settlement be clinched and its terms implemented? This chapter therefore assesses a certain type of preventive diplomacy, namely, efforts to keep peace processes on track. This approach effectively highlights the central issue of this book: the role of negotiation in preventive diplomacy.

Opportunities for Prevention

The debate on preventive action in ethnic conflicts—centering on questions of whether ethnic violence can be anticipated, whether sufficient responses can be generated, and whether the available and feasible instruments of diplomacy are up to the task—has yielded an important conclusion: Invariably, there are *myriad opportunities* for preventive action—particular points for action—to nip incipient escalation in the bud.[1] Preventive action can take place at various phases of a conflict: during the initial spiral of escalation, just as the threshold into violence is crossed, at a moment when action can contain the intensity and spread of violence, and, if settlement seems near or actually occurs, when violence can be kept from recurring. The key characteristic that distinguishes this type of diplomacy is engagement in crises to prevent their escalation into broader and more costly conflicts. In these instances, the likelihood of renewed violence is imminent, the time frame is short-term, and the principal objective is to prevent war (Jentleson 1996, 7).

Consequently, prevention is not a one-shot affair; on the contrary, the need for it is constantly with us. For example, even though preventive diplomacy was deemed successful in Congo-Brazzaville in 1992–93 (Lund 1996; Jentleson 1996, 2000; Stedman 1995), violent strife broke out in September 1997. Was the earlier preventive effort too transitory and unsustained, or did the 1997 clashes represent a new and altogether different missed opportunity to prevent violence?

Similarly, when does prevention end and a normal diplomatic effort to terminate war begin? During much of 1996, the simmering Hutu-Tutsi conflict in Burundi was the object of concerted action by the United Nations, global powers such as the United States, regional states and organizations, and nongovernmental organizations. Burundi, deeply divided between the Hutus and Tutsis (as is Rwanda) became the preventive diplomacy flavor of the month—propelled by the strong desire to prevent "another Rwanda." Burundi had held elections in 1993 that installed a Hutu-majority president, and officers in the Tutsi military began fomenting ethnic violence to undo their putative loss of power. To stem the growing tensions, a power-sharing pact that looked good on paper was reached, but it proved to be shaky and ultimately unworkable.

A 1996 coup d'état in Burundi restored Tutsi minority hegemony and military rule, and the violence quickly escalated into a renewed civil war. By early 1997, an estimated five hundred people were dying per week in widespread violence.

At what point did Burundi cease to be a problem of preventive diplomacy and instead become a problem of war termination? No one seems quite sure. In any event, Burundi had previously experienced recurring spasms of ethnic violence, and the civil war that erupted in 1996 was a new manifestation of a long-standing conflict. What was the international community seeking to prevent? It did not seek to avert an initial slide into violence but instead a recurrence of previous conflict. Precisely because of Burundi's nearly genocidal past, the prevention of renewed conflict was paramount. Unfortunately for Burundi, the international community's extensive efforts failed. So preventive diplomacy can mean different things at different moments in the life cycle of conflict.

Preventing the Recurrence of Violent Ethnic Conflict

Preventive action to keep a peace process on track occurs during a specific and limited phase of an existing negotiation process: after the conflict has escalated and begun to de-escalate through structured, formal talks but when backsliding and re-escalation are distinct and even likely possibilities.[2] The concern is focused less on the outcome than on the process of managing the conflict by pushing the dispute into an ongoing negotiation. The challenge of diplomacy in such instances is to prevent impasse and maintain progress via continuing negotiations.

Three cases are considered in this chapter. The situation in South Africa from 1990 to 1994 is an example of unambiguous success, in which concerted action through the United Nations at a moment of crisis helped prevent the peace process from derailing. The Sri Lanka situation in 1994 and 1995 is an unambiguous example of failure; sufficient preventive efforts were not forthcoming, the talks collapsed, and the civil war resumed—principally because the parties refused international mediation. In Northern Ireland, the peace train stalled and broke down several times during the negotiations, but the talks eventually led to a negotiated settlement (the April 1998 Good Friday Agreement) that was backed by majorities of both the Protestant and Catholic communities. In Northern Ireland, international mediation was conducted by individuals working in their private eminence, not as the representatives of states. More recently, U.S. president Bill Clinton has actively mediated attempts to prevent a total collapse of the accords.

Preventive diplomacy to keep peace processes on track suffers from many of the same difficulties faced by more narrowly conceived efforts that focus on the initial outbreak of violence (Lund 1996). Such difficulties include receiving and interpreting early warning indicators of an impending crisis; achieving a high-level and concerted response when the indicators are ambiguous or the conflict is not "hot" enough to warrant attention (the problem of political will); judging the seriousness of the crisis threatening to escalate; determining the timing of intervention initiatives and the appropriate ends and means of intervention; leveraging the parties with appropriate tactics; affecting the attitudes of elites and mass publics toward accommodation; and continuing the preventive intervention effort over time (Jentleson 2000).

Moreover, the instruments of preventive diplomacy—good offices and peacemaking, special envoys and representatives, summitry, fact-finding missions, deployment of monitors and observers, Security Council debates and resolutions—are largely the same. Similar, too, is the range of players involved: global powers such as the United States, middle powers, neighboring states, international organizations (often but not invariably the United Nations), regional organizations, eminent persons, and refugee, humanitarian, and ecumenical nongovernmental organizations. Finally, an assessment of this type of preventive action yields especially useful insights into the key issues of how preventive action relates to the stakes, attitudes, and tactics of parties to the conflict and third-party intervenors.

Peace processes, as the onset of formal negotiation, do not yield immediate peace. Political violence and the threat of violence continue to effect the scope, pace, and agenda of talks. Moreover, ongoing political violence is integrally linked to the process of negotiation;[3] violence is used as a beyond-the-table tactic by parties *at* the table as well as by "spoilers" (Stedman 1997) to bring about the peace process's demise. What happens on the street—continuing military engagements, death squad activity, terrorist bombings, assassinations, deadly riots and faction fighting—is related to what happens at the table, and what happens at the table is related to what happens on the street. Progress in talks (or the lack of it) often stimulates violence; and violence often affects whether talks will progress or backslide. The critical question in many peace processes is whether the discussions can be sustained in light of or even because of ongoing political violence.

Sharp upsurges in overall levels of political violence or critical events such as high-profile terrorist bombings are invariably vital turning points in negotiation processes.[4] Like crises that signal a conflict is about to turn violent, political violence during the course of de-escalation efforts also becomes the impetus for external intervention. That is, such events force the disputants to make critical choices—essentially, whether to recoil and fight or to hunker down, continue talking, and weather the storm. Dramatic political violence is *crisis inducing*, in that the parties are required to make critical choices on whether and how the peace process should progress. Following a particularly bloody event, will the peace process be derailed? The principal questions to ask are these:

- Under what conditions does crisis-inducing political violence prompt disputants to retract from talks, and under what conditions does it prompt disputants to continue talking as the way to stem the underlying causes of violence?

- What preventive actions can third-party intervenors—particularly diplomats seeking to avert a train wreck—take to turn crisis-inducing events into potential stimuli for quicker or continued progress in talks, as opposed to the derailment of the peace process?

To understand the conditions under which negotiations, once begun, will continue or fail to progress (and what preventive actions parties can take to keep them on track), certain questions should be asked in each case:

- *What was the nature of the initial pact to begin negotiations?* What brought the parties to the table, and how did they agree upon a structure or process for the negotiations?[5] The confluence of events that brought the parties to the table may help explain whether they will stay at the table and whether preventive action can reinforce these original compulsions.
- *What was the participant structure of the talks?* Who are the principal parties to the talks, and who are the principal rejectionists or spoilers?
- *What types of crises arose?* What type of political violence has threatened the peace process? Who has perpetrated this violence? Has it been committed by parties to the talks or by rejectionists? Who has been perceived culpable in the violence—negotiating parties hoping to exert power or destabilize adversaries, parties not in the talks but seeking a place at the table, or spoilers wanting to derail the peace process?
- *When crises erupted, what preventive diplomacy efforts were made?* Were international mediators deeply and/or persistently involved, and if so, how did they seek to prevent derailment of the peace process?
- *Did the peace process stay on track, or did it derail?* How were incipient crises diffused? Or did incipient crises escalate into full-blown crises that derailed the talks? Did the parties see the crisis-inducing violence as an impetus to continue talking ("If we don't continue negotiating, the violence will only get worse"), as a threat to talks ("We can't continue talking while this violence is destroying our communities"), or both, depending on the specific event? How did the parties react to mediator initiatives? Did preventive action take place? If so, did it work?

I have chosen contemporary cases that demonstrate alternative outcomes to the threats posed to peace processes by political violence—two instances when successful preventive action pre-empted a train wreck (South Africa and Northern Ireland) and one instance when the wreck was not averted and the conflict was reignited (Sri Lanka).[6] And I have sought some variance in the agency of preventive mediator interventions. Space prohibits an extensive review of every instance of political violence and each intervention in these cases (not all of which are publicly known in any event). Instead, my approach is to analyze what I believe are the key variables that affected the course of the peace process and the most important third-party action undertaken to prevent a recurrence of broader violence.

South Africa, 1990–1994

Resistance to the cruel polices of apartheid, the legally entrenched form of racial segregation that was implemented by South Africa's white minority government (the National Party [NP]), stimulated a wide antiapartheid, centralist revolt led primarily by the African National Congress (ANC). Between 1948 and late 1989, exacerbated by the Cold War, the conflict was characterized by a cycle of revolt and repression, with escalating levels of state violence and antiapartheid resistance and counterviolence (Sisk 1995). Significant upsurges in violent activities had occurred in 1960, 1976, and 1984–88.

A confluence of events, including the end of the Cold War, yielded a ripe moment in 1989. Peace talks began in early 1990, following an extensive period of prenegotiation (ca. 1984–90). Initially, the talks were bilateral—between the NP and ANC, led by F. W. de Klerk and Nelson Mandela, respectively—but they eventually became multilateral. The talks broadened to include parties to the right of the NP (notably, the white right-wing Freedom Front) and the ANC (notably, the Zulu-nationalist Inkatha Freedom Party [IFP]); small African nationalist parties on the radical Left, such as the Pan-Africanist Congress (PAC); and small, moderate, bridge-building parties, such as the Democratic Party (DP). Former homeland governments also participated in the multiparty talks; eventually (and especially at the time of the April 1994 elections that ended apartheid), the discussions included all the major political forces.

The most important interim pact was the Groote Schuur "minute" (agreement) of 1990, which linked renunciation of the ANC's armed struggle with normalization of political freedoms, the return of exiles, and the release of political prisoners. The pact defined "nonracial democracy" in a united South Africa as the ultimate outcome of the talks. Subsequent pacts on both procedural and substantive issues were reached in 1990, 1991, 1992, and 1993.

White right-wing militias and political parties, factions of the South African police and intelligence services, and elements and often the leadership of the IFP all openly rejected these agreements and fomented violence to bring them down. Similarly, during much of the negotiations, outbidders (political leaders who seek to outflank moderates with extremist rhetoric) on the ANC's left, such as the PAC, rejected the talks, and members of the ANC's combat wing continued to wage an armed struggle. Controversy continues over whether then President F. W. de Klerk and his senior cabinet officers sought to derail the accord by stoking political violence through clandestine security forces and agents provocateurs.

Political violence was an endemic feature of the transitional period. Fourteen thousand people lost their lives in political violence between 1990 and 1994. There were several crisis-inducing events that threatened the talks beginning in June 1990, just after the Groote Schuur pact was concluded. IFP-ANC faction fighting—mostly in the youth wings—was extensive, especially in greater Johannesburg and the Kwazulu-Natal region. A significant event was the June 1992 Boipatong massacre, which (along with a lack of progress in multiparty constitutional negotiations) prompted Nelson Mandela to withdraw from the talks. The failure of state security forces to prevent the killing implicated both the IFP and the NP in the incident. Later in 1992, after a bloody shoot-out in the town of Bisho that was blamed on the ANC leadership, the parties returned to the table and made an implicit agreement to negotiate despite (or even because of) the violence.

The April 1993 assassination of ANC and South African Communist Party leader Chris Hani by a white right-wing gunman failed to derail the talks despite widespread public protests. And efforts by white right-wingers to disrupt talks in June 1993 (they drove an armored vehicle through the window of the hotel where talks were being held) failed to prevent the Interim Constitution from being sealed that month. Significantly, a white right-wing bombing campaign and an eleventh-hour ANC-IFP shoot-out in downtown Johannesburg (the Shell House massacre) in the early months of 1994 failed to prevent the celebrated elections in April that brought Mandela to power and ended apartheid.

In South Africa, most mediation to keep the talks on track was internal, led by church and business leaders. After the June 1992 Boipatong incident, the United Nations dispatched Cyrus Vance as a special representative of the secretary-general on a fact-finding mission designed to prevent the talks from going astray. Had the talks been totally derailed, it was clear that levels of violence would escalate. Vance met with all the parties, implicitly (but not explicitly) mediating while the talks were frozen and while de Klerk and Mandela were engaged in vituperative exchanges of letters blaming one another for the breakdown in negotiations and engaging in mutual recriminations over the violence.

The Vance mission resulted in the August 1992 deployment of the sixty-member UN Observer Mission to South Africa (UNOMSA), which monitored political violence (but was barred from mediation). UN monitors were augmented by observers from the European Union, the Commonwealth, and the Organization of African Unity (OAU), about one hundred altogether. The OAU and Commonwealth observers were less constrained by their mandates, and they directly mediated a number of hot disputes, particularly the Hani assassination crisis and a virtual civil war then raging in Kwazulu-Natal. The observers did not directly mediate, but they were the critically important eyes and ears of the international community.

In the turbulent run-up to the April 1994 election, with the IFP vowing to violently disrupt the polling, eminent persons Lord Peter Carrington and Henry Kissinger were brought in to mediate between the NP, ANC, and IFP, but they left after several days without agreement on their terms of reference. Washington Okumu, a modest Kenyan professor who was part of the Carrington-Kissinger mission, stayed behind and brokered a last-minute accord in which the IFP agreed to contest the election and accept the settlement. Throughout the transition, Western diplomats and nongovernmental organizations also worked to backstop the talks. Had the preventive effort not been launched, the elections might have precipitated a bloodbath.

Violence clearly stalled the progress of the South African talks. Terrorist bombings and mass murders, faction fighting, assassination of midlevel political leaders, and rioting and mayhem all accompanied South Africa's transition. Prior to the Boipatong incident, violence had inhibited progress in the negotiations; Mandela's refutation of the talks after Boipatong is probably the best affirmation of this instinctive response. But after Boipatong, with the UNOMSA deployed, political violence failed to derail an agreement.

The ANC in particular changed its view and recognized that much of the violence was aimed at frustrating its pursuit of power. Especially after the Bisho massacre, the ANC resolved that upsurges in violence would not stall the long march to freedom. The group's changed position was summed up by key negotiator Kader Asmal, who told me in November 1993 that "we cannot hold the peace process hostage to violence and to the will of violent men." Thus, a settlement was clinched in June 1993 despite the ongoing strife on the streets. The two preventive diplomacy efforts—Vance's mission in 1992 and the eminent persons mediation of 1994—were clearly critical to the success of the South African transition.

Sri Lanka, 1994–1995

Since 1983, Sri Lanka has been embroiled in a civil war between a Sinhalese-led government and Tamil separatists, principally but not exclusively represented by the Liberation Tigers of Tamil Eelam (LTTE). The mostly Hindu Tamil minority represents 18 percent of Sri Lanka's seventeen million people, the majority of whom are Buddhist. Tensions grew in the postindependence era (i.e., after 1948), spurred on by an intolerance of Tamil language rights and educational opportunities that was inspired by Sinhalese clerics. Violence flared intermittently in 1958, 1977, and 1981. The ethnic strife, which escalated dramatically in July 1983, has claimed some thirty thousand victims, and Tamils have been "cleansed" from some areas of formerly mixed living. The Tamil-majority area of northeast Sri Lanka was, for some time, in the de facto control of the LTTE. A military stalemate ensued, with no side able to defeat the other.

Sri Lanka has a history of stalled and failed peace negotiations. Since the outbreak of the war in 1983, India's brokerage of an agreement in 1987—with considerable coercion, particularly applied to the LTTE—is the most significant negotiation effort. The Indo–Sri Lanka Accord led to the deployment of an Indian peacekeeping force for implementation. But tensions over Indian hegemony stimulated an insurgent reaction to the force, and the mission collapsed in a debilitating armed confrontation between the Indian soldiers and the LTTE; the only silver lining, however short lived, was the cooperation of the government of then Prime Minister Ranasinghe Premadasa and the LTTE to oust the foreign peacekeepers. The war between the regime and the LTTE resumed thereafter.

Direct talks began between the LTTE and the government of Sri Lanka in early 1994, following the assassination of Premadasa. As the November 1994 elections approached, ruling United National Party candidate Gamini Dissanyake and fifty-one other people were killed by a suicide bomber; the blast was attributed to the LTTE. Nevertheless—or perhaps *because of* the violence—Chandrika Bandaranaike Kumaratunga (daughter of a previous prime minister who had struck an accord with the Tamils) won the election on a peace platform. After her election, direct talks with the LTTE led to a January 8, 1995, cease-fire agreement, with a broad consensus that the government would eventually devolve significant power to the Tamils. Elements within both communities, however, opposed the peace process. Chauvinist Buddhist monks and the Sinhalese nationalist Janatha Vimukthi Peramuna (JVP), a Maoist revolutionary organization, worked to undercut the search for moderation. So, too, did elements within the LTTE, likely including the group's unpredictable leader, Velupillai Prabhakaran.

Sri Lanka has had more than its share of violence, including (and especially) that launched while nascent talks were under way. In early August 1995, Prime Minister Kumaratunga unveiled a long-awaited peace plan. The following day, suspected insurgents of the LTTE killed twenty-one people in an attack on a government building in Colombo, the capital. The bloody attack was equally directed at Kumaratunga's peace plan itself, the key plank in her effort to build a moderate core of Sinhalese Buddhist and Tamil constituencies to support the plan's aims and provisions.[7] The early August blast was followed by a sharp upsurge in bloodletting—both between the government and rebels and within the rebel movement itself. Justice Minister G. L. Peiris declared, "Now the government is at war with the LTTE. . . . In those circumstances we cannot confuse the picture by entering into any process of negotiation" (*International Herald Tribune* 1995).

The government of Sri Lanka, since the failed Indian attempt at peace, has consistently rejected external mediation or other forms of intervention (with the exception of the International Committee of the Red Cross and the United Nations High Commissioner for Refugees, which performed relief work with the internally displaced). However, in 1995, Kumaratunga sought the mediatory assistance of the government of France. The French refused to mediate but offered the services of eminent person François Michelle, who would be working in his private capacity. The LTTE rebuffed the government's effort, however, to allow third-party intervention, and Prabhakaran insisted that any mediator represent a government and not act as an individual. Apart from the work of Western ambassadors to keep the cease-fire, no other serious effort was mounted while elements within the LTTE continued terrorist attacks from April through August. The talks collapsed as a result.

Political violence during the nascent period of peace talks undercut the ability of Kumaratunga, despite her electoral mandate, to continue discussions with the LTTE. It was clear that the cease-fire of January 1995 was a momentary pause in the war and that the negotiations failed to progress beyond very initial and preliminary steps.

Kumaratunga's devolution plan for Tamil areas in November 1995 reflected an effort to woo Tamil moderates away from the LTTE and to possibly split the organization. Hard-liners within her own government and the Sinhalese majority rejected the plan as too generous, and the devolution scheme failed to gather momentum. In 1996, the Sri Lanka military launched a massive offensive that wiped out much of the LTTE's real estate holdings, although the military has not been able to "mop up" in the country's heavily jungled terrain. Many Tigers have fled the island, gathering strength to return to the fight. The war, therefore, continues. And there is little prospect that negotiations will be resumed. It is clear that the absence of sufficient international action was at least one factor in the failure of the talks to stem the conflict. Since 1995, the war has continued, but no victor has emerged. As of 2000, Norwegian diplomats were seeking anew to mediate a political settlement to Sri Lanka's devastating war.

Northern Ireland, 1994–2000

Northern Ireland, like South Africa, presents a remarkable situation in which a negotiated settlement was reached despite severe threats to the peace process. International mediation was vital in surmounting critical issues in the talks, especially on the decommissioning of arms. Between the Irish Republican Army (IRA) and Protestant Combined Loyalist Military Command cease-fires of late 1994 and the Good Friday Agreement of April 1998, continuous and extensive mediation helped keep the parties moving toward a settlement.

In Northern Ireland, the United Kingdom has, for nearly a century, controlled a disputed territory that features a slight Protestant majority (55 percent to 57 percent) on an Irish island that is overwhelmingly Catholic. Due to differential population growth rates, the Catholic-Protestant gap is shrinking, exacerbating the latter group's fears of vulnerability. The sectarian strife that pits nationalist, republican Catholics in the northern province against union-ist Protestants who favor continued British sovereignty has claimed nearly three thousand lives since "the Troubles" began in 1969. Unqualified majority rule has historically kept the two unionist parties—the Ulster Unionist Party (UUP) and the more virulent, pro-British Democratic Unionist Party (DUP)—politically dominant in the province, along with a heavy British mil-itary presence.

The British military and the Ulster security forces, along with unionist militias, have waged street battles and have traded bombings with the Irish Republican Army, the armed wing of the Irish republican nationalist party, Sinn Fein. The IRA, in particular, has waged an armed struggle marked by terrorist bombings, assassinations, and attempted assassinations on British government officials (including former Prime Minister Margaret Thatcher.) Still, the more mainstream party among Catholics is the Social Democratic Labor Party (SDLP), which advocates a more conciliatory republicanism. The relatively small Alliance Party seeks to bridge the chasm between the two communities.

The governments of the Republic of Ireland and the United Kingdom are implicitly or explicitly parties to the dispute, although they have acted both as disputants and mediators in recent years. There have been myriad attempts to mediate the Northern Ireland conflict and get the parties to reach a compre-hensive settlement, most notably the 1973 Anglo-Irish Sunningdale Agree-ment that failed to win the consent of the republicans or the unionists in the north. In recent years, the most significant efforts have been the initiatives of the United Kingdom's Northern Ireland secretaries (James Brooke and Patrick Mayhew) and the international eminent persons group, the Opsahl Commis-sion. The Brooke and Mayhew mediations in particular laid the groundwork for all-party talks, possibly including Sinn Fein, that could lead to a compre-hensive peace settlement.

In August 1994, after much prenegotiation and many back-channel talks but little high-profile external intervention, the IRA announced a unilateral cease-fire and issued a statement generally favoring talks on a future dispen-sation for the disputed territory. In response, weeks later, Ulster unionist mili-tias also agreed to cease the violence. Direct and public British–Sinn Fein talks began in December 1994, with the question of whether the IRA would sur-render its weapons in exchange for participation in all-party talks at the top of the agenda. The British government and the unionists insisted on the handing over of weapons prior to the talks; Sinn Fein and the IRA insisted that progress toward a settlement be reached before the arms caches would be dis-closed and dismantled.

A critical breakthrough in the Northern Ireland imbroglio occurred in February 1995 with the conclusion of the Anglo-Irish Framework Agreement between the governments of then Irish Prime Minister John Bruton and then British Prime Minister John Major. The proposals emphasized the notion of consent for any political changes in the territory and proffered a set of intra–Northern Ireland and cross-border institutions through which a comprehensive dispensation could be negotiated.

For more than a year, negotiations lagged over disputes relating to the sequencing of talks and the question of the IRA's capacity to wage an armed struggle. Once negotiations began in 1994, Sinn Fein representatives were excluded from discussions about decommissioning their weapons. Elements of Sinn Fein and factions within the DUP (possibly including the leadership of the Rev. Ian Paisley Jr.) opposed the talks, lacking trust that their respective adversaries were negotiating in good faith. Some have described war factions and peace factions within both communities, placing the blame for the conflict on the wicked ways of the respective war factions (George 1996). A report by the commission headed by the principal mediator, former U.S. senator George Mitchell—the most intrusive effort to date by the international mediator to keep the talks on track—failed to break the impasse.

In the few months of peace that followed the 1994 cease-fires, there were reports of increased violence within the IRA (attributed to score settling), although widespread intergroup violence stopped. As early as November 1994, Sinn Fein officials were said to be warning that if the peace process did not accelerate, violence could resume.[8] With efforts to convene all-party talks as envisaged in the framework agreement lagging, the IRA broke its cease-fire in February 1996 with a series of bomb attacks in England, the most dramatic of which was a blast in London's Docklands development, which killed two people. However, neither the IRA nor the unionist militias resumed their violence in Northern Ireland territory.

There are differing interpretations as to why the cease-fire was broken, although most observers say that the IRA military hawks were convinced that the armed struggle was a "use-it-or-lose-it" option. Delayed progress in the talks weakened their commitment to negotiation. Many believe that the precious months of peace in 1994 and 1995 were squandered. The IRA said British stalling and betrayal scuttled the talks; the British decried the IRA's bloodlust and demanded a reinstatement of the cease-fire.

In June, alleged IRA bombers struck in Manchester, effectively ending any dialogue with the British government. In October 1996, IRA terrorists are believed to have detonated a 500-pound bomb on a British military base near Belfast, further damaging the likelihood that direct talks would resume. A tit-for-tat response from the unionist militias ensued.

Clashes have also occurred over the practice of Protestant marching, whereby the Protestants essentially claim territory by insisting on the right to publicly parade through disputed neighborhoods. Catholics decry the marching as "triumphalism." In July 1996, for example, disturbances in the town of Portadown flared after the Orange Order unionists marched through town, and clashes with police and Catholics erupted. Rioting, mayhem, and fire-bombings spread to other cities, particularly Belfast and Londonderry, and one fatality was alleged to have been perpetrated by Protestant militias.

Along with Mitchell, the Clinton administration also facilitated negotiations in the Northern Ireland conflict, within the framework of Anglo-Irish efforts. President Clinton's celebrated November 1995 trip to the province was perhaps the high point of peace in Northern Ireland, although the U.S. leader was unable to secure an agreement on Sinn Fein's entry into talks prior to his visit, as was hoped. (Clinton had held a controversial White House meeting with Sinn Fein leader Gerry Adams.)

In June 1996, the all-party talks began in Belfast within the context of the Anglo-Irish Framework Agreement; they were chaired by Mitchell, acting in his personal capacity (i.e., as an eminent person—but with the implicit backing and considerable effort of the United States). Parties at the talks had been elected in a poll in May, which was remarkably free of widespread violence. (Significantly, Sinn Fein garnered 15.5 percent of the votes.) The talks, which began on June 10, were severely crippled, however, after the provocative IRA bomb attack six days later in Manchester, which injured two hundred. Mitchell kept a low profile on the question of violence and was not extensively engaged in managing the fallout of the Portadown incident and other marching-related crises. Preventive efforts took place but mostly behind the scenes.

In early 1997, Mitchell held extensive discussions involving David Trimble's UUP and John Hume's SDLP on the problem of decommissioning IRA arms, as well as the conditions for Sinn Fein participation in the negotiations. The all-party talks moved forward without Sinn Fein, although little was accomplished. With British and Irish elections anticipated in the first half of 1997, the talks were largely ceremonial—to prevent the appearance of a total derailment of the peace initiative—and back-channel negotiations between John Major's government and Sinn Fein failed to yield fruit on a reinstatement of the IRA cease-fire.

The return to political violence by the IRA and ongoing street violence crippled but did not mortally wound the peace process. The response of the British and Irish governments, as well as the unionist parties and Senator Mitchell, was to continue with the formal—some would say boring—talks while attempting to work directly with Sinn Fein on reinstating the IRA cease-fire. Although the uncertainty of the elections in late 1996 and into early 1997 kept the talks in a holding pattern, the negotiations were needed to give the impression that the momentum toward peace was being sustained.

With a Labour Party victory in Britain's May 1997 elections and a new sense of clarity after the June 1997 Irish elections, a turning point was reached. In May, newly installed Labour Party officials began discussions with Sinn Fein; the decommissioning issue and the reinstatement of the cease-fire comprised the most important elements on the agenda. But these talks would occur on parallel tracks, as proposed in the earlier efforts by Mitchell to prevent an impasse. By the end of the summer, the IRA had reinstated its cease-fire, Sinn Fein was invited to the talks, and the negotiations resumed; these discussions had a greater probability of reaching a comprehensive settlement than any effort since "the Troubles" first began almost thirty years earlier. Mitchell's approach of continuing the talks during a turbulent period of on-again, off-again violence by the IRA proved to be an effective tactic of preventive diplomacy.

A successful bid to impose a deadline on reaching a settlement helped focus the parties' minds on the need to grasp a rare opportunity for peace. What particularly informed the Northern Ireland talks was the experience of South Africa, in which a widely beneficial agreement was reached despite much higher levels of previous and ongoing political violence. The Northern Irish negotiators learned critical lessons that, when reinforced by the efforts of third parties such as George Mitchell, helped turned the tide toward peace. As Northern Irish scholar Paul Arthur (1998) has commented, talks facilitated by third parties, including negotiators from South Africa, led the Northern Irish participants to conclude that they could make better use of technical committees to resolve disputes. They also learned about the principle of "sufficient consensus," by which the talks went forward even if one of the major political parties did not concur.

The success of the Northern Irish peace process had much to do with the parties' realization that further violence would leave them marginalized from the negotiation process. Thus, the incentives for staying in the process were quite significant. These incentives for peace help explain the successful conclusion of this phase of talks, which yielded the celebrated April 1998 Good Friday Agreement. Moreover, it became clear in the referendum of May 1998 and the elections to the new Northern Ireland Assembly in June that the people of Northern Ireland backed the settlement by wide majorities. Given this basic conflict dynamic, quiet, behind-the-scenes mediation to prevent the peace process from derailing through the use of wise diplomacy proved effective. Unfortunately, the Good Friday Agreement has stumbled in the implementation phase despite valiant efforts of mediators to keep the process on track. The principal problem has been the unwillingness of the IRA to disarm. No party to the agreement is willing to vitiate the process altogether, but at the time of writing, the disarmament issue remains and the possibility of breakthrough seems remote.

Attitudes, Stakes, and Tactics

An assessment of prevention efforts used to keep peace processes on track can provide new insights into the overall issues of preventive diplomacy. The principal task in any such effort is to induce opposing parties to sustain negotiation and bargaining as the primary means for managing their conflicts. This entails channeling ethnic disputes into a structured negotiation process. The most serious danger to intergroup mediation is escalating political violence. Debilitating violence can be perpetrated by the parties to the talks—either as a means of exit or as a beyond-the-table tactic to affect the pace, agenda, or balance of power—or by rejectionists who oppose the very idea of negotiation and seek victory through revolution or the exhaustion and withdrawal of their adversaries. Whatever its source, violence usually results in at least one party withdrawing from the talks and asserting that negotiation in such a climate is intolerable.

Can preventive diplomacy—in these cases, a form of mediation within an ongoing negotiation—change attitudes, highlight the stakes of a recurring conflict, and reorient disputant tactics away from violence? It is clear that under some conditions, peace processes can weather the storm of such violence and strike a viable negotiated agreement, following which the conflict can be channeled through newly legitimate political institutions. Preventive efforts can help build a shelter to protect disputants during negotiation crises caused by political violence. South Africa and Northern Ireland, for example, successfully kept alive a nascent peace process threatened by violence. Clearly, in these two cases, the persistent efforts of third parties to prevent a recurrence of the violence made a difference.

Under other conditions, such as those in Sri Lanka, the talks break down, perhaps because one or all of the parties at the table were not really committed to reaching an agreement in the first place. Whether a more sustained effort at third-party mediation could have prevented the recurrence of violence in Sri Lanka is a counterfactual assessment that is difficult, if not impossible, to make.[9]

In assessing preventive action, I believe priority should given to analyzing the scope and strength of moderate, centrist elites committed to negotiations over violence *within* each of the contending parties, in addition to the more common focus on relations *between* the parties to the talks. Can a sustainable centrist coalition formed by moderates be struck and maintained? How vulnerable are the moderate elites who favor talks when an act of street violence induces a crises? The ability of political leaders, who are ostensibly committed to mediation, to control their own midlevel combatants is the most critical problem; after all, many of these midlevel functionaries have the most to lose from peace.

Moreover, it is important to analyze both the relationships between top and midlevel elites in each party to the talks and the relationships between them in terms of the broader groups they represent. Can elites, assuming they genuinely seek a settlement, carry their own organization's factions *and* their publics? Analyzing the relative strengths and weaknesses of the moderate coalition can also reveal the extent to which rejectionist violence will undermine moderates and exacerbate polarization to the point at which talks are no longer sustainable.

Thus, the focus of preventive action should be on the attitudes of these key elites, the stakes they perceive in terms of the relative costs and benefits of peace and violence, and the tactics that third parties might use to influence them. The focus of preventive efforts should be as much on the splits between hard-liners and moderates within each group or faction as on the differences between the groups in conflict.

If the target is the conflicts among elites within a group, on what issues should the preventive effort be focused? The principal explanation for the sustainabilty (or lack thereof) of the peace process in each of the cases presented in this chapter has been the extent to which the parties are motivated to *avoid a worse outcome* to negotiations (a return to open, violent conflict). The perception of the stakes involved in maintaining talks versus a regression to open violence is the most important variable. Are the key elites motivated to avoid the abyss? When this perception holds, a certain inevitability or sense of momentum is generated around the talks. Interventions designed to reinforce the perception that a worse outcome is to be avoided at all costs may bolster the moderates' basic instinct to avoid derailing the peace process and forestall a return to violent conflict.

The ability of preventive efforts to change attitudes and redefine the stakes in ethnic conflicts is, alas, highly limited. Such efforts are primarily effective at the margins. The principal factors that sustain the momentum of the talks are the strategic choices of the disputants themselves as they respond to (or sometimes foment) the crisis-inducing violence that threatens the negotiations. Whether they recoil and stall or end the talks or whether the violence spurs them to move toward a settlement is affected by several variables over which most external intervenors can exercise little control.

The first variable is *culpability*. Who is culpable or perceived to be culpable in fomenting the violence? When one party to a negotiation process is perceived by other parties as culpable in a crisis-inducing incident, digression occurs. When rejectionist parties or individuals are seen as culpable or when parties to a negotiation are perceived as equally culpable, crisis-inducing political violence can stimulate progress. The second variable is *uncertainty*. How clear is it where the peace process is headed? That is, how specific are the outcome parameters of the talks that were defined at the onset of negotiation? The greater the uncertainty in the expected ultimate outcome of the discussions, the greater the likelihood that crisis-inducing political violence will stimulate digression in the talks. Conversely, the greater the degree of certainty in the outcome, the greater the likelihood that political violence will stimulate progress.

The *timing* of the crisis and of third-party interventions is also critical. Does the violence surge right after talks have begun or only after the talks have been under way for some time and are nearing a settlement? Crisis-inducing violence at an early stage of the talks impedes progress more than violence at later stages. However, violence fomented by parties to a negotiation at a late stage of the talks stimulates digression. Crisis-inducing violence perpetrated by rejectionists at a late stage of the process can actually reinforce momentum toward a settlement, spurring progress.

These variables—culpability, uncertainty, and timing—count most in determining whether political violence will cause a peace process to derail and prevention efforts to fail. "It's really up to the parties," however, is hardly a sufficient assessment, since we know that in certain conflict settings, mediator interventions can serve myriad functions to increase communication, build confidence and trust, wield sanctions and incentives, and offer assurances or commitments in efforts to move the parties toward settlement (Rothchild 1997). Even if third-party preventive efforts are effective only at the margins, perhaps relative or marginal gains can keep talks going through a difficult period of violent turbulence. What can diplomacy do to help prevent peace processes from jumping the rails?

The inherent difficulties of preventive action designed to sustain a peace process mirror those of efforts to prevent escalation at an earlier stage of the game. The challenges of prevention are well known; possibilities and examples of successes are harder to come by. Parties are resistant to external influences if they believe intervention will force them to make costly concessions. And the more extensive and high-profile the intervention, the greater the likelihood that at least one party to the talks will not consent to it. Most uses of the tools of preventive diplomacy, as in the UN fact-finding mission in South Africa, the failed Michelle facilitation in Sri Lanka, and George Mitchell's mediation in Northern Ireland (backstopped by Clinton's personal diplomacy and interest in the conflict) demonstrate that preventive diplomacy efforts have some inherent weaknesses.

International mediators of peace processes in ethnic conflicts may not appropriately receive and interpret early warning indicators of an impending act of violence that will induce a crisis. These acts are organized and carried out in great secrecy, and at best, third parties can only seek to anticipate when the climate is right for a violent act (e.g., just prior to or just after an interim pact). Could the United States have anticipated the Sinn Fein return to armed struggle? To what extent could South Africa's high levels of transitional political violence have been anticipated? Similarly, even when there is a crisis, it may be difficult to garner a significant and concerted response when the indicators are ambiguous or the conflict is not "hot" enough or important enough to provoke sustained, high-level international attention.

Which of the many acts of violence in Sri Lanka, for instance, would be the last straw, bringing the talks to an end? What could have been done? Given the failure of the Indian peacekeeping troops in Sri Lanka during the mid-1980s, what foreign government would have been willing to put its troops in harm's way by contributing to a new peacekeeping force? In sum, there was no political will to extensively intervene in Sri Lanka's long-running fratricidal conflict.

Third parties may also be unsure whether the crisis is serious enough to escalate. In South Africa, the United Nations and others realized that a collapse of the talks was a critical event that demanded immediate and intense attention. In situations such as in Sri Lanka or Northern Ireland, it was clear that acts of violence were perpetrated by the parties to show that they wanted to terminate the talks or at least to exert power in them. Those seeking to mount preventive diplomacy also struggle with the appropriate means and ends of intervention. In other words, resistance by the parties limits the extent of intervention. Efforts to influence the opposing sides with tactics such as carrots and sticks, to affect the attitudes of elites and mass publics toward accommodation, and to continue preventive intervention over time are all carried out with very little leverage over the parties (especially when the intervenor is an eminent person). Success depends on persuasion: describing and manipulating the stakes, helping to shape attitudes, and determining the appropriate tactics—that is, deciding which instruments of preventive diplomacy to employ and when to use them.

Stakes and Attitudes

Preventive efforts are intended to convince the parties to the conflict that dire consequences will follow if efforts to manage the conflict *fail* to progress. That is, the stakes are defined as a return to a bloody past that, against the odds, the parties have begun to escape. How high are the stakes if the disastrous encounters of the past occur once again? Preventive action can help reframe the stakes to ensure that progress in the talks will be mutually beneficial and that failure to progress will precipitate a zero-sum situation. Stakes and attitudes in ethnic conflicts are related: When the stakes are so high that group elimination or subjugation is a real possibility, attitudes will remain essentialist—adversaries are to be beaten—rather than pragmatic. Attitudes are slow to change in ethnic conflicts such as those considered here, but the high stakes of violence may be enough to temper attitudes toward a "cold" cooperation.

In South Africa, Cyrus Vance and the UN-led international monitors helped focus the minds of South African negotiators on the stakes of failure; concomitantly, they offered assurances through the presence of observers that the costs of future violence would be managed and that any implementation of an agreement would be internationally monitored. In Sri Lanka, the parties did not agree that the stakes were so high that international mediation was necessary; they implicitly accepted the conclusion that the costs of failed talks would be bearable. Basically, the LTTE was not committed to peace, and Kumaratunga's coalition for peace was razor thin. The parties in Northern Ireland seemed to appreciate what was at stake if the peace process derailed, as indicated by the fact that the abrogated cease-fire of the IRA failed to induce the Protestant militias to abrogate their own cease-fire. Moreover, the talks resumed despite lingering essentialist attitudes on all sides.

Parties may fear the consequences of renewed violence, but they often fear the consequences of settlement even more. If preventive efforts are targeted at *reducing uncertainty*—for example, by seeking to put in place international confidence-building measures such as the deployment of an observer mission—it is more likely that the talks will be bolstered and that a recurrence of violence will be averted. Those who would prevent conflict may also amend the stakes by reframing the issue in non-zero-sum terms—mostly by exploring with the parties specific power-sharing options (Sisk 1996), such as creating an interim national unity or consensus-oriented government, and wielding leverage to induce them into such a pact. They may also buttress the commitment to continue negotiating with sweeteners, such as aid or recognition (a form of bestowing legitimacy) to change the payoff structure.

Who should be the agent? Although states may be able to offer rewards for clinching an agreement, eminent persons do not usually wield such authority by themselves (and the use of eminent persons is the most common form of mediation in these cases). Thus, the close tethering of eminent persons to a powerful state—such as Michelle's relationship with France or Mitchell's with the United States—seems likely to improve the chances for success. International organizations offer a comparative advantage if the principal problem is one of building confidence and limiting uncertainty via monitoring, observation, or military deployments.

Tactics

The tactics available for preventive efforts encompass a wide range of instruments. A standard response persists: dispatching a prominent envoy in the aftermath of a crisis, hoping that high-level international attention and facilitation will cap escalating tensions. In addition to the use of special envoys and eminent persons, there is an important place for ongoing, systematic international monitoring and observation. Permanent observation, such as the UNOMSA mission to South Africa, serves two purposes. First, it provides an on-the-ground early warning system to determine when and to what extent violence is likely to occur and what can be done to defuse it. Second, observer missions, if sufficiently large, can actually deter violence if the parties know that the eyes and the ears of the international community are turned toward them. Practical efforts to monitor human rights and diffuse community-level violence are prudent means of launching preventive action, in effect institutionalizing the intervention through a structure of ongoing engagement.

High-level summitry and attention was also used in at least two of the cases presented here, South Africa and Northern Ireland. The potential payoff of summitry is great. Leverage can be maximized, and symbolic breakthroughs can be dramatic. Summits can be conducted to create or stimulate a positive turning point in the negotiation process. Yet the potential for payoff does not come without considerable risk. Summits that fail can set peace processes back and make future progress more difficult to achieve. And even when summits succeed in making breakthroughs, mass publics become still more cynical if the peace process subsequently derails. High-level attention is necessary, and a very significant degree of coordination between states and envoys appears to be a prerequisite for success.

Conclusion

Preventive diplomacy, whether to calm a newly emerging ethnic conflict or to prevent a recurrence of violence in a long-standing one, must be more broadly conceived. In ethnic disputes, it should be aimed at preventing new disputes from spiraling into violence, but equal weight needs be given to those opportunities for taking preventive action to pre-empt the flare-up of an old conflict. Anticipating the opportunities and acting upon them is the key to successful intervention in both sets of cases; the problems and prospects are remarkably the same.

An accurate assessment of the parties' intentions is critical. In South Africa, preventive action was based on a correct assessment that the talks had only been snagged, not derailed. The eminent person's mediation by a special representative of the UN secretary-general made a critical difference at a key moment. In Sri Lanka, external parties were skeptical of the LTTE's commitment to peace; they doubted whether, given the latter's behavior, the peace process was really salvageable. There was no ability to generate sufficient political will to significantly intervene in Sri Lanka, especially when the parties were so resistant to third-party intervention. To determine whether allowing Sri Lanka to slip back into civil war was a failure of prevention or a justifiable unwillingness of the international community to become involved in a hopeless quagmire, one must assess the attitudes and intentions of tough ethnic forces, such as the LTTE.

If the parties *are* fundamentally motivated to avoid the abyss opening before them, third-party preventive efforts may help avert a recurrence of widespread violence. Preventive diplomacy has a chance if (1) the intervention is institutionalized in the form of an ongoing monitoring and observation mission, pursued by accepted, eminent, high-level envoys drawing their clout from close coordination with states or the United Nations, and (2) the intervention is aimed at reinforcing the basic beliefs of moderate elites that the risks of a negotiated settlement are preferable to the consequences of a return to war. Preventive action in these ethnic conflict circumstances, then, seems not only warranted but also necessary to provide a bridge leading from a repeated history of violent conflict to new opportunities for negotiated peace.

Notes

This chapter is based on a larger project begun during my 1995 term as a visiting fellow of the Norwegian Nobel Institute, whose support of this research is gratefully acknowledged. Research on which this chapter is based is also supported by a grant from the Program in Global Security and Sustainability of the John D. and Catherine T. MacArthur Foundation. I would like to thank the editor, members of the Processes of International Negotiation group, and especially Didier Bigo for their helpful comments on earlier drafts of this chapter.

1. On preventive diplomacy, see, for example, Lund (1996) and Jentleson (1996). The 1998 report of the Carnegie Commission on Preventing Deadly Conflict offers an extensive overview of the concepts and issues in preventive international conflict management. For a skeptical assessment of preventive diplomacy, see Stedman (1995).

2. In the literature on negotiation, this particular phase has generally taken a back seat to the difficult problems of getting the parties to the table and the substantive or outcome issues related to the nature of the comprehensive settlement (e.g., the terms of living together or the terms of separation or partition in centrist revolts). The difficulties of getting parties to the table has been explored in some length (Stein 1989; Saunders 1985), and so, too, has the implementation of peace agreements (Hampson 1996). However, the extremely risky and uncertain period after formal talks have begun and before an official, comprehensive peace agreement has been struck has not received sufficient attention as a distinct phase of negotiation in and of itself.

3. Steven Brams, in a *Theory of Moves* (1995), refers to the use of "threat moves" as a part of iterated bargaining.

4. On the concept of turning points, see Druckman (1986). When parties transform their relationship from one characterized by a zero-sum perception of the conflict (in which one side's gain is seen as the other side's loss) to a positive-sum perception (in which mutual gains are possible), they progress across thresholds or transition points that link phases of the negotiation process. That is, the phases of peace processes are connected by identifiable events or turning points that indicate the movement between stages. Because not all peace processes yield peace, it is clear that such events can lead toward violence as well as away from it. Roy Licklider wrote that "rather than a single pattern whereby civil violence is ended, it seems more useful to conceive of the termination of civil violence as a set of processes at which there are critical choice points. Selections at these points form alternative strategies of conflict termination" (1993, 18).

5. The structure of a negotiation finds its origins in agreements made during previous phases. That is, in order to assess the structure of negotiations toward a settlement, one must peer back to the prenegotiation phases, in which the shape and venue of the table, the sequences, and the outcome scenarios of the talks were determined.

6. In terms of the structured, focused comparison approach, I seek variance on the dependent variable—"progress" in negotiation stimulated by third-party intervention. *Progress* is defined as movement through the phases of bargaining, in this case from the onset of talks through the preliminary and formal stages of negotiation.

7. The peace plan unveiled in August was an attempt by the government to circumvent and undercut the LTTE's base by appealing directly to moderate Tamils and by retaining the support of a small progovernment Tamil party in the legislature. The peace plan offered to provide for greater autonomy by giving Tamils legislative powers over their own affairs in areas of law and order, land, and finance. Notably, the agreement was also strongly op-

posed by hard-line elements within the Kumaratunga cabinet and by Sinhalese nationalists led by Buddhist monks.

8. One incident, the IRA killing of a postal worker during a robbery in November 1994, was blamed on a breakdown in the chain of command.

9. See Jentleson (1996, 8) for an assessment of the methodological issues in assessing preventive diplomacy, including the inherent difficulties of counterfactual analysis.

References

Arthur, Paul. 1998. "Conflict Transformation—Theory and Practice in the Northern Ireland Conflict." United States Institute of Peace.

Brams, Steven. 1995. *A Theory of Moves.* New York: New York University Press.

Druckman, Daniel. 1986. "Stages, Turning Points, and Crises." *Journal of Conflict Resolution* 30: 327–60.

George, Alexander, and Timothy J. McKeown. 1985. "Case Studies and Theories of Organizational Decision-Making." *Advances in Information Processing in Organizations* 2: 21–58.

George, Terry. 1996. "Lost Without War in Northern Ireland." *New York Times,* July 17, 1996.

Hampson, Fen O. 1996. *Nurturing Peace: Why Peace Settlements Succeed or Fail.* Washington, D.C.: United States Institute of Peace Press.

Ilke, Fred C. 1971. *Every War Must End.* New York: Columbia University Press.

International Herald Tribune, August 8, 1995, p. 4.

Jentleson, Bruce W. 1996. "Preventive Diplomacy and Ethnic Conflict: Possible, Difficult, Necessary." Policy paper no. 27, Institute on Global Cooperation, University of California at San Diego.

———. 2000. *Opportunities Missed, Opportunities Seized: Preventive Diplomacy in the Post–Cold War World.* Lanham, Md.: Rowman & Littlefield.

Licklider, Roy, ed. 1993. *Stopping the Killing.* New York: New York University Press.

Lund, Michael. 1996. *Preventing Violent Conflicts: A Strategy for Preventive Diplomacy.* Washington, D.C.: United States Institute of Peace Press.

Putnam, Robert D. 1988. "Diplomacy and Domestic Politics: The Logic of Two-Level Games." *International Organization* 42, no. 3 (Fall): 427–60.

Rothchild, Donald. 1997. *Managing Ethnic Conflict in Africa: Pressures and Incentives for Cooperation.* Washington, D.C.: Brookings.

Saunders, Harold. 1995. "We Need a Larger Theory of Negotiation: The Importance of Pre-Negotiating Phases." *Journal of Conflict Resolution* 1, no 3 (Fall): 249–62.

Schelling, Thomas. 1966. *Arms and Influence.* New Haven: Yale University Press.

———. 1980. *The Strategy of Conflict.* Cambridge, Mass.: Harvard University Press.

Sisk, Timothy. 1995. *Democratization in South Africa: The Elusive Social Contract.* Princeton: Princeton University Press.

———. 1996. *Power Sharing and International Mediation in Ethnic Conflicts.* Washington, D.C.: United States Institute of Peace Press and the Carnegie Commission on Preventing Deadly Conflict.

Stedman, Stephen John. 1991. *Peacemaking in Civil War: International Mediation in Zimbabwe, 1974–1980.* Boulder: Lynne Rienner.

———. 1995. "Alchemy for a New World Order: Overselling Preventive Diplomacy." *Foreign Affairs* 74, no. 3 (Fall): 14–20.

———. 1997. "Spoilers in International Peace Processes." *International Security* 22, no. 2 (Spring): 5–54.

Stedman, Stephen, and Thomas Ohlson. 1995. *The New Is Not Yet Born: Conflict Resolution in Southern Africa.* Washington, D.C.: Brookings.

Stein, Janice Gross. 1989. "Getting to the Table: The Triggers, Stages, Functions and Consequences of Prenegotiation." In *Getting to the Table: The Processes of International Prenegotiation,* ed. Janice Gross Stein. Baltimore: Johns Hopkins University Press.

Wagner, R. Harrison. 1993. "The Causes of Peace." In *Stopping the Killing: How Civil Wars End,* ed. Roy Licklider. New York: New York University Press.

Wallensteen, Peter, and Margaret Sollenberg. 1996. "The End of International War? Armed Conflict, 1989–1995." *Journal of Peace Research* 33, no. 3 (June): 353–70.

Zartman, I. William. 1985. *Ripe for Resolution: Conflict and Intervention in Africa.* New York: Oxford University Press.

5

Divided States:
Reunifying without Conquest

Sukyong Choi

Yemen, Germany, and Korea were three nations whose externally imposed division brought conflict to the post–World War II world. The Korean War (1950–53) was the only direct superpower military confrontation of the Cold War. The Yemeni wars (1962–64, 1971–72, 1979, and 1993–94) repeatedly involved regional allies with great-power backing. That the German division did not break out into war only underscores its enormous potential for igniting World War III. Yemen and Germany achieved unification in 1990, but Korea is still waiting.

Preventive diplomacy was practiced on three types of occasions in these cases of national division: in preventing war from erupting between the two states, in preventing the wars that did erupt from spreading, and in reuniting the two halves of the nation. This chapter covers all three types but concentrates on the third, illustrated by the situation in Yemen and Germany and by the efforts made in South–North Korea in the 1990s. It also discuss the stakes, attitudes, and tactics involved in negotiating unification disputes of each of these three nations, in addition to explaining issues that have hindered further progress in the Korean dialogue and provided a breakthrough in June 2000.

Division of Yemen, Germany, and Korea

Yemen, Germany, and Korea were divided by Cold War politics, although the formal division of Yemen took place in the colonial period. In each instance, the division was an artificial, foreign-imposed separation within a single historical nation, but it was replicated in domestic politics. Thus, for domestic as well as international reasons, it carried the seeds of war.

Yemen

The division of Yemen was brought about by the foreign powers that had dominated the country since the nineteenth century: Britain in the south from 1939 until 1967 and the Turkish Ottoman Empire in the north until 1918. The division of the world after 1945 into two opposing international blocs led by the United States and the Soviet Union prolonged the partition of Yemen (Braun 1992). In North Yemen, the imam ruled until 1962, when he was ousted by republican forces and the Yemen Arab Republic was established. Civil war between royalists and republicans followed, with Gamel Abdel Nasser's Egyptian forces intervening to help the republicans and Saudi Arabia backing the royalists. The republicans eventually won (Burrowes 1987). Southern Yemen became independent in November 1967, combining Aden and the former protectorate of South Arabia. Before the British withdrawal, two rival factions fought for control: the National Liberation Front (NLF) and the Front for the Liberation of Occupied South Yemen (FLOSY). The socialist National Liberation Front prevailed and renamed the country the People's Democratic Republic of Yemen in 1970. Representatives of North Yemen made contact with South Yemenis with an eye to unification, but they failed to reach any agreement because of the ideological conflicts between moderate and radical socialists in South Yemen. The socialist radicalization in the South impelled many South Yemenis to move to the North. In North Yemen, traditional Islamic tendencies increased under Saudi Arabian influence. Thus, the two Yemens developed into different societies.

Germany

The division of Germany was created by the Allied powers after World War II. Toward the end of the war, the Allies agreed that upon the surrender of the Reich, they would assume authority over all of Germany, which would be divided into four zones of occupation, with joint control exercised from Allied headquarters in Berlin. But by 1947, the control ceased to function (Birnbaum 1973; Sowden 1975). The Soviet Union and the three Western powers–the United States, Britain, and France—then proceeded to establish German governments in their respective zones. The Western powers merged their three zones and established the Federal Republic of Germany (FRG) on September 21, 1949; the military occupation was then converted into a contractual defense relationship.

In the process, divided Germany came closest to war in 1948–49, as the three Western zones moved toward an autonomous government and on June 24, 1948, introduced a new common currency, the West German mark. Two days later, the Soviet Union closed all land routes to the Western sectors of Berlin. Faced with the options of shooting their way through on land and letting West Berlin starve into surrender, the United States and its allies decided to fly in supplies. For 462 days, until September 30, 1949, preventive diplomacy was practiced by avoiding the war-or-surrender choice and inventing a third option. The Soviet blockade ended on May 12, and negotiations were opened to restore ground communications and establish air corridors for civilian flights.

The Soviet zone declared itself the German Democratic Republic (GDR) a week after the airlift ended, on October 7, 1949, and was granted sovereignty by the Soviet Union on March 27, 1954. The Paris Agreement of 1954 gave sovereignty to the Federal Republic from May 1955. However, the four former occupying powers reserved their rights with regard to questions on Germany as a whole and its division. As for Berlin, the three Western sectors of the city were merged in 1949 into one unit, closely tied to West Germany but not completely merged with it. The area remained under the jurisdiction of the three Western powers until East and West Germany were reunified in October 1990.

Korea

As with Germany, the division of Korea was caused by the rivalry between the United States and the Soviet Union after World War II. The Yi dynasty was the last kingdom in Korea before the country was occupied by Japanese forces in 1905 and annexed by Japan in 1910. The surrender of the Japanese troops in August 1945 was received separately by the United States and the Soviet Union, and Korea became divided at the thirty-eighth parallel into two military occupation zones, with the Soviet forces in the North and the U.S. forces in the South. At the Moscow conference in December 1945, the United States and the Soviet Union agreed to a four-power trusteeship to last five years. However, the Soviet Union refused to take concrete measures to carry out the agreement.

The United States presented the question of Korean independence before the UN General Assembly, which adopted a favorable resolution on November 14, 1947, establishing the nine-nation UN Temporary Commission on Korea (UNTCOK). The UNTCOK arrived in Seoul but was refused admission to North Korea by the Soviet commander. Elections were held in South Korea in May 1948, and the Republic of Korea was inaugurated on August 15.

In the North, a Provisional People's Committee, led by Kim Il Sung of the Korea Communist Party, was established in February 1946. In July, the North Korean Worker's Party was formed from the merger of Kim's Communist Party and the New People's Party led by Koreans returning from exile in Yenan. In 1947, the Supreme People's Assembly was established, and Kim Il Sung became premier. A new assembly was elected in August 1948, and the Democratic People's Republic of Korea (DPRK) was proclaimed on September 9, 1948. Soviet forces withdrew from North Korea in December 1948. The following June, the Workers' Parties of North and South Korea were merged into one organization, the Korean Workers' Party, with headquarters in Pyongyang (Lee 1978).

On June 25, 1950, North Korean troops invaded the Republic of Korea. In the absence of the Soviet Union, the UN Security Council called for a cessation of hostilities and asked that all members provide military assistance to South Korea. After twenty-five months of war and negotiation, an armistice was signed on June 27, 1953, establishing a demilitarized zone around the thirty-eighth parallel (Acheson 1969; Joy 1964; Foot 1985; Chai and Zhao 1989; Fan 2000). This armistice continued for the rest of the century.

Reconciliation Between Divided Units of Yemen, Germany, and Korea

Contacts were made between the divided parts of Germany, Yemen, and Korea during the 1970s as an exercise in preventive diplomacy by both the divided state leaders and their external allies. Although these contacts prepared the base for later efforts, they failed to unite the nations because external conditions continued to support division and because the divided states' leaders were not strong enough to overcome external constraints on the stakes and attitudes involved even if they had wanted to do so.

Yemen

From November 1967, when South Yemen became independent, to the final phase of unity negotiations between South and North Yemen, repeated unity initiatives were advanced and two border wars broke out between the South and the North. The military clashes that occurred in the 1970s and 1980s were terminated through the mediation of the Arab League, which also tried to promote Yemeni unification. Intermittent fighting, beginning in early 1971, erupted into open warfare between the two Yemens in October 1972. North Yemen received aid from Saudi Arabia, and South Yemen was supported by the Soviet Union. Agreement on a cease-fire was eventually reached through Arab League mediation. At a meeting in Cairo on October 24, both sides agreed to unite the two Yemens within eighteen months. The leaders of South and North Yemen signed a second agreement the following month in Tripoli, defining the character of the new state and appointing members of various technical committees. However, the progress toward unity made in Cairo and Tripoli in 1972 did not continue (Dunbar 1992).

A second border war broke out in February 1979. Again, the war ended through Arab League mediation, and an agreement was signed in March 1979 in Kuwait. The agreement called for mutual troop withdrawal, noninterference, and rededication to the principles established in Cairo and Tripoli in

1972. The summit in Kuwait established a committee that produced a draft unity constitution and led to a series of agreements on cooperation in many fields. At the end of 1981, the constitution committee presented a draft plan for the establishment of a parliamentary democracy for a united Yemen. In the following years, South and North Yemen cooperated with each other and made extensive personal contacts through numerous unity-related meetings. However, such preparatory steps toward unification failed to yield practical results until 1989.

Germany

During the Cold War, West Germany demanded to be recognized as the sole legitimate representative of the whole Germany, but East Germany recognized the existence of two German governments. The East was isolated from the West because its government was not recognized as being democratically elected, and West Germany, according to the Hallstein Doctrine, did not maintain diplomatic relations with states recognizing East Germany. When Willy Brandt became chancellor of the Federal Republic in 1969, he made more conciliatory approaches to Eastern European countries, especially East Germany, in a démarche known as East Policy (*Ostpolitik*) (Hanrieder and Anton 1980). The following year, formal discussions were held between representatives of the East and West for the first time, and diplomatic contacts were made between West Germany and East European countries, including treaties with the Soviet Union and Poland. West Germany, however, would not ratify the treaties until a satisfactory solution of the Berlin question was reached by the Four Powers—France, Great Britain, the Soviet Union, and the United States.

The Four Powers finally signed an agreement on the status of Berlin in September 1971, in which the parties acknowledged that West Berlin was not a constituent part of West Germany but recognized that the ties between West Germany and West Berlin could be maintained. It was agreed that civilians and goods moving between West Berlin and West Germany could travel unimpeded through East Germany by road, rail, and waterway (Merkl 1974–1975; Birnbaum 1973; Catudal 1978; Mahnke 1973; Keithly 1985). In December 1972, West and East Germany signed the Basic Treaty. In it, they pledged to maintain normal and good-neighborly relations; uphold sovereign equality and self-determination; discontinue the West German claim to speak for the whole Germany; cooperate in economic, scientific, and cultural matters; and exchange permanent missions. Though West Germany recognized the East as a government and pledged to deal with it on the basis of equality, it was not willing to treat East Germany as a foreign state. West Germany stated that there was only one German nation and that relations between East and West could not be the same as those between foreign states. Both countries became members of the United Nations in September 1973. In 1974, West and East Germany agreed to establish permanent representative missions in Bonn and East Berlin.

Following the Basic Treaty, a number of agreements were signed between the two Germanies, leading to diverse interactions between East and West Germans. From 1975 to 1989, West Germans (half of them inhabitants of West Berlin) made about 6.3 million visits to East Germany, including East Berlin. About 1.3 million East Germans over retirement age, plus 40,000 younger people, were officially permitted to visit West Germany. The volume of East-West German trade increased from 4.5 billion clearing units in 1970 to 14.4 billion in 1987 (Kindermann 1991).

Korea

Official peaceful contacts between South and North Korea began in the early 1970s. The Nixon Doctrine of 1970 signaled the lessening of the Cold War and the advent of détente in the international system and on the Korean Peninsula. On August 12, 1971, the president of the South Korean National Red Cross proposed direct South–North negotiations to arrange for the reunion of family members separated by the division of the country. His proposal was accepted by the president of the Red Cross of North Korea. North Korea, seeking peaceful coexistence with the West, also proposed a North–South Korean dialogue. On July 4, 1972, in a joint communiqué published simultaneously by Seoul and Pyongyang, the two parties agreed (1) that unification should be peaceful and achieved through independent Korean efforts not subject to external imposition or interference, and (2) that unification should transcend differences in ideas, ideologies, and systems. In addition, a South–North coordinating committee was established.

South Korea has been a permanent observer at the United Nations since 1951, and North Korea obtained observer status in 1973. South Korean president Park Chung-hee announced on June 23, 1973, that his country would not object to entering the United Nations together with North Korea, provided that this would not hinder national unification. President Park made it clear that this policy was to be considered an interim measure before national unification and did not signify recognition of North Korea as a state. The South Korean government preferred a gradual approach to a unified state.

North Korea put forward the five-point Peaceful Unification Program in response to the June 23 statement, proposing joint entrance into the United Nations under the single name "Confederal Republic of Koryo," along with the creation of a great national assembly. The North argued that concurrent admission to the United Nations would lead to a permanent division of the country, and it advocated a rapid step to unification. Unification talks were suspended in 1973, and a series of clashes between North and South Korean vessels occurred in disputed waters the following year. In October 1978, the UN Command accused North Korea of threatening the 1953 armistice after discovering an underground tunnel beneath the demilitarized zone.

In the 1980s, international changes promoted cooperation between South and North Korea. With the emergence of Mikhail Gorbachev in the Soviet Union, which weakened the Cold War system, North Korea needed to improve its relations with the United States. Its leaders therefore suggested tripartite talks on unification in June 1984, involving North and South Korea and the United States. The offer signaled a significant change in the North Korean position because it included South Korea for the first time. However, the proposal was rejected by the South, which favored direct, bilateral South–North talks instead.

After the explosion of a South Korean airplane over Southeast Asia in November 1987, with the loss of many lives, South Korea accused North Korea of sabotage. Although Pyongyang denied the accusation, it indicated that unless the North and South resolved their differences, a military confrontation was likely; the North's leaders then proposed a joint conference. In August 1988, a series of talks were held at Panmunjom between North and South Korean legislators. The negotiations produced no constructive results.

Negotiating National Unification Disputes in Yemen and Germany

Tactics

South and North Yemen were united from the top down by the two established leadership groups, through step-by-step agreements and then military action. Following unification, the makeup of the leadership changed.

North Yemen president Ali Abdallah Saleh and South Yemen general secretary Ali Salim al-Baid discussed the unification of their two countries in April and May 1988 and agreed to revive the unification process and to reduce tensions in the frontier area. As a result, both nations withdrew troops from their common border and created a demilitarized zone for a joint investment project; their citizens were permitted to cross the border using only identification cards.

The following year, North Yemen proposed the merger of the foreign and defense ministries of the two countries as a first step toward unification. President Saleh and General Secretary al-Baid signed an agreement to unite the two states within a year on the basis of the 1981 constitutional draft; an organizational committee was set up to work out procedural arrangements. The existing political organizations in the two states, the Yemen Socialist Party (YSP) in the South and the General People's Congress (GPC) in the North, were to be retained.

The allocation of senior posts in the new government proved difficult. The principle of a fifty-fifty split and the assignment of deputies from one part of the country to department heads from the other was maintained. Saleh and al-Baid were named president and vice president for the five-man Presidential Council, and South Yemen's head of state, Haydar Abu Bakr al-Attas, became prime minister. The two legislatures were amalgamated to form the House of Representatives.

Commissions were entrusted in January 1990 with the task of preparing for the integration of the armed forces and the internal security apparatus. Negotiations were held on finance, economic, and other portfolios. The central banks, postal and customs services, and news agencies, among others, were amalgamated in early 1990, and both currencies were to be valid at a fixed exchange rate. Unification entailed many structural changes in South Yemen, including the lifting of the ban on political parties, liberalization of the economy, and freedom of the press.

Unification ran into renewed difficulties in August 1993, however, when the YSP leader al-Baid withdrew from government activities in protest against the growing marginalization of the South, especially with regard to the distribution of oil revenues. The political deadlock continued in spite of the efforts of French, Omani, Jordanian, Palestinian, and U.S. diplomats to mediate. Al-Baid declared the independence of the new Democratic Republic of Yemen, with Aden as its capital, in May 1994, and the northern army attacked in response. The UN Security Council then passed a unanimous resolution (no. 924) calling for a cease-fire.

Fierce fighting followed, and the oil refinery in Aden was damaged by two bombing raids from the South. The foreign ministers of the Gulf Cooperation Council declared that the unity of Yemen should not be imposed militarily. However, northern forces maintained their pressure on Aden, which came under their control in July. Many of the southern leaders fled to neighboring countries as the civil war ended. Since then, Yemeni elections have been hailed as the most democratic in the Arab world (Omalia et al. 1993, 1997; Mermier 1997).

East and West Germany were united under democratic pressure, which brought about leadership changes in the East during the unification process within the context of the transformation of the Soviet Union and the ending of the Cold War. Tactics employed concerned, above all, the establishment of agreement on the negotiability of unification among the proper parties. Federal (West) German chancellor Helmut Kohl organized the process, first using the East German people to undermine their government, then gathering support from the United States, and finally turning to the negotiation of terms of an agreement with the Soviet Union. Starting in July 1989, many thousands of East German citizens fled to West Germany through other East European countries. Spontaneous demonstrations and church meetings took place in East Germany in the fall and winter of 1989, with citizens vociferously demanding human rights, self-determination, and political, social, and economic reforms. The New Forum (*Neues Forum*) was established in September 1989 with support from opposition groups and a goal of opening a dialogue with the communist rulers of East Germany. Erich Honecker resigned as prime minister and general secretary of the Socialist Unity Party one month later and was replaced by Egon Krenz, who offered concessions to the opposition and initiated a dialogue with the New Forum and church leaders. When one million East Germans demonstrated in East Berlin in November 1989 to demand free elections and democratic reforms, the government and politburo members resigned. The Berlin Wall was brought down by enthusiastic crowds from both sides on November 9. Four days later, Hans Modrow was confirmed as the new prime minister by the East German Parliament, and he pledged to introduce political and economic reforms and hold free elections in 1990.

The process of finding an *interlocuteur valable* on the East German side continued into 1990, as the East German Parliament removed constitutional provisions that protected the single-ruling-party status of the Communist Party (SED) renamed the Democratic Socialist Party (PDS) in February. As the political situation became unstable, the party politburo and the Central Committee and Chairman Krenz of the Council of State all resigned. Continuing pressure from the citizens and opposition parties forced the passage of laws required for changing the constitution as well as the election law on February 20. The first free elections in East Germany took place on March 18, 1990. The winners were an alliance of three conservative parties with ties to the West and led by the East German Christian Democratic Union (CDU); although the alliance failed to obtain an absolute majority, a coalition government was formed in April 1990, with Lothar de Maiziere as prime minister. Negotiations could begin.

First, however, it was necessary to determine just who would participate in those negotiations. Because of the international status of East and West Germany and their membership in opposing military alliances (NATO and the Warsaw Pact, respectively), the process of German unification had to include negotiations with the Four Powers. At the Malta Summit of December 1989, U.S. president George Bush convinced Soviet party secretary Mikhael Gorbachev to enter into negotiations, but Gorbachev preferred to keep the matter between the four occupying powers. It was not until the end of January 1990 that the Soviet Union agreed to include the two Germanys in the negotiations along with the Big Four, by a procedural formula known as "2 + 4." In February, representatives of twenty-three NATO and Warsaw Pact countries endorsed the 2 + 4 talks, in which East and West Germany would handle the internal aspects of German unification and the Four Powers would deal with the external aspects (Szabo 1992; Kohl 1997; Treverton 1992).

Stakes

The unification of Yemen, originally scheduled for November 1990, was achieved on May 22, six months ahead of schedule. Unification was made possible by the changes in stakes produced by internal and external developments in the late 1980s. First, changes in Eastern Europe and the rapid disintegration of the socialist community of states, within which South Yemen was integrated ideologically, economically, and militarily, removed external support for the South Yemeni government. The Soviet Union dropped its reservations about Yemeni unification in March 1990.

Internally, the economy of Yemen was dysfunctional. Land reforms resulted in a reduction in agricultural production, industrial production fell, and the petroleum sector almost went bankrupt. Soviet military and economic aid, which was vital to South Yemen, was drastically reduced. Pressures for unification from South Yemen citizens continued in spring 1990. As a result, the South Yemen government had very limited options. The regime was divided into factions opposed to one another along regional and ideological lines. In this state of confusion, the leadership thought that achieving a rapprochement with North Yemen was the best way to stay in power (Dunbar 1992, 464–67).

Changes also occurred in North Yemen. The tribes in the North had opposed unification in the late 1960s, which caused the failure of the Cairo and Tripoli agreements. Tribal opposition also stalled North Yemen's initiative following the 1979 border war. The tribes were hostile to the socialism of South Yemen, convinced that the socialist system indicated a decline in moral standards, and they were joined by Islamic forces and conservative business circles in their opposition. They were also strengthened by financial backing from Saudi Arabia. In the 1980s, the situation began to change; the government began to control the northern and eastern tribes, and the collapse of socialism reduced their fears. Furthermore, the Saudi government no longer opposed the unification efforts. Thus, unification was made possible through negotiations between North and South Yemen and cooperation from Saudi Arabia. However, the case of Yemen also shows that unification can be threatened if some of the parties are dissatisfied with its results.

In East Germany, the Communist Party had ousted its old leadership, apologized to the people, and promised reforms in order to regain the public's confidence. In spite of these efforts, German people continued to rebel until the government leaders gave up the absolute status of the Communist Party and consented to free elections. They were then voted out of power in the elections of March 1990 by the parties demanding immediate unification. The East German people thus redefined the stakes, first changing their system from dictatorship to democracy through their own efforts in order to change the relations from division to unification.

Despite the 2 + 4 formula, the real negotiations over unification took place between one of the "2"—West Germany—and one of the "4"—the Soviet Union. Here, two questions were in play: What was at stake for the Soviet Union? And what was the price of unification (i.e., of losing East Germany)? That price was termed "security," but that concept needed to be operationalized. First, the Soviet Union defined it as German withdrawal from NATO or neutralization, then changed the definition to mean membership in both NATO and the Warsaw Pact. Shortly thereafter, Moscow said it meant membership in a NATO with changes, but then in June, the Soviet Union backtracked to its previous position and called for German membership in both NATO and the Warsaw Pact for five years. That position was rejected both by West Germany and by the Four Powers in the June 1990 2 + 4 meeting. Finally, on July 15, Kohl and Gorbachev reached an agreement that a united Germany would be free to join whatever military alliance it wished, thus permitting it to become a full member of NATO. The Soviet Union pledged to withdraw its armed forces from East German territory within four years, and all sides agreed that NATO troops would not be in East Germany during this period; it was also agreed that a united Germany would reduce the strength of its armed forces to 370,000 troops and forswear nuclear, biological, or chemical weapons, all components of the security that the Soviet Union bargained for in exchange for inevitable unification.

But the process of redefining the stakes continued, with a new focus. A formula of "unification in exchange for security" was not enough. Less than a week before the signing of the Treaty on the Final Settlement with Respect to Germany, scheduled for September 12, 1990, Gorbachev told Kohl of the difficulties he was facing inside the Soviet Union; Kohl understood and raised his offer from DM 5 million to DM 8 million to house the returning Soviet troops, against the DM 16–18 million asked by Gorbachev. The Soviet leader intimated an impasse over the aid matter, and three days later, Kohl raised his figure to DM 11–12 million, while Gorbachev talked of DM 15–16 million. Gorbachev noted specifically that it was unification that was at an impasse. Kohl then added to the DM 12 million offer another DM 3 million as credits without interest. The sum of DM 15 million was thus reached as the price for reunification, and the new formula became "unification in exchange for payment." The Treaty on the Final Settlement with Respect to Germany was signed on schedule.

Article VII, paragraph 2 of the treaty stipulates the united Germany has full sovereignty over its internal and external affairs. The treaty entered into force on March 15, 1991, when the Soviet Union, as the last party, ratified it. The 2 + 4 treaty, which provided an international legal framework for German unification, has helped Germany to unite without war, suffering, and conflict.

The unification of Germany was thus made possible because the Soviet Union was brought into the argument through two successive formulas. In the late 1980s, Gorbachev abandoned his nation's policy of hegemonic imperialism and control in Eastern Europe, allowing the East European countries to decide their own futures (Kindermann 1991). But the prospect of the German unification created worries in the Soviet Union. Moscow wanted Germany to remain neutral after unification. However, recognizing that only Germany would be able to grant economic assistance to the Soviet Union for restructuring its economy, Gorbachev gave in and allowed Germany to choose its own alliances. A change in the Soviet position also came about as the Gorbachev administration grew convinced that a united Germany controlled within an alliance—even a Western one—was less of a threat than if it were on its own, loose in the heart of Europe.

Attitudes

In the 1980s, the North Yemen government began to change the attitudes of northern tribes. The government constructed schools and hospitals in the tribal areas and provided services and jobs for tribal members. Its new relationship with the tribes permitted the government to freely pursue unification. In the South, public opinion grew to support the unification process in the late 1980s, while the leadership began to see unification in its interest in the current domestic and international context.

Even though negotiation brought about the unification of Yemen, it did not produce peaceful results when that unity was later threatened by the dissatisfied part of the new state. When the southern part of Yemen tried to secede from the central government after unification, the mediation of the UN Security Council and the outside powers was not able to find a peaceful resolution to the conflict. The northern armed forces finally reimposed the unity of Yemen militarily.

In East Germany, the government tried to pursue a pre-emptive policy of giving in to popular demands, but the public used each concession as a stepping stone and was always one step ahead of the leaders. To reduce pressure from its people, East Germany opened the borders in November 1989, hoping that the most dissatisfied citizens would go to West Germany and that those who chose to remain could be brought under control. However, contrary to the government's expectations, the people demanded a change of system.

Seizing on the rapidly evolving situation in the East in 1989, West German chancellor Helmut Kohl stepped up a persistent campaign for reunification. He publicly proposed the end—reunification—and the means—negotiation—before the West German Parliament on November 16 and received a Soviet go-ahead the next day. He then presented a ten-point plan for the future of Germany on November 28, suggesting a confederal structure with the ultimate aim of federation. On December 19 in Dresden, Kohl and Modrow proposed a contractual community between the two Germanys.

German unification was achieved through direct negotiation between the two German democratic governments. This was possible because the East German people, through their own efforts, were able to compel the communist government to hold free elections, by which the communist dictatorship was transformed into a democratic system in a peaceful manner. West Germany's long-term strategy of informing the East Germans about the situation of West Germany and the outside world by radio and TV changed attitudes and contributed to the unification of Germany.

In May 1990, the Parliaments of East and West Germany approved the Treaty Between East and West Germany Establishing a Monetary, Economic, and Social Union, which went into effect on July 1, 1990. The Treaty Between East and West Germany on the Establishment of German Unity was signed two months thereafter, stipulating that East Germany would accede to West Germany on October 3, 1990, in accordance with Article 23 of the Basic Law of 1949.

Negotiating the National Unification Disputes of Korea

Attitudes

As in other divided states, the new international environment of the post–Cold War era changed some of the attitudes involved in the Korean division. South and North Korea agreed to build a new relationship through their prime ministers' meetings in the early 1990s. In September 1990, North Korean Premier Yon Hyong-muk visited Seoul for discussions with South Korean Prime Minister Kang Young-hoon. The meeting represented the highest-level contact between North and South Korea since the end of the Korean War. Subsequent talks between the two premiers were held in October and December 1990 and, after a hostile delay, in October 1991.

A Basic Agreement on Reconciliation, Non-Aggression, Exchanges, and Cooperation between South and North Korea was signed at the conclusion of the fifth round of prime ministerial talks in Seoul in December 1991. Under the agreement, South and North Korea pledged to discontinue their mutual slander, to promote economic cooperation and the reunion of family members, and to work toward a full peace treaty to replace the 1953 armistice agreement. The agreement became effective in February 1992 during the sixth round of negotiations, held in Pyongyang, when the two parties for the first time accepted each other as legitimate partners in negotiation (Kihl 1992). South and North Korea realized that peace and unification were interrelated and that peaceful coexistence between the two parties had to precede national unification. The Basic Agreement provided a framework for cooperation and exchanges between the South and the North to build a foundation for the unification.

North Korea applied for UN membership in May 1991, in a change from its earlier insistence that the two Koreas should occupy a single UN seat. Both Koreas became members of the UN separately in September 1991.

Stakes

Despite the 1991 Basic Agreement, North and South Korea face two important political issues that complicate the stakes involved in unification: the nuclear status of North Korea and the transformation of the Korean armistice regime.

North Korea officially joined the International Atomic Energy Agency (IAEA) in September 1974. It joined the Non-Proliferation Treaty (NPT) in December 1985 and signed the nuclear safeguards agreement with the IAEA in January 1992. The North Korean Supreme People's Assembly ratified the agreement in April 1992. Meanwhile, the Bush administration declared it would withdraw nuclear weapons from South Korea in September 1991. The prime ministers of South and North Korea signed the Joint Declaration of the Denuclearization of the Korean Peninsula on January 20, 1992, designed to eliminate the danger of nuclear war through denuclearization and to create an environment and conditions for a peaceful unification of Korea. According to the declaration, South and North Korea shall not test, manufacture, produce, receive, possess, store, deploy, or use nuclear weapons and nuclear reprocessing and uranium enrichment facilities, and they shall use nuclear energy only for peaceful purposes.

To permit verification of the denuclearization of the Korean Peninsula, the parties agreed to conduct inspections of the objects selected by the other side and agreed upon between the two sides in accordance with procedures and methods determined by the South-North Joint Nuclear Control Commission. After the ratification of the nuclear safeguards agreement in North Korea, the first international inspection team arrived at the North's nuclear facilities at Yongbyon. The inspection team found evidence that North Korea was not complying with its NPT obligations. Eventually, the confrontation between North Korea and the IAEA came to a deadlock, leading to Pyongyang's decision to pull out of the NPT altogether in March 1993. At that point, the United States felt compelled to open a direct dialogue with North Korea on nuclear matters (Mansourov 1995; Mazarr 1995; Reiss 1995; Sigal 1998, 2000). The first result was a statement, issued in June 1993 in Geneva, that suspended the North Korean withdrawal from the NPT. In return, the United States pledged not to use or threaten to use nuclear weapons against the North.

After subsequent negotiations that benefited from a roadblock-breaking intervention by former President Jimmy Carter, the United States and North Korea signed the Agreed Framework on the Nuclear Issue in Geneva on October 21, 1994 (Carter 1994; Oberdorfer 1997; Zartman and Michishita 1996). With this agreement, North Korea promised to dismantle its potential military application of the nuclear program. In accordance with this pact, the North also froze its nuclear program on November 1, 1994, and pledged to dismantle its graphite-moderated reactors by 1998 (Paik 1995).

A North Korean submarine landed on the eastern coast of South Korea in September 1996, and twenty-six armed infiltrators went ashore. Later, North Korea apologized to the South for the incident and promised to make efforts to ensure that it would not recur. The apology opened the way to a resumed dialogue between North and South Korea and contributed to the reduction of tensions on the Korean Peninsula. The next day, North Korea agreed to talk with the South and the United States about negotiating a formal end to the Korean War. North Korea also agreed at the same time (December 30, 1996) to store spent nuclear fuel rods safely rather than reprocessing them for plutonium, in keeping with a 1994 agreement. North Korea and a U.S.-led consortium called the Korea Energy Development Organization (KEDO) signed the protocols on January 8, 1997, for the construction of two light-water nuclear reactors. KEDO was formed in 1995 after the 1994 U.S.–North Korean agreement to freeze the North's suspected nuclear weapons program in exchange for the reactors.

In return for the nuclear agreement, North Korea gained economic, political, and military benefits. Economically, Pyongyang exchanged the nuclear freeze for economic assistance worth US$4.5 billion, a Western pledge to transfer some advanced technologies to North Korea, a ten-year supply of oil, and an easing of economic sanctions. As in the case of Germany but several steps away from unification, stakes were redefined, and the formula for agreement became "removal of obstacles in exchange for payment." Politically, the nuclear deal with the United States allowed North Korea to break out of international isolation; among other things, this paved the way for an improvement in its relations with major Western countries and the application for membership in international organizations such as the International Monetary Fund (IMF), the World Bank, the Asian Pacific Economic Cooperation (APEC) forum, and the World Trade Organization (WTO). Militarily, North Korea obtained the U.S. guarantee that Washington would not use or threaten to use nuclear weapons against it as long as it remained in the NPT.

Despite the 1994 accord, however, North Korea was suspected of developing nuclear weapons at the Kumchangri underground site near Yongbyon. The United States had been pressing since August 1998 for access to the site. The Clinton administration was obliged by the U.S. Congress to clear up all suspicions by the end of the following May; if not, Congress was set to suspend the use of federal funds to supply North Korea with heavy oil as an alternative energy source, thus damaging the 1994 framework agreement.

In a major breakthrough, North Korea agreed on March 16, 1999, to provide the United States satisfactory access to the Kumchangri site by allowing an initial visit by a U.S. delegation in May 1999 and additional visits later on to remove any concern about the site's future use. The United States, in turn, agreed to take steps to improve political and economic relations and also offered six hundred thousand tons of grain to North Korea through the World Food Program (*Korea Times,* March 17, 1999).

In relation to the nuclear issue, North Korea missile development has raised tensions in the peninsula and more broadly in the region. Since 1985, North Korea has been conducting missile tests, including the Scud B tests in 1985, Scud C tests in 1990, and Rodong I tests in 1993. The United States has held negotiations with the North since 1996 in order to freeze the North Korean ballistic missile program and halt the export of its missiles to countries in the Middle East and south Asia. In August 1998, North Korea test-fired a newly developed Taepodong I ballistic missile into the open seas off the coast of Japan; it also developed the Taepodong II missile, capable of reaching the West Coast of the United States. The Taepodong I missile test was intended as a show of force by North Korea in the midst of its dealings with the United States.

During his visit to the North in May 1999, former Secretary of Defense William Perry, appointed by President Clinton to prepare a report on U.S. policy toward North Korea, offered economic and political incentives in return for an end to missile development. In August, Pyongyang expressed its willingness to negotiate over its missile development. There is a possibility that North Korea has undertaken its missile program as a bargaining chip, in order to trade it off against economic and political benefits being considered by the United States, although the foreign missile sales are economically rewarding. If the benefits offered are sufficient, North Korea, in difficult economic straits, may have no alternative but to accept the deal offered by the United States (*Korea Times,* September 1, 1998; *Korea Herald,* August 27, 1999).

The transformation of the Korean armistice regime into a peace treaty is seen as the way to change the stakes from security between hostile neighbors to joint security and prosperity through unification. The 1953 armistice has come under serious threat since 1974 as North Korea has raised its demand for a peace treaty with the United States. Until the late 1990s, South Korea held the position that issues related to replacing the current armistice regime with a new peace structure were to be discussed through a dialogue between South and North Korea. South Korea wants to be actively involved in the resolution of the armistice issue. At a summit meeting between President Clinton and South Korean president Kim Yong-sam in April 1996, the two leaders proposed the convening of a four-party meeting of the representatives of South and North Korea, the United States, and China "as soon as possible and without preconditions" to "initiate a process aimed at achieving a permanent peace agreement." They agreed that this process should also address a wide range of tension-reduction measures (*Korea Herald,* April 17, 1999; *International Herald Tribune,* April 17, 1999).

China's initial response to the proposal was positive; it indicated it was willing to play a constructive role as a signatory to the armistice agreement. However, as time went on, China made it clear that the four-party talk could only be realized when the parties directly concerned, that is, South and North Korea, settle their differences. China would not press North Korea to accept the proposal. The South Korea–U.S. Joint Announcement also made it clear that the two Koreas should take the lead in a renewed search for a permanent peace agreement and that separate negotiations between the United States and North Korea on peace-related issues on the Korean Peninsula cannot be considered.

The opening rounds of four-party talks were held in Geneva in December 1997 and March 1998, focusing mainly on how to proceed with the four-party talks. At the third round in October 1998, the parties agreed to deal with concrete and substantive issue and to set up two subcommittees to discuss the establishment of a peace regime and tension reduction on the Korean Peninsula. The sixth round of four-party talks made little progress in August 1999; North Korea insisted that the agenda include its demand for the U.S. troop withdrawal from South Korea and a peace treaty between North Korea and the United States.

In sudden change of policy in the North, South Korean President Kim Dae-jung and North Korean National Defense Commission Chairman Kim Jong-il held summit talks from June 13 to 15, 2000 in Pyongyang. Their joint declaration endorsed inter-Korean reconciliation and unification, eased tension, and promoted peace on the Korean Peninsula, helping reunited separated family members and broaden exchanges in economic, social, and cultural fields. The two Koreas moved toward implementing the provisions of the 1991 Basic Agreement that pledged to transform the state of armistice into a state of peace between the two sides and to abide by the armistice until peace is realized.

Tactics

South Korean policy favors a gradual approach to unification: first, confidence building and peaceful coexistence between the two Koreas and, later, nation unification. South Korean president Kim Dae-jung suggested a sunshine policy toward North Korea, asking the North to open its door to South Korea and the outside world and indicating that South Korea would not seek to absorb the North. The Pyongyang response was very defensive. North Korean leaders said that they would pursue their own policy of opening the door to the outside world in their own way, and they criticized South Korea's attempt to liberalize the North through its sunshine policy. North Korea's main concern at this stage is to maintain its own political system and avoid changes such as those occurring in the rest of the former communist bloc, especially Eastern Europe.

North Korea has used nuclear and missile threats to obtain aid from the United States and other countries in order to overcome its tremendous economic difficulties. Experiencing it own economic difficulties at the turn of the twenty-first century, South Korea is also worried about maintaining its system. Both South and North Korea seek to maintain the status quo. However, each side needs a more stable international environment to do so. Thus, both need to establish a peace regime in the peninsula.

The four-party meetings can be utilized as an opportunity to enhance the peace and stability and facilitate unification of the Korean Peninsula. But on the question of transforming the current Korean armistice regime into a peace regime (Paik 1995), South and North Korea have differed on tactical issues, such as the parties to the negotiation and the role of the current armistice regime. South Korea has maintained that the transformation of the armistice regime should be discussed between the two parties concerned, as stated in the 1991 Basic Agreement on Reconciliation, Non-Aggression, Exchanges, and Cooperation between South and North Korea.

North Korea has insisted that a peace treaty should be negotiated between North Korea and the United States, excluding South Korea. The armistice agreement was signed by the supreme commander of the Korean People's Army and the commander of the Chinese People's Volunteers, on the one hand, and the UN commander, on the other; because the Chinese People's Volunteers have withdrawn from Korea and the UN forces in South Korea are, in fact, U.S. troops, the real parties to the armistice agreement are the DPRK and the United States, and, according to North Korea, these would be the parties to conclude a peace treaty. Moreover, the North contends that South Korea cannot become a signatory to the peace treaty because it did not sign the armistice agreement. Thus, South and North Korea differ as to who should negotiate on the transformation of the armistice agreement regime into a peace regime.

The four-party meetings were intended to harmonize the U.S.–North Korean talks and the inter-Korean dialogue. The United States was in a dilemma, needing to meet Pyongyang's demand for direct talks while simultaneously allaying South Korean concerns. The four-party meeting proposal was presented as a practical solution to the dilemma. To the extent that North Korea continues its pro-U.S./anti–South Korean policy approach, the discussions can function as a supplementary device to encourage South–North dialogue on the establishment of a peace arrangement.

Initially, there had been differences in South and North Korean approaches to unification. South Korea suggested a confederation calling for two systems and two governments, while North Korea advocated one federal state. At the 2000 South–North Korean summit talks, North Korea changed its position and agreed to the idea of confederation. Both South and North Korean leaders recognized that peaceful coexistence between the two Koreas is more important at this stage than immediate unification. The two agreed to implement easy things first, such as mutual exchanges and reunion of separated families, and save for later difficult things, such as building a peace regime on the Korean Peninsula.

Conclusion

Preventive diplomacy seeks to prevent the escalation of conflict and violence. In two of the three divided states—Yemen and Korea—war was not prevented on several occasions—between the Koreas in 1950–53, between the Yemens in 1971–72, 1979, and 1993–94, and within North Yemen in 1962–65 and South Yemen in 1965–70.

Between the two Germanies, however, war *was* prevented on an ongoing basis and most notably in 1948–49, as both sets of external supervisors took measures to avoid direct confrontation with each other (Sinn and Sinn 1996). In general, war and other forms of violent confrontation were averted by repeated and renewed efforts to create a unification process. When violent incidents and tension that threatened to escalate into violence disrupted these efforts, energies were deployed to get the process back on track.

Ultimately, escalation and violence were prevented by conflict resolution and transformation, in other words, by simply eliminating the conflict through negotiated unification. A number of conditions made this possible, and a number of policies built on those conditions. Stakes changed as the economy collapsed on one side of the divide and as that side's elites realized they would acquire new and better fortunes by joining the opposition. Attitudes changed when the external sponsors no longer supported division, when the weaker side's sponsor dropped its sponsorship, and when public pressure rose in favor of unification. Leaders on both sides—whether incumbents or new replacements—then began to negotiate the steps to unification, making sure that its benefits were shared, that its procedural uncertainties were eliminated, and that the outcome would clearly be more advantageous than continued division. The parties then negotiated two sets of procedures— a transitional regime to accomplish unification and a permanent constitutional regime for relations within the newly unified state.

Many of the same conditions existed in the Korean Peninsula, but they have not as yet produced the same results. In fact, they have led the weaker side to dig in and even to increase tensions and threats of war. As a result, the stronger side has grown more wary of unification. Some progress was made in South–North Korean relations through a series of prime ministerial talks between the disputants in the early 1990s. The Basic Agreement between South and North Korea in 1991 suggests that peaceful coexistence between the two nations can eventually lead to unification.

The nuclear problem of North Korea recently raised tensions in the Korean Peninsula, but the problem was managed through the negotiations between North Korea and the United States in 1994 and 1999. The issue of transforming the armistice regime into the peace regime has not been resolved between South and North Korea. The main obstacles in the South–North Korean dialogue are Pyongyang's demands for the withdrawal of U.S. troops from the

Korean Peninsula and for a U.S.–North Korean peace treaty. In addition, North Korea keeps adding new stakes or reviving old ones whenever progress is made. Meanwhile, the leaders in Seoul contend that peace can be established only when attitudes are changed and confidence is built between the South and the North.

Each side sticks to its uncompromising position. South Korea seeks to achieve peaceful coexistence and carry out exchanges with North Korea, believing that this will eventually lead to unification talks between the two parts of the peninsula, somewhat as occurred in Yemen. North Korea, however, is hesitant to open its society to South Korea and the outside world, as this may lead to systemic changes in the North. It therefore seeks to maintain its own system as its first priority.

However, North Korea agreed to hold the South–North Korean summit talks in June 2000. North Korea needed to cooperate with South Korea to overcome its economic crisis. It changed its approach to unification and accepted the South Korean concept of peaceful coexistence and a gradual approach to unification. The South–North Korean summit talks suddenly opened up the prospect of a Korean reconciliation and cooperation.

In order to prevent war and reduce tension on the peninsula, South and North Korea need to form a bilateral military committee to discuss nonaggression, reduction of tension and other issues related to peace on the peninsula. When the two Koreas succeed in building confidence through arms control negotiations, and peaceful coexistence becomes predominant, the need for reconciliation and cooperation will become evident as the next step. This spirit of cooperation will eventually lead to the peaceful unification of Korea, as occurred in the cases of Yemen and Germany.

References

Acheson, Dean. 1969. *The Korean War.* New York: Norton.

Birnbaum, Karl E. 1973. *East and West Germany: A Modus Vivendi.* Farnborough, England: Saxon House.

Braun, Ursula. 1992. "Yemen: Another Case of Unification." *Aussenpolitik* 43, no. 2: 174–84.

Burrowes, Robert D. 1987. *The Yemen Arab Republic.* Boulder: Westview.

Carter, Jimmy. 1994. *Report of Our Trip to Korea.* Atlanta: Carter Center.

Catudal, Honoré, Jr. 1978. *The Diplomacy of the Quadrapartite Agreement on Berlin.* Berlin: Berliner Verlag.

Chai, C., and Y. Zhao. 1989. *Panmunjom Negotiations.* Beijing: PLA.

Cheon, Seongwhun. 1996. "The Four-Party Peace Meeting Proposal." *Korea and World Affairs* 20, no. 2 (Summer): 179.

Cummings, B., ed. 1983. *Child of Conflict: The Korean-American Relationship, 1943–1953.* Seattle: University of Washington Press.

Dunbar, Charles. 1992. "The Unification of Yemen: Process, Politics, and Prospects." *Middle East Journal* 46, no. 3: 456–76.

Fan, Xibo. 2000. "China and the United States Negotiating the End of the Korean War." In *Power and Negotiation*, ed. I. William Zartman and Jeffrey Z. Rubin. Ann Arbor: University of Michigan Press.

Federal Republic of Germany Press and Information Office. 1978. *Documentation Related to the Federal Government's Policy of Détente*. Bonn: Press and Information Office.

Foot, Rosemary. 1985. *The Wrong War*. Ithaca: Cornell University Press.

———. 1990. *A Substitute for Victory*. Ithaca: Cornell University Press.

Hanrieder, Wolfram, and Grame Anton. 1980. *The Foreign Policies of West Germany, France, and Britain*. Englewood Cliffs, N.J.: Prentice-Hall.

Henderson, Gregory, Richard Ned Lebow, and John G. Stoessinger. 1974. *Divided Nations in a Divided World*. New York: David Mckay.

Hwang, Byong-Moo, and Young-Kwan Yoon, eds. 1996. *Middle Powers in the Age of Globalization*. Seoul: Korean Association of International Studies.

Joy, C. Turner. 1964. *How Communists Negotiate*. Stanford: Hoover.

Keithly, David. 1985. *Breakthrough in Ostpolitik: The 1971 Quadripartite Agreement*. Boulder: Westview.

Kihl, Young Whan. 1992. "New Environment and Context for Korean Reunification." *Korea and World Affairs* 16, no. 4 (November).

Kindermann, Gottfried-Karl. 1991. "The Peaceful Reunification of Germany." *Issues and Studies* 27, no. 3 (March 1991).

———. 1997. "Never Give Up Hope and Practically, Always Remain Prepared." *Diplomacy* 23, no. 8.

Kohl, Helmut. 1997. *Uniting Germany*. Pekka Kalevi: Pekka Kalevi Hamalainen.

Laird, Robbin. 1991. *The Soviets, Germany and the New Europe*. Boulder: Westview.

Lee, Chong Sik. 1978. *The Korean Worker's Party: A Short History*. Stanford: Stanford University Press.

Mahnke, Dieter. 1973. *Berlin im geteilten Deutschland*. Munich: Oldenbourg Verlag.

Mansourov, Alexander Y. 1995. "The Origins, Evolution and Future of the North Korean Nuclear Program." *Korea and World Affairs* 19, no. 1 (Spring).

Mazarr, Michael. 1995. *North Korea and the Bomb*. New York: St. Martin's.

Merkl, Peter H. 1974–1975. "The German Janus: From Westpolitik to Ostpolitik." *Political Science Quarterly* 89, no. 4 (Winter): 803–24.

Mermier, Franck, ed. 1997. "Yemen: L'État face à la démocratie," special issue of *Maghreb-Machrek* 155 (January).

Oberdorfer, Don. 1997. *The Two Koreas*. Boston: Addison-Wesley.

Omalia, Thomas, et al. 1993. *Promoting Participation in Yemen's Election*. Washington, D.C.: National Democratic Institution.

———. 1997. *The April 27, 1997 Parliamentary Elections in Yemen*. Washington, D.C.: National Democratic Institute.

Paik, Jin Hyun. 1994. "The Geneva Framework Agreement and South Korea's Strategy of Engagement." *Korea and World Affairs* 18, no. 4 (Winter): 631.

———. 1995. "Building a Peace Regime on the Korean Peninsula." *Korea and World Affairs* 19, no. 3 (Autumn): 408–12.

Reiss, Mitchell. 1995. *Bridled Ambition*. Washington, D.C.: Woodrow Wilson Center Press.

Republic of Korea National Unification Board. 1992. *A White Paper on South-North Dialogue in Korea*. Seoul: Republic of Korea National Unification Board.

Rubin, Barnett. 1995. *The Search for Peace in Afghanistan*. New Haven: Yale University Press.

Sigal, Leon. 1998. *Disarming Strangers: Nuclear Diplomacy with North Korea*. Princeton: Princeton University Press.

——. 2000. "Nuclear Diplomacy with North Korea." In *Nuclear Negotiations,* ed. Rudolf Avenhaus, Gunnar Sjöstedt, and Victor Kremenyuk. Laxenburg, Austria: International Institute of Applied Systems Analysis.

Sinn, Gerlinde, and Hans Werner Sinn. 1996. "What Can Korea Learn from German Unification?" In *Middle Powers in the Age of Globalization,* ed. Byong-Moo Hwang and Young-Kwan Yoon. Seoul: Korean Association of International Studies.

Sowden, J. K. 1975. *The German Question, 1945–1973*. New York: St. Martin's.

Szabo, Stephen. 1992. *The Diplomacy of German Unification*. Washington, D.C.: American Institute for German Studies.

Treverton, Gregory. 1992. *American, Germany and the Future of Europe* . Princeton: Princeton University Press.

Vreeland, Nena, ed. 1975. *Area Handbook for South Korea,* 2nd ed. Washington, D.C.: Government Printing Office.

Yun, Kun-Shik. 1975. "A Comparative Study of East-West German and South-North Korea Relations." *East Asian Review* 2, no. 2 (Summer):120–44.

Zartman, I. William, and Narushije Michishita. 1996. "Two Korea's Negotiating Strategies Revisited: Focusing on the Nuclear Issue." In *Middle Powers in the Age of Globalization,* ed. Byong-Moo Hwang and Young-Kwan Yoon. Seoul: Korean Association of International Studies.

6

Disintegrating States:
Separating without Violence

P. Terrence Hopmann

The end of the Cold War did not bring an end to conflict in the world. But the more recent disputes often have a somewhat different character from those that predominated in previous periods of history. Even as interstate conflicts have decreased in relative frequency on the global scene, intrastate disputes have sprung up in many parts of the world. One of the most common sources of these internal conflicts is the breakup of states along the lines of ethnicity, with language and religion most often being the main markers of identity; affiliation with a region or clan sometimes serves this function as well. The reshuffling of global politics as a result of the end of the Cold War has brought forth and made more open demands for self-determination by peoples who had previously been considered minorities in other, larger states or by peoples who had not considered themselves minorities until being thrust into this new status when larger states broke apart. This phenomenon is certainly not altogether new: With the end of colonialism in much of Africa and Asia, movements for self-determination arose within some of the newly independent states in those regions, as, for example, was the case with Katanga Province in the former Belgian Congo or with Bangladesh in Pakistan.

However, the disintegration and reshuffling of state structures took on significant proportions with the demise of the communist system after 1989. Most notable was the collapse of the Soviet Union itself, whereby one of the two global superpowers split into fifteen independent pieces. Within many of these states, significant groups of people did not identify with the new entity to which they belonged, and they, too, demanded self-determination. A similar process occurred as Yugoslavia broke apart into its constituent elements, and Croatia and Bosnia-Herzegovina experienced severe internal conflict over the identity of the new state. Such ethnonational conflicts serve as the primary focus of this chapter.

Of particular significance is the fact that disintegration took very different forms in different situations: In some cases, the process was accompanied by intense violence; in others, there was no bloodshed. At the opposite extremes are the situations of Czechoslovakia, on one hand, and Bosnia and Herzegovina, on the other. Czechoslovakia split voluntarily and peacefully into two states, the Czech Republic and Slovakia, in what has generally been described as the "velvet divorce." After the collapse of communism, Czechoslovakia had reconstituted itself as the Czech and Slovak Federal Republic, with the Czech entity being constituted primarily by the historical regions of Bohemia and Moravia. But, as I. William Zartman (1998) has pointed out, federations with two members tend to be unstable, and the easiest resolution to this problem was to accept the division of the country into two independent states. By contrast, Bosnia and Herzegovina became independent from Yugoslavia, when the tenuous federation of six republics fell apart in 1991–92, only to find itself embroiled in an intense and violent conflict among its three principal ethnic components, with culture and religion serving as the primary identity markers—Serbs (predominantly Eastern Orthodox), Croats (mostly Roman Catholics), and Bosniaks (mostly Muslims). The very different outcomes to similar disintegrative processes in nearby regions raise the question of how to explain this difference: What accounts for the peaceful dissolution of some states and the violence in others? This chapter will explore whether preventive diplomacy by outside parties or effective negotiation directly between disputing parties can, in part, produce such divergent outcomes. I do not claim that diplomacy is the single or even the most important factor explaining this difference. I only examine whether it constitutes at least one significant factor, possibly among many. There are two major hypotheses:

1. The greater the extent to which parties to an ethnonational dispute utilize problem-solving techniques for bilateral diplomacy in the early stages of an escalating conflict, the greater the likelihood that they will be able to accommodate their differences without violence.
2. The greater the availability of third parties or international institutions to serve as mediators between disputing ethnonational parties, the more they intervene early in developing disputes, and the more committed they are to promote a problem-solving approach to negotiations, the greater the likelihood of a nonviolent resolution of the conflict.

Preventive Diplomacy and the Breakup of the Former Soviet Union

It is commonly asserted that conflicts over state disintegration are easier to resolve before, not after, they become violent. This view has been expressed forcefully by Max van der Stoel (1997,16), the High Commissioner on National Minorities of the Organization for Security and Cooperation in Europe (OSCE): "It is evident from the experience of Bosnia, of Chechnya, of Nagorno-Karabakh,[1] of Georgia and elsewhere, that once a conflict has erupted, it is extremely difficult to bring it to an end. In the meantime, precious lives have been lost, new waves of hatred have been created and enormous damage has been inflicted. It is my firm belief that money spent on conflict prevention is money well spent, not only because it is cheaper, but especially because it saves so many lives."

Preventive diplomacy offers the possibility of avoiding a good deal of the pain and suffering typically associated with violent conflict and the tense stalemate that often follows such violence. If it is usually necessary to wait until a "hurting stalemate" is recognized by the disputing parties before a mediator can intervene and initiate meaningful negotiations, it is also important to recognize that a much earlier point of intervention may also have been available, before the conflict turned violent in the first place. Furthermore, intervention at an earlier stage is also more likely to lead to mutual accommodation than any intervention after a period of violent conflict or even after the development of a hurting stalemate. Michael Lund (1996, 15) has enumerated some of the most important reasons for this assertion in his recent book on preventive diplomacy: "The issues in the dispute are fewer and less complex; conflicting parties are not highly mobilized, polarized, and armed; significant bloodshed has not occurred, and thus a sense of victimization and a desire for vengeance are not intense; the parties have not begun to demonize and stereotype each other; moderate leaders still maintain control over extremist tendencies; and the parties are not so committed that compromise involves loss of face."

The difficulty with preventive diplomacy, however, is that there is often only a very narrow window of opportunity during which parties may intervene to avert violence. At early stages in a conflict, the gravity of the situation may not be recognized so that no stimulus to intervene arises. Furthermore, premature intervention may actually create a self-fulfilling prophecy and even stimulate conflict in the minds of disputing parties. But if outside parties wait too long before intervening, the threshold of violence may be crossed before preventive diplomacy can be engaged. And once that threshold has been crossed, the opportunity to resolve the conflict may not present itself until a long time later. Thus, timing the engagement of preventive diplomacy is an extremely critical, yet elusive, factor in the etiology of a conflict.

A number of prerequisites must be satisfied if preventive diplomacy is to be effective in forestalling conflict. First, the relevant parties must be aware early on that a conflict is developing. Many indicators provide an early warning, including riots and demonstrations by dissident groups, statements or declarations of an intent to secede and form an autonomous state, intense debates over language laws or religious customs that might advantage one group at the expense of another, and political restructuring of the state or of a particular regime that brings one national group into a dominant position.

Second, warnings of real conflicts must be distinguished from false alarms. As Alexander George and Jane Holl (2000, 29) have noted, the problem for preventive diplomacy often is not a failure to identify potential trouble spots but rather an inability to understand "such situations well enough to forecast which ones are likely to explode and when." However good may be their intentions, states and multilateral organizations can antagonize important constituencies by crying wolf too frequently. They also may alienate parties if they try to intervene in situations that do not seem to warrant early intervention from the outside. And they may exhaust both their willpower and their limited resources by trying to intervene in more conflicts than they can handle at any one time.[2]

Third, someone must be available to attend to the warnings. In certain cases, it may be the disputants themselves. An advantage of placing the primary responsibility for effective preventive diplomacy upon the disputing parties is their greater knowledge of the conflict at hand. The background of the dispute and the nature of the opposing factions are almost always best understood by the parties themselves, and the disputants do not have to make a special effort to adapt to the specific requirements of local custom. For the involved parties to take heed of early warnings, however, a stable political leadership is essential, as regimes occupied with internal disorder and chaos may not be able to recognize and respond to such warnings. At times, the blindness of involvement may cause political leaders to ignore or deny the need for preventive action to head off an approaching disaster (Rapoport 1960, 259–72). They therefore must be able to see that beyond the present turmoil, there are greater risks to their well-being and leadership if preventive action is not taken rapidly. Furthermore, the political leadership must not be single-mindedly committed to one specific outcome; they must avoid black-and-white thinking as well as the tendency to stereotype the issues and the other parties; and they must be willing to sacrifice whatever benefits might accrue to them from "winning" the conflict in order to prevent larger losses from "losing" through a further escalation and violence. Needless to say, wise leadership of this type is seldom present in situations that reach such a crisis that the disintegration of the state itself is threatened.

In other cases, the relevant parties may be outside the dispute but capable of lending a hand in its resolution—that is, they may be the typical third parties that are able to step between the disputing groups and mediate a solution. For such parties to attend to the conflict, they must have an interest in it either because they have an institutional role in its resolution or because they have a direct stake in the outcome. They must not be restricted from intervening by bureaucratic or domestic political constraints, and they must not be preoccupied with so many competing crises that their commitment to prevention is weakened. Undoubtedly, one of the reasons for the collapse of preventive diplomacy in 1990–92, when many conflicts appeared throughout the former communist world, is that the rapid pace of change and the frequency with which crises appeared in various parts of Eurasia overloaded policymakers in international institutions and in key countries such as the United States. This made it difficult for them to attend to, much less respond to, the many events that were occurring at such a rapid pace simultaneously.

The inability of outside parties to respond quickly was particularly apparent in the former Soviet Union as it was breaking apart. Although Russia may have formally been an outside power in some cases, as in the conflict in Georgia, for example, it was seen as too deeply involved in the disputes themselves to claim effective third-party status. At the same time, outside the former Soviet Union, other parties were reluctant to become engaged in the early stages: In addition to being overwhelmed by the number of potential problems for preventive diplomacy that arose more or less simultaneously, especially in Central and Eastern Europe, they did not want to enter too quickly into a region that had so recently been dominated by one of the global superpowers, especially when the status of the new states remained somewhat ambiguous. It was impossible for an unprepared world to respond to such sudden and dramatic change very effectively. As a consequence, local preventive action was, in many cases, the only alternative to rapid escalation.

A general principle that underlies the central hypotheses is that a special kind of intervention and specific negotiating techniques are required to cope with the conflicts of state disintegration. That is because most of these are not simple conflicts of interest, in which parties may try to trade off various stakes to find an acceptable solution, but almost invariably involve issues of identity. Ethnonational conflicts develop because at least one group feels that its identity is jeopardized and perhaps even at risk of being extinguished. At moments of social and political upheaval, identities may be especially vulnerable. Therefore, as Zartman (1998, 318) has emphasized, it is essential that the state develop "an identity principle to hold its people together and to give cognitive content to the institutional aspects of legitimacy and sovereignty. Without such a regime, it will fall apart in continuing and renewed conflict; without an identity principle, it becomes merely a bureaucratic administration with no standard terms for expressing allegiance."

As I have argued, such problems of identity are virtually impossible to settle through negotiations based on a traditional bargaining process; instead, they require a problem-solving approach to negotiations (Hopmann 1997). In this method, the parties must view the conflict as a problem to be solved jointly with the other parties, rather than as a conflict to be won.[3] This requires that they treat the dispute essentially as a non-zero-sum game—one in which both parties stand to lose from escalation and in which both may gain from mutual accommodation. They must avoid attitudes that stereotype the other party to the conflict. Tactically, they must show sufficient flexibility to achieve progress in negotiations without appearing weak and thus vulnerable to exploitation. They must use persuasion to get their needs satisfied rather than hard bargaining tactics designed to intimidate the other party into making concessions.[4] The message of this chapter is that preventive diplomacy will be most effective if it creates a negotiation process that avoids hard bargaining and facilitates and even encourages joint diagnosis of the problem and a common search for solutions that will serve mutual needs and interests.

In encouraging this process, third parties can be most effective by influencing the psychological and attitudinal components of the impending dispute. Often, their assistance is needed by the disputants to reframe the issues so that they no longer appear so zero-sum in nature, to help them overcome stereotyped images of their "enemies," to aid them in identifying possible formulas that merge their joint interests rather than divide them, or even to help them make concessions that will not entail losing face or opening themselves to exploitation by the other party.[5] Thus, the third party may assist the disputants in changing attitudes and reevaluating stakes so that they can resolve their problems in ways that they would not have come upon by themselves. Very often, the perceived absence of formulas reflecting joint interests is what led to the conflict in the first place. Moreover, stereotyped images of the opponent make it hard to work *with* the other party to find potential common ground, and the fear of exploitation by the opposition leads to a paralysis in which neither side takes the initiative to make concessions. Without some ability to reformulate the stakes in various outcomes (or to perceive outcomes that were not previously identified), to modify attitudes of implacable hostility, and to avoid counterproductive tactical maneuvers, negotiations are unlikely to be successful either at forestalling conflict in the first place or in preventing its escalation once conflict has broken out.

Too often, third parties focus primarily on seeking substantive solutions when, in fact, these can usually best be discovered by the parties themselves, who know the issues and their stakes most intimately. Thus, outside parties are normally most effective in creating a process through which the disputants can find ways of meeting their fundamental needs and securing their interests (especially preserving and protecting their identity as viable social units) at the lowest possible cost and with the least possible physical violence. Whenever feasible, it is important that the parties to a dispute feel ownership of the solution: Participants on both sides should believe that the agreement was one that *they* developed to solve the problem rather than one that was imposed on them from outside. If they own the solution, they have a responsibility to see it implemented effectively, whereas if they see it as externally imposed, their only obligation will be to do whatever is necessary to avoid opprobrium and sanctions associated with noncompliance.

Given the nature of the post–Cold War world, there are literally dozens of cases that could be chosen to investigate the role of preventive diplomacy in conflicts involving the disintegration of states. To facilitate comparisons, however, this chapter will focus exclusively on cases arising within the former Soviet Union, so as to establish a maximum control for external variations. The following three paired cases will provide the basis for the focused comparison in this chapter:

1. Abkhazia and Ajaria in Georgia
2. Transdniestria in Moldova and Crimea in Ukraine
3. Chechnya and Tatarstan in the Russian Federation

Abkhazia and Ajaria in Georgia

Abkhazia

Abkhazia occupies the western tip of Georgia, bordered on the north by the Russian Federation and on the south by the Black Sea. When the Soviet Union broke up, only 17 percent of the population of Abkhazia consisted of Abkhazians, a people whose language is related to that of mountain peoples of the Northern Caucasus. The Abkhazian people, whose origins can be traced back at least to the fifth century B.C., were widely dispersed, killed, or deported by the Russian colonizers. Abkhazians share a common language and culture but not a common religion, as some are Muslims, some are Eastern Orthodox Christians, and a large percentage retain "pagan" practices and beliefs. The proportion of Abkhazians in Abkhazia diminished steadily over the twentieth century. These adverse demographic trends help to explain why the Abkhazians fear for their survival as a distinct people.

In the early Soviet period, Abkhazia had a peculiar status vis-à-vis Georgia[6] in which neither party was subordinated to the other, but Joseph Stalin reduced Abkhazia to an autonomous republic within Georgia in 1931. Many Abkhazians wished to have it regain its former status. Beginning as early as 1989, they sought its separation from Georgia. They objected to Georgia's attempts to assimilate them into Georgian society, especially the effort to have the Georgian language predominate in Abkhazia, so their leaders appealed to Moscow to grant them the status of a full union republic. Georgians rallied to support the integrity of their own nation and the interests of the ethnic Georgians (who composed about 45 percent of the population of Abkhazia) by organizing a national demonstration in Tbilisi in April 1989, which was initially aimed against the Abkhazians but quickly generated demands for Georgian secession from the Soviet Union. Georgian Communist Party officials appealed to Moscow to provide assistance in putting down this demonstration, and Gen. Igor Rodionov was sent to Tbilisi to organize army and internal security forces. On April 9, those forces launched an attack upon the demonstrators, using tear gas and chemical weapons. Nineteen people were killed and thousands were injured by the chemicals in what became known in Georgia as "bloody Sunday in Tbilisi" (Batalden and Batalden 1997, 127–28). Partially in reaction to these events, the Georgian Supreme Soviet declared sovereignty in August 1989, prompting fears in Abkhazia that Georgia would exploit this opportunity to no longer recognize the Abkhazians as a distinct people.

With the proclamation of sovereignty, however, Zviad Gamsakhurdia, an intellectual and former dissident who headed a political faction known as Round Table/Free Georgia, emerged as a national hero. He and his followers called for new parliamentary elections and demanded the restoration of the constitution that had governed Georgia from 1918 through 1921, when the nation had temporarily achieved independence after the collapse of czarist Russia and prior to the consolidation of Soviet control over the Southern Caucasus. In elections for the Georgian Supreme Soviet in 1990, Gamsakhurdia's Round Table/Free Georgia faction gained 56 percent of the vote, in contrast to 24 percent for the Georgian Communist Party (Fuller 1990, 13–16).

Georgia declared its independence from the Soviet Union on April 9, 1991, and Gamsakhurdia emerged as its first leader. Having headed Parliament since November 1990, he was elected as Georgia's first president in May 1991, appealing to nationalist themes. As his power grew, he became more and more overtly authoritarian and nationalistic, describing himself as sent by God to make Georgia a moral example for the entire world (Batalden and Batalden 1997, 128). He attacked his political opponents strongly and sought to limit participation in the electoral process only to parties that had support throughout the entire country. Gamsakhurdia's personality and positions increased fears among national minorities across Georgia, not only in Abkhazia. He began his attack on minority regions by abolishing the autonomous status of the South Ossetian Autonomous Oblast, and he sent Georgian troops to the regional capital of Tskhinvali to establish Georgian authority over the region.

Meanwhile, opposition to his authoritarianism began to mount in Tbilisi. Coming full circle, Gamsakhurdia ordered National Guard troops to fire on peaceful demonstrators there in September 1991. This set off a power struggle within Georgia, pitting the president and his followers against elements of the National Guard, led by Tengiz Kitovani, and other internal security forces known as the Mkhedrioni. Together, these forces launched a coup d'état that ousted Gamsakhurdia but was followed by a bloody civil war between Gamsakhurdia's supporters and the newly installed State Council of Georgia. In an effort to restore order and national unity, the State Council called on Eduard Shevardnadze, former first secretary of the Georgian Communist Party and later Soviet foreign minister under Mikhail Gorbachev. He was named to head a new interim state council, in which Kitovani served as minister of defense, and he formed a new political coalition that led him to victory in the presidential election held in October 1991. Shevardnadze immediately sought and received, in early 1992, international recognition for the state of Georgia within its boundaries from the Soviet period, but the struggle for control of this government continued through many months of civil strife (Otyrba 1994, 287).

In the midst of this internal crisis in Georgia, the issue of Abkhazia also came to a head. As early as 1988, Abkhazian leaders had appealed to Gorbachev to re-create the Abkhazian Soviet Socialist Republic, with treaty ties to Georgia but with complete rights of self-government. In August 1990, the Abkhazian Supreme Soviet, with ethnic Georgian deputies absent, declared the region to be sovereign and offered to negotiate with Georgian leaders about a federal relationship that would preserve the formal territorial integrity of Georgia. In December 1990, the Abkhazian Supreme Soviet elected Vladislav Ardzinba as its chair. In early 1991, Abkhazian leaders negotiated with the government of Gamsakhurdia, proposing the creation of a two-chamber parliament for Abkhazia. One chamber would represent the population on a proportional basis; the other would represent the various national groupings within Abkhazia. After a period of negotiations, legal experts from the two sides agreed that Abkhazians would be entitled to 28 seats in a 65-member chamber, compared to 26 for Georgians and 11 for other minorities. These proposals were rejected by Georgians within Abkhazia and ultimately by the central government authorities as well.

As the negotiations were falling apart, the strife within Tbilisi entangled the Georgian government in civil war. Ardzinba and his colleagues saw in the breakdown of authority in Georgia an opportunity to consolidate Abkhazian independence, this time without negotiating any special relationship with Tbilisi. Ethnic Georgian officials and parliamentarians were removed from their positions within Abkhazian structures, and Abkhazians claimed the right of the titular group to rule in spite of the ethnic composition of the region, in which they were a clear minority. The Parliament restored a 1925 draft Abkhazian constitution, which declared that Abkhazia was not part of Georgia. However, on August 12, 1992, the Abkhazian Supreme Soviet agreed to negotiate future federal relations between Abkhazia and Georgia (Otyrba 1994, 287). In spite of this conciliatory gesture, the presidium of the Georgian State Council sent Georgian troops into Abkhazia, ostensibly to free hostages held by Gamsakhurdia's forces and to protect highways and railroads from sabotage by them.

Despite some disagreement, there seems little doubt that Shevardnadze participated in the initial decision to send forces into Abkhazia, taken by Kitovani and his ally Jaba Ioseliani, head of the Mkhedrioni military group, both of whom who were later removed from office by Shevardnadze and eventually jailed (Nodia 1997, 51–52). But Shevardnadze's responsibility for subsequent events that quickly escalated out of control is less clear. When the Georgian military forces entered Abkhazia, they encountered resistance. Led by Kito-vani, they fought back and entered Sukhumi/Sukhum, the capital of Abkhazia, where they went on a rampage, attacking civilian targets and killing at least fifty people. They took control of Sukhum(i) and declared that the Abkhazian Supreme Soviet was dissolved. Abkhazian leaders took refuge in Gudauta, where they organized their military resistance to the Georgian "invasion." They began mobilizing a military response and calling for volunteers from throughout the region. Young men from the Northern Caucasus (including Chechnya), Abkhazians from Turkey, and Russian Cossacks joined in the fighting. Many Georgians also believed that Russian troops in the region pro-vided at least indirect support for the separatist forces and perhaps even fought directly on their side. Kitovani asserted that Georgia had to be a uni-tary state and rejected any proposals for federal solutions. By December 1992, even Shevardnadze acknowledged that a peaceful solution was impossible and that the dispute could only be settled by military means (Otyrba 1994, 290).

Georgians in Abkhazia had generally been supporters of Gamsakhurdia, and thus they were caught in the middle in the fighting. As many as three hundred thousand Georgians fled their homes in Abkhazia and became refugees within their own country; the two sides debate whether these individuals withdrew will-fully or were forced out, but it is apparent at least that they fled to avoid what they feared would be death at the hands of the Abkhazian forces. The intense fighting ended when the Georgians fled Sukhum(i) in September 1993, resulting in a clear victory for the Abkhazians. A peacekeeping force from the Commonwealth of Independent States (CIS), consisting solely of Russian troops, under the ob-servation of a UN mission, has maintained a tense cease-fire ever since (Trofimov 1995, 78–83). Those Georgians who have attempted to return to their homes in the Gali district of Abkhazia have encountered harassment and violence, and they have received little assistance from the CIS peacekeepers (MacFarlane, Min-ear, and Shenfield 1996, 26–27). Although several meetings took place in the 1990s to try to negotiate a solution to the crisis, by early 2000 no agreement had been reached and Abkhazia remained isolated.

The stakes in this conflict for both sides are intense and deeply emotional: Both parties quite literally feel that their identity is at stake. Indeed, the Ab-khazians believe that their very survival as a people is threatened by Georgian efforts to assimilate them into Georgian culture and destroy their language, their traditions, and their separate identity as a distinct group living in the re-gion for some two and a half millennia. Autonomy along the lines of the sta-tus quo ante is unacceptable to them because it would continue to leave them a small minority in their own land. The return of ethnic Georgians to Ab-khazia would mean that Georgians could dominate the region politically, re-establish all ties with the central government and Tbilisi, and continue the Georgian national project of constructing a unitary Georgian nation with all minorities assimilated within that majority culture and national identity.

As Ghia Nodia (1997, 37–38) has pointed out, this conflict is not strictly ethnic but is the product of a collision of competing "national projects" that could not be realized simultaneously. But he also has noted that these projects did not *have* to lead to violence. At least at first, the Abkhazians did not insist on full independence; their bottom line was tied to the fear of extinction as a separate ethnic community. There was a basis for negotiation because most Georgians also were willing to acknowledge the legitimacy of the Abkhazians as a distinct people living on the territory of the Georgian state. Indeed, as Nodia (1997, 38) pointed out, it was widely recognized among Georgian elites that "the Abkhaz are an indigenous population and have no other homeland, thus that it is legitimate for them to have some sort of special territorial-political arrangement which would guarantee preservation of their identity." The Abkhazian attitudes also embraced a positive image of their people's status under the Soviet Union, and they saw Moscow during Soviet times as their chief protector against Georgian imperialism. Throughout that period, "Georgia and Georgians exclusively filled the slot of the 'enemy image' [for Abkhazians]" (Nodia 1997, 31).

At the same time, most Georgians do think of Abkhazia as part of Georgian territory. As citizens of a small, new country, they fear that their project of creating a state is threatened by disintegrative tendencies throughout their territory, not only in Abkhazia but also in South Ossetia (where violence also occurred), in Ajaria (as discussed later in this chapter), in Javakheti (a region populated primarily by ethnic Armenians), and among other Muslim peoples such as the Azeris and Meshkhetians living in Georgia. Independence for any of these entities undermines the territorial integrity of the Georgian state and risks setting off a chain reaction of independence movements throughout Georgian territory. Some Georgians have gone so far as to attack the distinct nature of Abkhazian identity or, in the case of Gamsakhurdia, to argue that the Abkhazians' native land was really in the Northern Caucasus and not within Georgia at all. Gamsakhurdia had offered to support Abkhazian autonomy within the Northern Caucasus (that is, within the Russian Federation), just as he supported the Chechen struggle for autonomy against the Russians.

There are, of course, material stakes in this conflict, but these are relatively minor. Abkhazia does, indeed, contain some of the best Black Sea beaches of the former Soviet Union, and some Abkhazians maintain that an independent Abkhazia has the potential to become a kind of Monaco on the Black Sea.[7] Abkhazia sits across major land transportation routes connecting Georgia with Russia, Ukraine, and Western Europe—routes that do not cross the rugged Caucasus Mountains. But all of these material factors are trivial in comparison to the fundamental ethnopolitical conflict, a conflict that, as Nodia (1997, 16) has suggested, stems from competing national projects in which "pre-modern ethnic identities are reconstructed into modern national ones, so they can fit into the modern system of nation-states."

Within this context, the tactics utilized by both parties were confrontational and coercive. After the outbreak of violence, no direct negotiations took place between the opposing sides until the summer of 1997. The outbreak of the war in 1992 came at a time when there was virtually no communication between the parties, and the war was halted largely due to the intervention (or, in another interpretation, the changing role) of Russian military forces, which eventually established themselves as peacekeepers under mandate from the Russian-led CIS. After the cease-fire was achieved, a UN mission was established to oversee the peacekeepers, to assist in the resettlement of refugees, and to promote dialogue. Talks were begun in earnest under UN auspices in Geneva in 1997, four years after the end of the violence and when the existence of a hurting stalemate had become apparent to most observers. Yet none of this can be considered to constitute preventive diplomacy in any normal sense of the word. The UN and, to a lesser degree, the OSCE (which has focused primarily on South Ossetia) have engaged in some efforts at preventive diplomacy to forestall a resumption of open hostilities, but preventive diplomacy normally refers to the effort to avert the outbreak of violence in the first place. In this regard, these later efforts might more appropriately be described as attempts to find a basis for the settlement of the conflict rather than as preventive.

In summary, the fighting in Abkhazia broke out amid widespread political chaos and anarchy throughout much of Georgia. If there was any early warning of the outbreak of this violence at the international level, it clearly was not heeded. Few, if any, serious or sustained efforts at preventive diplomacy were undertaken by the parties to the dispute themselves, by outside interested parties (such as Russia, which is widely believed to have stimulated rather than restrained violence), or by international institutions. In September 1992, President Boris Yeltsin invited the parties to Moscow to try to bring an end to the fighting, but that effort failed. Thus, Abkhazia constitutes a classic case of the failure of diplomacy to prevent a violent conflict that, as the preceding analysis of the events leading up to the conflict suggests, *could have been prevented*. It also illustrates vividly how the intense bitterness that ensued in the aftermath of the violence has made a peaceful settlement of the dispute far more difficult to negotiate than it probably would have been had constructive, problem-solving negotiations been seriously undertaken as the region began to drift into chaos and anarchy in 1991. Not surprisingly, partisans of each side argue that they were interested in negotiations that could have produced a peaceful settlement, and each blames the other for not taking up those negotiations. But the simple fact is that, regardless of who was responsible, the parties never really engaged one another in meaningful negotiations, and outside entities did not offer their assistance to help the parties overcome their differences until after the violence had broken out and the hurting stalemate had become entrenched.

Ajaria

Ajaria is a primarily Muslim enclave nestled between Georgia, Turkey, and the Black Sea. It was dominated by the Ottoman Empire for centuries until it was annexed by the Russian Empire in 1878. During the Turkish period, most of the Georgian population of the region converted to Islam, and it has remained Muslim ever since. Except for this religious difference, however, Ajarians have generally considered themselves to be Georgians, and Georgian is their principal language. Like Abkhazia, Ajaria had the status of an autonomous republic within the union republic of Georgia from Soviet times, a status formalized by a treaty between Soviet Russia and Turkey in 1921 (Suny 1994, 321–22).

During the perestroika period in the Soviet Union, Islam experienced a revival in the Ajarian region, after decades of Soviet propaganda against religion. By 1989, separatist movements also began to appear in the political life of Ajaria, and a political organization was created to resist any attempt that might be made to abolish Ajarian autonomy. Such moves were opposed by Georgian nationalists who feared that they would work against their efforts to promote a sense of Georgian "national consciousness" at a time when the central Soviet authority was clearly eroding (Fuller 1991, 8). Georgia's new leader, Gamsakhurdia, threatened to abolish the Ajarian Autonomous Soviet Socialist Republic (ASSR) as a separate entity within Georgia when his country succeeded in gaining its independence. In response, the Ajarian Supreme Soviet modified its election laws to restrict anyone who was not a permanent resident of Ajaria from voting. In January 1991, this provision was overruled by the Georgian Constitutional Court, which found that the provision violated the Georgian constitutional provision that citizens of Georgia can vote in any state elections.

As voting for the Ajarian Parliament approached in late April 1991, increasingly pro-Soviet themes were prominent in the arguments of Ajarian nationalists, in contrast to the more anti-Soviet themes of the Georgian separatists. Demonstrations and heated confrontations took place, and voting was twice postponed. At the beginning of June, Gamsakhurdia traveled to Ajaria and struck a conciliatory note. He emphasized that Ajaria was the "cradle of Georgian Christianity," but he also stressed that his government was committed to religious freedom "not only on paper, but in practice"; Ajarians themselves had to decide whether to retain or abandon their autonomous status, which would not be taken away unilaterally by Tbilisi, and he urged them to join with other Georgians in their common struggle against the "imperial forces" (Fuller 1991, 12). He also engaged in an active program to proselytize on behalf of Christianity in the region. When the elections for the Ajarian Supreme Soviet were finally held on June 23, the turnout was so low that the results had to be invalidated in many districts under the Ajarian and Georgian electoral laws. Very few candidates had an absolute majority, and the required

runoff elections, held on a weekday, had an even lower turnout. Gamsakhurdia nonetheless interpreted the results as a victory for his faction because it
had an overall plurality of the votes and of the total seats (32 out of 79 overall). In truth, however, given that a majority of Ajarians had voted for the
Communist Party in the all-Georgian elections in October 1990 and still refrained from voting for Gamsakhurdia's Round Table coalition in the Ajarian
election of June 1991, the results actually signaled the low support for Gamsakhurdia in Ajaria.

Meanwhile, newly appointed parliamentary chairman Islan Abashidze, a
descendent of a family that more or less ruled Ajaria from 1463 until the late
nineteenth century, began consolidating his own power within Ajaria. His increasingly pro-Islamic pronouncements and his close ties with the Russian
military forces in the region created considerable fear and hostility in Tbilisi.
The press in Tbilisi began accusing the Russian military of both supporting
Gamsakhurdia (now in exile and fighting to return to power) and propping
up Abashidze and his clannish and autocratic regime in Batumi, capital of
Ajaria (Fuller 1993, 24). Within Ajaria as well, Abashidze was confronted with
an increasingly restive opposition, especially among intellectuals. However, he
responded that he was not seeking to destroy Georgian territorial integrity but
only to assure the autonomy of the Ajarians within Georgia and their right to
practice their own religion without domination by Georgian Christians. His
political party, the All-Georgian Revival Union Party, claimed that it was not
a regional faction but one that represented Georgians across the nation. At the
same time, Abashidze affirmed his support for the stationing of Russian
troops in Georgia as the only guarantors of stability in the region. Clearly, the
Russian military had a strong stake in Ajaria. It felt a duty to protect both the
Russians who constituted almost one-third of the population of Ajaria and
the large quantity of weapons and ammunition stored in the area. The region's
proximity to Turkey also gave it special geopolitical importance to Russian
strategists (Fuller 1993, 25).

Abashidze managed to work out a political rapprochement with the new
Georgian government of Shevardnadze. He was careful not to challenge the
basic principle of the territorial integrity of Georgia, which had been the primary cause of the violence in both Abkhazia and South Ossetia. He also played
a useful role in mediating several short-lived cease-fire agreements between
Shevardnadze and Gamsakhurdia, due to his fairly good relations with both, although this effort to bring an end to the long-running civil war in Georgia was
fruitless until the death of Gamsakhurdia. Abashidze's ties with Moscow and especially with the Russian military also gave him considerable influence in negotiating with the Georgian president. Shevardnadze depended heavily on the
Russian military to aid him in the civil confrontation with the Gamsakhurdia
forces and to stabilize the situation in Abkhazia and South Ossetia. Indeed, Shevardnadze is reported to have offered Abashidze the position of Georgian prime

minister in 1993, which he declined (Fuller 1993, 26). Instead, Abashidze focused his attention on achieving de facto independence for Ajaria without insisting on converting that into a legal status. He also promoted Batumi as a port for a new pipeline for Caspian Sea oil from Azerbaijan.

Ever since Georgia's civil war and two secessionist conflicts began to settle down and Shevardnadze consolidated his own political position in Tbilisi, the issue of Ajarian autonomy has largely disappeared from the political agenda. Efforts of the central government to remove the formally autonomous status have, for the most part, ceased, although little effort has been made to negotiate the details of relations between the center and Ajaria, in contrast to the case of Tatarstan and Russia that is examined later in this chapter. Rather, the situation has largely settled into a standoff in which neither side threatens or causes pain to the other. The national leadership in Tbilisi continues to deal with the government in Batumi more or less as one might with leaders of an independent country with which one has fairly good relations. Given the absence of a contest over the de jure status of Ajaria, the situation has remained peaceful and fairly stable since 1993.

In short, the stakes in the conflict involving Ajaria had more to do with identity than with material issues. During the period of turmoil as the Soviet Union was falling apart, Georgian national leaders were embarked upon a program of nation building, an effort to create a distinct Georgian consciousness in contrast to the Soviet identity. For many, this required ending the autonomy of Georgia's regions and creating a unitary regime in Tbilisi. Because this explicitly threatened the autonomous status that Ajaria had enjoyed since 1921, it threatened the survival of the Ajarian identity as such. More explicitly, Ajarians feared that they might lose their freedom to pursue Islam, which was experiencing a rebirth in the region, and that they would become assimilated in Georgian Christendom. Unlike Abkhazians and South Ossetians, however, the Ajarians were more interested in the practical advantages of their autonomy than in achieving full legal independence, and their sense of being Georgians, albeit of the Islamic faith, also moderated their demands for complete separation from Georgia. Furthermore, as long as the Ajarian leadership did not challenge directly the principle of the territorial integrity of Georgia, there was room for compromise.

Other stakes in the region were at least partially shared. Batumi, the capital of Ajaria, was one of the most popular Black Sea resorts from the Soviet period, but restoring its status as a tourist destination required peace and stability. Because Tbilisi would undoubtedly also benefit from a return of tourism to the region, this interest was largely shared by the central government. Similarly, the construction of an oil pipeline from Baku to Batumi would bring considerable economic benefit to both parties. In addition, each party, at least in 1993, saw the presence of the Russian army in the region as a stabilizing factor, both internally and in terms of preventing interference from countries on or near their borders where the Islamicist movement had taken on a more radical political coloration. Although government leaders in Tbilisi have since grown weary of the role played by the Russian army in their country and would like to see it removed, there is little doubt that this shared belief in Russia's stabilizing role helped to reduce tensions at the critical juncture when Shevardnadze took power in Georgia.

Perhaps one of the most significant factors affecting the peaceful outcome in Ajaria was that attitudes never reached the stage of open hostility; with the exception of a few radical elements on each side, neither party perceived the conflict in zero-sum terms. The common language and shared identity of being Georgian overcame religious differences and kept each side from stereotyping its opposition. In the end, the parties developed a live-and-let-live approach, rather than trying to force their political will on each other. In this climate, violence never seemed necessary or desirable.

The tactics utilized in this conflict were primarily political in nature, for the most part involving the interaction and involvement of each party in the internal political divisions within the other. Gamsakhurdia's government tried to influence the outcome in Ajaria by manipulating the electoral process and by helping his allies gain control of the key political institutions in the region. This was a much more effective strategy than pursuing hard bargaining and even coercion against a recalcitrant regime in Batumi. Similarly, especially after Abashidze consolidated his control in Batumi, the Ajarian side also played a role in the politics of the central government, first with Gamsakhurdia, then as a mediator between the opposing sides in Georgia's civil war, and finally with Shevardnadze. In the end, Abashidze's All-Georgian Revival Union Party collaborated with the Shevardnadze government in Parliament on a wide range of issues. As the interests of political elites in both entities tended to merge, any grounds for violent conflict between them by and large disappeared. Furthermore, since 1993, most relations have been conducted in a constructive, problem-solving atmosphere rather than in one of stark competition.

Comparison of Abkhazia and Ajaria

In some crucial respects, the situations of Abkhazia and Ajaria started from similar points. The two regions were the only autonomous parts of Georgia in Soviet times, and their continued autonomy was threatened by Georgian independence and the resultant effort to create a unified Georgian state. Both were divided from the Georgian majority by important markers of ethnic identity: language and culture in the case of Abkhazia and religion in the case of Ajaria. Both became embroiled in the conflict and anarchy that tore apart Georgian society itself, especially the civil war in 1991–92 between Gamsakhurdia and his opponents, eventually led by Shevardnadze; the chaos in Tbilisi provided an incentive for different militarized factions to threaten the periphery as well as opportunities for the peripheral regions to seek greater independence from the center and receive military assistance to do so from outside Georgia. Given these significant similarities, it is notable that the outcomes of the two conflicts were quite different. Several factors seem to have contributed to this difference.

First, the stakes were perceived differently. Abkhazians felt direct threats to their survival as a separate people because they were a small minority within Georgia and even in the region bearing their name. By contrast, the Ajarians felt that they were Georgians in some important ways, albeit Georgians who had converted to Islam under Ottoman occupation, for they share a common language and many other cultural values.

Second, the conflicts became rapidly polarized in Abkhazia, whereas political linkages between Tbilisi and Batumi provided channels for communications and negotiations. Radical political leaders on both sides sought to exploit the situation in Abkhazia, but more moderate political forces surfaced to replace nationalist extremists in Ajaria and Tbilisi. President Shevardnadze, after he ousted the radicals who instigated fighting in Abkhazia, and the chair of the Ajarian Parliament, Abashidze, eventually sought reconciliation with one another.

Third, tactics in Abkhazia were highly provocative on both sides, whereas they were more conciliatory in Ajaria. The violent intervention of the Georgian National Guard in Abkhazia in August 1992, for example, was clearly a provocative action, and both sides quickly gave up hope for a peaceful settlement of the dispute and sought to pursue their conflict through military means. All diplomatic efforts were overwhelmed by military actions and counteractions that rapidly escalated to large-scale violence.

Transdniestria in Moldova and Crimea in Ukraine

Transdniestria

The region on the left (or east) bank of the Dniester River has long had a separate identity from other parts of what was to become the union republic and then the Soviet successor state of Moldova. This narrow strip of land lies mostly between the Dniester River and Ukraine on the east, and in 1990, it had a population of some six hundred thousand people, about two-thirds of whom were ethnically Slavic, mostly Russians and Ukrainians. As long ago as 1791, the Peace of Iasi established the Dniester River as the border between the Russian and Ottoman Empires. The region west of the Dniester was known as the Moldovan (or Moldavian) Province and was itself cut in two by the Prut River. In 1812, Russia conquered most of the portion of Moldova located between the Dniester and Prut Rivers and called the area Bessarabia. In 1878, the newly independent state of Romania obtained the part of Moldova located west of the Prut River without granting it any distinct political or administrative status (Kolstø and Edemsky 1993, 977). It remains part of Romania to the present day. Following World War I, the region of Bessarabia fell under the jurisdiction of the Romanian crown, and the region east of the Dniester became incorporated in the Soviet Union as the autonomous Moldovan republic under the union republic of the Ukraine. This region, however, contained very little of the territory that historically had been known as Moldova. Moscow gained control of the west bank and Bessarabia under the Ribbentrop–Molotov Pact in 1940, when the enlarged Moldova was granted the status of a union republic within the Soviet Union.[8] After the war, the unity of the republic was retained, but most of the cultural differences between the regions on opposite sides of the Dniester also endured (Kolstø and Edemsky 1993, 978–79). The area east of the Dniester was heavily industrialized and thoroughly Russified, and it developed its primary links with Russia and Ukraine rather than with the weaker economic potential represented by Moldova (Perrins n.d., 6–7).

During the perestroika period, Moldovan nationalists began to call for independence, and activists from the Moldovan Popular Front pushed for union with Romania. The titular language, which had officially been called "Moldovan" under the Soviet Union, was renamed "Romanian," and its alphabet was changed from Cyrillic to Latin. Even though the language law maintained the status of Russian as a language of interethnic communication, the Slavic populations of the Transdniester region were not satisfied, for they were fearful of Romanian irredentism and of the dominance of the Romanian-Moldovan language in public spheres. Russian speakers were concerned that the new language law would mean that their jobs would be given to ethnic Moldovans.

Increased popular agitation led Moscow to send troops to Moldova in 1989 and remove Semen Grossu as first secretary of the Moldovan Communist Party in November of that year. In the elections for the Moldovan Supreme Soviet held in March 1990, supporters of the Moldovan Popular Front received 40 percent of the seats and took control of the Parliament.[9] In June 1990, following Russia's declaration of independence from the Soviet Union, the Moldovan Supreme Soviet declared the republic to be sovereign, Soviet "occupation" was declared to be illegal, and the Soviet military draft was discontinued (Batalden and Batalden 1997, 67). The change in the language law led to changes in place-names, so that, for example, the name of the capital city was changed from Kishinev to Chisinau. Mircea Snegur was chosen as president of the Moldovan Republic, and he strongly opposed Gorbachev's efforts to revive the dying Soviet Union through a new union treaty. The Moldovan government formalized its claim to independence following the failure of the attempted coup in Moscow in August 1991, and the Republic of Moldova was admitted to the United Nations. The Snegur government also opened negotiations with Moscow regarding the complete removal of Soviet troops; a treaty was eventually signed in November 1994, but because it was never ratified by the Russian Duma, most troops and large quantities of ammunition remained in Transdniestria three years later when the withdrawal was to have been completed.

Meanwhile in Transdniestria, the predominantly Slavic population reacted strongly against Moldovan efforts at independence. This opposition began with strikes in the fall of 1989, extended to a boycott of the Moldovan Parliament after the Popular Front took control in the spring of 1990, and led to the proclamation of a "Transdniester Moldavian Soviet Socialist Republic within the Soviet Union"—which implied that Transdniestria was no longer part of the Moldovan Republic—in the fall of 1990. The first major activity of the new Transdniester Republic government under President Igor Smirnov was to adopt a trilingual policy, making Russian, Ukrainian, and Moldovan all state languages (Tishkov 1997, 99). After proclaiming their republic in September 1990, the government held elections for a Supreme Soviet and created a Transdniestrian militia, which became embroiled in several violent clashes with Moldovan police along the Dniester River and in Chisinau. The Moldovan leaders in turn kidnapped some prominent figures in Ukraine, including Smirnov, the unrecognized president of Transdniestria, and Gen. Gennadii Yakovlev, former commander of the Russian Fourteenth Army. Both were taken to Moldova and subsequently released. During the attempted Moscow coup of August 1991 and even after it failed, the leaders in Transdniestria supported the putschists, and the Communist Party remained an influential force in the region even after it collapsed in Moscow.

In the spring of 1992, Moldovan president Snegur issued an ultimatum demanding full compliance with the laws of Moldova on the east bank, and fighting broke out with units of the Transdniestrian Republican Guard, supported by elements of the Russian Fourteenth Army stationed in Transdniestria. Although the extent of the Russian soldiers' active involvement in combat is debated, there appears to be little doubt that Russian armaments, including armored personnel carriers and tanks, were obtained by the Transdniestrian forces. Smirnov, as the leader of Transdniestria, invited officers and soldiers from the Fourteenth Army to join the force of 12,000 soldiers that he sought to build, and it seems likely that at least some troops, especially those from the immediate region, did so, in addition to groups of volunteers from Russia (primarily Cossacks) (Nahaylo 1992, 2). Skirmishes broke out in March, leaving about three hundred people dead (EEN 1992, 1–4). On April 5, Russian vice president Alexander Rutskoi visited Tiraspol (the capital of Transdniestria) to show support for the Russian enclave and declared that "the Dniester Republic exists and must exist," a statement that elicited a hostile response from the government of Moldova; he then returned to Moscow and urged the Russian State Duma to recognize the Dniester Republic (Nahaylo 1992, 6). Shortly thereafter, the Moldovan military attacked Transdniestrian enclaves lying on the west bank of the Dniester in Bendery. When Gen.

Alexander Lebed took command of the Fourteenth Army in June 1992, he voiced strong support for the regime in Tiraspol and referred to Transdniestria and even the west bank town of Bendery as constituting "a small part of Russia" (Kolstø and Edemsky 1993, 988).[10]

Leaders of the government of Ukraine sought to mediate the conflict. They called a meeting of specialists from Ukraine, Romania, Hungary, Russia, and Moldova to try to defuse the situation, and they sought the intervention of Jiri Dienstbier of Czechoslovakia, the chairman-in-office of the Conference on Security and Cooperation in Europe (CSCE). At the time, the CSCE was just beginning to set up its Conflict Prevention Center in Vienna, and it was overwhelmed with the escalating crisis in the former Yugoslavia. Thereafter, Moldovan president Snegur met with Russian president Yeltsin, Ukrainian president Leonid Kravchuk, and Romanian president Ion Iliescu in an attempt to bring an end to the conflict. At their summit in Moscow on July 6 and 7, 1992, the parties agreed to call a cease-fire and to send in a peacekeeping force consisting of Russian, Moldovan, and Transdniestrian troops. At this time, President Yeltsin argued that a Yugoslav-type solution was inappropriate in Moldova, which he considered to be a single state; he also noted that the people of Transdniestria were mostly Russians, but he concluded that the interests of Russians in states outside the Russian Federation could not be defended by military means but only by using political methods (Perrins n.d., 22). The mediating presidents failed to find any lasting resolution to the conflict, although fighting was soon brought to a halt, leaving some seven hundred to eight hundred people dead and the two regions even more bitterly divided.

On February 4, 1993, the CSCE set up a mission to Moldova, mandated "to facilitate the achievement of a lasting, comprehensive political settlement of the conflict in all its aspects . . . , based on the reinforcement of the territorial integrity of the Republic of Moldova along with an understanding about a special status for the Trans-Dniester region" (OSCE 1997, 11). The CSCE mission also observed the activities of all military forces in the region, including the "peacekeepers" (Kirillov 1995, 59–64). In addition, the OSCE's High Commissioner on National Minorities became active in Moldova and Transdniestria in December 1994, trying to focus mostly on problems faced by ethnic minorities in both regions of the country (FIER 1997, 68–70). However, all of these interventions came after the outbreak of violence and the subsequent cease-fire, and they have necessarily focused on postconflict management and negotiation as well as on the prevention of renewed violence. Negotiations continued into 2000 under the mediation of the OSCE, the Russian Federation, and Ukraine. Substantial progress was made, especially in the area of confidence building between the two parts of Moldova. The parties agreed to form a "common state" in which both will cooperate, but differences remained over the definition of the common state, with Moldova preferring a unitary state with regional autonomy for Transdniestria and the negotiators from the left bank preferring a state composed of two formally equal entities. The OSCE and the Russian peacekeepers nonetheless successfully prevented any recurrence of the large-scale violence that broke out between the parties in 1992.

The stakes in this conflict are fairly clear-cut. The government in Chisinau wishes to consolidate its new state. Following the general practice that has been adopted by the international community after the breakup of the Soviet Union, post-Soviet states have been recognized only within the borders of the former union republics. To realize their sovereignty, the Moldovan authorities believe that the territorial integrity of their country must be preserved. Some within Moldova also clearly wish to preserve the option of unifying their state with Romania, even though that objective may seem less likely several years after independence than it did when the Soviet Union was falling apart. Moldovan attitudes toward the leadership of Transdniestria also tend to be hostile. Not only are the Transdniestrians considered separatists who are trying to tear the new state apart, they are also perceived to represent the legacy of the former Soviet Union. Most in Moldova view Transdniestria as a haven for unreformed former communists—ethnic Russians or Ukrainians who want good relations with their home countries but also seek to turn back the changes that occurred at the beginning of the 1990s and instill a Soviet-style system in their own region even if they cannot bring back the Soviet Union in all its former glory.

By contrast, the stakes for Transdniestria generally reflect the Russian speakers' desire to retain their linguistic identity in an independent country after the disappearance of their Soviet homeland. As the majority peoples of the Soviet Union, they almost overnight found themselves relegated to a minority position within a newly independent country. Furthermore, their region had been a center of Soviet industry, with relatively good jobs and a comfortable lifestyle by Soviet standards. The nationalistic excesses of the Moldovan majority at the outset of independence, especially as represented by the initial language laws, exacerbated these natural tensions and threatened the Slavic peoples not only with the loss of their dominant positions in society and the economy but also with the possibility of losing their jobs and identity. The final straw appeared to be the movement toward reunification between Moldova and Romania; although this step was not favored by many Moldovans, the fear that it might completely submerge Slavic identity in Romanian culture appears to have caused panic and hardened the attitudes of ethnic Slavs vis-à-vis the Moldovan authorities. The attitudes of the Russian population were further sharpened by widespread rumors that Ukraine and Romania were preparing to give the Transdniestria region back to Ukraine in exchange for the return of former Romanian territory now within Ukrainian borders, despite insistent denials by the government of Ukraine.

Within Transdniestria, there is not necessarily a complete unanimity of attitudes between the Russian and Ukrainian populations. The latter are generally less enthusiastic about the attachment of the Russian plurality to the old Soviet state or even to present-day Russia. Ukrainians, who tend to come from the more rural areas of the region, generally identify more closely with Ukraine, which borders the entire region on the east. As violence was breaking out in the spring of 1992, many of these people appealed to the Ukrainian government to assist in preventing a wider conflict. In March 1992, the Ukrainian government protested the influx of Russian Cossacks into Transdniestria, even though some Ukrainian paramilitary forces joined in the battle alongside the Cossacks. It also protested the violation of Ukraine's borders by the separatist forces and threatened appropriate action, closing its border with Transdniestria (Nahaylo 1992, 3).

Nonetheless, it is the tactics adopted by both parties that, more than any other factor, seem to have contributed to the violent turn of events in Moldova. Apparently, there was no significant direct contact or attempt at negotiations between the parties to the conflict. Each side sought to strengthen its own military position in order to be able to coerce the other to accept its preference. Both sides sought allies outside the country, with Transdniestria turning to elements in Russia (especially in the military and in nationalistic elements in the State Duma) and Moldova seeking the assistance of Ukraine, Romania, and Hungary. Both parties also exchanged acrimonious assertions about each other's motives. Moldovans accused the Transdniestrian separatists of being old-fashioned, hard-line communists who represented the interests of reactionary elements within Russia, whereas Transdniestrians accused the Moldovans of being agents of Romania, seeking to romanize the entire region and to destroy Slavic culture. Moldova tried to resolve the crisis by issuing ultimatums, and the Transdniestrians responded with force and violence against Moldovan interests. All of these hostile tactics made serious direct negotiations between the parties impossible, and only the intervention of neighboring states such as Russia and Ukraine enabled the establishment of a shaky cease-fire and a temporary separation of forces until conditions became ripe for serious negotiations.

Crimea

Although Crimea is located within Ukraine, its population is about 67 percent ethnic Russian. In fact, Crimea, originally the homeland of the Crimean Tatars who were deported to Central Asia during World War II, was part of Russia until 1954, when it was given as a gift to Ukraine by Nikita Khrushchev. There are at least two sources of conflict within Crimea: between the Crimean Russians and the central government in Kiev and between Crimean Slavs and returning Crimean Tatars. Indeed, the Tatars have tried, often unsuccessfully, to gain Kiev's support for the protection of their own rights vis-à-vis the Russian-speaking majority in Crimea (Bremmer 1993, 25–26).

Even before the breakup of the Soviet Union, a referendum in Crimea indicated an overwhelming desire to create an autonomous Soviet republic outside Ukraine. At that time, there were still differences of opinion about whether this republic should be a truly independent state or an autonomous region within the Russian Federation, but there was a general consensus that it should separate from Ukraine. In the last days of the Soviet Union, the Supreme Soviet of the Ukrainian Soviet Socialist Republic (UkrSSR) granted Crimea's request to be made an autonomous republic within the UkrSSR, and this provision was entered into the Crimean constitution on June 6, 1991. Clearly, even at that late date, Ukraine's leaders did not foresee the sudden collapse of the Soviet Union or the consequences of an autonomous Crimea within an independent Ukraine.

In Crimea, a citizens' movement among the ethnic Russian population opposed to being part of an independent Ukraine began to organize in the spring of 1992. In an interview on May 1, 1992, Anatolii Los, head of the Russian Society of Crimea, declared that the group's purpose was nothing less than "the recreation of the USSR. . . . Crimea will play its historic role, just as it did two thousand years ago, giving the people of Russia—that is, the people of Rus' and among them the people of Ukraine—spirituality, culture, and religion" (quoted in Pikhovshek 1995, 42). In Ukraine, this was perceived as a virtual declaration of war by Russia, not just by Crimean Russians, and, indeed, the actions of the Crimean separatists were viewed with favor and even enthusiasm by many nationalists in Russia. Soon thereafter, the Russian Supreme Soviet proclaimed the 1954 transfer of Crimea to Ukraine to be lacking in legal force. The first reactions of Ukraine's leaders were moderate, and they agreed to grant Crimea full political autonomy (but not territorial separation) and more economic rights vis-à-vis the government in Kiev. However, Crimeans began to press for even greater concessions from Ukraine, which, in turn, caused Ukrainian nationalists to get their backs up about the status of Crimea as an integral part of Ukraine.

As the confrontation grew, Crimea adopted an act of state independence on May 5, 1992, and the following day adopted a constitution proclaiming the Republic of Crimea to be a sovereign state that would deal with Ukraine as an equal. A referendum was called for August 1992 to ratify the declaration of independence. On this basis, the Supreme Council of Crimea proposed to negotiate treaty arrangements with Ukraine. But on May 13, the Ukrainian Rada ordered that the Crimean act be annulled within two weeks. In June, the Ukrainian Parliament passed a new law delineating the division of power between Ukraine and Crimea. In return, Crimea agreed to drop its referendum on independence. This ended the immediate crisis, but the issue continued to simmer within Crimea.

In January 1993, President Kravchuk of Ukraine appointed his special representative to Crimea, and negotiations continued at the grassroots level. But the president also threw his political support behind a former colleague from the Soviet era, Mykols Bahrov, who had been first secretary of the Crimean Communist Party (Jaworsky 1995, 142). Bahrov, however, was soundly defeated by an unabashedly pro-Russian candidate, Yuri Meshkov, who became the first president of Crimea in January 1994. Meshkov set out on a confrontational path, and the Crimean Parliament responded on May 20, 1994, by reconstituting those sections of the 1992 constitution that maintained that Crimea was not an integral part of Ukraine.

The CSCE (later renamed the Organization for Security and Cooperation in Europe [OSCE]) first became involved in the situation in Crimea in late 1993, when the High Commissioner on National Minorities initiated contacts with Ukrainian authorities regarding the status of ethnic Russian populations in various parts of Ukraine. Ambassador Max van der Stoel paid his first visit to the region in February 1994, followed by a visit to Donetsk in the Donbass region of eastern Ukraine and to Simferopol, capital of Crimea, in May 1994. On May 15, 1994, he addressed a letter to Ukrainian foreign minister Anatoly Zlenko in which he recommended a settlement based on principles that would "reaffirm the need to maintain the territorial integrity of Ukraine, but . . . contain a complete programme of steps to solve various issues concerning the implementation of the formula of substantial autonomy for Crimea, especially in the economic field" (van der Stoel 1994). Zlenko replied on June 7, agreeing to most of van der Stoel's recommendations but also noting that the May 20 decision by the Crimean Parliament violated the Ukrainian constitution. He stated bluntly, "This illegal decision provoked by the irresponsible policy of the present leadership of the Crimea and aimed at undermining the constitutional order of Ukraine and its territorial integrity cannot be qualified other than an obvious attempt by separatist forces to put the internal political stability of Ukraine at risk and provoke tension in the relations between Ukraine and Russia" (Zlenko 1994).

In part on the basis of the report of the High Commissioner to its Committee of Senior Officials in Prague, CSCE created a mission of long duration to Ukraine in August 1994, with a special focus on the problems of Crimea and with headquarters in Kiev and a regional office in Simferopol. Its mandate included "providing objective reporting . . . on all aspects of the situation in the Autonomous Republic of Crimea (Ukraine), or factors influencing it, and efforts towards the solution of its problems; . . . to facilitate the dialogue between the central government and the Crimean authorities concerning the autonomous status of the Republic of Crimea within Ukraine; preparing reports on the situation of human rights and rights of persons belonging to national minorities in the Autonomous Republic of Crimea (Ukraine)" (OSCE 1997, 19). The limited mandate permitted the CSCE's mission in Ukraine to engage only in the process of facilitating negotiations rather than in active mediation or other measures of preventive diplomacy, but it has at least provided an additional and neutral channel for communications between the parties.

In September, Crimean president Meshkov began to issue a series of unilateral declarations and abolished the Supreme Council of Crimea as well as local councils. However, the Presidium of the Supreme Council declared that Meshkov had violated the laws of both Crimea and Ukraine by acting in this fashion. At that point, President Leonid Kuchma of Ukraine stepped in and told both Meshkov and Sergei Tsekov, chair of the Supreme Council, that he would "not allow the use of force to settle the conflict between the branches of government in Crimea." He ordered his deputy prime minister, Yevhen Marchuk, to go to Crimea to mediate between the Crimean president and Parliament (Pikhovshek 1995, 47–48). In September 1994, the Ukrainian Rada passed a law giving Crimea only until November 1 to bring its constitution fully in line with the Ukrainian constitution. In early 1995, the Supreme Council of Crimea stepped up its challenge by declaring that the state property of Ukraine in Crimea belonged to Crimea and by threatening to hold a referendum on independence during the April municipal elections. This led to a reaction by the Ukrainian Rada, which sought to dismantle Crimean autonomy. On March 17, 1995, it annulled the 1992 Crimean constitution, abolished the Crimean presidency, and brought criminal charges against President Meshkov. President Kuchma also decreed that the Crimean government was to be subordinated to the Ukrainian government.

These rising tensions caused the CSCE's High Commissioner on National Minorities to step up his work in the region. He became actively engaged as a go-between in helping the parties adjust their constitutions so that they might conform with one another. On his initiative, the OSCE organized a conference in Locarno, Switzerland, from May 11 to 14, 1995, which came on the heels of the Crimean Parliament's announcement of its intention to hold a referendum on the reinstatement of the 1992 constitution. On May 15, van der Stoel proposed a deal to try to head off escalating tensions between the parties. He suggested that the Crimeans agree not to proceed with the referendum. He also expressed support for a number of provisions in a draft Ukrainian law of June 1992 on the division of powers, which had not gone into force. Specifically, he suggested that certain principles of this draft text should be incorporated in parallel constitutions of Crimea and Ukraine, granting Crimea unrevokable autonomy in many key areas, a right to appeal to the Ukrainian Constitutional Court if it considered that Ukrainian legislation infringed on those competencies, and recognition as an autonomous republic within the state of Ukraine. He also proposed that the Parliaments of Ukraine and Crimea create "an organ of conciliation with the task of suggesting solutions to differences arising in the course of the dialogue about relevant legislation" (van der Stoel 1995). These recommendations were generally well received by the leaders in Kiev, and they acknowledged that the Simferopol authorities' decision to cancel the referendum seemed to have served as "evidence of a certain influence of recommendations developed in Locarno" (Udovenko 1995).

Based on this success, a second round table was held in September 1995 in Yalta, focusing on the narrower topic of the reintegration of deported peoples (Tatars) who were returning to Crimea. In 1996, the High Commissioner concentrated on both the constitutional issue and provisions for the education of minorities (both Ukrainians and Tatars) in Crimea (FIER 1997, 75–77).

The Crimean leadership acquiesced in most of Kiev's demands, for a variety of reasons (FIER 1997, 46–53). Not the least of the factors enabling Ukraine to preserve its territorial integrity was the fact that the Crimean separatists received little support from the Yeltsin government in Moscow. In addition, their almost complete economic dependence on financial support from Kiev made autonomous action virtually impossible to sustain. And there was also little public outcry in Crimea; fewer than two hundred people showed up to protest the dismissal of President Meshkov (Pikhovshek 1995, 51), and in July 1995, the speaker of the Crimean Parliament, Tsekov, lost a vote of confidence in the Parliament and was replaced by a much more conciliatory speaker, Yevhen Supruniuk (Bukkvoll 1997, 48). Furthermore, the central government had carefully gained control of the law enforcement agencies in Crimea, especially the structures of the Ministry of Interior throughout the region. And as the Crimean Parliament abolished the presidency and created the post of prime minister instead, Kiev successfully maneuvered to have a sympathetic candidate, Anatolii Franchuk, elected premier.

The more moderate leadership that took over from Meshkov was also more inclined to follow the recommendations of the OSCE's High Commissioner. The new constitution on the status of the Autonomous Republic of Crimea, adopted on November 1, 1995, incorporated many of the suggestions from the Locarno conference, except that it failed to guarantee representation for the Crimean Tatar community as the High Commissioner had strongly advised (Packer 1998).

After 1995, the Crimean Russians renewed their demands for autonomy, but they stressed negotiation with Kiev as a means to achieve their goals. The new parliamentary leader, Supruniuk, pursued a more conciliatory policy than his predecessors, simultaneously trying to assure Kiev that the separatist threat was over while seeking to gain the greatest autonomy possible for Crimea through adoption of the new Crimean constitution and assertion of Crimean control of its own internal economic policy (Bukkvoll 1997, 53).

To speed up the process of closing the remaining gaps, the OSCE's High Commissioner on National Minorities organized a third round table in the Netherlands at Noordwijk from March 14 to 17, 1996. Key participants from both disputing parties were brought together, along with four technical experts on topics such as law and economics, selected by the High Commissioner. This conference revealed agreement on most of the essential issues; of the remaining twenty points of dispute, only a few were of major significance. On the basis of this discussion, the High Commissioner again wrote to the Ukrainian foreign minister on March 19, 1996, urging the government of

Ukraine to adopt the constitution of the Crimean Autonomous Republic without delay, except for those specific provisions that remained in dispute. Following a visit to Ukraine on April 3 and 4, 1996, he addressed yet another letter to Ukrainian authorities on April 5, suggesting specific provisions to try to overcome the remaining issues in dispute. He essentially recommended that matters such as defense, security, and control over the continental shelf should remain under the exclusive jurisdiction of the central government in Kiev, but that many other functions should come under Crimean jurisdiction. He proposed that most disputes on economic matters be referred to outside experts for adjudication (Packer 1998).

Immediately thereafter, the Ukrainian Rada adopted a new law concerning Crimea that accepted 116 of the 136 articles of the Crimean constitution. On June 28, 1996, after intense debate, the new Ukrainian constitution was adopted, reconfirming the status of Crimea as an autonomous republic within Ukraine. Negotiation on harmonizing the two constitutions continued through 1998 with the ongoing assistance of the High Commissioner. At the end of the year, a new Crimean constitution was adopted that was effectively consistent with the Ukrainian constitution, bringing the crisis to an end, at least for the moment. As long as relations between Russia and Ukraine continue on an even keel, this agreement is likely to endure. However, a change in that bilateral relationship could cause ethnic tensions to reappear. And the further deterioration of the already serious economic conditions could particularly exacerbate the situation, especially regarding the integration of Crimean Tatars into regional politics.

The stakes in this conflict, like most others of this type, included issues of identity, but more material matters, for an array of parties, were entailed as well. There were economic incentives to build closer ties with Russia. After the breakup of the Soviet Union, trade in industrial goods between Crimea and Russia declined to about one-third of its previous level, and shipbuilding industries suffered particularly heavy losses when Russian orders for both military and civilian vessels ceased. The more rapid process of economic reform in Russia compared with the stagnation of Ukrainian economic policy also seemed to make Russia a more attractive economic partner over the long run, although, apparently paradoxically, most Crimean Russians opposed economic reforms and favored the continuation of a Soviet-style economy in spite of the rapid changes taking place in Russia.

Crimean Russians felt their identity was threatened by Ukrainian independence. The fact that Crimea had been transferred from Russian to Ukrainian jurisdiction within the Soviet Union carried few practical consequences for most residents of Crimea. As part of the Soviet Union, dominated by ethnic Russians, Crimean Russians could still feel that they were first-class citizens; theirs was the dominant culture and language of one of the world's two superpowers. When the Soviet Union fell apart, however, they felt themselves slipping to a subordinate position within Ukraine. In spite of their similarities, Russian and Ukrainian culture and language are not identical, and Ukrainian nationalists sought to magnify the differences in their project of creating a new sense of Ukrainian identity in an independent state. Crimean Russians felt that they were first and foremost a part of greater Russia, and their identity was threatened not only by Kiev but by the return of Crimean Tatars, who claimed that the peninsula was *their* homeland, not the homeland of Russians or Ukrainians. Furthermore, the Russians felt frustrated and abandoned by Moscow, which refused to press the claim for Crimean autonomy largely out of fear of provoking greater moves for autonomy from regions within the Russian Federation. This sudden decline in status and the fear of being marginalized largely fueled the separatist movement among Crimean Russians.

The Crimean Tatars also had a stake in this drama because the return of Crimea to Russia or even independence would almost certainly entail their continued subordination to Russians. The returning Tatars have been beset by serious economic problems, and neither the government in Kiev nor that in Simferopol seem to be prepared to deal with them. But in spite of these problems, the Tatars in Crimea formed a tactical alliance with the government and key political parties in the Parliament in Kiev to preserve the unity of Ukraine, notwithstanding the lack of enthusiastic support for the Tatar cause from the central government in Kiev (Bremmer 1993, 24–28).

Ukrainian stakes also included the consolidation of identity as a newly independent state based upon the territorial boundaries of the former Ukrainian Soviet Socialist Republic. There was a significant Ukrainian minority in Crimea, and psychologically, Crimea had been seen as part of Ukraine since 1954. Acquiescence in all of the demands of Crimean separatists might also have encouraged potential separatist movements in other regions of Ukraine heavily populated by ethnic Russians, including the Donbass region in the east and the area around Odessa in the south. Ukraine also had economic and strategic stakes in the Crimean peninsula, which offered significant economic potential through its industrial strength and its important Black Sea resorts. But perhaps it was Crimea's status as the base for the former Soviet Black Sea fleet that caused the greatest competition for control of Crimea. The division of the fleet and the status of Sevastopol, the city where it is based, were the subject of intensive negotiations between Russia and Ukraine.

The issue of the Black Sea fleet was an intense one within Russian domestic politics. As the Crimean crisis was developing, Ukraine and Russia also found themselves at loggerheads as each state claimed full control over the fleet and its port facilities. Of all of the separatist movements outside the Russian Federation, it is likely that none tempted the Russians to intervene in support of separatist aims more than that in Crimea. This region was clearly a part of the Slavic culture, with a majority population of ethnic Russians, and the Black

Sea Fleet was one of the few remaining symbols of the military might of the former superpower. Pressures from nationalistic circles and the remnants of the military-industrial complex within Russia were undoubtedly exerted on President Yeltsin to encourage him to take a confrontational stance with Ukraine over the status of Crimea. Although the Russian government consistently resisted these pressures and refrained from making provocative gestures, the Russian Duma frequently did so, especially by making territorial claims on Sevastopol, site of the major Russian naval base in Crimea. Indeed, in July 1993, Ukraine took the matter to the UN Security Council, which confirmed the territorial integrity of Ukraine under the UN Charter. The issue was eventually resolved through negotiations between Yeltsin and Kravchuk and later Kuchma; first, the Black Sea Fleet was divided equally between the two parties, and then, Ukraine "sold" part of its share to Russia in payment of debts owed and Sevastopol was leased to the Russian navy. An apparent but unstated quid pro quo was that Russia would reaffirm Ukrainian sovereignty throughout Crimea, clearly aiding the peaceful resolution of this conflict.[11]

Attitudes varied widely among the members of each party to the dispute, between intensely nationalistic elements on each side and those with more pragmatic or centrist orientations who sought to avoid a full-scale confrontation. Within Crimea, confrontational attitudes were displayed most clearly by organizations of Russian citizens such as the Russian Society of Crimea and the National Salvation Front, to whom President Meshkov largely owed his election in 1994 and whose positions he adopted. Similarly, nationalist Ukrainian elements, especially radical right-wing parties such as the Ukrainian National Assembly in the Verkhovna Rada, for the most part viewed the Crimean separatists as agents of the ultranationalists within the Russian Federation who sought to restore something approximating the former Soviet Union. By contrast, more problem-solving attitudes emerged in the Crimean Supreme Council after Supruniuk became speaker and Franchuk, supported by Ukrainian President Kuchma, became prime minister. Similarly in Kiev, both Presidents Kravchuk and Kuchma generally tried to manipulate the situation in Crimea behind the scenes, establishing control from within so as not to have to resort to force from without to achieve their objective of preventing the complete separation of Crimea from Ukraine.

Tactically, both parties in this dispute failed to pursue any clear and consistent policy, largely due to internal infighting. In Kiev, rivalries between the president and Parliament and changes made between the governments of Presidents Kravchuk and Kuchma accounted for much of this inconsistency. As John Jaworsky (1995, 140) noted, "During Leonid Kravchuk's presidency the absence of a clear strategy with respect to Crimea meant that Ukraine's representatives greatly weakened their bargaining position by behaving in a haphazard and sometimes irresponsible fashion during negotiations." Although it was slow in developing a tactical posture toward Crimea, the government in Kiev under President Kuchma eventually pursued a policy of trying to undermine the Crimean position from within, a policy that was at least temporarily successful due to the political divisions that appeared in Simferopol. Crimean leaders were themselves very divided over their ultimate objective in the conflict, and alternations in leadership between extreme nationalist leaders and more conciliatory ones also accounted for numerous shifts in policy. The split that appeared in the Crimean leadership in particular opened a wedge that the government in Kiev was able to exploit in subsequent bargaining. As a major external player, Russia was also divided between the more conciliatory factions in the presidential administration and the coalition of communists and nationalists who dominated in the Duma. Ultimately, Moscow accepted the basic principle insisted upon by the Ukrainian government, namely, preservation of the territorial integrity of the state.

In conclusion, preventive diplomacy seems to have played a significant role in avoiding the violent escalation of the Crimean dispute. Perhaps most significant was the role of High Commissioner on National Minorities van der Stoel, who made numerous trips to both Ukraine and the Crimean region. He organized three workshops among participants in the conflict and offered a series of recommendations for resolving specific differences, especially on the constitutional question of how to secure the status of Crimea as an autonomous region while preserving the territorial integrity of Ukraine with Crimea as an integral component. The workshops appeared to succeed in changing attitudes, and the High Commissioner was able to develop "identity formulas" that incorporated the needs and interests of both parties to this dispute. His flexibility, his ability to respond on a moment's notice when tensions appeared to be running high, his willingness to listen to the parties and then span their differences by formulating principles (often based on objective criteria and expert opinion), and his quiet approach have enabled both sides to find face-saving ways to back down from confrontations and to emerge from this potentially dangerous situation without any significant, organized violence.

However valuable van der Stoel's role may have been in averting violence, it is unlikely that the outcome in Crimea would have been nonviolent had it not also been for structural considerations within Ukrainian domestic politics and within Russia. The latter's self-interest in preventing the further disintegration of post-Soviet space, even when this might have served its own immediate interests, was obviously a key factor in the relative stability in the region. Crimea's economic dependence on Ukraine and the ability of the leadership in Kiev to control security forces in Crimea were also undoubtedly important factors affecting this conflict. As Tor Bukkvoll (1997, 53) has pointed out, however, none of these structural factors is permanent, and changes in one or more of them could readily create a new wave of Crimean separatism. The need to improve mechanisms of preventive diplomacy in this area thus remains as great as ever, for there is no certainty that the next crisis in Ukrainian-Crimean relations will be resolved as nonviolently as the previous ones have been.

Comparison of Transdniestria and Crimea

In summary, Transdniestria and Crimea are both autonomous regions within different but geographically proximate states in post-Soviet space. Neither region has a long and deep history of connections with the state of which they have recently become a part, and both are heavily populated by ethnic Russians. The explanation for the peaceful transition in Crimea thus far in contrast to the violent outcome in Transdniestria is therefore an interesting one, involving two basic factors: the different role of preventive diplomacy and the diverse structural conditions, especially in terms of the part played by a third state—Russia.

In Moldova, there was little effective diplomacy in the early stages of the dispute, and the conflict escalated through a series of unilateral declarations and ultimatums issued by each of the parties, followed by unilateral and provocative actions by security and paramilitary forces. Threats and other tactics of hard bargaining were utilized, and apparently, no attempt was made to initiate problem-oriented negotiations. Ukraine tried briefly to perform a mediating role and to bring in the CSCE, which was just in the process of developing a capacity for preventive diplomacy; however, the CSCE was slow in responding and did not really become engaged in this conflict until after violence had occurred. Since the cease-fire was brokered, the OSCE mission has played an important role in preventing the resumption of fighting between the parties, and it has recently assisted in efforts to promote an agreement to resolve the underlying conflict. But it entered the situation too late to prevent the initial escalation to violence.

By contrast, the crisis in Crimea developed somewhat more slowly and at a later stage in the post-Soviet development. As the conflict was escalating in 1993, 1994, and again in 1995, the intervention of the High Commissioner on National Minorities was of critical importance in assisting the parties to find at least partial solutions, sufficient to prevent the full-scale escalation of the crisis to violence. Ambassador van der Stoel played an information-sharing, problem-solving role in organizing workshops to explore various formulas that might satisfy the fundamental needs of both parties to have their identity recognized and their basic interests realized. His recommendations regarding both the Crimean and Ukrainian constitutions helped the parties overcome significant differences over the legal status of Crimea within the Ukrainian state. The OSCE's long-term mission in Ukraine has also provided transparency to the conflict, not only in relations between Kiev and Simferopol but also with regard to the potential instability resulting from the influx of Crimean Tatars. No comparable efforts were made to suggest possible solutions for the terms of Transdniestrian autonomy within a Moldovan state, and through the early stages of that dispute, both parties maintained their absolute positions: Transdniestrian leaders insisted on complete autonomy or union with Russia, while Moldovan leaders insisted that Transdniestria was an integral part of Moldova, subject to its legal jurisdiction.

But preventive diplomacy might not have been successful in the Crimean case had the structural conditions surrounding the conflict not also been different from those present in the Moldovan conflict.

1. The Russian role in the two cases was quite different, and that difference was important. In Moldova, the Russians actively supported the separatists in Transdniestria, and the Russian Fourteenth Army was present in the region and was probably a major factor in its ability to consolidate its separatist position. In the Crimean situation, although the Russian military played a significant and high-profile role, the authorities in Moscow eventually reached a political settlement with the government of Ukraine (including bilateral agreements about the Black Sea Fleet and the status of Sevastopol) in which they recognized Ukrainian sovereignty over Crimea. Under these circumstances, the Crimeans lost their best potential supporter for their goal of complete independence; they were left to deal with Kiev on a bilateral basis, taking from a multilateral institution such as the OSCE whatever support they could get for their autonomy but in no case for their independence.

2. Fear of a loss of ethnic identity, a significant issue in both conflicts, was probably more intense in Transdniestria than in Crimea. But a major factor in the violent escalation of the Moldovan conflict was the possibility that Russians and Ukrainians in Transdniestria would be integrated into a non-Slavic state and perhaps even into greater Romania. If this happened, the people had serious reasons to fear that their cultural and linguistic identity could be completely submerged in Romanian culture. In Crimea, by contrast, the prospect of integration into Ukrainian society did not entail assimilation into such a radically different culture. Furthermore, the presence of large Russian minorities in other parts of Ukraine and of large populations of Russified Ukrainians throughout the country, as well as the presence of the Russian Federation along large portions of Ukraine's eastern border, served as a tacit deterrent to any schemes Ukrainian authorities might have contemplated to mount a campaign for the predominance of Ukrainian language and culture in the region.

3. Because its economy was heavily dependent upon its relationship with Ukraine and because it was unable to reorient itself toward Russia for economic sustenance, Crimea was forced to seek some form of accommodation with Kiev. By contrast, almost all economic resources in Transdniestria were tied into the Russian and Ukrainian economies and

had little relationship to the Moldovan economy. Thus, the government in Chisinau had fewer means by which to influence Transdniestrian policy than did the government in Kiev regarding Crimea. In addition, there appears to have been greater political unity within the regime in Tiraspol than that in Simferopol. Thus, the Moldovans were doomed to fail in any effort to pressure the separatists in Transdniestria to reach an accommodation, whereas the regime in Crimea was vulnerable to Ukrainian influence and could therefore be more easily manipulated into adopting a more accommodating policy toward the central government.

Chechnya and Tatarstan in the Russian Federation

Chechnya

Chechnya is a predominantly Sunni Muslim province in the Northern Caucasus. The Chechens are traditionally mountain people who adopted Islam in the fourteenth century, and Sufi orders have long been influential. Chechens are divided into clans, which are, in turn, united into larger groups, but there is not a strong class hierarchy within the society. Martial skills have been valued in Chechnya throughout history. The Chechens resisted Russian conquest in 1763 at great cost in human suffering, and only after a war of almost one hundred years did they succumb to Russian occupation in 1859. There was, however, a division between the Chechens from the mountainous regions to the south, who resisted subjugation more fiercely, and those from the plains clans of the northern region, who more readily assimilated into the Russian Empire.

Although the Chechens generally supported the Bolshevik Revolution at the outset as a potential liberation from czarist domination, they soon realized that, in fact, it meant the loss of broader freedoms, especially in terms of the private farming and communal pastures that had been the basis of their traditional economy. Therefore, they fiercely resisted collectivization in the 1930s, and when World War II opened, they took up guerrilla warfare against the Soviet regime. They were deported to Central Asia by Stalin in 1944, further embittering relations with Russia and also completely disrupting the social order within the Northern Caucasus. Many died during the deportations, but most of those who survived returned to Chechnya in the 1950s when the Chechens were rehabilitated after the death of Stalin (Arutiunov 1995). After their return, they became part of the restored Chechen-Ingush Autonomous Soviet Socialist Republic within the Russian Federation.[12] In the last Soviet census of 1989, there were a little over one million people in Chechnya, of whom about 65 percent were Chechens and 25 percent were Russians, mostly concentrated in the capital of Grozny ("The Terrible"), where they constituted a majority of the population.

In the confusion following the failed attempt at a coup d'état in Moscow in August 1991, Gen. Dzokhar Dudayev rose to power in Chechnya, overthrowing Doku Zavgayev, the republic's Communist Party boss. Dudayev, formerly a Soviet air force general stationed in Estonia, had built close relations with the Estonian national liberation movement. In 1990, he founded the Chechen National Congress and adopted a staunchly nationalistic stance. He was opposed at the outset by Vice President Rutskoi of the Russian Federation and Ruslan Khasbulatov, the ethnic Chechen speaker of the Russian Duma. Moscow continued to recognize Zavgayev as the legal leader of the Autonomous Republic of Chechnya and insisted that he must be a party to any negotiations in what they often referred to as an inter-Chechen conflict (Guldimann 1997, 3). Shortly thereafter, the Russian army withdrew from Chechnya, leaving behind large stocks of arms that were later appropriated by Dudayev's forces. Yeltsin issued an ultimatum insisting that Dudayev conform to constitutional procedures, to which Dudayev responded by forming a national guard and announcing a general mobilization. He proceeded with presidential and parliamentary elections on October 27, 1991, in which he claimed victory with 85 percent of the vote. A week later, he declared independence formally under the title of the Chechen Republic Ichkeria. Yeltsin responded by declaring a state of emergency and sending a small number of Russian troops into Chechnya. They were withdrawn, however, a few days later when the Russian Parliament refused to ratify Yeltsin's state of emergency (Hanson and Seeley 1996, 17–18).

Thereafter, economic conditions, which deteriorated rapidly in Chechnya as in many other parts of the former Soviet Union, were worsened by a Russian blockade. Although it cut off legal commerce, however, the blockade did little to stop smuggling and probably strengthened the criminal elements that had been operating in Chechnya for some time. The Russian leaders continued their efforts to develop an alternative to Dudayev, and they supported Umar Avturkhanov, a protégé of Zavgayev, who organized a provisional council in 1993 as a potential alternative to the Dudayev government. In January 1993, a Russian mission to Chechnya, headed by Vice Premier Sergei Shakhrai and Chairman of Soviet Nationalities Ramazan Abdulatipov, refused to meet with Dudayev, dealing only with Chechen Vice Premier Yaragi Mamodayev, whom Dudayev subsequently accused of treason (Payin and Popov 1995, 4). Fighting broke out between the two factions allied with these men, and Chechen religious leaders voted to declare a holy war in the event of Russian intervention in support of their client in the north. Two further coup attempts failed to unseat Dudayev in 1993, and the Russians began massing military forces on their border with Chechnya. The full extent of any private negotiations that occurred during this period is not known, but at least one official meeting took place between Dudayev and the Russian defense minister, Gen. Pavel Grachev, in which the latter promised that, in exchange for the release of some Russian prisoners, he would not pursue a military solution to the dispute (Payin and Popov 1995, 23–24).

Throughout the developing conflict, Dudayev refused to participate in negotiations on the Federation Treaty advocated by Yeltsin. At the same time, Ingushetia separated from Chechnya and agreed to sign the treaty in a futile attempt to get Russian assistance for the return of the Prigordny region from North Ossetia, populated mainly by Ingush. Throughout 1994, the Russians provided extensive military and financial support to the armed Chechen opposition, which included some Russian mercenaries. In November, these opposition groups mounted an attack on Grozny. The attack failed miserably, and Dudayev's forces captured the Russian mercenaries and showed them on television as evidence of Moscow's efforts to defeat him, further humiliating the already diminished Russian pride. On December 9, 1994, Yeltsin signed a decree authorizing the use of "all available means to assure the security of the state," and on December 11, some forty thousand Russian troops entered Chechnya from Ingushetia, North Ossetia, and Dagestan, resulting in full-scale warfare. The apparent reasons why no earnest negotiations were attempted were well summarized by Sergei Arutiunov (1995, 11):

> Proclaiming independence, Dudayev undoubtedly did not seriously consider the meaning of independent existence. The proclamation of independence was seen by him as a symbol of the position for further negotiations with Russia, in the course of which he apparently would have been prepared to accept confederation status as an associate member, or even the Tatarstan variation of bilateral relations. However, Russia did not want to pursue serious negotiations with Dudayev; it restricted itself to declaring the illegitimacy of his regime and refused to recognize Chechen independence. A strange situation developed in which Chechnya's independence was not recognized, though it actually existed.

There is a great deal of speculation, mostly in Russia, about the reasons for Dudayev's survival and the reluctance to open serious negotiations. Dudayev clearly had ties with criminal organizations and elements of the former Soviet State Security Committee (the KGB), giving him an independent power base in Moscow. A significant amount of drug trafficking into Russia is believed to have gone through Chechnya, and Dudayev clearly had powerful friends in Moscow. At the same time, opposition to Dudayev began to mount in Chechnya, which the Kremlin failed to exploit, contrary to the recommendations from Yeltsin's expert advisers on interethnic relations (especially those from the analytical center directed by Emil Payin). Some believe that by the time the war began, Dudayev was supported only by the clan grouping with which he had the closest ties and the criminal organizations with which they were associated. Although not all specialists agree with Arutiunov's (1995, 13–14) assessment of the situation at the time, it is, indeed, a provocative argument: "The regime could have quickly collapsed on its own. And what is more, in this case true democrats could have seized power in Chechnya, and not the puppets. But this is precisely what the military-adventurist junta—which today [January 1995] exerts absolute influence over Yeltsin—did not want to allow to happen. And therefore it unleashed this absurd, bloody and dirty war, which once again made the suppressed majority of the Chechen people comrades-in-arms with Dudayev."

The stakes of the parties in this conflict are somewhat difficult to sort out. At one level, of course, the dispute seemed to be an ethnonational conflict, similar to many others that arose during the period of transition that accompanied the fall of communism throughout Central and Eastern Europe. Yet this interpretation fails to provide a sufficient explanation for the violent outcome of this conflict: As the Tatarstan comparison clearly illustrates, there were many such situations, but most did not result in the high level of violence that occurred in Chechnya. Furthermore, although Islam was stronger in Chechnya than in many other post-Soviet regions, it was still not a major factor in Chechen life during the Soviet period, and the revival of Islam would seem to be more a consequence rather than a cause of the conflict with the powerful Russian neighbors. After the war reached its height, of course, the Chechens were fighting for their very existence as a people, but it is unlikely that the stakes in the conflict were widely perceived in such terms prior to the full-scale Russian invasion. Few people in Chechnya were probably aware of the high-stakes game in which they were to become involved until violence broke forth in its full fury.

Although the Russian government of President Yeltsin was under considerable domestic pressure to prevent the further disintegration of Russia, public opinion polls generally suggested that most Russians did not feel that military action in Chechnya was justified to preserve their notion of the integrity of the Russian state. Indeed, Arutiunov (1995, 19) reported that public opinion polls showed up to 65 percent of the Russian public opposed military action in Chechnya in 1995. Yeltsin certainly was influenced in his refusal to negotiate seriously by the rise in Moscow of the nationalist opposition, evidenced by Vladimir Zhirinovsky's strong showing in the parliamentary elections in December 1993. After that time, he became more subject to influence by the military and less inclined to rely upon his more liberal advisers.

Certainly, there were significant economic issues at stake in the conflict. Although Chechnya is a relatively poor, agrarian region, it has great economic potential. Significant deposits of high-quality oil and gas lie below its surface. The major pipeline for the transport of oil and gas from the Caspian Sea and the Tengiz oil fields to the Russian Black Sea ports bisects Chechnya along the east-west line. Major highway and rail lines cut through Chechnya in a north-south direction, connecting the Russian heartland with the Southern Caucasus, especially Georgia and Armenia, where Russian troops remained stationed near the border with one of Moscow's traditional enemies, Turkey. Control of these resources, however, is probably not to be measured so much in terms of their contribution to national wealth as in terms of the private wealth of the individuals and organizations that control those resources. Especially given the close links between many of Russia's top political elites and the oil and gas industry, there was a great deal at stake both for the economy and for them personally. Also, for those members of the military who still dreamed of one day restoring something approximating the Russian Empire, control of these strategic routes was of great importance. It hardly matters that their interests did not necessarily reflect a wider consensus in either Moscow or Grozny; they did reflect the personal interests of those individuals having the greatest control over relations between the Russian Federation and Chechnya, and they provided a significant obstacle to opening serious negotiations.

In the end, however, the stakes in the conflict were probably much more complex and clouded in intrigue than these traditional explanations would suggest. Moreover, they probably had more to do with personal rivalries for power and wealth than with national interests as generally portrayed in much of the international relations literature. The full scale of the involvement of criminal organizations, remnants of former intelligence and security institutions, large economic enterprises, and military officers still intent upon re-creating the former glory of the disappeared elite of the Soviet army may never be fully known. But what is clear is that those involved in these complex linkages and symbiotic relationships all had a common interest in avoiding an unambiguous political settlement to the conflict over Chechnya's legal status in relation to the Russian Federation, and this shared interest in avoiding a negotiated settlement had the most direct impact on the actual events.

Attitudes are also difficult to discern in this case, though they clearly reflected the stereotyped and simplistic views each party held about the other. Russians on the whole viewed Chechens as a primitive mountain people who were not a serious threat to them over the long term. Gen. Oleg Lobov is reported to have told a deputy to the Russian State Duma that "we must absolutely have a little victorious war" (Arutiunov 1995, 16–17). Like the Germans and Austrians in World War I, the United States in Vietnam, and the Soviets in Afghanistan, the Russian army, however depleted and demoralized it might have been following the breakup of the Soviet Union, was universally expected to overwhelm this little ragtag band of mountain guerrillas. Indeed, many saw the Chechen conflict as a small war to restore national pride and to set aside the "Afghanistan syndrome," just as many in the United States saw the invasions of Grenada and Panama as easy military operations designed to overcome the "Vietnam syndrome." And it is likely that some of Yeltsin's advisers believed that such a military victory would shore up the president's lagging electoral support. In other words, a short and easy military victory seemed to these Russians likely to produce a much more favorable outcome than could be achieved through a negotiated settlement.

Although the Chechens, especially at the onset of the conflict, generally got along well with the ethnic Russians living in their midst, they held somewhat different attitudes about the government in Moscow, which had sought to suppress them in various ways over centuries. As Arutiunov (1995, 8) noted, the Chechens "see in Russian authority, Russian soldiers and particularly in Russian officers and generals the embodiment of evil and a danger to humanity. That is what history has taught them." And, of course, the more the policies of the Yeltsin government seemed like a repetition of traditional Russian imperialism, the more these hostile images of the Russian state were reinforced. However much they recognized their economic dependence on Russia, Chechens also came to realize that Russia still represented a threat to their very existence as a people with a unique identity.

The tactics utilized by both sides have already been summarized. They included mutual attempts to intimidate one another, threats, guerrilla attacks, and ultimatums. Although some sporadic negotiations did take place, the two opposing leaders—Yeltsin and Dudayev—adamantly refused to meet together, and one or the other consistently scuttled any compromises that might have been worked out by their underlings. At the same time, Russia sought to neutralize the influence of international organizations that might attempt to intercede and offer to mediate by insisting on the legal formality that the Chechnya situation was an internal matter within the Russian Federation. Attempts by some organizations such as the OSCE to raise humanitarian objections to Russian policy—especially their disregard for the newly adopted Code of Conduct on Politico-Military Aspects of Security, which emphasized that "armed forces will take due care to avoid injury to civilians or their property" (OSCE 1994, 9)—or to criticize Russia for potential violations of confidence- and security-building measures in their unannounced concentration of troops near the Chechen border largely fell on deaf ears. Within these institutions, Russia was effectively able to block concrete actions by preventing the formation of a consensus to take any action, including mediation. The Russian leaders' confidence that they could win more on the battlefield than at the negotiating table probably reinforced their desire to keep outside actors from intervening to provide good offices or other third-party assistance. Nongovernmental organizations (NGOs) were also looked upon with some suspicion by the very self-reliant Chechens, which reduced the NGOs' ability to play an effective role in inducing the parties to seek a nonviolent solution to their differences.

The war lasted for almost two years and resulted in a great deal of destruction and loss of life, especially in the civilian population. Furthermore, issues between Russia and Chechnya were complicated by internal conflicts within the Chechen leadership. Zavgayev had formed a government-in-exile in Moscow, and Russia insisted until August 1996 that representatives of his government participate in the negotiations. Therefore, direct negotiations between the opposing sides did not open until well into the violent stages of the conflict. In fact, serious negotiations only began following the attack by Chechen guerrillas and the taking of hostages at the hospital in Budennyovsk in southern Russia in June 1995. With the aid of the OSCE Assistance Group in Chechnya, which had been established in April, a military accord was signed in Moscow by Yeltsin and Dudayev on July 30, though it was frequently broken over the next year. Finally, in May 1996, following Dudayev's death during a Russian rocket attack and with the assistance of OSCE mediation provided by the head of mission, Ambassador Tim Guldimann of Switzerland, direct negotiations were opened between Russia's short-term national security adviser, Gen. Alexander Lebed, and Chechnya's Aslan Maskhadov. They agreed to a cease-fire on August 13, 1996, to be followed by parliamentary and presidential elections in Chechnya on January 28, 1997. On August 31, a political agreement was signed in Khasavyurt in which the issue of Chechnya's formal status in relation to the Russian Federation was deferred for eventual settlement by 2001 (Guldimann 1997, 3). Of course, the negotiations at that point, which included the OSCE, no longer constituted third-party preventive diplomacy in any meaningful sense. Instead, they consisted of traditional mediated talks to bring an end to an armed conflict and to provide for a period of tension reduction during which political differences could be sorted out. But by that time, many thousands of people were dead, and Chechen society was torn apart to such an extent that anarchy and violence reigned throughout the country following the Khasavyurt agreement. Although the elections in January 1997 went off peacefully and elected Aslan Maskhadov president of the Chechen Republic, he was unable to establish control over the powerful warlords and competing factions within Chechen society. By 1999, radical leaders assaulted Russian military bases in neighboring Dagestan, and the Chechens were also blamed for a series of apartment bombings in Moscow. This enabled the Russian army to resume its military campaign in Chechnya in the fall of 1999, which by early 2000 led to a Russian military conquest of all but the southern, mountainous regions of the republic. But this military victory came at a high price, as Chechnya was virtually destroyed, several hundred thousand Chechens became refugees in neighboring republics, and the Russian Federation was charged with numerous violations of international accords in its brutal military action throughout the region. Thus, "preventive diplomacy" failed a second time in the decade, at huge human cost, leaving the prospects for any normal political life in Chechnya extremely remote for the foreseeable future.

Tatarstan

Tatarstan is another Muslim republic in the Volga region of the Russian Federation. The Kazan Tatars had arrived on the banks of the Volga early in the thirteenth century, where they established a khanate, compelled their Russian neighbors to pay them tribute, and assimilated and Islamicized the indigenous peoples in the region (Musina 1996, 195). They fell under Russian control in 1552 under Czar Ivan the Terrible. Subsequently, the Tatars were dispersed and ended up comprising less than 50 percent of the population of the autonomous republic that bears their name. However, following the breakup of the Soviet Union, the Tatarstan government under the former first secretary of the Communist Party, Mintimer Shaimiev, refused to sign the Federation Treaty (Tatarstan and Chechnya were the only two republics to do so), and a referendum led to a vote in support of Tatarstan's sovereignty. For the ethnic Tatars, the survival of their ethnic identity in a recognized territory was at stake. They constitute the second largest ethnic group within the Russian Federation, although some 75 percent of them live outside the territorial boundaries of Tatarstan. Nonetheless, the republic stands as a symbol of a homeland for some seven million Tatars living within the Russian Federation, and it embodies the cultural and political center of the Tatar "nation" (Musina 1996, 197).

There were, however, important differences in the attitudes expressed by Tatar nationalists and the majority of government officials. The former strongly resented the centuries of Russian domination and sought complete independence. The latter did not seek complete independence but rather pursued the goals of increasing their control over local resources and distancing themselves from a government in Moscow that they did not find responsive to their needs (Musina 1996, 206). They resented the fact that foreign currency earned by their raw materials and industries all went into the coffers in Moscow and that their many productive industries were controlled by central authorities rather than locally. For these more moderate elements, therefore, the issue was more one of local control rather than complete independence (Sheehy 1992, 2). Finally, Tatar leaders believed that the prospects for democratization were greater if they were able to break as fully as possible from the traditional Soviet structures. As Raphael Khakimov (1996, 71), head negotiator and principal adviser to the president of Tatarstan, put it: "Tatarstan has always viewed decentralization and federalization of Russia as a means of dismantling the state structures of the empire, enabling a change towards truly democratic foundations of life."

For the Russians, the stakes in the conflict with Tatarstan were also extremely high. First, there was the issue of preserving the territorial integrity of at least the Russian Federation, following the disintegration of the Warsaw Pact and then the Soviet Union. Nationalist political forces in Russia were highly critical of the earlier defeats of the Gorbachev period and blamed Yeltsin for the breakup of the Soviet Union. But the absolute limit seemed to be set at preserving the territorial integrity of the Russian Federation. Any Russian political leader who acquiesced in this next step in the disintegration that had swept across the region would have faced increasingly vocal and powerful opposition at home. Second, Tatarstan, like Chechnya, was of particular strategic value to the Russian Federation as well, more so than most other territories that might have broken away. Tatarstan straddles the most significant river system in Russia, connected with the Volga and also east-west communications lines, including the trans-Siberian railroad. It is the major link between Russia's industrial heartland in the west and the sources of raw materials in the east. Over one-quarter of Russia's oil is produced in Tatarstan. Furthermore, although some 49 percent of the population of Tatarstan consists of ethnic Tatars, some 43 percent are ethnic Russians, 86 percent of whom live in the cities. Thus, the major urban areas of Tatarstan are predominantly Russian cities, whereas Tatar culture really dominates only in the countryside (Musina 1996, 197–98). Consequently, as was the case in Chechnya, Russian political leaders could not face the prospect of abandoning a Russian-dominated urban and industrial center to the control of an autonomous Muslim republic.

The conflict in Tatarstan came to a head on August 30, 1990, when the Supreme Soviet of Tatarstan adopted a declaration of sovereignty. This move followed the same procedure that the Russian Federation had adopted only three months previously to assert its sovereignty within the Soviet Union, and it was probably intended only to upgrade Tatarstan to the status of a union republic, on a par with Russia and the fourteen other entities with that status. Nonetheless, the move generated opposition from within the Russian Federation, which still considered Tatarstan to be an integral part. The leaders in Tatarstan pushed the issue further, however, when they held presidential and parliamentary elections in June 1991. Many Tatar nationalists were elected at that time, although most moderated their programs after being elected to office.

Moscow refused to recognize the sovereignty declaration or the elections, prompting the leaders in Kazan to hold a referendum on the status of the republic in March 1992. This referendum was declared unconstitutional by the Russian Constitutional Court because it would have limited the applicability of federation law on the territory of Tatarstan. In a strongly worded statement, Valerii Zorkin, chairman of the Constitutional Court, ordered the authorities in Tatarstan to conform to the court's ruling. President Yeltsin himself launched a strong publicity campaign against the referendum, which inflamed interethnic tensions within the republic. Nonetheless, the referendum took place quietly, and 61.4 percent of the voters, or 50 percent of the population of Tatarstan, agreed with the proposition that "the Republic of Tatarstan is a sovereign state and a subject of international law that should structure its relations with the Russian Federation and other republics and states on the basis of equal treaties" (Musina 1996, 204). After the vote, Chairman Zorkin threatened criminal charges against Tatarstan's president Shaimiev and Farid Mukhametshin, chairman of the Parliament. At the same time, Yeltsin recommended that all parties remain calm, and he agreed that Russia should negotiate a bilateral treaty with Tatarstan in addition to the Federation Treaty. Shaimiev responded, however, that Tatarstan must not sign the Federation Treaty with Russia and instead must negotiate a bilateral treaty in which a confederal relationship would be created; through that relationship, Tatarstan would then delegate certain powers, such as defense and border patrols, to the federal government in Moscow (Sheehy 1992, 3–4).

Negotiations between the Tatar government and Moscow began on August 12, 1991, and they took place in four stages over the next two and a half years. The initial Russian position was to insist upon holding a referendum, which the Tatar side quickly accepted. As noted earlier, the results of that referendum on March 21, 1992, gave considerable support to Tatar autonomy, apparently much to the surprise of the Russian side. Having counted on the support of the ethnic Russian population in Tatarstan for preserving the federation intact and having been disappointed by the actual results, the Russian bargaining position was substantially undercut.

The principal Russian negotiator, state secretary Gennady Burbulis, then proposed negotiating a bilateral treaty incorporating the basic framework of Yeltsin's federal treaty, which the Tatar side had already refused to sign. But the Russians insisted that power ought to be shared by the center and by the republics and that three separate categories of powers should be demarcated: (1) powers belonging to the Russian Federation, (2) joint powers, and (3) full powers of the republics. The Tatar side agreed to this principle but argued that the categories assigned to the Russian Federation in the federal treaty were so comprehensive that they would inevitably lead to Moscow's domination of the regions (Malik 1994, 16).

The second round of negotiations began after the referendum, but at the outset, the Russian delegation appeared to be hopelessly divided. Burbulis was attacked in the Russian Supreme Soviet for being "soft on the republics," and one member of the negotiating team, Sergei Stankevich, led the attack on him in the Supreme Soviet. Burbulis was then removed and replaced, first by the ethnographer Valery Tishkov and shortly thereafter by Sergei Shakhrai, who would later become Russia's vice premier. During this period of confusion on the Russian side, the Tatarstan delegation, headed by Raphael Khakimov, submitted a proposal that declared Tatarstan to be a sovereign entity "which independently executes all state authority" (Malik 1994, 18). Throughout the entire negotiations, the leadership of the Tatar negotiating team remained virtually unchanged (Khakimov 1996, 75).

The third phase of negotiations followed a visit by Shakhrai to Kazan in which he persuaded President Shaimiev of Tatarstan to attend the constitutional conference of the Russian Federation, which the Tatars had previously boycotted. At the conference, Shaimiev and Yeltsin negotiated face to face. The Tatar president asserted his position that Tatarstan was a sovereign state, subject to international law, and "associated with" (but not "part of") the Russian Federation (Malik 1994, 18). Yeltsin responded by putting financial pressure on the Tatars to make them realize how economically dependent they were on Russia. Being completely surrounded by Russia, Tatarstan would have found it difficult to achieve true economic independence without close Russian cooperation. The Russians discontinued all financial inputs into the significant military-industrial complex in Tatarstan, so that defense conversions came to a virtual standstill; state orders for Tatar products were also drastically cut back. This caused Tatarstan to concede to joint controls of the military-industrial complex, with two exceptions: Russia would retain sole jurisdiction over weapons that were fully under its control, and Tatarstan would retain full control of the civilian production. At the same time, Shaimiev insisted that Tatar laws had precedence over Russian laws, and he further set about trying to establish diplomatic relations with other states. Tatarstan negotiated an especially comprehensive economic agreement with Crimea, including especially the sale of Tatar oil to the region.

Yeltsin's tough stand against the Russian Parliament in October 1993 appears to have softened Tatarstan's negotiators, who were impressed by the Russian president's determination and willingness to use force to get his way. When the referendum on the Russian constitution was held on December 12, 1993, only 14 percent of the eligible electorate voted in Tatarstan, and the constitution was not approved. Russia's leaders again reacted by putting additional economic pressure on the regime in Kazan, this time by threatening to close off the oil pipeline conveying Tatarstan's most valuable export commodity to the outside world. The strong electoral victory of Vladimir Zhirinovsky and his Liberal Democratic Party in the December elections for the Russian State Duma also frightened the Tatar leaders (Malik 1994, 26).

The fourth round of negotiations began shortly thereafter and concluded with an agreement on February 15, 1994. Both sides made substantial concessions in the final round. As Elizabeth Teague noted; "Moscow's main concession seems to have amounted to dropping its demand that Tatarstan sign the Russian Federal Treaty, while Tatarstan relinquished its declared aim of an agreement under which all powers not specifically granted to the federal center would remain with the republic" (cited in Malik 1994, 26). This agreement was patterned after the original Russian proposals in that it delimited three spheres of authority, but it differed in that Tatarstan emerged with a much wider range of powers than the Russians had proposed two years earlier, based on the model of the Federation Treaty.

Specifically, the agreement gave Tatarstan a "special status" as a state "*united with*" (but not *within*) the Russian Federation (italics added); this language implies somewhat closer ties than the original Tatar language, which had called for Tatarstan being "associated with" the Russian Federation. The agreement gave the Tatars substantial autonomy with regard to fifteen specific areas (primarily involving cultural, educational, social, and economic affairs), whereas twenty-two areas of joint authority were enumerated, such as crime control and environmental affairs; finally, seventeen specific areas were listed as belonging to the sphere of the federal authority of the Russian Federation, including defense and security, foreign policy, and questions of war and peace (Malik 1994, 25). One month after the treaty was signed, elections were held in Tatarstan to select two representatives to Russia's federal council, and President Shaimiev and Chairman Mukhametshin of the Supreme Soviet of Tatarstan were elected (Malik 1994, 26).

Although the communists and nationalists in Russia attacked the treaty for giving too much power to the regions, the reaction in Russia was generally rather positive, as the strong centrifugal forces that appeared to be tugging away at the Russian Federation were brought under some control. Indeed, many argued that the Russian-Tatar treaty should serve as an example to other regions that sought autonomy, not the least of which was Chechnya. At a minimum, there was relief that, unlike the case of Chechnya, Tatarstan and Russia were able to solve their differences peacefully, without the intervention of the Russian military (Shabad 1995, 15–17).

The Tatarstan lead negotiator, Raphael Khakimov, has reflected on the negotiations. A major factor for their success, he has contended, is that they were conducted simultaneously on three levels: (1) the top political level, which worked on the general formula for federal relations; (2) the government level, where implementing principles were worked out; and (3) the ministerial level, where details were negotiated. This three-tiered approach, he has suggested, made it possible to broaden participation and to create the kind of supporting coalitions necessary to reach agreement. This was especially critical for the Russian side. As Khakimov (1996, 75) has noted: "In Russia there was considerable opposition to the 'separatist' deal with Tatarstan. ... That is why it was so important to have allies on all levels in the circle of President Yeltsin's co-workers, in the government, in the parliament. Otherwise the great effort by both sides on the summit level could be brought to naught on the lower level: in the government and especially in the ministries."

Comparison of Chechnya and Tatarstan

This final pair of cases contrasts two autonomous regions within the Russian Federation that had a significant population of Islamic peoples and pursued independence from Russia after the breakup to the Soviet Union. In one case, a limited separation was negotiated peacefully, whereas in the other, negotiations broke down and an extremely bloody war resulted. These two cases seem to represent the clearest extremes of the peaceful resolution of differences and of large-scale warfare in two situations that, at the outset, bore some remarkably similar features. Several factors seem to account for the differences:

1. Yeltsin and the Russian leadership found it easier to negotiate with a respected politician from Soviet times, President Shaimiev of Tatarstan, in contrast to the upstart general from Chechnya, Dudayev, whom Yeltsin refused to recognize.

2. Internal unity within Tatarstan and continuity in its negotiating team gave it an effective negotiating position vis-à-vis the Russian Federation, whereas internal divisions within Chechnya tempted the Russian leadership to try to exploit those divisions rather than negotiate with the most powerful Chechen leader. In Tatarstan, radical nationalists were largely marginalized, whereas in Chechnya, they attained the center stage. Russian leaders were effectively able to manipulate interclan conflicts in Chechnya but failed to mobilize the Russian population of Tatarstan against the Tatar leaders.

3. The conflict in Chechnya quickly became militarized, in contrast to the purely political nature of the conflict in Tatarstan. Indeed, the long history of the militarization of the Chechen-Russian conflict contributed to the rapid militarization of this, its most recent, manifestation.

4. Shaimiev and his negotiators worked well with the Russian negotiators at all levels—from the experts, who were generally academic specialists on interethnic relations to the highest political leaders, including President Yeltsin. Jointly, they sought a formula that would permit Tatarstan to claim full sovereignty while actually blurring the sovereignty issue in the details. They largely adopted a problem-solving approach to the negotiations. By contrast, the Chechens and Russians adopted a confrontational approach almost from the beginning, and Dudayev refused to consider anything less than full sovereignty and independence; he denounced as traitors any colleagues who might consider a compromise solution. At the same time, the Russian specialists on the Caucasus increasingly lost influence over the relationship with Chechnya, and military leaders and others within the Russian government who had direct and often personal interests in Chechnya became dominant; these individuals saw little, if anything, to be gained by a negotiated settlement and preferred military victory, which some believed could be achieved with relative ease. They thus spurned attempts at negotiation in favor of efforts to coerce Chechen compliance with Russian priorities in the region. Although negotiations were pursued sporadically at lower levels, the negotiators on both sides had little support for reaching an agreement from their top political leadership. As a result, a long and bloody war broke out that settled nothing and left Chechnya in a state of ruin and anarchy, completely outside Moscow's control and with no prospect of negotiating a final settlement.

Conclusion

The most general conclusion reached in this chapter is that preventive diplomacy was neither a necessary nor a sufficient condition for the avoidance of violence but that it did seem to facilitate the peaceable resolution of disputes and to help avert their escalation to overt violence. Good preventive diplomacy was clearly not a necessary condition: In the case of Ajaria, for example, a tense situation did not escalate into violence even in the absence of a significant preventive effort. The argument that preventive diplomacy was not a sufficient condition for the avoidance of violence is somewhat more difficult to establish because problem-solving preventive diplomacy was seriously employed in only two of the six cases studied here—Crimea and Tatarstan—and in both situations, the outcome was nonviolent. In these two cases, structural factors and other conditions also made it possible for preventive diplomacy to be engaged effectively and aided the diplomats in reaching nonviolent solutions; it seems unlikely that violence would have been avoided had these factors not been present. Of course, this argument can only be sustained with confidence if a case is identified in which violence occurs in spite of the employment of problem-solving mechanisms of preventive diplomacy.

At the same time, a substantial case can be made that preventive diplomacy substantially facilitates nonviolent outcomes when other conditions are also favorable to peaceful resolution. Even this conclusion, though, must be tempered by one essential methodological caveat regarding the analysis of phenomena such as preventive diplomacy: It is always harder to analyze why something did *not* happen than why it *did*.

In the tensions between Tatarstan and the Russian Federation, it appears that effective bilateral diplomacy played an important role, in combination with other factors, in averting the escalation of the conflict. In particular, the modest demands of the Tatarstan leaders, their willingness to pursue a problem-solving approach to find an appropriate formula for Tatarstan's autonomy, and the consistent pursuit of a diplomatic solution by a coherent and moderate leadership in Kazan made a negotiated agreement possible. These negotiations were facilitated by the personal ties between the two parties that had existed in Soviet times and provided for a stable negotiating environment between leaders who knew one another well as individuals.

In Crimea, third-party preventive diplomacy was engaged at several key points of high tension in the dispute, and it played a significant role in averting the escalation of these tensions into violence. In particular, the assistance provided by the OSCE's long-term mission and especially the High Commissioner on National Minorities was vital in assisting the parties to overcome some of their most serious differences, especially regarding the legal status of Crimean autonomy within Ukraine. At the same time, the outcome in Crimea also appears to be a consequence of divisions within the Crimean leadership and of the eventual refusal of the Russian Federation to provide any backing for Crimea's efforts to achieve full independence and sovereignty. Crimean leaders were thus resigned to accept far less than optimal outcomes as a result of their inability to manipulate the negotiations in directions they preferred or to solicit outside aid to help them move the talks along a more promising path. This certainly facilitated the mediator's ability to urge restraint on the government in Kiev and to extract significant concessions from the Crimean leaders.

In Ajaria, the major factor accounting for the peaceful outcome was probably that Ajarian leader Abashidze was quite content to settle for autonomy and being left alone to govern more or less unilaterally within his own enclave, in exchange for agreeing not to challenge the formal territorial integrity of the Georgian state. Although Abashidze developed extensive political ties with Georgian president Shevardnadze, these linkages would normally not be considered negotiations so much as joint political consultations and coordination to achieve the objective of political stability, which served the interests of both parties.

Although effective diplomacy may not have been the decisive factor in any of the three instances of peaceful resolution, it is clear that there was generally some form of continuing communications among the parties and that, in at least two of the cases, significant attempts at problem solving were made. This contrasts with the three cases that turned violent: Chechnya, Transdniestria, and Abkhazia. In some of these disputes, diplomacy was tried, but it was never pursued consistently or with any apparent determination to seek a negotiated outcome to the conflict. For the most part, negotiators used hard bargaining rather than problem-solving tactics, and they sought to use negotiations to advance their own unilateral goals rather than to forge mutually acceptable agreements. The parties often became antagonistic, their attitudes toward one another were stereotyped and black-and-white, and their tactics became dominated by threats and provocative actions rather than attempts to identify common positions. In these cases, the claim for complete self-determination collided directly with the assertion of the territorial integrity of states that emerged after the breakup of the Soviet Union, and between these two absolute principles, there was little room for compromise or for identifying an overarching identity principle that would bridge the differences between the parties. In these circumstances, the conflicts had to reflect a far more typical etiology of escalating tension, the outbreak of overt violence, unstable ceasefires, and the eventual appearance of a hurting stalemate before the opportunity became ripe for opening serious negotiations to manage or resolve the conflicts. Diplomacy at this stage must generally concentrate on conflict management and confidence building to lay the foundation for constructive negotiations, rather than on preventive diplomacy as normally defined.

This analysis has demonstrated that preventive diplomacy does have a significant role to play in facilitating the nonviolent outcome of ethnonational conflicts in disintegrating states. It is extremely hard to do a useful counterfactual analysis of what might have happened in the three conflicts that turned violent had effective preventive diplomacy been engaged at the outset. One of the most difficult aspects of the disintegration of large states or empires such as the Soviet Union is that it is often very difficult, even in the best of circumstances, to bring the tools of preventive diplomacy to bear in a timely fashion. But this analysis certainly suggests that the early diagnosis of developing conflicts and intervention in the initial stages of those conflicts can increase the likelihood of averting much of the pain and suffering that has accompanied the disintegration of the Soviet state and the complex problems of building new nations in its aftermath.

New multilateral institutions and regimes are being developed and strengthened to support these tasks, but it is also important that knowledge from the social sciences be brought to bear in order to improve the process of keeping Humpty-Dumpty whole rather than always having to put him back together again. Even in the cases that did not lead to violence, more effective preventive diplomacy might have assisted a more rapid and long-term settlement of the disputes, and early intervention and effective implementation of preventive diplomacy might have kept some of the most serious conflicts that have accompanied the disintegration of the Soviet Union from turning violent. This analysis emphasizes how difficult it is even to engage in the preventive effort, much less to pursue it to a favorable result, especially in tough cases such as the identity conflicts that frequently accompany the disintegration of multinational states. The task before us, therefore, is to redouble the efforts of governments, NGOs, multilateral security institutions, and parties in regimes to engage in effective and timely preventive diplomatic action before the outbreak of violence makes the resolution of these identity conflicts even more difficult to achieve.

Notes

I am extremely grateful to Dominique Arel and Stephen Shenfield, my two colleagues in the Global Security Program at Brown University's Watson Institute, for their invaluable assistance in the preparation of this chapter, for this research draws a great deal from a joint research project we conducted. As specialists on the post-Soviet region, they have assisted in providing a great deal of source materials (especially from scholars in the area), in commenting on a draft of this text in great detail, and especially in helping me resolve apparent contradictions between different accounts of the same events. In short, this chapter could not have been written without their assistance and valued comments. Nonetheless, I assume full responsibility for the final version and its conclusions, and any errors of fact or interpretation are solely my responsibility.

The research on which this chapter was based was conducted primarily under a grant to the Watson Institute from the Carnegie Corporation of New York's Program on the Prevention of Deadly Conflicts, and I am grateful to David Speedie and Astrid Tuminez at the

Carnegie Corporation for their support. In addition, at the time this chapter was written, I was the recipient of a Fulbright Senior Research Fellowship to the Organization for Security and Cooperation in Europe, based at the Austrian Institute of International Affairs (AIIA) in Vienna, Austria. I am grateful to the Fulbright Program and to the director of the AIIA, Otmar Höll, for their support as well. As always, the views expressed are exclusively my own.

1. This region is commonly referred to by its Russian name, Nagorno-Karabakh. I have found, however, that one of the few things upon which the Armenian and Azeri parties to this dispute agree is that the region should *not* be referred to by its Russian name because it is no longer in anyone's mind a part of Russia; instead, it should be called "Mountainous Karabagh."

2. In an interview with me in The Hague on November 18, 1997, Ambassador Max van der Stoel, OSCE High Commissioner on National Minorities, expressed concern about the problem of the continuing crisis in the Kosovo region of the Former Republic of Yugoslavia. There, international agencies including the OSCE warned of a potential crisis at least since 1991, but few major global actors took heed. Indeed, there was an appearance of relative calm compared to neighboring regions, at least until 1997. However, he noted that the international community had become complacent about the dangers inherent in the situation, and he argued strongly that firm action by institutions such as the OSCE and the political leaders of Western Europe and the United States was necessary at that time to head off a rapidly brewing crisis as tensions mounted between an increasingly radicalized Kosovar Albanian movement and the government in Belgrade. Sadly, his warnings were largely ignored until late 1998, when the situation had escalated to the point at which violence was extremely hard to prevent. If preventive diplomacy had been engaged actively by late 1997 or early 1998, it is at least possible that the eleven-week NATO-led aerial campaign over Serbia and the forced expulsion from Kosovo of ethnic Albanians by Serb forces might have been avoided. The costs in lost lives, human suffering, and economic resources necessary to provide security and rebuild Kosovo in the aftermath of the conflict exceed by incalculable amounts what would have been required to engage timely preventive diplomacy in this crisis in late 1997 or early 1998 (cf. Brown and Rosecrance 1999, where Kosovo is only mentioned briefly).

3. For a discussion of the difference between these two styles of negotiation, see Hopmann 1995, 24–47.

4. This only constitutes a brief introduction to the processes of problem-solving negotiations. For further elaboration on the kinds of approaches and tactics associated with this form of negotiation, see Hopmann 1996.

5. For a review of the literature on third-party roles, see Hopmann 1996, chapter 12.

6. In the 1920s, the whole Transcaucasus region was treated as one political unit within the Soviet federation, along with the Russian, Ukrainian, Belarusian, and the Central Asian republics. Abkhazia's status was always lower than that of these union republics, but its relative status vis-à-vis Georgia in the first decade of the Soviet Union remains in dispute.

7. This view was argued by Daur Bargandjia, lecturer in economics at Abkhazia State University, in a presentation at a conference entitled "Georgians and Abkhazians: The Search for a Settlement and the Role of the International Community" at the Free University of Brussels, June 12, 1997.

8. Meanwhile, the territory west of Bessarabia, also part of the geographic region known as Moldova, remained within the borders of Romania.

9. Only one party, the Moldovan Communist Party, was registered for these elections, but opposition candidates were allowed even though many of them were still Communist Party members. Once in Parliament, the Communists split along nationalist-nonnationalist lines, which explains why the Popular Front managed to control the agenda.

10. General Lebed subsequently modified his views in his autobiography (1997, 331) and became critical of the leadership of Transdniestria and especially of President Smirnov, whom he accused of creating a "little principality" to exploit the popular urge for freedom.

11. Russia formally recognized the territorial integrity of Ukraine by signing the Russian-Ukrainian Partnership Treaty in May 1997.

12. Shortly after the collapse of the Soviet Union, Chechnya and Ingushetia became separate republics of the Russian Federation. I refer to Chechnya throughout the text even though the formal entity was called Checheno-Ingushetia through much of this period.

References

Arutiunov, Sergei. 1995. "Chechnya: Origins and Prospects for the Crisis." Trans. Eileen Kane. Moscow: Russian Academy of Sciences, Institute of Ethnology and Anthropology, Investigations in Applied and Current Anthropology.

Batalden, Stephen K., and Sandra L. Batalden. 1997. *The Newly Independent States of Eurasia.* Phoenix: Onyx.

Bremmer, Ian. 1993. "Ethnic Issues in Crimea." *RFE/RL Research Report* 2, no. 18 (April).

Brown, Michael E., and Richard N. Rosecrance, eds. 1999. *The Costs of Conflict: Prevention and Cure in the Global Arena.* Lanham, Md.: Rowman & Littlefield.

Bukkvoll, Tor. 1997. *Ukraine and European Security.* London: Royal Institute for International Affairs.

EEN. 1992. "Moldova Fused." *Eastern European Newsletter* 6, no. 6 (March 16).

FIER (Foundation for Inter-Ethnic Relations). 1997. *The Role of the High Commissioner on National Minorities in OSCE Conflict Prevention.* The Hague: FIER.

Fuller, Elizabeth. 1990. "Round Table Coalition Wins Resounding Victory in Georgian Supreme Soviet Elections." *Report on the USSR* 2, no. 46.

———. 1991. "Georgia's Adzhar Crisis." *RFE/RL Institute Report* 3, no. 32 (August 9).

———. 1993. "Aslan Abashidze: Georgia's Next Leader?" *RFE/RL Research Report* 2, no. 44 (November 5).

George, Alexander, and Jane Holl. 2000. "The Warning-Response Problem and Missed Opportunities in Preventive Diplomacy." In *Opportunities Missed, Opportunities Seized: Preventive Diplomacy in the Post–Cold War World,* ed. Bruce W. Jentleson. Lanham, Md.: Rowman & Littlefield.

Guldimann, Tim. 1997. "The OSCE Assistance Group to Chechnya." Paper presented at a meeting of the Carnegie Endowment for International Peace, Washington, D.C., March 11.

Hanson, Greg, and Robert Seeley. 1996. *War and Humanitarian Action in Chechnya.* Occasional Paper no. 26. Thomas J. Watson Jr. Institute for International Studies, Providence, R.I.

Hopmann, P. Terrence. 1995. "Two Paradigms of Negotiation: Bargaining and Problem Solving." *Annals of the American Academy of Political and Social Science,* no. 542 (November).

———. 1996. *The Negotiation Process and the Resolution of International Conflicts.* Columbia: University of South Carolina Press.

———. 1997. "New Approaches for Resolving Europe's Post–Cold War Conflicts." *Brown Journal of World Affairs* 4, no. 1 (Winter-Spring).

Jaworsky, John. 1995. "Crimea's Importance to Ukraine and Its Future." In *Crimea: Dynamics, Challenges, and Prospects,* ed. Maria Drohobycky. Lanham, Md.: Rowman & Littlefield.

Khakimov, Raphael S. 1996. "Prospects for Federalism in Russia: A View from Tatarstan." *Security Dialogue* 27, no. 1.

Kirillov, Victor. 1995. "The Conflict in the Trans-Dniestr Region." In *Crisis Management in the CIS: Whither Russia?* ed. Hans-Georg Ehrhart, Anna Kreikemeyer, and Andrei V. Zagorsky. Baden-Baden, Germany: Nomos Verlagsgesellschaft.

Kolstø , Pål, and Andrei Edemsky, with Natalya Kalashnikova. 1993. "The Dniester Conflict: Between Irredentism and Separatism." *Europe-Asia Studies* 45, no. 6.

Lebed, Alexander. 1997. *My Life and My Country.* Chicago: Regnery.

Lund, Michael. 1996. *Preventing Violent Conflicts: A Strategy for Preventive Diplomacy.* Washington, D.C.: United States Institute of Peace.

MacFarlane, S. Neil, Larry Minear, and Stephen D. Shenfield. 1996. *Armed Conflict in Georgia: A Case Study in Humanitarian Action and Peacekeeping.* Occasional Paper no. 21. Thomas J. Watson Jr. Institute for International Studies, Providence, R.I.

Malik, Hafeez. 1994. "Tatarstan's Treaty with Russia: Autonomy or Independence?" *Journal of South Asian and Middle Eastern Studies* 18, no. 2 (Winter).

Musina, Roza N. 1996. "Contemporary Ethnosocial and Ethnopolitical Process in Tatarstan." In *Ethnic Conflict in the Post-Soviet World,* ed. Leokadia Drobizhava, Rose Gottenmoeller, Catherine MacArdle Kelleher, and Lee Walkers. Armonk, N.Y.: M. E. Sharpe.

Nahalyo, Bohdan. 1992. "Moldovan Conflict Creates New Dilemmas for Ukraine." *RFE/RL Research Report* 1, no. 20 (May 15).

Nodia, Ghia. 1997. "Causes and Visions of the Conflict in Abkhazia." Paper presented at a conference at the Free University of Brussels, Belgium, June.

OSCE (Organization for Security and Cooperation in Europe). 1994. *Code of Conduct on Politico-Military Aspects of Security.* Vienna: OSCE.

———. 1997. "Survey of OSCE Long-Term Missions and Other OSCE Field Activities." Vienna: OSCE, October 7.

Otyrba, Gueorgui. 1994. "War in Abkhazia: The Regional Significance of the Georgian-Abkhazian Conflict." In *National Identity and Ethnicity in Russia and the New States of Eurasia,* ed. Roman Szporluk. Armonk, N.Y.: M. E. Sharpe.

Packer, John. 1998. "Autonomy Within the OSCE: The Case of Crimea." In *Autonomy: Applications and Implications,* ed. Markku Suksi. The Hague: Kluwer Law International.

Payin, Emil, and Arkady Popov. 1995. "Russian Policy in Chechnya, Part 3." *Izvestiya,* February 9.

Perrins, Michael. N.d. "Moldova and the Trans-Dniester Region: The Anatomy of Conflict." Balrugg Paper no. 13, Centre for Defence and International Security Studies, Lancaster University, Lancaster, United Kingdom.

Pikhovshek, Viacheslav. 1995. "Will the Crimean Crisis Explode?" In *Crimea: Dynamics, Challenges, and Prospects,* ed. Maria Drohobycky. Lanham, Md.: Rowman & Littlefield.

Rapoport, Anatol. 1960. *Fights, Games, Debates.* Ann Arbor: University of Michigan Press.

Shabad, Anatol. 1995. "A First Hand Account of Russian Military Action in Chechnya." In *Central Asia,* ed. Roald Z. Sagdaev and Susan Eisenhower. Chevy Chase, Md.: CPSS.

Sheehy, Ann. 1992. "Tatarstan Asserts Its Sovereignty." *RFE/RL Research Report* 1, no. 14 (April 3).

Suny, Ronald Grigor. 1994. *The Making of the Georgian Nation,* 2nd ed. Bloomington: Indiana University Press.

Tishkov, Valery. 1997. *Ethnicity, Nationalism, and Conflict In and After the Soviet Union: The Mind Aflame.* London: Sage.

Trofimov, Dmitri. 1995. "The Conflict in Abkhazia: Roots and Main Driving Forces. In *Crisis Management in the CIS: Whither Russia?* ed. Hans-Georg Ehrhart, Anna Kreikemeyer, and Andrei V. Zagorsky. Baden-Baden, Germany: Nomos Verlagsgesellschaft.

Udovenko, Hennady. 1995. Letter to Ambassador Max van der Stoel, June 30. OSCE Reference no. HC/4/95.

van der Stoel, Max. 1994. Letter to Foreign Minister Anatoly Zlenko, May 15. OSCE Ref. Com. no. 23.

———. 1995. Letter to Foreign Minister Hennady Udovenko, May 15. OSCE Reference no. HC/1/95.

———. 1997. "Minorities in Transition." *War Report,* no. 48 (January-February).

Zartman, I. William. 1998. "Putting Humpty-Dumpty Together Again." In *The International Spread of Ethnic Conflict,* ed. David Lake and Donald Rothchild. Princeton: Princeton University Press.

Zlenko, Anatoly. 1994. Letter to Ambassador Max van der Stoel, June 7. OSCE Ref. Com. no. 23.

7

Cooperative Disputes: Knowing When to Negotiate

Fen Osler Hampson

The proposition that friends or allies will behave differently from adversaries in a bargaining or crisis situation obviously has a certain amount of intuitive appeal. We would like to think that a cooperative relationship is based on trust, reciprocity, and feelings of mutual respect such that when a dispute arises, parties will sit down at the negotiating table to settle their differences amicably and peacefully. Alas, too much evidence of a historical, circumstantial, and even biblical nature suggests that friends, allies, or family members will not necessarily behave in that way and that a conflict between close associates can escalate out of control. The Bible, for example, is filled with accounts of close relationships that turned sour as a result of a breakdown in interpersonal relations (Judas's betrayal of Jesus) and crises in which family members failed the test of loyalty and friendship (Cain and Abel, Job and his three sons, Isaac and his two sons, Joseph and his brothers). Likewise, the history of international politics is filled with stories of similar kinds of conflicts (though usually not with such high moral drama), including those involving betrayal between allies or good friends. In some instances, these conflicts have escalated and led to a major disruption in relations; in others, disputes have been handled more or less successfully through negotiation and other means of dispute resolution.

This chapter examines a particular kind of conflict in international politics, namely, disputes between allies or countries that enjoy close relations with each other and whose relations are otherwise characterized by a propensity to engage in joint decision-making. Although a more formal definition will be offered, these conflicts are referred to as "cooperative disputes" because of the good relationship and commitment to joint decision-making that existed between the parties prior to the onset of conflict. In looking at the preventive use of negotiation, three interrelated questions are addressed: First, what are the roots or origins of cooperative disputes and can we make any systematic generalizations about the nature, stakes, and attitudes of these conflicts and the way parties will respond to them? Second, what kinds of bargaining and negotiating strategies and tactics are available to manage such disputes? Third, when is it desirable to enter into formal negotiations to manage these conflicts and when is it not?

Definition of a Cooperative Dispute

Any discussion about managing a conflict must begin with a clear understanding of what is meant by the term *cooperative dispute.* In a classic study of a friendly relationship that, for a brief time, turned sour, Richard Neustadt suggested that a cooperative dispute is one that occurs in a peacetime relationship between allies. Relations between such allies are marked neither by indifference nor enmity but by what Neustadt called "variegated" and "tight" ties between governments, as well as a network of connections between polities at the nongovernmental level. In the case of Anglo-American relations, which were the focus of Neustadt's study, the relationship between Britain and the United States was considered to be a special one because of the close association these countries enjoyed through two major international crises (World Wars I and II) and "connections between Washington and London [that] ran both wide and deep." In addition, in Neustadt's (1970, 2–3) words, "history and language and acquaintance added a special qualitative strength to those entanglements. So did a sense of shared external interests, global in scope. Beneath all these, supporting all, were foundations of felt need."

In Neustadt's notion of a cooperative dispute, the parties have already developed mechanisms and institutions (formal and informal) for coordinating behaviors and interests such that when real conflicts of interest do occur, they do not destroy the relationship, even though they may test the institutional foundations and personal relations that go to the heart of that association. Relatively few cases meet all the conditions specified in Neustadt's definition of a cooperative relationship. But his description is useful because it draws our attention to the complex array of jointly managed institutions that coordinate behavior and expectations between close allies or associates. Neustadt also reminds us that the mere existence of a cooperative relationship does not mean that conflicts will not arise between the parties.

Leigh Thompson has pointed out that, unlike noncooperative decision-making situations (such as the Prisoner's Dilemma, in which parties are making unilateral choices that affect themselves and others), cooperative decision-making is characterized by "joint, non-coerced behavior." Thus, "situations are known as 'cooperative' because the outcome is not enforceable until and unless both parties voluntarily agree to it," usually through a process of negotiation (Thompson 1996, 398).

Cooperative disputes typically emerge in what Thompson (1996, 397) called "lose-lose" situations in which "people in an interdependent decision-making situation all prefer one settlement over another but fail to achieve that settlement." The reasons for this may lie in a zero-sum belief—that is, in an assumption that one's interests in an interdependent decision-making situation are completely opposed to those of the other party (Thompson 1996, 404). Lose-lose situations can also arise if the parties agree in their beliefs but falsely assume that they disagree; if more than one outcome is feasible (i.e., if there are multiple equilibriums); and if parties are free to communicate their preferences but are not able to verify that the information is complete, truthful, or believed (Thompson 1996, 398–99). These characteristics bring out more specific implications of decisions in institutional, allied relationships.

Although social psychologists typically stress the importance of cognitive, social, and organizational variables in accounting for these kinds of joint decision-making failures (Kramer, Shah, and Woerner 1995; Murnighan and Pillutla 1995; Thompson, Peterson, and Kray 1995), a negative outcome can also arise when parties adopt bargaining strategies that are inappropriate to the market failure or coordination problem in question. Even if parties are committed to joint (as opposed to unilateral) decision-making in a cooperative dispute, they may still fail to reach an agreement or fall into a lose-lose situation if they do not fully understand the implications of their dispute in terms of negotiation strategy. As Thompson recognized, such disputes can arise when parties are presented with multiple equilibriums but have difficulty coordinating their preferences because they disagree about which outcome is best. But multiple alternatives with multiple preferences represent only one kind of cooperative dispute. The various dispute types are considered in the next section.

Varieties of Disputes

Many potential sources of friction can arise between states in situations of complex interdependence, in which a basis for cooperation already exists because the parties are involved in some form of joint decision-making. These frictions, in turn, may trigger demands to negotiate new institutional arrangements and develop new coordinating mechanisms to manage relations and coordinate expectations between and among the states. However, in the process, these frictions may also generate conflict (Caporaso 1993; Yarborough and Yarborough 1990). The growing literature on international regimes and the political economy of institutions, much of which has focused on the sources of cooperation in international politics (Keohane 1984, 1995), suggests a way of identifying and grouping the different kinds of disputes that may emerge in a cooperative relationship. The following categorization is intended to be suggestive rather than inclusive or exhaustive.[1]

Public Goods Disputes

The provision, distribution, and consumption of public goods can generate a number of different kinds of disputes in a cooperative situation. In the case of so-called pure public goods (in which jointedness and nonexcludability coexist), the benefits are consumed by all members of a community almost as soon as they are produced for or by any one member. Conflicts may arise between the provider of the public goods and the "free riders" who consume without contributing or paying compensation. For example, the provision of security (a public good) by the hegemonic leader in an alliance can lead to friction if smaller allies are seen as taking a free ride and not living up to their alliance responsibilities by providing for their own security or contributing their purportedly fair share to an alliance undertaking.

Open confrontation is more evident in an area such as modern communications and information systems, which have made it relatively easy for firms to take technological innovations developed elsewhere (often in another country) and incorporate them into their own product lines. In the absence of patents or licensing laws, companies making use of these innovations have acted as free riders because they have employed those innovations at no extra cost to themselves and without having to compensate the original knowledge producers.

Information systems and communications technologies are increasingly viewed as an important source of national comparative advantage in international trade. The free-rider problem is thus a major (and growing) irritant in relations between key trading partners (Canada and the United States, the United States and Japan, the United States and China). Ongoing negotiations to address this problem have been directed at developing an international property rights regime based on the extension of domestic patent legislation to cover foreign firms, as well as crafting bilateral treaties and strengthening the World International Patent Organization (WIPO), which was set up to register patents and copyrights internationally.

In the case of international joint goods, disputes can arise between members over the size and membership of the club (that is, over who should be in the club and who should be excluded). The General Agreement on Tariffs and Trade/World Trade Organization (GATT/WTO) system, for example, has extended trade liberalization, but GATT/WTO rules only apply to members; those who are not members are denied key benefits of membership (e.g., the extension of most-favored-nation trading status). Whether to expand present club membership to include countries such as China and Russia is currently a matter of active discussion, revealing strong differences of opinion among WTO members.

There is an obvious tension in any club agreement between the optimal size of the club and the marginal cost of savings for existing members. Adding members may also have other consequences (such as inducing changes in distributional and allocative relations) that may be deemed undesirable by current members. Some of these tensions are evident in current concerns about the implications of adding new members from Eastern and Central Europe to the European Union (EU). This is particularly true among the smaller states of the EU, who worry openly about their political and economic clout with the addition of new members and the diversion of investment funds away from the Union's poorer members (Greece, Spain, Portugal).

Some of the more serious and contentious issues in these kinds of clubs relate to leadership, not only in terms of how it is exercised but also in terms of who should provide the public good, especially when it is being supplied by more than one state, as in the case of Duncan Snidal's (1986) privileged "K" group. Serious disputes may also arise over the terms on which the public good is provided, particularly when the hegemon in such clubs decides unilaterally to change the terms of the bargain or to withdraw the good being offered. For example, one of the most serious disputes in the recent history of international monetary relations occurred when Washington decided unilaterally to take the United States off the gold standard and to suspend convertibility of the dollar in order to establish a new international monetary order (Odell 1982).

A "nested" version of the more traditional public goods dispute lies within the "security dilemma," whereby a state's efforts to increase its security only decrease it by making other states take measures to make themselves more secure in response (Jervis 1978, 1983). States may respond to this dilemma by forming alliances and taking various military measures, which may set in motion an escalatory dynamic as they seek to provide for their own security (Solingen 1996; Downs, Rocke, and Siverson 1986). Or they may try to curb the security dilemma by such means as confidence-building measures or by the creation of arms-control regimes, which is only one governance option in a variety of responses (Price 1995). The escalatory dynamics of security dilemmas "can be checked by unilateral measures designed to reduce critical uncertainties for the other side regarding its own actions" (George, Farley, and Dallin 1988, 671). Political concerts (e.g., the Concert of Europe), balances of power, and other approaches are alternative pathologies associated with the security dilemma (Jervis 1983; Kupchan and Kupchan 1991).

A less studied aspect of the security dilemma but surely a no less important one concerns the way in which the dilemma affects relations between allies and the kinds of disputes that can surface in their attempts to deal with it either through regimes negotiated with adversaries or through collective defense regimes. For example, allies may have profound disagreements about the level and depth of the security dilemma, about where the threats lie, and about how they should respond to them. During times of global transition when old threats disappear, such disputes may be especially acute if there is no shared consensus about who should take what action to address new and emerging security problems elsewhere (e.g., the allied, especially French, view versus the U.S. view about how to deal with current conflicts in the Great Lakes region of Africa). Likewise, the question of granting membership to new parties will be highly contentious, as we have seen in the issue of expanding the North Atlantic Treaty Organization (NATO).

Serious conflicts and disputes may also erupt over burden sharing and decision sharing in an alliance and over who is providing the public good—security—and who is getting a free ride (public goods and distributional conflicts). During the Cold War, for example, Canada was criticized by some of its larger NATO partners for spending too little on defense. If an ally decides to defect from a formal alliance or if it takes a course of action that jeopardizes the security interests of its partners, this may also lead to a crisis in interalliance relations. The 1956 Suez crisis, one of the subjects of Neustadt's study, is a perfect illustration of this problem. In that case, the combined British, French, and Israeli intervention to recapture the Suez Canal was seen by the United States as a betrayal of allied interests and a move that exposed the alliance to great danger, because the Soviets, under the cover of allied preoccupation with Suez, invaded Hungary.

Externality Disputes

International externalities may also be a source of conflict between countries if those externalities are the unintended and uncompensated by-products of cooperative transactions. A negative externality or an external diseconomy occurs when actions create nonexcludable and uncompensated costs for third parties. Most international pollution problems are negative, aggregate externalities or what might be called "collective social bads." Examples include acid rain resulting from industrial emissions carried across interstate borders or the pollution or depletion of shared water resources among neighboring riparian states.[2] Such externalities have been identified as a major and potentially serious source of international conflict not just between traditional adversaries but also between friendly states (Homer-Dixon 1994).

The externality problem is perhaps most severe in the case of common property resources—the "tragedy of the commons." An efficient property rights structure has four characteristics: universality (all resources are privately owned), exclusivity (there are no spillovers), transferability, and enforceability (Tietenberg 1984). In most externalities, the market failure involves the exclusivity characteristic. However, for common property resources, the universality characteristic is not met. As a result, these resources tend to be overexploited, their scarcity rent is dissipated, and their net benefit to society is competed down to zero. The overfishing in the North Atlantic is one manifestation of this problem. In recent years, intense disputes have arisen between a number of countries regarding the depletion of a common property resource, Atlantic cod. Depletion has occurred in spite of the existence of the Northwest Atlantic Fisheries Organization (NAFO), which ostensibly fosters the rational management and conservation of fisheries resources. In some instances, allies have even resorted to the use of force to prevent excessive exploitation, as happened in Britain's cod wars with Iceland or, more recently, the fishing dispute between Canada and Spain.[3]

Coordination Disputes

In some conflicts, the actors' dominant strategies directly conflict, leading them to Pareto-suboptimal outcomes, as occurs in a public goods dispute (or the classic Prisoner's Dilemma Game). In coordination disputes, by contrast, the actors seek to *avoid* the same outcome even though they may not prefer to *achieve* the same outcome (dilemmas of common aversion and divergent interests) or are indifferent to any particular outcome when presented with multiple equilibriums (dilemmas of common aversion and common indifference) (Stein 1990; Fearon 1988). As noted by Snidal (1986), in dilemmas of common aversion with divergent interests, in which parties prefer different outcomes when presented with multiple equilibriums, the incentives to defect usually rise over time, particularly if the game is iterative; hence, more formal, institutional mechanisms (norms, rules, and possibly even sanctions) are needed to coordinate behavior and to promote convergent expectations, eliminate ambiguity, or predetermine which actor gets the preferred equilibrium. But this creates an impossibility theorem if such a regime is to be reached through formal negotiation. As we will see, negotiation theory suggests that if parties are to successfully negotiate an agreement, there must be some convergence of expectations around a shared focal point that is informed by shared norms or values. Lacking that, negotiations run the risk of continuing endlessly and never reaching an agreement. If shared norms are absent, it may be difficult to negotiate new regimes, defined as norms, rules, and principles around which expectations can converge (Krasner 1983, 2).

The coordination problem and the sorts of disputes that arise under dilemmas of common aversion and divergent interests are illustrated by the difficulties industrialized states have experienced in coordinating their macroeconomic policies. It is widely recognized that domestic macroeconomic policies neither fully insulate economies from external shocks nor protect neighboring countries from macroeconomic spillovers. The fully autonomous policies practiced in the 1930s, including competitive devaluations, bank panics, and insufficient money creation, were a prime cause of the Great Depression. The

International Monetary Fund (IMF) and the World Bank were formed as parts of the Bretton Woods monetary regime to cushion and control the effects of autonomous macroeconomic policies. As John Ruggie has argued, under the "compromise of embedded liberalism" inherent in Bretton Woods, nation-states were supposed to pursue Keynesian macroeconomic policies internally without disrupting international stability (Ruggie 1983, 1996; Gilpin 1987).

The collapse of the Bretton Woods agreement has been widely studied, but the international monetary regime that emerged from it is less well charted. International monetary coordination through central banks, particularly by the big G-7 members (Japan, Germany, and the United States), has played a key role in dampening international macroeconomic instabilities. Disputes about conflicting macroeconomic policy objectives and the need to coordinate policies because of the time lags between the choice of a policy direction and its effects on the system have also been the subject of ongoing discussions by the G-7. But a macroeconomic stabilization regime built on policy cooperation does not exist and will probably be difficult to form because of the same problems of regime coordination (Cooper 1986).

Distributional Disputes

Distributional disputes are conflicts in which gains by one party necessarily imply losses for the other (i.e., bargaining is taking place at the Pareto frontier, and no further joint gains are possible). This is not to say that it is impossible to arrive at a fair solution, such as a Nash solution, that establishes some form of parity between claimants as measured by their relative gains in utility (Nash 1950). The real problem is that there are too many solutions. Before they can negotiate, parties somehow have to agree on the rules for allotting fair shares of a given good: Will the good be allocated according to a utilitarian criterion of distributive justice (the Nash solution), on the basis of need (social justice), on the basis of which groups are the worst off in society (Rawlsian justice), or according to some other formula or criterion? These rules themselves are the subject of negotiations within institutionalized allied relationships. A problem of this type is less serious in a domestic setting because most societies have rules enshrined in law for settling certain kinds of disputes (e.g., disputes about property and inheritance) (Young 1994). However, such rules are less well developed in the international setting, even though there is a large and developing body of international case law. One only has to look at some of the difficulties negotiators have experienced in dealing with the distributional aspects of a problem such as global warming to see that there is no consensus in the international community about the principles that should be used to assign responsibility and share costs for adaptive or preventive response strategies (Hampson and Reppy 1996).

Distributional disputes lie at the heart of many interstate conflicts and frequently arise between close trading partners or countries whose relations are marked by close dependence, as in North–South relations. In fact, distributional disputes between North and South have been at the core of virtually every major international negotiation since the early 1970s, particularly in UN forums such as the United Nations Conference on Trade and Development (UNCTAD). In spite of the high levels of rhetoric in the North–South debate, these conflicts have not demonstrated any great propensity to escalate because (1) the South has deep asymmetries in structural power and has failed to use linkage and other bargaining tactics and strategies effectively, and (2) the relationship itself has a constraining value (Zartman 1985, 1987; Rothstein 1984; Bacharach and Lawler 1986).

Distributional conflicts also lie at the heart of many property rights disputes in international relations, especially those involving territories that former colonial powers have been reluctant to give up (e.g., the Falklands/Malvinas in the South Atlantic, long controlled by Britain). When these sorts of disputes arise within cooperative arrangements between allies (as happened in Britain's conflict with Spain over the status of Gibraltar), their spillover effect on the cooperative regime makes them more, not less, difficult to resolve.

The deliberate framing of a conflict in distributional terms also makes it more difficult to reduce tensions even when close allies are involved and the basic issue itself is not distributional. Consider, for example, the effect of the Helms-Burton legislation in the United States. Because of that legislation, what was once a difference in outlook between the United States and its Canadian and European allies vis-à-vis dealing with Cuba has become a major dispute over property rights. Components of the legislation that call for the extraterritorial application of U.S. law and the imposition of tough penalties on foreign investors who do business in Cuba are based on the premise that these business transactions are illegal because they use the expropriated assets and properties of exiled Cuban Americans. Thanks to issues raised by those provisions, what was hitherto a rather general disagreement between allies about whether to engage Cuba or isolate it has been turned into a zero-sum dispute about property rights and restitution for Cuban Americans who lost their holdings when Fidel Castro seized power.

In identifying the different kinds of disputes in a cooperative relationship, it should be emphasized that the categories just mentioned represent ideal types. Most cooperative disputes typically contain elements of more than one category, as in the case of security dilemma/public goods disputes between allies. But for analytical purposes and for addressing the role of negotiation as an instrument of preventive diplomacy in dealing with these disputes, such distinctions are useful.

The Role of Negotiation in Preventing Cooperative Disputes

In critiquing institutional analysis and the political economy approach to the study of international cooperation and the formation of international regimes (Keohane 1984; Krasner 1983; Rittberger 1995), some scholars are greatly frustrated by the fact that these theories offer remarkably few insights on the way in which regimes are negotiated and on the bargaining processes that give rise to institutions (Odell 1997; Hampson and Hart 1995). In much of the scholarly literature, there is an unfortunate tendency to assume that once a market failure of some sort has been correctly identified, international regimes or some other international governance mechanism will more or less automatically emerge. Some correctives are, of course, found in the recent work of scholars who have approached the problem of negotiating regimes from a negotiations analysis perspective (Zartman 1994; Hampson and Hart 1995). However, the theoretical and conceptual linkages between formal institutional theory about the sources of cooperation and the bargaining and negotiating strategies that work best in a cooperative setting remain undeveloped. The previous discussion has shown that differences and disputes within cooperative relations can escalate and lead to serious conflict, particularly because betrayal of cooperation compounds injury with insult. Although this type of conflict may not reach the intensity seen in some of the other issue areas treated in this volume, violence is not always excluded. Moreover, conflict at any level is all the more serious because it runs counter to the expectations created by the context of cooperation.

It is useful to consider this matter in terms of the two major bargaining paradigms that inform much of the negotiation literature. Richard Walton and Robert McKersie (1965) call these the "distributive" and "integrative" models or paradigms of negotiation (Zartman 1978; Hopmann 1995). The distributive paradigm is based on the work of scholars who treat negotiations as a mixed-motive or zero-sum game (Schelling 1960; Raiffa 1982); the integrative paradigm is based on the work of scholars who view the negotiation process as an exercise in problem solving and integrative bargaining (Walton and McKersie 1965; Zartman and Berman 1982; Fisher, Ury, and Patton 1991; Fisher 1994; Young 1986).

Under the conditions specified in a distributive bargaining model, the negotiation process is characterized, following P. Terrence Hopmann (1995, 26), "by bargaining, in which (1) initial offers are made by each party to the other, (2) commitments are made to certain positions in an effort to hold firm, (3) promises of rewards and threats of sanctions are issued to induce other parties to make concessions, (4) concessions are made as one party moves closer to another, (5) retractions of previous offers and concessions are issued as parties draw apart, and (6) finally, when the dynamics of concession making overcome the pressures to diverge, the parties tend to converge upon agreement somewhere between their opening offers," despite asymmetries in power, bargaining resources and capabilities, and so forth. At the core of the distributive paradigm is the notion of concessions. From an analytic standpoint, the challenge is to explain how parties can move to an agreement that maximizes their own return by manipulating initial offers and the rate and size of concessions (Raiffa 1982, 128–30). Concession theory is derived largely from game theory, and most models are based on two-person games (Hamner and Yukl 1977). Different strategies of concession making are identified in the literature. These include tough strategies, moderately tough or intermediate strategies, soft strategies, and fair strategies (Brams 1990).

In contrast, the integrative model treats negotiation as a process in which the challenge is not to claim value, as in distributive bargaining, but to create it (Lax and Sebenius 1986). In metaphorical terms, the task is to bake a bigger pie instead of rushing to divide up the one you already have. Integrative bargaining is characterized by high levels of uncertainty, Pareto-inferior bargaining outcomes, the potential for multiple equilibriums, and nonstrategic behavior (Young 1989). Success in institutional bargaining situations will depend on the extent to which issues lend themselves to contractual interactions, the salience of the issues, arrangements that all participants can accept as equitable, clear-cut and effective compliance mechanisms, and effective leadership (Young 1989, 367–73).

Thus, under the integrative model, the main challenge and activity of negotiation is to search for a creative formula that satisfies competing or rival interests. I. William Zartman and Maureen Berman (1982) defined a formula as "a shared perception or definition of the conflict that establishes terms of trade, the cognitive structure of referents for a solution, or an applicable criterion of justice," on the grounds that a formula is more than just a concession or a compromise based on a series of fixed moves and positions. To be effective, they argued, a formula or agreed solution must be "framed by a relatively simple definition or conception of an outcome" that encompasses the essential demands of the parties concerned. A "balanced" formula is one that brings together competing interests in a way that is considered fair while meeting certain standards or criteria of justice. These criteria can be substantive, procedural or impartial, equitable, compensatory, or subtractive (Zartman and Berman 1982; Young 1991). Whatever criteria underlie the formula, in order to achieve a stable outcome parties must "come away [from the negotiation] with the sense that their primary concerns have been treated fairly" (Young 1989, 368; Friedman 1994; Friedman and Shapiro 1995). This is more important than the achievement of allocative efficiency.

Which of these two general approaches to bargaining and negotiation—the distributive or the integrative approach—is likely to work best in the different kinds of disputes mentioned earlier? Taking each of the categories in turn, it is clear that some strategies are preferable to others.

Public Goods and Externality Disputes

Disputes about the provision of public goods and externalities are more conducive to a distributive approach to bargaining, particularly if the problem involves getting other parties to internalize costs (e.g., with problems of burden sharing in an alliance or cross-border pollution). In these instances, there will be strong incentives to use threats, sanctions, and distributive bargaining tactics in order to wrest concessions from one's negotiating partners. If these threats are made by the hegemon who, as a last resort, threatens to withdraw the public good or unilaterally change the terms on which it is offered, the incentives to comply will be quite strong. For example, on a number of occasions during the Cold War, the United States threatened to reduce its troop commitments in Western Europe unless the Europeans carried more of the defense burden. Such was the case in 1984 when Sen. Sam Nunn introduced an amendment in the U.S. Senate that called for a phased reduction of U.S. troops in Europe unless West European members of the alliance assumed a greater share of the collective defense costs.

That being said, it is possible to envisage situations in which opening gambits based on a problem-solving approach to negotiation might be interpreted by one's negotiating partners as a sign of weakness (Pruitt 1991). Parties to such disputes also tend to have strong and well-defined best alternatives to a negotiated agreement (BATNAs), and therefore, the use of threats and sanctions in a bargaining relationship is credible (White and Neale 1991). Because public goods disputes involve problems of allocative efficiency in which there is (theoretically) a Pareto-optimal bargaining solution, concession-convergence tactics are also warranted as the Pareto frontier is approached, for no further joint gains are possible once that frontier is reached (Raiffa 1982, 139).

A key assumption in these scenarios, however, is that parties have abundant or nearly perfect information about each other's bargaining utilities or preferences and understand their respective bargaining capabilities. When such information is lacking, these kinds of strategies may be more difficult to sustain and will be associated with greater levels of risk and enhanced conflict. Further, to the extent that there is more uncertainty in a relationship (even a close one), the potential for misperception and miscalculation cannot be discounted (Lebow and Stein 1994; Neustadt 1970; Bazerman and Neale 1985). Rather than inviting concessions, parties may hold out for a better deal, and threats may escalate. To continue with the previous example, even in a close alliance such as NATO, cooperation among the allies could not be taken for granted. Successive U.S. administrations—if not the U.S. Congress—widely recognized the need for judicious consultation and consensus building among allied governments and within member states to reconcile differences over the ways, means, and goals of enhancing NATO's conventional defense capabilities.

Coordination and Distributional Disputes

If caution is advisable in resorting to distributive bargaining strategies and techniques in disputes over public goods and externalities—even when the incentives to use these strategies and tactics are strong—it may be inadvisable to employ these techniques in the early stages of negotiation in coordination and distributional disputes. As noted earlier, coordination disputes are characterized by the existence of multiple equilibriums and, therefore, no clearly optimal bargaining outcome. If parties have serious disagreements about which outcome is preferred, the application of distributive bargaining techniques, including threats and sanctions intended to raise one's security point in the negotiation, will likely prove ineffective. Strategic behavior may simply drive parties away from the negotiating table when they are faced with multiple alternatives and multiple preferences (Fearon 1988). Within the Organization for Economic Cooperation and Development (OECD), the failure of negotiations to reach a multilateral agreement on investment (MAI) that would enhance mobility of capital can be understood, in part, as a coordination dispute characterized by serious differences among the parties. Specifically, the parties differed on the scope and applicability of the agreement (e.g., whether and how to include "cultural" industries), the chief mechanisms appropriate for liberalization, and what the appropriate negotiating forum should be (the United States preferred to adopt standards within the OECD, but Canada and the European Union preferred to negotiate binding rules within the World Trade Organization) (Smythe 1998).

Although the strategy of pre-emption is one possible solution to the dilemma of common aversions, it will only work if the other actors have no choice but to go along and/or if the preemption is based on firm knowledge and the assumption that other parties will go along (e.g., the pre-emption of radio frequencies within accepted wavelengths) (Stein 1983). But if there are other choices or if such knowledge is not available, different strategies must be considered.

Similarly, in a distributional dispute, a concession-convergence approach to bargaining is likely to be ineffectual at best and counterproductive at worst if there are no shared norms or values about how the pie is to be divided, as well as about the general principles and conceptions of justice by which distribution will be decided. The use of threats and bullying tactics in order to force the issue or get one's way will only escalate the dispute or encourage the other side to walk away from the table in frustration. This problem was all too evident in the decade-old dispute between Canada and the United States over Pacific salmon, which was only resolved in 1999. Although elements of the dispute lay in the 1985 Pacific Salmon Treaty between Canada and the United States, which was badly drafted and had a weak mechanism for setting allocations, the conflict also involved the concept of equitable sharing, which, according to Linda Rief (1998), had never been properly established or agreed upon. As salmon stocks declined in the late 1990s, the dispute intensified, with Canada arguing that the U.S. fishers were catching more salmon than the Canadians and fishers in both Alaska and Canada upping their catch rate when talks broke down. The British Columbian government poured oil on the fire by announcing that it would cancel a U.S. lease of a weapons testing ground, and British Columbian fishers took matters into their own hands by blockading a U.S. ferry in Prince Rupert harbor (Rief 1998, 275).

Standards of fairness and justice cannot be imposed or developed through threats or strategic bargaining behavior, as that case illustrates; they have to be created through a search for mutual accommodation and consensus. Even so, methods of conflict resolution and negotiation are unlikely to work if the parties are wedded to fundamentally different views about the basis of equity and about what constitutes a "fair" solution—as in the case of the Pacific salmon dispute. In a highly asymmetrical bargaining situation, the stronger side may try to force the other to concede to its view about who should get what and on what conditions, but this is not negotiation as typically conceived, nor does it promote a fair solution. In coordination and distributional disputes, the more productive bargaining strategy is one in which the parties adopt an integrative approach to negotiation—at least in the early stages of the talks. In a coordination dispute, an integrative approach to the problem entails a search for shared norms that allow the parties to settle on a common focal point in later negotiations. In a distributional dispute, the main challenge of negotiation is to identify principles and standards of fairness and justice on which the parties agree and on which an allocative formula can be based and subsequent negotiations can center. This can only come about through the exchange of views and the development of shared understandings. If the parties are far apart on just what those principles are or should be, any attempt to force the issue through threats, sanctions, or bribery will be counterproductive, particularly if the agreement is intended to be the product of joint, noncoerced behavior (Thompson 1996, 398).

Obviously, different opinions are expressed in the negotiation literature about what specific techniques and tactics are most appropriate within an integrative bargaining framework. As Hopmann (1995, 27) pointed out, whereas some scholars emphasize the importance of "principled" negotiations "based on interests rather than positions," other scholars stress a cautious, exploratory approach to negotiation based on problem recognition and understanding prior to the onset of formal discussions. All scholars are in agreement, however, that bargaining strategies involving threats, sanctions, and inducements are usually not effective in creating value.

In sum, from a theoretical vantage point, the effective use of different bargaining strategies and tactics in a cooperative dispute may well depend upon the characteristics of the kind of conflict that lies at its heart. Disputes over public goods and externalities (as well as certain kinds of disputes among allies about how to address the security dilemma) may, in some situations, call for a distributive approach to bargaining, subject to the caveats indicated earlier. But coordination and distributional disputes require an integrative approach to bargaining if there is to be any prospect of reaching an agreement and reducing tensions.

In practice, however, the choices are not likely to be so clear-cut because, as discussed earlier, there are very few (if any) pure disputes. And even if the parties in a negotiation come to recognize that the proverbial pie is expanding and that there are joint gains to be realized through cooperation and an integrative approach to bargaining, the question of how the pie should be divided remains. As James Sebenius (1984, 73) noted, "Integrative bargains engender distributive ones. If interests make up a negotiation's basic data and alternatives place limits on it, then joint gains from agreement, regardless of how they are shared, constitute its potential." Once a common focal point has been settled upon in a coordination dispute or after certain norms or principles of justice are agreed upon in a distributional dispute, distributive bargaining strategies, including the use of concession-convergence tactics, may be involved in hammering out the details of a final settlement.

The choice and availability of different bargaining strategies and techniques will also be affected by the parties' perceptions about the long-term nature of their relationship and the value they place on friendship and trust. If friendship is valued, parties may actively avoid threats and brinksmanship even if a distributive approach to bargaining is warranted by the dispute at hand (e.g., public goods). They may also be less concerned about balancing concessions over the short term because they believe reciprocity will eventually be rewarded (Hirsch 1976).

Likewise, if negotiations take place within the context of an existing regime in which negotiating forums are clearly identified and a culture or climate of accommodation already exists and/or formal dispute and negotiating mechanisms are clearly identified, parties may be more predisposed to pursuing integrative (rather than distributive) bargaining, to deferring contentious issues to a later date, or to combining both approaches (Winham 1990). But we should also be aware that when the provision and distribution of public goods is involved or when externalities lie at the core of a cooperative dispute, parties have strong incentives to employ distributive bargaining as they struggle to reach the Pareto frontier.

Choosing When to Negotiate in a Cooperative Dispute

One of the most fundamental decisions in any kind of negotiation is deciding when to negotiate. In the literature on conflict resolution, this issue has received an enormous amount of attention. Zartman, for example, has offered the important insight that many conflicts have a self-sustaining dynamic of their own. For third-party mediation efforts to be effective, the conflict has to reach the level of a mutually hurting stalemate. This is the point at which the parties no longer feel they can use force to gain a unilateral advantage and instead become willing to consider other options because they perceive the costs and prospects of continued confrontation will be more burdensome than the costs and prospects of a settlement (Zartman 1985; Haass 1990). The notion of ripeness is also relevant to cooperative and distributive disputes—that is, a variety of conditions must be met before formal negotiations can proceed. These include a consensus about norms and a convergence of attitudes on issues of fairness and allotment.

Coordination and Distributional Disputes

A decision to start negotiations in a coordination dispute, for example, requires an extremely careful assessment about whether the parties have achieved enough of a consensus (or convergence of views) so that expectations will meet around the same focal point in the negotiations that follow. Likewise, in a distributional conflict, some convergence of attitudes about the principles of fairness and justice that will inform negotiations is required *before* the parties begin to negotiate, much like the case of buying a car or a house when a convergence of values exists between buyer and seller as to what kind of give-and-take (offer and counteroffer) is required to reach a fair deal. In the international setting, however, such norms may be absent because there is no consensus on the rules or principles on which the pie should be divided or how costs for dealing with highly complex problems such as global warming should be assigned. In these instances, negotiators will simply go round and round the problem in an effort to open negotiations. Until they begin to develop a shared sense of justice or fairness, they will never reach an agreement. Moreover, increasing frustration and anger may poison the well for any future negotiations and alienate parties even further. In effect, this is what has happened in UNCTAD (Zartman 1987).

In these kinds of disputes, the best preventive strategy is to defer negotiations until such norms emerge or enough of a consensus on negotiating principles is reached to allow formal discussions to begin. This does not mean, though, that parties should not talk to each other or try to sound each other out through a process of prenegotiation. In fact, a prolonged period of prenegotiation within the institutions of cooperation may be just what is called for to (1) help the parties define the problem more clearly, (2) encourage the parties to think about new solutions that have to be invented to address their interests, (3) identify new norms that will help develop focal points in subsequent negotiations, and (4) strengthen the parties' commitment to formal negotiations (Zartman and Berman 1982; Kriesberg, Northrup, and Thorson 1989; Stein 1990). As indicated earlier, this is, in effect, what the G-7 have decided to do through their annual summit meetings, at which they continue to discuss their differences over macroeconomic policy rather than trying to negotiate formal agreements.

Public Goods and Externality Disputes

In disputes over public goods or externalities, by contrast, the incentives to prenegotiate generally tend to be lower and the incentives to begin formal negotiations sooner rather than later are correspondingly higher because of the allocative nature of such disputes and the need to maximize efficiencies through cooperative solutions. Delay in beginning negotiations and reaching an agreement will only increase the costs to the parties if the underlying problem is left unattended. Again, this assumes the parties have perfect or nearly perfect knowledge and information about what those costs are. When that knowledge is lacking or information is incomplete, there may be less urgency to reduce such costs and a correspondingly greater need to gather information that identifies strategies as well as principles (including distributive justice) for joint action. This was noted by M. J. Peterson (1996) in her discussion of recurrent efforts to renegotiate a new international regime on whaling, and it is evident in the problems negotiators have had in reaching an effective international agreement on global warming because of contending assessments about the magnitude of the problem and appropriate response strategies (Hampson and Hart 1995).

Conclusion

In this chapter, I have argued that cooperative disputes represent a special kind of conflict in international relations because of the nature of the relationship between the negotiating partners. Such disputes arise in joint decision-making situations in which parties have strong incentives to cooperate but fail to reach an agreement through negotiation. Recognizing that the exact nature of these conflicts will vary considerably from one setting to another, I have contended not only that there are different kinds of cooperative disputes—public goods disputes, externality disputes, coordination disputes, and distributional disputes—but also that preventive diplomacy to reduce each type of conflict may require different negotiating strategies and tactics. In some disputes—coordination and distributional ones—negotiation is not always a good thing, and the preferred strategy may be to have the parties cooperate in prenegotiations. Although disputes over public goods and externalities create strong incentives for distributive bargaining, such an approach should not be employed indiscriminately because of the risks of miscalculation and because distributional and other kinds of conflicts often lie at the heart of these disputes. In negotiating with friends or allies, we must choose our strategies and tactics carefully.

Notes

In the course of writing this chapter, I have benefited greatly from conversations with Pamela Aall, Max Cameron, Vivek Dehejia, Philip Hampson, David Long, Dane Rowlands, Martin Rudner, and William Zartman.

1. Some elements of the following discussion are drawn from an essay I coauthored; see Eden and Hampson 1997.
2. See chapter 9 by Bertram Spector in this volume.
3. See Habeeb 1988, especially chapter 6 on the cod wars.

References

Bacharach, Samuel B., and Edward J. Lawler. 1986. "Power Dependence and Power Paradox in Bargaining." *Negotiation Journal* 2, no. 2: 167–74.

Bazerman, Max H. 1983. "Negotiator Judgment: A Critical Look at the Rationality Assumption." *American Behavioral Scientist* 27, no. 2: 220–28.

Bazerman, Max H., and Margaret A. Neale. 1985. "Perspectives for Understanding Negotiation: Viewing Negotiation as a Judgment Process." *Journal of Conflict Resolution* 29, no. 1: 33–55.

Brams, Steven J. 1990. *Negotiation Games: Applying Game Theory to Bargaining and Arbitration.* New York: Routledge.

Caporaso, James A. 1993. "International Relations Theory and Multilateralism: The Search for Foundations." In *Multilateralism Matters: The Theory and Praxis of an Institutional Form,* ed. John Gerard Ruggie. New York: Columbia University Press, pp. 51–90.

Cooper, Richard N. 1986. "The Prospects for International Policy Coordination." In *International Economic Policy Coordination,* ed. Willem Buiter and Richard D. Marston. Cambridge: Cambridge University Press, pp. 366–72.

Downs, George W., David M. Rocke, and Randolph M. Siverson. 1986. "Arms Races and Cooperation." In *Cooperation Under Anarchy,* ed. Kenneth A. Oye. Princeton: Princeton University Press, pp. 118–46.

Eden, Lorraine, and Fen Osler Hampson. 1997. "Clubs Are Trump: The Formation of International Regimes in the Absence of a Hegemon." In *Contemporary Capitalism: The Embeddedness of Institutions,* ed. J. Rogers Hollingsworth and Robert Boyer. Cambridge: Cambridge University Press, pp. 361–94.

Fearon, James D. 1988. "Bargaining, Enforcement and International Cooperation." *International Organization* 52, no. 2: 269–305.

Fisher, Roger. 1994. "Deter, Compel, or Negotiate?" *Negotiation Journal* 10, no. 1: 17–32.

Fisher, Roger, William Ury, and Bruce Patton. 1991. *Getting to Yes: Negotiating Agreement Without Giving In,* 2nd ed. New York: Penguin Books.

Friedman, Raymond A. 1994. "Missing Ingredients in Mutual Gains Bargaining Theory." *Negotiation Journal* 10, no. 3: 265–80.

Friedman, Raymond A., and Debra L. Shapiro. 1995. "Deception and Mutual Gains Bargaining: Are They Mutually Exclusive?" *Negotiation Journal* 11, no. 3: 243–54.

George, Alexander L., Philip J. Farley, and Alexander Dallin. 1988. *U.S.-Soviet Security Cooperation: Achievement, Lessons, Failures.* New York: Oxford University Press.

Gilpin, Robert. 1987. *The Political Economy of International Relations.* Princeton: Princeton University Press.

Haass, Richard N. 1990. *Conflicts Unending: The United States and Regional Disputes.* New Haven: Yale University Press.

Habeeb, William Mark. 1988. *Power and Tactics in International Negotiation.* Baltimore: Johns Hopkins University Press.

Hamner, W. Clay, and Gary A. Yukl. 1977. "The Effectiveness of Different Offer Strategies in Bargaining." In *Negotiations: Social-Psychological Perspectives,* ed. Daniel Druckman. Beverly Hills, Calif.: Sage, pp. 137–60.

Hampson, Fen Osler, with Michael Hart. 1995. *Multilateral Negotiations: Lessons from Arms Control, Trade, and the Environment.* Baltimore: Johns Hopkins University Press.

Hampson, Fen Osler, and Judith Reppy. 1996. *Earthly Goods: Environmental Change and Social Justice.* Ithaca: Cornell University Press.

Hirsch, James. 1976. *The Social Limits to Growth.* Cambridge, Mass.: Harvard University Press.

Homer-Dixon, Thomas F. 1994. "Environmental Scarcities and Acute Conflict." *International Security* 16, no. 2: 5–40.

Hopmann, P. Terrence. 1995. "Two Paradigms of Negotiation Bargaining and Problem Solving." *Annals of the American Academy of Political and Social Science* 542 (November): 24–47.

Jervis, Robert. 1978. "Cooperation Under the Security Dilemma." *World Politics* 30, no. 2: 167–214.

———. 1983. *Perception and Misperception in International Politics.* Princeton: Princeton University Press.

Keohane, Robert O. 1984. *After Hegemony: Cooperation and Discord in the World Economy.* Princeton: Princeton University Press.

———. 1995. "The Analysis of International Regimes: Towards a European-American Research Program." In *Regime Theory and International Relations,* ed. Volker Rittberger. Oxford: Oxford University Press, pp. 23–48.

Kramer, Roderick M., Pri Pradhan Shah, and Stephanie L. Woerner. 1995. "Why Ultimatums Fail: Social Identity and Moralistic Aggression in Coercive Bargaining." In *Negotiation as a Social Process,* ed. Roderick M. Kramer and David M. Messick. Thousands Oaks, Calif.: Sage, pp. 285–308.

Krasner, Stephen D., ed. 1983. *International Regimes.* Ithaca: Cornell University Press.

Kriesberg, Louis, Terrell A. Northrup, and Stuart J. Thorson. 1989. *Intractable Conflicts and Their Transformation.* Syracuse, N.Y.: Syracuse University Press.

Kupchan, Charles A., and Clifford A. Kupchan. 1991. "Concerts, Collective Security, and the Future of Europe." *International Security* 16, no. 1: 114–61.

Larrick, Richard P., and Sally Blount. 1995. "Social Context in Tacit Bargaining Games: Consequences for Perceptions of Affinity and Cooperative Behavior." In *Negotiation as a Social Process,* ed. Roderick M. Kramer and David M. Messick. Thousands Oaks, Calif.: Sage, pp. 268–84.

Lax, David, and James Sebenius. 1986. *The Manager as Negotiator.* New York: Free Press.

Lebow, Richard Ned, and Janice Gross Stein. 1994. *We All Lost the Cold War.* Princeton: Princeton University Press.

Lund, Michael S. 1996. "Early Warning and Preventive Diplomacy." In *Managing Global Chaos: Sources of and Responses to International Conflict,* ed. Chester A. Crocker and Fen Osler Hampson, with Pamela Aall. Washington, D.C.: United States Institute of Peace Press, pp. 379–402.

Murnighan, J. Keith, and Madan M. Pillutla. 1995. "Fairness Versus Self-Interest: Asymmetrical Moral Imperatives in Ultimatum Bargaining." In *Negotiation as a Social Process,* ed. Roderick M. Kramer and David. M. Messick. Thousands Oaks, Calif.: Sage, pp. 240–67.

Nash, John F. 1950. "The Bargaining Problem." *Econometrica* 18, no. 1: 128–40.

———. 1975. "Two-Person Cooperative Games." In *Bargaining: Formal Theories of Negotiation,* ed. Oran J. Young. Urbana: University of Illinois Press.

Neustadt, Richard. 1970. *Alliance Politics.* New York: Columbia University Press.

Odell, John S. 1982. *US International Monetary Policy: Markets, Power, and Ideas as Sources of Change.* Princeton: Princeton University Press.

———. 1997. "Policy Beliefs and International Economic Negotiation." Paper presented at the annual meeting of the International Studies Association, Toronto, Canada.

Peterson, M. J. 1996. "Whalers, Cetologists, Environmentalists, and the International Management of Whaling." In *Knowledge, Power, and the International Management of Whaling,* ed. Peter M. Haas. Columbia: University of South Carolina Press, pp. 147–86.

Price, Richard. 1995. "A Genealogy of the Chemical Weapons Taboo." *International Organization* 29, no. 1: 73–104.

Pruitt, Dean G. 1991. "Strategy in Negotiation." In *International Negotiation: Analysis, Approaches, Issues,* ed. Victor A. Kremenyuk. San Francisco: Jossey-Bass, pp. 78–90.

Raiffa, Howard. 1982. *The Art and Science of Negotiation: How to Resolve Conflicts and Get the Best out of Bargaining.* Cambridge, Mass.: Harvard University Press.

Rief, Linda C. 1998. "Environment Policy: The Rio Summit Five Years Later." In *Leadership and Dialogue: Canada Among Nations,* ed. Fen Osler Hampson and Maureen Appel Molot. Toronto: Oxford University Press, pp. 267–85.

Rittberger, Volker. 1995. *Regime Theory and International Relations.* Oxford: Oxford University Press.

Rosenau, James N. 1990. *Turbulence in World Politics: A Theory of Change and Continuity.* Princeton: Princeton University Press.

Rothstein, Robert L. 1984. "Regime-Creation by a Coalition of the Weak: Lessons from the NIEO and the Integrated Program for Commodities." *International Studies Quarterly* 28, no. 3: 307–28.

Ruggie, John Gerard. 1983. "International Regimes, Transactions, and Change: Embedded Liberalism in the Postwar Economic Order." In *International Regimes,* ed. Stephen D. Krasner. Ithaca: Cornell University Press, pp. 423–88.

———. 1996. *Winning the Peace: America and the New Order.* New York: Columbia University Press.

Schelling, Thomas. 1960. *The Strategy of Conflict.* Cambridge, Mass.: Harvard University Press.

Sebenius, James K. 1984. *Negotiating the Law of the Sea.* Cambridge, Mass.: Harvard University Press.

Smythe, Elizabeth. 1998. "The Multilateral Agreement on Investment: A Charter of Rights for Global Investors or Just Another Agreement?" In *Leadership and Dialogue: Canada Among Nations,* ed. Fen Osler Hampson and Maureen Appel Molot. Toronto: Oxford University Press, pp. 239–66.

Snidal, Duncan. 1985. "The Limits of Hegemonic Stability Theory." *International Organization* 39, no. 4: 579–615.

———. 1986. "The Game Theory of International Politics." In *Cooperation Under Anarchy,* ed. Kenneth A. Oye. Princeton: Princeton University Press.

Solingen, Ethel. 1996. "The Domestic Sources of Regional Regimes: The Evolution of Nuclear Ambiguity." *International Studies Quarterly* 38, no. 2: 305–38.

Stein, Arthur A. 1983. "Coordination and Collaboration: Regimes in an Anarchic World." In *International Regimes,* ed. Stephen D. Krasner. Ithaca: Cornell University Press, pp. 115–40.

Stein, Janice Gross, ed. 1989. *Getting to the Table.* Baltimore: Johns Hopkins University Press.

Thompson, Leigh. 1990. "Negotiation Behavior and Outcomes: Empirical Evidence and Theoretical Issues." *Psychological Bulletin* 108, no. 3: 515–32.

———. 1996. "Lose-Lose Agreements in Interdependent Decision-Making." *Psychological Bulletin* 120, no. 3: 396–409.

Thompson, Leigh, Erica Peterson, and Laura Kray. 1995. "Social Context in Negotiation: An Information Processing Perspective." In *Negotiation as a Social Process,* ed. Roderick M. Kramer and David M. Messick. Thousands Oaks, Calif.: Sage, pp. 5–37.

Tietenberg, Tom. 1984. *Environmental and Natural Resource Economics.* Glenview, Ill.: Scott, Forsman.

Walton, Richard E., and Robert B. McKersie. 1965. *A Behavioral Theory of Labor Negotiations.* New York: McGraw-Hill.

White, Sally Blount, and Margaret A. Neale. 1991. "Reservation Prices, Resistance Points, and BATNAs: Determining the Parameters of Acceptable Negotiated Outcomes." *Negotiation Journal* 7, no. 4: 379–88.

Winham, Gilbert R. 1990. "The Prenegotiation of the Uruguay Round." In *Getting to the Table,* ed. Janice Gross Stein. Baltimore: Johns Hopkins University Press, pp. 280–303.

Yarborough, Beth V., and Robert M. Yarborough. 1990. "International Institutions and the New Economics of Organization." *International Organization* 44, no. 2: 235–59.

Young, Oran R. 1986. "International Regimes: Towards a New Theory of Institutions." *World Politics* 39, no. 1: 100–22.

———. 1989. "Politics of International Regime Formation: Managing Natural Resources and the Environment." *International Organization* 43, no. 3: 349–76.

Young, Peyton H. 1991. "Fair Division." In *Negotiation Analysis,* ed. Peyton H. Young. Ann Arbor: University of Michigan Press, pp. 25–46.

———. 1994. *Equity.* Princeton: Princeton University Press.

Zartman, I. William. 1978. "Negotiations as a Joint Decision-Making Process." In *The Negotiation Process,* ed. I. William Zartman. Newbury Park, Calif.: Sage.

———. 1985. *Ripe for Resolution: Conflict and Intervention in Africa.* New York: Oxford University Press.

Zartman, I. William, ed. 1987. *Positive Sum: Improving North-South Negotiations.* New Brunswick, N.J.: Transaction.

———. 1994. *International Multilateral Negotiation: Approaches to the Management of Complexity.* San Francisco: Jossey-Bass.

Zartman, I. William, and Maureen R. Berman. 1982. *The Practical Negotiator.* New Haven: Yale University Press.

8

Trade Wars:
Keeping Conflict Out of Competition

Gunnar Sjöstedt

The Great Depression of the early 1930s generated "beggar-thy-neighbor policies" and mounting protectionism in leading economic powers. Governments in these countries closed their borders to imports in order to achieve economic growth by means of domestic policy measures. Consequently, they exported unemployment. Instead of cooperating to expand international markets, governments resorted to unilateralism and engaged in an escalating trade war. Such trade policies exacerbated the world economic crisis and increased tensions between the great powers (Kindleberger 1987). It is generally believed that these developments indirectly contributed to the onset of World War II.

The worldwide depression of the 1930s vividly illustrated the meaning of *trade war* and its potentially devastating effects. Memories of the global depression have lingered and have probably influenced economic policy-making until the present time. The Bretton Woods institutions and the General Agreement on Tariffs and Trade (GATT) created after the end of World War II were motivated by a widely perceived need to establish international institutions that would facilitate cooperation between the great powers and prevent a new world economic crisis (Eichengreen 1996; Dam 1970). When, on occasion, such a crisis seemed to be unfolding, politicians and academic analysts recalled the specter of the Great Depression in a call for prudence and cooperative solutions. The economic repercussions of the so-called first oil crisis of 1973 were one such chain of events. Other examples include the recession of the early 1980s and the global financial crises of the late 1980s and the 1990s. On each of these occasions, multilateralism and intergovernmental cooperation triumphed (James 1996). Indeed, since the end of World War II, no economic crisis has occurred to repeat the events of the Great Depression of the 1930s.

The explanation for this state of affairs is not that world economic relations have remained harmonious and nonconflictual. In fact, despite the free trade objectives of the international trade regime, many governments have pursued policies of managed trade that have generated a multitude of interstate disputes.[1] In addition, several waves of neoprotectionism have occurred during recent decades (Tumlir 1985; Baldwin 1986; Ray 1989). And governments have also intervened to monitor trade flows for security reasons: For example, control of trade flows was employed as a political weapon by CoCom against the Soviet Union and its allies during the Cold War, by Arab states against Israel, and by the United Nations against Iraq after the 1991 desert war (Forland 1991; Simons 1996). Numerous episodes of economic sanctions involving various countries have occurred since the end of World War II (Hufbauer, Schott, and Elliot 1990; Cortright and Lopez 1995; Doxey 1996). The media have also reported on so-called trade wars involving one or more of the present world economic great powers—the European Union (EU), Japan, and the United States.

When such conflicts have occurred, commentators have often been quick to make comparisons with the worldwide economic crisis of the 1930s. However, on no occasion since World War II has a trade conflict involving one or more of the economic great powers escalated out of control. Although some trade wars have intensified, the conflicts have been carefully managed by at least one of the parties involved. The chief focus of this chapter is on the circumstances and actions that have contributed to preventing post–World War II trade wars from escalating into a situation similar to the Great Depression.

Preventive diplomacy is given a wide interpretation in this book, referring to the type of negotiation strategy used to forestall an emerging confrontation or halt the escalation of an ongoing conflict (see chapter 1). Because of the practical difficulties of identifying trade conflicts that would have occurred unless preventive measures had been undertaken, the study of actual cases is primarily focused on preventing the further escalation of existing disputes.[2] The analysis of the prevention of the *occurrence* of trade wars has been carried out in more general terms, without reference to particular cases. The perspective on preventive diplomacy is partly open-ended, in the sense that it does not stipulate a priori what kinds of state action might represent preventive diplomacy associated with a trade war.

Considering the special circumstances of the issue area of international trade, it is important to distinguish between actions that produce direct preventive effects and those that produce indirect preventive effects. Mediation in an ongoing trade conflict that arrests its further escalation exemplifies a direct preventive effect (Bercovitch and Rubin 1992; Kleiboer 1997). In contrast, indirect preventive effects are typically separated in time and space from the diplomatic measures generating them, and they usually originate in the operation of international regimes. International institution building has often been the result of arduous negotiations containing strong elements of conflict resolution. However, once institutions have been established, they may have a considerable impact on the behavior of states without further negotiations between the nations concerned. Hence, a market-share settlement between the main producers of a particular good may eliminate the incentives for conflict within this group of nations for a certain period of time.[3] An international regime may identify the common interests of member countries in such a way that cooperation prevails in their mutual relationship. Value distribution becomes subordinated to value creation. Regimes and other forms of international agreements may, therefore, generate preventive effects either through their initial establishment or through their operation. In the analysis of trade wars, both direct and indirect effects of preventive diplomacy must be considered. This chapter only covers the period after World War II and is particularly concerned with trade wars engaging the present great economic powers.

What Is a Trade War?

Trade war has been given a narrow interpretation in this chapter as a conflict in which national governments with diverging interests try to monitor trade flows in order to achieve trade policy objectives other than those attained on the market.[4] A typical pure trade war situation exists when (1) the government of nation A introduces illegitimate trade obstacles in order to circumscribe the penetration of A's domestic markets by companies from nation B, and (2) government B responds in kind. The trade policy measures of a country are illegitimate when they are inconsistent with the international obligations that this nation has accepted in the General Agreement on Tariffs and Trade/World Trade Organization (GATT/WTO) and other international agreements.[5]

This definition of a trade war has fundamental implications that need to be highlighted at the outset. An emerging conflict in which at least one of the parties uses military power or political leverage to promote trade objectives is not a pure trade war. Neither is a situation in which warfare manifests itself as the manipulation of trade flows—sanctions—for purposes outside the realm of trade policy. For example, the trade sanctions that were in place for many years to force South Africa to abandon the apartheid system were not part of a trade war (Doxey 1996).

In spite of these limitations, the definition of a pure trade war as a conflict situation in which parties use trade policy measures in order to achieve trade policy objectives remains too vague and general for the analytical purposes of this analysis. The word *war* indicates an atypical situation in which parties resort to extraordinary measures. But conflict as such is not atypical for international commerce, despite the fact that trade is often mentioned as a prime example of international cooperation. According to the predominant free trade doctrine, formalized in GATT/WTO, competition—conflict of interest—is a main driver of the world economy (Lusztig 1996). It is true that companies as well as governments have taken steps to manage trade, by means of cartels and neoprotectionism, for instance (Sjöstedt and Sundelius 1986). Although such measures have reduced the unrestricted competition of a truly free market, the struggle for market shares is still a basic characteristic of all international trade.[6] The recurrent multilateral trade negotiations in GATT/WTO have disclosed considerable differences of interest among many trading nations, not least of all between the economic great powers. A main function of the GATT rounds has been to cope with such major conflicts related to international trade and trade policy (Gilpin 1987; Winham 1986). Nevertheless, the GATT rounds are not considered to represent a trade war.

Accordingly, the critical element of a trade war is not the presence of a conflict of interest but the way the parties involved perceive it and behave toward one another in order to cope with the tensions between them. Thus, a trade war is a process that involves an exchange of threats and sanctions—that is, pressure and coercion—by two or more competing parties.

Trade wars concern businesses in two or more countries, for international commerce is the transboundary exchange of goods and services among individual companies. Business competition on international markets can sometimes have warlike attributes, in the sense that companies may use various "dirty" measures (such as economic espionage or character assassination) to promote their interests (Brégeon and Luchaire 1988). However, in this chapter, a trade war is considered to be a confrontation of states.

A Characterization of Pure Trade Wars

The political processes related to the international trade regime are primarily multilateral in character: For example, almost one hundred nations participated in the Uruguay Round (1986–1994) (Croome 1995). In contrast, pure trade wars are two-party confrontations. Many trade conflicts have been motivated by differences of broad interests. Numerous disputes between the European Union and the United States regarding specific agricultural or tropical products, for instance, have related to the overall agricultural policies of these two great powers or to the EU's preferential economic treatment of former colonies in Africa and the Caribbean (Josling 1996; Lemesle 1996; Mailafia 1997). However, a typical feature of emerging trade wars after World War II has been the very specific issues they usually address. Generally speaking, they involve particular products or product groups as well as specific trade policy measures such as tariff treatment, the regime for a special commodity (e.g., sugar), import measures, production aid, or internal regulations with an impact on international trade (Petersmann 1997; Baldwin and Hamilton 1988). Although all sorts of states, industrialized as well as developing, have been engaged in emerging trade wars, the larger economic powers seem to have been over-represented, particularly the European Union and the United States (Bhagwati 1991).

A trade war begins when one country tries to hurt another via trade policy measures. Any trade war begins with nation A taking an offensive posture and imposing illicit trade policy measures to pressure country B. This is the first-strike stage of an unfolding trade war.[7] Further developments depend on the reaction of the target hit by this first strike. In theory, nation B has several options—it can ignore, comply, retaliate, accept mediation, or bargain. These responses correspond to a number of scenarios for the further evolution of a potential trade war after the first-strike stage: abortive trade war, blitzkrieg, multilateralization, rule-based dispute settlement, rule making, and escalation.

Abortive Trade War

An abortive trade war is totally inconsequential after the first-strike stage. In this scenario, one country introduces illicit trade policy measures that do not have any significant impact on the target nation. It is even possible that the governments of some developing countries may not be fully aware of certain trade policy measures directed against them.

Blitzkrieg

The blitzkrieg is also a brief episode. It is different from an abortive trade war in the sense that it includes a reaction on the part of the target nation.

The first strike of the offensive party (A) leads to an immediate victory as the target party (B) chooses to comply with A's demand without further resistance. The frequency of successful trade blitzkriegs can be gauged by the so-called voluntary intergovernmental agreements that result, in which one of the two parties restricts its exports of certain clearly defined products or product groups.

Many of the known voluntary export restraint (VER) agreements have common attributes indicating that they are the outcome of rising trade wars (Choi, Hwa, and Marian 1995; Tumlir 1985; Baldwin 1986; Hamilton 1990; Krueger 1995; Chen 1995). First, the accords that result from the negotiations are heavily skewed in favor of nation A, the offensive party in the encounter, with the main objective being to limit the exports of nation B, the target party, to A, in disregard of B's own interests. Second, the agreements are highly specific in their stipulations. Third, they are valid for a limited period of time. Fourth, they become increasingly institutionalized and more legitimate over time; the history of the Multi-Fibre Agreement that is being dismantled since the close of the Uruguay Round (1986–1994) is a telling example. Fifth, the voluntary agreements negotiated in the trade blitzkriegs are typically signed by countries of quite different size and power. The offensive party, nation A, is invariably an industrialized country, usually one of the great powers.[8] In contrast, nation B is, in most cases, a developing country with little leverage in international trade politics.

These five characteristics may explain why so many trade wars have almost immediately been won by the offensive party. For weak instigators, the best alternative to a negotiated agreement (BATNA) is clearly a more costly or riskier outcome than voluntary export restraint. The alternative confronting the nation B is typically unilateral action by A in the form of import restrictions with a broader coverage, with no time limit and a legal form that makes their removal difficult.

Multilateralization

Emerging bilateral trade conflicts have sometimes become partly or completely integrated into a parallel multilateral process dealing with trade questions. For example, in the Uruguay Round, gray area measures—a common designation for various "voluntary" arrangements to manage trade with sensitive products—were an important issue. The concepts of a "standstill" and a "rollback" were introduced into the special language of the Uruguay negotiations: Under a standstill, countries participating in the Uruguay Round were supposed to refrain from introducing new gray area measures, and under a rollback, parties were to begin eliminating existing gray area measures (Croome 1995).

The preceding example of gray area measures indicates a scenario in which emerging two-party confrontations over trade issues are discontinued because they become reframed and transferred to a new multilateral context.[9] Seemingly, the multilateralization that defuses an emerging trade war need not produce a binding agreement that includes the parties concerned. Multiparty processes of policy harmonization and coordination in, for example, the World Trade Organization (WTO) or the Organization for Economic Cooperation and Development (OECD) may likewise absorb or interrupt emerging trade wars (Dobson 1991; Croome 1995).

Rule-Based Dispute Settlement

In general descriptions of the significance of the new WTO, its instrument for dispute settlement has often been emphasized. However, WTO's instrument was not an innovation but was transferred from the General Agreement on Tariffs and Trade (GATT) (Petersmann 1997).[10] For many years, trade disputes have been handled in GATT panels, the critical component of the instrument: In 1980, there were five panels, in 1981 four, in 1982 eight, and in 1983 six (Bhagwati 1991).[11]

Rule Making

Rule making is a recurrent but not permanent function of the international trade regime (Wiener 1995). It takes place in special negotiating bodies set up outside the permanent institutional framework (Winham 1986). The multilateral negotiations of the GATT rounds have been used to cope with bilateral disputes between lead trading nations in a larger context, involving more countries and a multitude of issues. Hence, all the successful GATT rounds since the creation of the European Economic Community (EEC) have been used as instruments for coping with EU-U.S. trade problems (Baldwin and Hamilton 1988). The rule-making scenario may be seen as a variation of the multilateralization scenario. However, it includes an important additional element—the creation of new or modified rules representing solutions to complicated or sensitive trade issues that have been difficult to deal with in a bilateral setting.

Escalation

Target party B's retaliation represents escalation if it will increase the scope (number of issues), rate of participation (number of actors), or intensity (higher costs or risks) of a conflict. Escalation may be understood as upward movement on a ladder, with each rung representing an action or response by one of the contenders, A or B.

Trade is driven by competition—continuous conflict—among businesses. Governments become involved in the continuous "economic warfare" on international markets because they support and defend companies based in their respective countries. Recurrent government intervention generates contention between the countries. Most of these controversies are managed and resolved at a very early stage: Either they are settled soon after they have manifested themselves, as in the blitzkrieg scenario, or they are managed in an orderly way through established institutions, such as formal dispute settlement mechanisms or multilateral negotiations. Only a few of the multitude of emerging disputes evolve into an exchange of threats or sanctions. Such trade wars share a number of critical characteristics. Escalation occurs only at the low end of the ladder. Threats and counterthreats are exchanged, and actual sanctions start to be implemented. In the emerging stage, conflict intensity is high and rising, and parties are aggressive and recalcitrant. Escalation appears to be imminent. However, the intensity in escalation has not passed the threshold at which the risk for a larger and more destabilized interaction between the parties increases radically.[12]

The Oilseeds Trade War

The typical process character of an emerging trade war between great powers is illustrated by the confrontation between the European Union and the United States known as the oilseeds trade war. This conflict concerned subsidies to European farmers and took place in the autumn of 1992.[13] Process initiation occurred on September 2, 1992, when the U.S. administration announced that support to U.S. wheat producers would be increased. One declared motive was the need to demonstrate more assertiveness against the EU in the negotiations about the liberalization of agricultural goods going on in the Uruguay Round at the time. A week later, the French government cautioned Washington that the U.S. initiative represented a threat to the multilateral trade negotiations. A month thereafter, it was announced that immediate negotiations were forthcoming in Brussels between the EU and the United States on the issue of agricultural subsidies. The French government declared its firm resolution to block any EU concession to the United States. In Washington, U.S. spokespeople explained the necessity of reaching an agreement before the upcoming U.S. presidential election on November 3.

Participants in bilateral talks between the EU and the United States, which were held in Brussels from October 10 to 12, failed to reach a settlement. A meeting of the EU heads of government on October 15 in Birmingham, England, confirmed the dissent existing between the major European powers. Germany and the United Kingdom expressed the need for a swift settlement, but France continued to refuse to make concessions to the United States. President George Bush sent a message to the European meeting, stressing that the United States had done everything possible to facilitate an agreement: Now, it was up to the EU to lead the way. On the following day, the president of the European Commission responded by noting that the United States had not made any concessions in the negotiation, and he asserted that the EU governments must have the courage to defend their legitimate interests against the United States. The EU meeting in Manchester, England, two days later was followed by consultations in Ontario between the major players in the GATT talks: the United States, the EU, Canada, and Japan. One day later, the French government insisted Washington's argument that it was necessary to reach a solution before the U.S. elections in November should not be accepted.

The ongoing dialogue between the EU and the United States broke down a few days later, on October 21. Washington warned the next day that unless the EU agreed to reduce the controversial economic support to producers of vegetable oil, the United States would introduce import surcharges on French wine and cheese, at a cost of $350 million. This threat put pressure on the EU countries to activate the bilateral direct talks with the United States on November 2, but the discussion broke down the following day.

On November 5, lame-duck President Bush signaled that within thirty days, the United States would introduce 200 percent surcharges on imported French white wine. The European Commission responded with threats of reprisals, although it was clear that the leading EU countries were highly divided on this issue (with France taking a hard stance and Germany and the United Kingdom favoring an agreement with the United States). On November 11, the director-general of GATT, Arthur Dunkel, indicated that he was now engaged as a mediator in the EU-U.S. conflict, holding direct discussions with the key decision-makers in Brussels and Washington during the following week. An agreement was reached on November 20 between the EU and the United States. It was rejected by France, but three days later, the French government acknowledged that it could not veto the position taken by the other EU countries. On December 3, a U.S. delegation went to Brussels to finalize the technical details in the U.S.-EU treaty, definitely settling the transatlantic dispute on vegetable oil.

The 1992 U.S.-EU oilseeds dispute demonstrates a number of typical properties of pure trade wars. Like most outspoken disputes between economic great powers, it was initiated by the United States: Washington performed as the *demandeur* and was responsible for sustaining the conflict. Neither the EU nor Japan has launched a trade war against the United States, although Washington has usually argued that it has reacted against protectionist or unfair policies developed by the other party to the emerging trade war.

The transatlantic oilseeds conflict revealed the recurrent difficulties the EU has had in establishing and retaining a common position against the United States in an emerging crisis. As usual, France was intransigent, whereas both Germany and Britain argued for a compromise settlement of the dispute. The oilseeds conflict was focused on extremely specific and narrow issues with regard to both products and trade policy measures, but those issues were clearly linked to more fundamental and larger values. In fact, the connection with the multilateral trade negotiations in GATT was referred to openly by the parties themselves. The oilseeds war may, therefore, be seen as a surrogate for a much larger and riskier conflict pertaining to agricultural trade generally or even the overall agenda of the Uruguay Round. The link to the GATT context also opened the way for third-party intervention, in this case mediation by the director-general of GATT.

During the oilseeds war, threats to institute sanctions were exchanged. In fact, the United States actually began to enact sanctions, but they did not have time to affect the target party, the EU, before a settlement was reached. All trade wars between great economic powers since 1945 have unfolded and finished in a similar way. They have been relatively brief processes of hostile diplomatic interaction, culminating with an exchange of threats and sometimes sanctions. At that point, the trade wars have appeared menacing and destabilizing. However, trade conflicts have invariably been terminated before sanctions and retaliation have begun to hurt either party.

Prevention of Trade Wars: Instruments and Conditions

In international trade, conflicts have generally been managed and resolved very effectively. Furthermore, conflict prevention seems to have been important and successful with regard to contentious trade issues. How, then, has prevention functioned? What instruments and tactics have been employed to prevent the occurrence or the further escalation of a pure trade war? Three facets of this process need special consideration: weak motive forces supporting the escalation of conflicts, successful preventive intervention, and preventive impact of the international trade regime.

Weak Motive Forces Supporting the Escalation of Conflicts

When governments employ threats and sanctions to get their way in trade disputes, they accrue costs and take risks. Regulated imports increase costs to consumers and may also elevate production costs in domestic companies that are forced to buy more expensive components on the home market (Baldwin 1986). Threats and sanctions may also involve substantial political risks, particularly when such measures are used by an economic great power (Robinson 1996). An aggressive government may, for instance, contribute to reducing the credibility of the international trade regime in the eyes of other governments.

Thus, there are cost constraints for the rational employment of threats and sanctions in the context of trade politics. The relationship between, on the one hand, the costs and risks and, on the other, the magnitude of the stakes of potential trade wars will determine the will of governments to initiate confrontations and to escalate conflicts (Hufbauer, Schott, and Elliot 1990). Accordingly, governments may abstain from escalating an emerging trade war because such action is not cost-effective. This hypothesis is supported by the highly specific and circumscribed issues that have typified trade wars involving economic great powers.

However, the specificity and narrowness of issues does not necessarily exclude a wider salience. The particular issues that emerge in an unveiled conflict between leading economic powers such as the EU, Japan, or the United States have often been a manifestation of much broader and more fundamental differences (Mason and Turay 1991; JETRO 1991; Baldwin and Hamilton 1988). For example, the initiation of the oilseeds war should be seen as a U.S. offensive directed more generally against the EU's Common Agricultural Policy (CAP) (Josling 1996). The offensive was also linked to the deadlock in the parallel Uruguay Round, in which one of the main sticking points concerned the liberalization of trade with agricultural products. Clearly, then, specified narrow questions of emerging trade wars have often represented much wider differences of interest with major political importance and strategic significance. Thus, a general conclusion that issues in a trade war have been so relatively insignificant that they have not motivated a strong response to a first strike is not warranted.

Preventive Effects of Diplomatic Interaction

Eventually, the director-general of GATT became a mediator in the oilseeds trade war between the EU and the United States. His intervention occurred just before the parties made a settlement, but it is hard to determine exactly what role the GATT director performed in this crisis. Seemingly, the GATT attempt at mediation was essentially symbolic in character. The main function of the intervention was to recall the significance of the international trade regime. Trade wars have usually been terminated by the parties themselves, without significant support by a third party.

Preventive diplomacy in the trade sector has usually not taken the form of direct intervention in a particular conflict. Instead, multilateral interaction has prevented a multitude of trade disputes from evolving into trade wars. Three types of multilateral exchange have been especially important in this regard: recurrent GATT rounds, formalized dispute settlements, and trade policy reviews.[14]

Formally, *multilateral trade negotiations* at the level of world politics after 1960 have been organized in a sequence of autonomous rounds: the Kennedy Round (1964–1967), the Tokyo Round (1973–1979), and the Uruguay Round (1986–1994) (Preeg 1970; Winham 1986; Croome 1995). In reality, the multilateral trade negotiations have been an almost continuous diplomatic process, during which the rounds have represented particularly intense and decisive stages. The rounds have been linked by periods of preparatory work for the next round, as well as by various forms of postnegotiations related to the implementation of decisions made in the earlier round (Winham 1986). Multilateral trade negotiation in GATT/WTO has evidently been an appealing alternative to bilateral conflict resolution. A multilateral approach is less risky with regard to political costs, and a multiparty context makes it possible to involve countries other than the two initial contenders in an emerging trade dispute. Such circumstances may present at least two advantages. First, the multilateral environment encourages problem solving and integrative negotiations and opens possibilities for creative solutions to an emerging stalemate in a bilateral confrontation (for example, with the help of trade-off arrangements among several or many countries). Second, many arrangements designed to cope with a trade problem disturbing the trade relations between two of the economic great powers need to involve other trading nations as well, in order to establish viable international rules of the game (Zartman 1994).[15]

The *instrument of dispute settlement* in GATT has an obvious potential for conflict prevention (Petersmann 1997). It represents an alternative to a trade war as an approach to resolve a bilateral trade dispute.

Trade policy reviews were introduced into the international trade regime in connection with the transformation of GATT into the new World Trade Organization.[16] This instrument of policy assessment was, however, no novelty to industrialized countries with market economies, and it had been used for a long time in the OECD. One purpose of policy reviews is to give advice to individual countries on how they should pursue their trade policies. Measures related to this objective may help to decrease the likelihood that conflict will be initiated or escalated by indicating for the country under review how other governments react to its trade policies. Another aim of the country review is to teach individual governments about the trade policies and conditions of other nations. Such consultations may create a mutual understanding about trade policies, which can, in turn, be expected to decrease the risk for brutal trade wars.

Preventive Impact of the International Trade Regime

The international trade regime secured in GATT/WTO has evidently had an important effect on preventing potential trade wars. The rules of the GATT/WTO regime constrain the formulation of trade policies at the national level (Chayes and Chayes 1995).[17] And compliance with GATT/WTO rules contributes to conflict prevention in at least two ways. First, the existence of accepted rules of the game decreases the risk that one country will undertake trade policy measures that other states will consider threatening. Through respected rules, governments have agreed, in detail, on what they can and cannot do with regard to trade policy. Second, the accepted rules also reduce uncertainty in the trade policy area, as national trade policies become fairly predictable. Transparency in policy-making reduces the risk of pseudo-conflicts, in which misunderstanding may unnecessarily enhance conflictual behavior (Jackson 1996; Krasner 1983; Levy, Young, and Zürn 1996; Hasenclever, Mayer, and Rittberger 1997).

The exact extent to which trading nations have complied with the rules of GATT/WTO, as well as other regimes, has been debated in the literature (Chayes and Chayes 1995). It is always possible to find examples of countries that have not fully respected the rules in a particular situation. Some authors have been worried that a decreasing U.S. hegemony in the world trading system has begun to dilute the authority of the international trade regime; according to these authors, international regimes will not function effectively unless they are policed by a hegemon (Gilpin 1987). However, there seems to be wide agreement among analysts of GATT/WTO that its rules are complied with by most nations most of the time (Hudec 1993; Petersmann 1997). In fact, this trade regime is exceptionally strong in comparison to other regimes relating to international economic questions and also in comparison to other regimes generally. Consequently, the capacity of the GATT/WTO regime to prevent the occurrence of escalating and destabilizing conflicts is likewise relatively forceful.

Other elements of the GATT/WTO regime besides rules have also helped prevent the occurrence or escalation of trade wars. According to a standard theoretical approach, regimes can be regarded as issue-specific systems of "rules, norms, principles and procedures around which actor expectations converge" (Krasner 1983). Norms give general direction to policy-making without representing formal and binding obligations. In the trade area, a leading norm is that governments should promote world economic growth by using economic resources efficiently (Hudec 1993). Principles represent a widely accepted understanding—or consensual knowledge—about issues covered by the regime. In the GATT/WTO regime, one important element of the principles is the free trade regime that explains why and how the elimination of obstacles to the uninhibited transboundary exchange of goods and services contributes to increase world economic growth (Sjöstedt and Sundelius 1986; GATT 1986). Finally, procedures include organizational bodies and established working methods for the management and evolution of the regime (Jackson 1996).

In addition to having formal and highly specified constructions in its rules and procedures, the GATT/WTO regime also features norms and principles that have been explicitly expressed (GATT 1986). Although the four regime elements are distinguishable from one another, there is a strong and complex interaction between them. Thus, one of the main functions of both norms and principles in the context of regime dynamics is to support the operation of regime rules, that is, essentially to increase the likelihood that an actor will comply with them. However, norms and principles also have other regime functions, which have also had an important preventive effect on emerging—or potential—trade wars.

The norms specified in the GATT/WTO regime have been important in conflict resolution in that they have identified common objectives for the parties involved. In an emerging conflict, the GATT/WTO norms may help steer two parties away from a confrontation with a potential for escalation.

The principles—consensual knowledge—of the GATT/WTO regime may contribute to conflict prevention in different ways. For example, the free trade doctrine at the heart of GATT/WTO principles provides governments with authoritative arguments that they can use in domestic political debates against powerful sectoral interests requiring protectionist measures (Lusztig 1996). However, the most important contribution of regime principles to conflict resolution relates to their function as a common doctrine and a transnational, conceptual framework for those who make trade policy in both national governments and international organizations. This professional language code has created substantial transparency in national trade policies (Sjöstedt and Sundelius 1986). It has also improved the capacity of national governments to assess the consequences of offers, requests, and new policy measures. A particularly important function of the conceptual framework has been its capacity to help national governments identify and evaluate common interests and objectives. Furthermore, the consensual knowledge that represents the main component of regime principles facilitates the communication between parties when they strive to describe their own concerns and particular interests (Haas 1990; Spector, Sjöstedt, and Zartman 1994). The consensual knowledge embedded in GATT/WTO is unusually specified and acknowledged for an international regime. It has significantly facilitated constructive intergovernmental discussions of sensitive and complex trade issues, which, in turn, has seemingly prevented the escalation of trade conflicts.

Conclusion

Since World War II, a large number of bilateral disputes have surfaced in the sector of international trade, many of which have concerned highly important values. On a number of occasions, trade disputes involving economic great powers have started to evolve in the direction of intensive trade wars. In such cases, the escalation under way has invariably been terminated before the parties have started to hurt each other. Such prevention has not primarily been the achievement of the brilliant intervention of hero-diplomats; rather, it has resulted from the daily work of heroic institutions. A variety of successful approaches to conflict management have been established. Effective conflict management appears to have been a positive condition for the prevention of serious and destabilizing conflicts.

One may ask if the lessons from the trade sector could not be applied in other issue areas. This prospect should certainly be investigated. However, when lessons are drawn from the trade sector, it has to be kept in mind that in certain respects this sector has special conditions for policy-making, international cooperation, and preventive diplomacy. For instance, under the label of competition, conflict has a much more positive role with regard to international trade than it has in most other issue areas. Moreover, trade issues can usually be expressed in quantitative terms and are therefore comparatively easy to handle at the negotiation table. An exceptionally strong link exists between the international trade regime and a widely supported free trade doctrine guiding policy-making in the large majority of trading nations. Finally, the stability of the background factors for effective conflict prevention must be carefully investigated. For example, what will happen to the trading system when developing countries become stronger and more assertive in discussions about export restraint? How will the GATT/WTO regime be affected if the doctrine of fair trade continues to dilute the doctrine of free trade? And will the forces of conflict prevention weaken if the trade regime becomes increasingly less potent?

Notes

1. Recall that the essence of a "free trade policy" has been to eliminate obstacles for the uninhibited transboundary exchange of goods and services. The essence of a free trade policy has been nonintervention by state authorities in international markets.

2. See Note 12.

3. A commodity agreement of states may be compared with a deal to create an oligopoly market, in which a group of leading firms reduce competition between themselves by sharing the market. A commodity agreement typically has a limited duration, which is specified in the parties' contract.

4. This interpretation is derived from a definition proposed by J. Conybeare: A trade war, he stated, "is a category of intense international conflict where states interact, bargain and retaliate primarily over economic objectives directly related to the traded goods or service sectors of their economies, and where the means used are restrictions on the free flow of goods and services" (Conybeare 1987).

5. The notion of gray area policy measures indicates the difficulty of always distinguishing between legitimate and illegitimate elements of a national trade policy. Some confrontations of states in the trade area have been genuine disputes over the interpretation of regime rules.

6. Note that the present understanding of the term *trade war* represents an interesting paradox with respect to the role of competition on international markets: A more intense conflict between states (an emerging trade war) tends to create less intensive conflict among firms (managed competition).

7. The initial stages of a full-fledged trade war can, in reality, only be identified after the conflict has manifested itself clearly. The first strike of the trade war may have at least two different functions for the nation that launches it—either to derive benefit from a neoprotectionist commercial advantage or to punish the target nation.

8. In textile trade, the system of voluntary export restraint became quasi-legitimate by means of multilateralization through the Multi-Fibre Agreement and its couplings to GATT. This arrangement helped smaller industrialized nations ask developing countries for voluntary restraint with respect to textiles. The quasi-legitimate character also appears to have supported neoprotectionist measures in sectors other than textiles.

9. The so-called Dillon Round in 1960 is considered a failure. Thereafter, three consecutive, successful GATT rounds took place: the Kennedy Round (1964–1967), the Tokyo Round (1973–1979), and the Uruguay Round (1986–1994) (Preeg 1970; Winham 1986; Croome 1995; Sjöstedt chapter in Zartman 1994).

10. The transfer of the instrument for dispute settlement from GATT to WTO was combined with certain reforms intended to enhance the effectiveness of that instrument. These reforms have generally been considered successful. At the same time, the differences between the instrument of GATT and that of WTO should not be exaggerated. The accomplishments of dispute settlement in GATT should not be underestimated.

11. To the GATT panels should be added an unknown number of cases that were handled by the instrument for dispute settlement but could be resolved by means of consultations between the parties concerned.

12. The following trade war cases have been considered: The chicken war at the time of the Kennedy Round (U.S.-EEC); the oilseeds war in the midst of the Uruguay Round (U.S.-EC); voluntary export restraint regarding exports of cars and information technology (IT)

products (U.S.-Japan-EC countries-EU); cooperation regarding the development and construction of aircraft and the Airbus (U.S.-EC); the construction of a Japanese military aircraft (U.S.-Japan); the merger of Boeing and Douglas (U.S.-EU); and access to Japanese and U.S. harbors (U.S.-EU).

13. The story of the oilseeds war has been reconstructed primarily on the basis of two sources: *Keesings Record of World Events* and the *New York Times Index*.

14. This is not a complete inventory of conflict preventive multilateral instruments. There are, for instance, a number of such institutions at the regional level, particularly in Europe and North America. The cited categories should be understood as three principal models, each of which produces a preventive impact in a somewhat different way.

15. The three latest GATT rounds were initiated by the United States. It is significant to note that a main motive behind the U.S. initiative was a need to cope with trade problems pertaining to the EU-U.S. relationship.

16. A considerable number of member states have already been assessed in country reviews; see, for instance, GATT 1996.

17. The rules of a trade regime are specified in the legally binding Articles of the World Trade Organization, in the same way that they were stipulated in the General Agreement on Tariffs and Trade.

References

Baldwin, R. 1986. *The New Protectionism: A Response to Shifts in National Economic Power.* Cambridge, Mass.: NBER.

Baldwin, R., and C. Hamilton, eds. 1988. *Issues in US-EC Trade Relations.* Chicago: University of Chicago Press.

Bercovitch, J., and J. Z. Rubin, eds. 1992. *Mediation in International Relations: Multiple Approaches to Conflict Management.* New York: St. Martin's.

Bhagwati, J. 1991. *The World Trading System at Risk.* New York: Harvester/Wheatsheaf.

Brégeon, J., and F. Luchaire. 1988. "Quelle défense économique." *Défense nationale* 44, no. 12 (December): 93–100.

Chayes, A., and A. Chayes. 1995. *The New Sovereignty: Compliance with International Regulatory Agreements.* Cambridge, Mass.: Harvard University Press.

Chen, T.-J. 1995. *Bilateral Negotiations and Multilateral Trade: The Case of Taiwan-US Trade Talks.* Cambridge, Mass.: National Bureau of Economic Research.

Choi, Y.-P., S. C. Hwa, and N. Marian, eds. 1995. *The Multi-Fibre Arrangement in Theory and Practice.* London: Frances Pinter.

Conybeare, J. 1987. *Trade Wars: The Theory and Practice of International Commercial Rivalry.* New York: Columbia University Press.

Cortright, D., and G. Lopez, eds. 1995. *Economic Sanctions: Panacea of Peacebuilding in a Post–Cold War World.* Boulder: Westview.

Croome, J. 1995. *Reshaping the World Trading System: A History of the Uruguay Round.* Geneva: World Trade Organization.

Dam, K. 1970. *The GATT: Law and International Economic Organization.* Chicago: University of Chicago.

Dobson, W. 1991. *Economic Policy Coordination: Requiem or Prologue?* Washington, D.C.: Institute for International Economics.

Doxey, M. 1996. *International Sanctions in Contemporary Perspective.* Basingstoke, England: Macmillan.

Eichengreen, B., ed. 1996. *The Reconstruction of the International Economy, 1945–1960.* Cheltenham, England: Elgar.

Forland, T. 1991. *Cold Economic Warfare. The Creation and Prime of CoCom, 1948–1954.* Oslo: University of Oslo.

GATT. 1986. *The Contracting Parties to the General Agreement on Tariffs and Trade.* Geneva: GATT.

———. 1996. *Trade Policy Review: Brazil (1996).* Geneva: General Agreement on Tariffs and Trade.

Gilpin, R. 1987. *The Political Economy of International Relations.* Princeton: Princeton University Press.

Haas, E. 1990. *When Knowledge Is Power: Three Models of Change in International Organizations.* Berkeley: University of California Press.

Hamilton, C., ed. 1990. *Textiles Trade and the Developing Countries: Eliminating the Multi-Fibre Arrangement.* Washington, D.C.: World Bank.

Hasenclever, A., P. Mayer, and V. Rittberger. 1997. *Theories of International Regimes.* Cambridge: Cambridge University Press.

Hudec, R. 1993. *Enforcing International Trade Law: The Evolution of the Modern GATT Legal System.* Salem, N.H.: Butterworth Legal.

Hufbauer, G., J. Schott, and K. Elliot. 1990. *Economic Sanctions Reconsidered.* Washington, D.C.: Institute for International Economics.

Jackson, J. 1996. *GATT and the World Trade Organization.* London: Royal Institute of International Affairs.

James, H. 1996. *International Monetary Cooperation Since Bretton Woods.* Washington, D.C.: International Monetary Fund.

JETRO. 1991. *Handy Facts on EC-Japan Economic Relations.* Tokyo: JETRO.

Josling, T. 1996. *Agriculture in GATT.* Basingstoke, England: Macmillan.

Kindleberger, C. 1987. *The World in Depression.* Harmondsworth, England: Penguin.

Kleiboer, M. 1997. *International Mediation: The Multiple Realities of Third-Party Intervention.* Boulder: Lynne Rienner.

Krasner, S., ed. 1983. *International Regimes.* Ithaca: Cornell University Press.

Krueger, A. 1995. *Trade Policies and Developing Nations.* Washington, D.C.: Brookings.

Lemesle, R.-M. 1996. *La Convention de Lomé: Principaux objectifs et examples d'action, 1975–1995.* Paris: CHEAM.

Levy, M., O. Young, and M. Zürn. 1996. *The Study of International Regimes.* Laxenburg, Austria: IIASA.

Lusztig, M. 1996. *Risking Free Trade: The Politics of Free Trade in Britain, Canada, Mexico and the United States.* Pittsburgh: Pittsburgh University Press.

Mailafia, O. 1997. *Europe and Economic Reform in Africa: Structural Adjustment and Economic Diplomacy.* London: Routledge.

Mason, D., and A. Turay, eds. 1991. *US-Japan Trade Friction: Its Impact on Security Cooperation in the Pacific Basin.* Basingstoke, England: Macmillan.

Petersmann, E. U. 1997. *The GATT/WTO Dispute Settlement System: International Law, International Organizations and Dispute Settlement.* London: Kluwer Law International.

Preeg, E. 1970. *Traders and Diplomats: An Analysis of the Kennedy Round of Negotiations Under the General Agreement on Tariffs and Trade.* Washington, D.C.: Brookings.

204   Gunnar Sjöstedt

Ray, E. 1989. *US Protectionism and the World Debt Crisis.* New York: Quorum.

Robinson, S. 1996. *The Politics of International Crisis Escalation: Decision-Making Under Pressure.* London: Tauris Academic Studies.

Simons, G. 1996. *The Scourging of Iraq: Sanctions, Law and Natural Justice.* Basingstoke, England: Macmillan.

Sjöstedt, G., and B. Sundelius, eds. 1986. *Free Trade—Managed Trade? Perspectives on a Realistic International Trade Order.* Boulder: Westview.

Spector, B., G. Sjöstedt, and I. W. Zartman, eds. 1994. *Negotiating International Regimes: Lessons Learned from the United Nations Conference on Environment and Development (UNCED).* London: Graham & Trotman/Martinus Nijhoff.

Tumlir, J. 1985. *Protectionism: Trade Policy in Democratic Societies.* Washington, D.C.: American Institute for Public Policy Research.

Vermulst, E. 1987. *Antidumping Law and Practice in the United States and the European Communities: A Comparative Analysis.* Amsterdam: North-Holland.

Wiener, J. 1995. *Making Rules in the Uruguay Round of the GATT: A Study of International Leadership.* Aldershot, England: Dartmouth.

Winham, G. 1986. *International Trade and the Tokyo Round Negotiations.* Princeton: Princeton University Press.

Zartman, I. W., ed. 1994. *International Multilateral Negotiation: Approaches to the Management of Complexity.* San Francisco: Jossey-Bass.

9

Transboundary Disputes: Keeping Backyards Clean

Bertram Spector

Transboundary problems often contain the seeds for both conflict and cooperation. Such problems can be perceived as threatening the well-being, the security, and even the sovereignty of a nation, stimulating hostile and conflictual responses. Yet a transboundary dispute may be resolvable through cooperative, interdependent action among the states that share the problem. Negotiation used early and preventatively can generate a consensus for integrative solutions.

Many transboundary issues—including drug trafficking, population migration, support to insurgency movements, organized crime, and energy or economic development projects situated near a border—can cause tension between states. In recent years, environmental and resource concerns have been among the most prominent of such transboundary issues. They hold the potential for unleashing interstate conflict and regional instability, but if conditions are ripe and if political willingness and technological capacity are available, conflicts can be prevented or mitigated through cooperative mechanisms such as negotiation. Environmental early warning indicators and the use of preventive techniques including negotiation can help to halt the maturation of disputes beyond critical thresholds, thus reducing the severity of potential security problems (Lonergan, Gustavson, and Harrower 1997). This chapter focuses on the use of negotiation as a preventive mechanism when environmental threats jeopardize security.

The relatively new field of environmental security (Homer-Dixon 1994; Spector et al. 1996; Woodrow Wilson Center 1995, 1996) examines several competing, multidimensional models that seek to explain the conditions under which transboundary environmental problems evolve into interstate or intrastate conflicts. Researchers are also beginning to explore the use of preventive mechanisms to avert the negative consequences of disputes at an early stage. A multinational North American Treaty Organization (NATO)/Partnership for Peace research project is under way to examine the policy options available to deal with environmentally unstable situations that may threaten national security.[1] This project adds the related policy concept of "preventive defense" to the concept of "preventive diplomacy." Within the U.S. government, several agencies, including the Central Intelligence Agency, the National Security Council, the National Intelligence Council, the Department of Defense, and the State Department, have all begun to examine the policy options available in the face of environmentally provoked threats (Marcus and Brauchli 1997).

Environmental stresses usually do not operate alone. Along with social, political, economic, military, ethnic, and cultural factors, they trigger or contribute to the emergence of risks to the national security and well-being of the state. Results of one of the major research projects on the subject (Homer-Dixon and Percival 1996) suggest that environmental scarcity is rarely the *sole and direct* cause of violent conflict (except in the case of shared river waters, in which dams or other water-related projects have caused major relocations of peoples that yield violent conflicts and turmoil). Rather, environmental problems influence conflict *indirectly* through secondary political, social, and economic effects.

For example, security risks may be triggered by environmental scarcities. Those scarcities may cause economic decline, decreased agricultural production, or population migration, which, in turn, may generate civil strife, insurgencies, and state collapse. The triggering environmental elements and the subsequent effects are often transboundary problems, involving shared water, land, or atmosphere and the cross-border migration of population groups.

This chapter examines models, issues, and cases that can help to explain the nature and utility of negotiation approaches as preventive mechanisms in situations with the potential to spark transboundary environmental conflict. It explores the various schools of thought on the relationship between environmental problems and conflict. The chapter also turns to the preconditions for and processes of preventive negotiation—a reframing of the stakes, attitudes, and tactics needed for pre-emptive problem solving.

Characterizing Transboundary Environmental Problems

Significant changes in the characteristics or utilization of environmental resources in one country that have negative consequences for a neighboring country or region give rise to transboundary environmental security conflicts (Trolldalen 1992). Difficulties can arise from the mere perception of a change, as well, if one party believes another has caused a deviation from what was considered a mutually acceptable environmental baseline (Shaw et al. 1997).

Negative environmental changes can be natural or caused by humans. If the changes are a result of natural events (floods or droughts, for example) or if they stem from unpremeditated human actions (for instance, the deposit of toxic industrial emissions across a border due to a shift in wind patterns), then the affected countries share a joint problem. If, however, the changes are premeditated, such as the diversion of a river flow or the siting of a nuclear plant at a border, then a hostile action has occurred. In both situations, negotiation can be used to address the resulting problems and avert further risks. But depending on the origins and extent of the negative environmental change, the parties' framing of the problem and their degree of cooperation is likely to influence how the negotiations progress and whether an integrative solution is possible.

Four categories of environmental change can result in potential transboundary problems:

1. Degradation (pollution)
2. Scarcity (shortage)
3. Maldistribution (inequitable allocation)
4. Disaster or accident (natural or caused by humans)

Each of these problem categories involves an important change from a previous status quo marking the availability of environmental resources. When these resources are shared among countries and their availability becomes threatened, the potential for transboundary conflict exists. But a change in environmental resource availability is not inherently a cause for conflict; as a growing literature demonstrates, such changes may also enhance the potential for increased cooperation among nations (Elhance 1996b).

But environmental change is a continuous natural occurrence. What distinguishes trivial and significant environmental changes? *Reference values* identify the thresholds at which changes over time in environmental indicators are transformed from being beneficial or neutral to being negative, costly, unsafe, or risk-provoking along some dimension (World Bank 1995). These values are popularly thought of as benchmarks, standards, or rules of thumb that clearly differentiate when an indicator that is being monitored has changed in a major, stepwise way and represents the early stages of regime building.

Reference values for key environmental indicators can be conceived of in three ways. First, they can simply be scientific expressions. For example, the availability of a certain amount of water may be determined as the basic minimum human requirement for sustainable health in a particular country. If the country can deliver to its population more than the reference value, it is operating in a sustainable fashion. If, however, it fails to deliver up to the level of this reference value, human suffering may ensue, and stability and security will be negatively affected. Second, reference values may be conceived of in terms of policy targets. These reference values usually place scientific evidence in the context of a country's economic interests, technological capacity, and political will. The result is a policy target that is sought by the country. Most international environmental agreements and national environmental laws and regulations specify such targets. Third, the public perception of an environmental threshold can sometimes play a more significant role than the scientific benchmark or policy target. For example, let us say that it is scientifically determined that 50 liters of water per person per day is the basic minimum human requirement. If a country that typically consumes 150 liters of water per person per day suddenly experiences a drop in available supply to 75 liters (still above the basic minimum), a perceived reference value may be reached and the perception of scarcity may be high, even though the scientific minimum has not been reached. However, if a country that consumes 55 liters per day drops to 45 (below the minimum), the impact may not be perceived as severe enough to trigger a crisis even though the population may sense the change.

In these three conceptions, reference values help to establish a foundation against which to judge the meaning of changes in environmental trends (Hammond et al. 1995). They make it easier to assign policy significance to indicators and to knowledgeably interpret change. They assign meaning to increases or decreases in environmental indicators, thus offering the ability to analyze such trends against policy goals and make meaningful comparisons over time and across regions or countries. The consequences of environmental change can be viewed in terms of improving or worsening environmental problems that, in and of themselves, may present a threat, generate the conditions for increased threat, or influence other contextual factors, which, in combination, may trigger a larger security or instability problem (Tunstall, Hammond, and Henninger 1994).

Several examples help characterize how environmental change can be captured through reference values. Reviewing a wide range of scientific studies that assessed the minimum water requirements for human and ecological functions, Peter Gleick (1996) concluded that, on average, basic needs (water for drinking, for human hygiene, for sanitation services, and for household needs in preparing food) can be met at 50 liters per person per day, contingent on climate and distance from the water source. If a country's provision of water falls below that threshold, as happens in fifty-five nations, "large-scale human misery and suffering will continue and grow in the future, contributing to the risk of social and military conflict" (p. 83).

The United Nations Commission on Sustainable Development (1996) has recently produced a set of over 130 sustainable development indicators and identified "targets" for most of the indicators. These targets are a mixture of scientific benchmarks and policy goals that are based on scientific rules of thumb. Some examples of these targets include:

- The wood-harvesting intensity required to maintain a sustainable yield of timber—not more than 70 to 80 percent of the total annual increment of forests

- The optimal amount of biodiversity-protected area as a percentage of total area—not less than 10 percent protected area for each major ecological region in a country as a percentage of the total area
- The desirable reduction in greenhouse-gas emissions—no less than an immediate 60 percent reduction in emissions is required to stabilize atmospheric concentrations of carbon dioxide at present levels

Other benchmarks are set for fisheries, greenhouse-gas concentrations, emissions of sulfur oxide and nitrogen oxide, ozone-depleting substances, and World Health Organization (WHO) air-quality guidelines in urban areas. Additionally, many scientifically based targets for particular environmental indicators are set forth in Agenda 21, in international agreements, and in national legislation. Preventive action in the form of negotiations may be useful if the monitoring of such reference values reveals negative trends.

The characteristic that is central to all of these trends is that they easily spill over borders, not via military attack but by processes that are both nontransparent and difficult to recognize in the early stages. Change in environmental features (such as alterations in freshwater access, environmental accidents, changes in the disposal and handling of hazardous or nuclear wastes, increasing transboundary pollution, greater soil erosion, intensified deforestation, and accelerated climate change) can directly or indirectly harm a bordering nation, thereby redistributing costs. In these cases, *both* countries usually lose; in fact, transboundary environmental disputes are often negative-sum situations.

Characterizing Water Conflicts in the Middle East: An Example

Issues surrounding the availability of transboundary water in the Middle East offer a good example of how environmental change can evolve into actual and perceived environmental threats to interstate security.[2] Shared freshwater resources have long been a source of both local and regional conflict in the Middle East. Indeed, water, more so than land, is often believed to hold the key to peace in the region. In the contemporary Middle East, the volatile politics, unfavorable demographics, and limited quantity of freshwater may combine in the future to bring many of the region's water conflicts to a crisis point.

Water shortages represent a primary issue of concern, as the region's population increases and economic development leads to greater industrial and agricultural demand for water. At this time, only Iraq and Lebanon have adequate water resources relative to their populations. In most other countries of the region, withdrawals exceed renewable supplies (World Bank 1993, 9). Pressure on the water supply comes primarily from irrigation. In Jordan, the West Bank, and Israel, where water demand exceeds supply by 20 to 50 percent, approximately two-thirds of this water is used in agriculture (Clawson 1992, 87). Given the present inefficiences in water use by the agricultural sector, there is some hope that technical solutions and a redirecting of water resources may resolve future water shortages. However, shifting resources out of the agricultural sector runs up against political and cultural obstacles.

Meanwhile, the demand for water in urban areas is expanding rapidly as well. Given current population projections, most experts predict that by 2020, renewable water supplies absorbed by urban areas will need to increase between 10 to 20 percent or more simply to maintain present use rates (World Bank 1993, 9). Incidental demographic changes will tax water resources in the region even more. And further progress in the peace process is expected to increase immigration into Israel and the West Bank and Gaza Strip; following the Gulf War, Jordan absorbed three hundred thousand Palestinians from Kuwait (Wolf and Ross 1992, 957). These numbers mean a greater drain on already overtaxed water resources.

Degradation of water quality is another major source of contention in the region. Water quality can be compromised through the seepage of untreated domestic and industrial waste, landfill and saline agricultural drainage from the surface into water bodies, and overdrafts of groundwater that result in intrusions from the sea.

Conflicts over the *ownership and usage of surface (river) water* focus on three major watersheds: the Jordan, the Nile, and the Tigris-Euphrates Rivers. The Jordan River is relatively small, but it supplies five riparians—Lebanon, Jordan, Syria, Israel, and the Palestinian territories. Control of the Jordan and its headwaters to the north has played a role in prompting some of the region's most intense conflicts, and allocation of the water's use is the subject of multilateral negotiations in the Arab-Israeli peace process. In the Nile basin, water abundance is coming to an end. Increasing population, economic growth, environmental degradation, and climatic change have all combined to put pressure on water resources in the valley. Egypt is extremely vulnerable to unilateral upstream withdrawals by Sudan and Ethiopia, who, in turn, are concerned about the legal implications of Egypt's desert reclamation plans, making future negotiations over Nile waters more complex (Waterbury 1979). In the Tigris and Euphrates valleys, Turkey possesses the most commanding riparian position and the greatest military power (Naff and Matson 1984, 96). Exploiting the Euphrates for hydroelectric power and irrigation holds appeal for Turkey as a means of developing the long-neglected southeastern part of the country, but the Southern Anatolian Project would significantly reduce water flow to Syria and Iraq, causing tension among the three nations.

Conflicts also occur over the *control and use of groundwater*. For example, the natural recharge areas for groundwater supplying both Israel and the West Bank are situated in the mountainous center of the West Bank. Two-thirds of the West Bank water resources are used inside Israel, supplying one-third of Israel's total water needs. An overdraft of groundwater resources in the West Bank would result in saltwater intrusion along Israel's coastal plain and eventually into the mountain aquifers (Wolf and Ross 1992, 944). However, since

1967, the Palestinian population on the West Bank has increased by 84 percent, yet Palestinian access to water has increased by only 20 percent. Establishing an agreement on the equitable use of the aquifers will become a vital element in any peace plan for the establishment of a self-governing Palestinian entity in the West Bank.

Disputes among government authorities, local communities, industry, farmers, and nongovernmental organizations (NGOs) over *water access* can also result in tensions and instability. The siting of wastewater treatment plants, development of sewer systems, establishment of wastewater treatment standards for irrigation reuse, operation of irrigation systems, regulation of private groundwater wells, and municipal water supply issues are public policy matters that concern many local stakeholders with conflicting interests. If all the stakeholders participate early on in efforts to resolve these issues, they are less likely to later perceive that a policy has been imposed on them or that they have somehow been coerced—perceptions that could lead to friction and civil unrest.

Water disputes in the Middle East are, in large part, couched in terms of *ownership rights*. Most attempts at preventive diplomacy to date have tried to settle the issue of rights. The Johnston Plan, formulated between 1953 to 1955 between riparians of the Jordan River, provided water allocations that have generally held to this day, with adjustments worked out by U.S. negotiator Philip Habib in the early 1980s. As a consequence of the Johnston Plan, Israel and Jordan have sent technical representatives to regular "picnic table talks" to work out day-to-day hydrologic operations. Another example of successful negotiation is the 1959 Nile Waters Agreement between Egypt and Sudan. Despite its disproportionate quota ratios favoring Egypt, the agreement has promoted cooperative development, allowed for construction of the Aswan Dam, and established a legal basis for water usage between the two countries. Nevertheless, economic analysis suggests that, however important such rights may be, water ownership and water usage are analytically independent and should not be confused (Fisher 1994). Ownership is a win-lose proposition, but by using the alternate definition of the problem as one of water usage, creative and collaborative problem solving and negotiation may be possible.

Linkage Models of Environmental Change and Conflict

Recently, several conceptual models have been developed to explain when and why the preceding elements of environmental change had to conflict. Each model has different implications for preventive negotiations.

Probably the most popular framework is the *scarcity model* (Homer-Dixon 1994),[3] which holds that three factors produce environmental scarcity: depletion and degradation of a country's natural resource supply, increased demand for and consumption of resources, and uneven distribution of those resources among the population. The resulting scarcity can affect other economic, social, or cultural conditions in a country. For example, agricultural production can decline, economic hardship can increase, migration can occur, ethnic tensions can flare, and already weak governments can fail. These effects, in turn, can lead to violent conflict. Disputes resulting from the dearth of freshwater in the Middle East are often cited as examples of the scarcity model. Preventive diplomacy based on this model's logic would seek to change the stakes by increasing or redistributing resources to yield an allocation that levels the playing field and reduces the potential for conflict between states.

A competing framework is the *modernization model,* which is based on the assumption that the push for economic growth and development in less developed countries can lead to an overly intensive use of natural resources and pollution of the environment (Porter and Brown 1996; Trolldalen 1992). The Rio Conference on Environment and Development in 1992 addressed these problems of unsustainable economic development. For example, heavy industrial and municipal waste discharges and the degradation of the water supply in cities along the Black Sea coast have created potential conflicts among the littoral states and spurred cooperative programs to avert conflict. Preemptive negotiations based on this model would seek to change the stakes and create environmental sustainability through technological advancements, investments, and the assistance of foreign donors.

According to the *spillover model,* environmental conflicts begin as domestic disputes but quickly cross boundaries to cause disputes with other countries (Wilkenfeld 1973). In the process, the nature of the conflict may change from an environmental problem to a social, economic, or political dispute. For example, the deforestation that occurred in Haiti to supply firewood to the population resulted in massive soil erosion and unreclaimable agricultural land. As a consequence, a large proportion of the population migrated from the countryside to the cities and then fled by boat to the United States. Prominent pre-emptive solutions in this model are attitudinal, often involving socioeconomic responses to change lifestyles or reduce excessive population growth so that transboundary environmental risks do not create unmanageable and unstable situations.

Finally, the *leading-edge model* depicts environmental problems as the trigger for "hotter" conflicts brewing under the surface or as the straw that breaks the camel's back (Trolldalen 1992). For example, Senegal and Mauritania have often been at odds because of the scarcity of arable agricultural land and the threat of drought in the Senegal River valley. In 1989, disputes over claims to arable land triggered a spiral of retaliatory attacks that severely threatened regional stability, caused the deaths of hundreds, and turned thousands of citizens into refugees. The implied solution set for this model is tactical—to deal with the latent conflicts in the early stages.

Although each of these models has merit, each also exhibits certain flaws (Gleditsch 1998). First, each model focuses on a certain set of factors that are deemed critical in explaining conflictual outcomes produced by transboundary environmental problems, and each ignores factors that are seen as significant in the others. A synthesized model would be more useful. Second, many of these models ignore situational conditions that either facilitate, inhibit, or moderate the impact of the environmental problems. Third, these models generally assume that environmental disputes will yield violent outcomes, but research has instead shown that (1) although environmental problems may be important contributors or triggers of transboundary disputes, adding fuel to the fire in political, economic, ethnic, or military disputes, they rarely operate in isolation, and (2) transboundary problems may, in fact, stimulate the principal disputants to seek interstate cooperative solutions, avoiding conflictual (let alone violent) outcomes altogether.

Negotiations Concerning Transboundary Threats

The catch-22 of any preventive diplomatic effort is gaining the principal parties' *early recognition and acceptance* of the fact that they face a sufficiently dangerous and imminent threat, even though the effects of that threat have yet to be experienced or, if nothing were done, might never emerge. The principal parties must reframe their stakes in the situation, their attitudes about the conflict and the other side, and the tactics and timetable they will use to deal with the problem. Moreover, both the leaders and their domestic constituencies must be willing to reframe the situation perceptually. Leaders cannot easily begin negotiations and make compromises on problems that their constituencies do not believe are imminent and dangerous. It may be difficult, for instance, to convince constituencies that taking precautionary action against a potential "resource grab" by a neighboring country is better than waiting, since the predicted worst outcome (violent conflict) has not yet happened and may never occur at all.

Another precondition for preventive action is the recognition of *superordinate goals* (Sherif 1967). States affected by the transboundary environmental problem could take a conflictual path and escalate the dispute, or they could take a problem-solving path, seeking to resolve the environmental problem through joint, interdependent action. In many cases, the transboundary nature of the problem makes it impossible for only one party to effectively and independently deal with the environmental root cause. For example, if riparian states control access to or pollution of a shared river system, cooperative action may be the only way to resolve the environmental resource availability problem. Self-interest is met through a recognition of transboundary superordinate goals.

Preventive action must also take place in the *"potential" and limited stages of the dispute,* when it is still possible to avert conflict; otherwise, actions become only postemergent containment. Environmental problems that begin as disparate, localized, and low-level conflicts of interest (incipient conflicts) may, over time, fester and induce secondary socioeconomic-political effects in the country and in the region and ultimately emerge as manifest conflicts (Trolldalen 1992). Early recognition that transboundary environmental change carries a potential security threat is a critical requirement in commencing negotiations and orienting them preventatively. In addition, threats can escalate through space as well as time. Localized conflicts can rise to national and then regional levels, drawing in new disputants, issues, and complexities at each stage. Prevention is easiest if the dispute is dealt with at the local levels.

Negotiation intervention is appropriate at several points and can be accomplished in several ways:

- *By dealing directly with the anticipated environmental problems.* Negotiations can deal with the transboundary environmental change itself, a change that might result in scarcity, degradation, maldistribution, or disaster.
- *By treating conditions associated with the environmental problem.* Negotiations can deal with secondary conditions that, if left untreated, could lead to environmental problems and disputes, including socioeconomic conditions that might aggravate problems and cause them to escalate. This category of negotiations is concerned, for example, with development assistance, technology transfer, investment, economic assistance, and social development assistance.
- *By addressing the security threats involved.* Negotiations can address the transformation of the environmental problems into national security problems—for instance, by dealing with population migration and resulting ethnic unrest rather than with the scientific aspects of the environmental issues.

The general purpose of negotiation mechanisms used to prevent the escalation of transboundary environmental threats is to build regimes through *norm creation* or *norm adjustment,* finding agreed principles of conduct within a particular policy area. Abiding by such norms and participating in the regimes that maintain and govern them over time is the preferred approach to averting future transboundary problems triggered by environmental change.[4]

Negotiations to create new norms are the building blocks of new regimes; they are the institutional structures by which norms are maintained over time. The recent proliferation of regimes, especially concerning environmental issues, suggests the international community is increasingly interested in norm creation as a preventive tool to resolve environmental problems and stop them from escalating into major transboundary threats. Such negotiations may be spurred by the scientific identification of a transboundary environmental problem, such as the ozone hole or global warming; sometimes, negotiations may be stimulated by a sudden crisis, such as the nuclear accident at Chernobyl in 1985. Negotiations to create new norms involve the participation of new nontraditional actors (such as nongovernmental organizations), multiple linked issue sets, coalition building, consensus formation, and the policy assessment of continually changing scientific information, among other factors (Spector, Sjöstedt, and Zartman 1994b).

Where norms already exist, postagreement negotiations can be conducted to adjust or extend them. Broadly stated norms may require additional specification over time, and if scientific knowledge increases or the results of past action are evaluated, a major change or extension of existing norms may be recommended, again warranting further negotiation. Negotiations to modify existing norms have their own dynamics (Spector, Sjöstedt, and Zartman 1994a). They operate at the international and domestic levels simultaneously and deal more with implementing details than establishing new formulas. Within the context of existing agreements and relationships, they address issues that have proven to be the sticking points in previous negotiations.

In the sector of transboundary water resources alone, over two thousand treaty instruments and regimes establish norms and seek to govern primarily bilateral relationships concerning transboundary waterways in a cooperative and preventive manner (McCaffrey 1993). Across these instruments, common expectations, principles of justice, and norms of behavior have developed between states to prevent conflicts (Zartman et al. 1996). Most reflect the principle of "equitable utilization," whereby the use and benefits of the shared water resource are apportioned in an "equitable" manner. Another basic norm established in these treaties is the principle of doing no harm, that is, that no state should engage in activities concerning waterways that would negatively affect other states using them.

The institutionalization of norms through regional and international regimes has fended off potentially critical environmental security threats. For example, the 1986 Vienna Convention on Early Notification of Nuclear Accidents developed a mechanism for the rapid exchange of information when nuclear accidents occur to avoid the spread of misinformation and the generation of crises. Similarly, the multilateral talks on Middle East water issues focus on developing preventive norms and actions that will help to avert the evolution of violent conflicts. One case of true preventive negotiations concerns the Zambezi River system: Negotiations have led to the creation of a regional regime to manage the economic development of shared water resources among eight riparian states far in advance of even the symptoms of transboundary conflict.

Examples of Preventive Negotiation
Concerning Transboundary Water Problems

Selected examples from water or water-related resource use are offered here to illustrate how negotiation mechanisms have been employed in a preventive fashion to reduce transboundary environmental threats to security. Examples could also be drawn from other environmental domains—land resources, forestry, biodiversity, desertification, atmosphere—but more research is available on interstate problems related to water.

Over two hundred river basins in the world are shared by two or more sovereign states, but few formal treaties or accords exist to govern the joint use of their resources (Elhance 1996b). Thus, there are many opportunities for incompatible goals and conflicts to develop. The examples that follow are limited to negotiation and mediation efforts undertaken to forestall overt interstate conflicts stemming from environmental change.[5]

The Aral basin includes five states that share the Aral Sea and the catchment and drainage areas of the two major rivers that drain into the sea—Kazakhstan, Kyrgyzstan, Tajikistan, Turkmenistan, and Uzbekistan. In 1991, these five states agreed to deal with their growing problems of water shortages, desertification, and environmental degradation—specifically, poor water- and land-management practices, water and land pollution resulting from the use of agrochemicals, and water-intensive agricultural practices (Elhance 1996a). The many economic and resource dependencies that exist among these five countries heighten the potential for escalating conflict as a result of severe environmental problems. In fact, several internal armed conflicts in recent years can be attributed to water-related problems—between Kyrgyz and Tajiks in Kyrgyzstan (1989) and in the Osh region of Kyrgyzstan (1990). The 1991 agreement developed a regime with a set of procedures and mechanisms that seek to resolve conflicts over shared transboundary water resources; the regime is based on the principle of equality among the five states in terms of exploiting their common resources. What motivated the agreement was a mutual understanding of the potential for both severe environmental conditions and the secondary conflicts that might emerge as a result. The opportunity to secure significant rewards—an influx of financial and technical assistance—from national and international donors was a significant complementary motive. An important catalyst influencing the operation of the agreement has been the development of nongovernmental organizations that work at a micro level to effect change.

The Zambezi River System Action Plan (ZACPLAN), concluded in 1987, encompasses eight riparian states—Angola, Namibia, Zambia, Zimbabwe, Botswana, Congo, Malawi, and Mozambique. Remarkably, the negotiations that resulted in this regime were conducted in the absence of any major manifest conflict over the Zambezi among the signatories; prevention of transboundary environmental conflict clearly is the regime's watchword. However, the latent potential for disputes was recognized, and the various parties wanted to establish mechanisms to deal with possible future conflicts (Trolldalen 1992). As the area's population grows, the associated food demand will increase, and improved living standards will raise the level of water use; therefore, there is a heightened risk of perceived resource grabs, unsustainable development projects (especially for generating hydroelectric power), environmental pollution, and environmental conflicts.

Some of the motivation to negotiate a cooperative river-management regime was generated externally. First, the United Nations Environment Program (UNEP) promoted such a regional regime within its Environmentally Sound Management of Inland Waters Program, and it provided initial funding for ecological studies and workshops. Other external donors (including several Nordic countries) expressed interest in funding the new regime's activities. Second, the Southern African Development Coordination Conference (SADCC), a regional organization, offered its services to include the regime under its umbrella. This placed ZACPLAN within an existing transboundary framework in which dialogue, rather than conflict and competition, was the norm. Third, there was a common external "enemy"—South Africa—which served to unify the riparian states in a common goal to limit South African dominance in the region and to counter the proposed South African water diversion projects (including the Chobe-Vaal Water Project) that threatened downstream countries. Together, these factors helped the riparian nations reframe their interests and attitudes and stimulated the preventive negotiations that resulted in the establishment of the regime.

Another transboundary environmental dispute, the U.S.-Mexico tuna conflict, emerged in 1990 when Washington unilaterally restricted the import of yellowfin tuna from Mexico. The authorities cited a U.S. law, the Marine Mammal Protection Act, that imposes import restrictions on tuna caught in purse seine nets, which catch and drown dolphins as they snare tuna (Trolldalen 1992). Mexico filed a complaint with the contracting parties to the General Agreement on Tariffs and Trade (GATT) under its dispute-resolution provisions. A panel established to arbitrate the dispute found that U.S. domestic laws restricting imports from other countries were contrary to GATT, an agreement to which the United States is a signatory; the United States was then asked to bring its domestic law into conformity with its obligations under GATT. As a result of the finding, GATT has begun a major reassessment of the relationship between environment and trade. In this case, a transboundary conflict was adjudicated within the framework of an existing regime. Although a conflict actually had to emerge before the regime's dispute-resolution provisions came into play, the fact that GATT was in place and the complaint could be aired before its representatives early on prevented the dispute from festering and escalating. As a consequence, the nature of the finding put a new process in motion that is likely to reshape the regime itself and yield postagreement negotiations within GATT aimed at modifying its norms, principles, and procedures.

The Canada-Spain fishing dispute arose in 1995 over fishing rights beyond the 200-nautical-mile zone of Canada. Canada fired warning shots at a Spanish fishing vessel in the Grand Banks off Newfoundland, impounded the vessel, and arrested the captain on charges that Spain was systematically disregarding an agreement negotiated through the Northwest Atlantic Fisheries Organization (NAFO), which established catch quotas for the European Union and Canada. Spain sought to bring the matter up for adjudication before the International Court, but Canada withdrew its recognition of the court's jurisdiction over the fishery. Spain then sought EU sanctions against Canada but ran into opposition from other EU members. Ultimately, negotiations conducted directly between the EU and Canada defused the situation by increasing the catch quota available to the EU but at the same time enhancing the monitoring and enforcement provisions of the NAFO agreement to prevent cheating on the quotas. Again, negotiations were conducted within the context of a regime in which the disputing parties had made previous commitments. The regime mechanism was not capable of preventing the conflict, but it *was* able to provide a diplomatic mechanism by which escalation could be averted.

The seeds for violent conflict between India and Pakistan over the Indus River were planted in the 1948 partition of the region (McDonald 1988). After years of tension, the Indus Water Treaty was signed in 1960 under the mediative leadership of the World Bank, which offered major financial support to the two protagonists. The bank also persuaded Australia, Canada, New Zealand, West Germany, the United Kingdom, and the United States to pledge substantial grants and loans to India and Pakistan to induce them to cooperate.

The Beagle Channel dispute over three islands between Argentina and Chile was mediated by the Vatican (McDonald 1988). Hostilities were imminent in 1978 when the mediation efforts began, but the pope's moral authority and pledge of confidentiality helped to produce a treaty in 1985.

The Icelandic fisheries dispute began in 1958 when Iceland announced that it was extending its territorial limits from 4 to 12 miles offshore, thus constraining UK fishing (McDonald 1988). Several incidents ensued, involving the exchange of gunfire between UK trawlers and destroyers and the Icelandic coast guard. The matter was raised at the Law of the Sea Conference in 1960, but the parties to the dispute were directed to conduct bilateral talks to resolve this matter. Agreement was reached in 1961 to restructure the status of the territorial dispute, whereby the United Kingdom accepted Icelandic sovereignty over the expanded limits but Iceland provided special waivers for UK fishing in those waters during several months of the year.

In 1968, Uruguay announced the planned development of oil and natural gas fields on the continental shelf under the Plata estuary (McDonald 1988). Argentina protested, laid claim to the territory, and occupied it. Through negotiations, an agreement was crafted in 1973 that facilitated joint economic exploitation of the oil resources, established the legal boundary between the countries as the middle of the river, distributed the territory of the river's islands, and provided for the international use of the river's channels.

Construction of the Gabicikovo and Nagymaros Dams on the Danube River in Slovakia and Hungary, respectively, began in the 1970s and was almost completed in the early 1990s, just as the Cold War was ending. At that point, Hungary decided it did not want the dams to be put into operation, ostensibly because of their negative environmental impact but more deeply because of ethnic-related, legal, and economic conflicts between the two countries. In fact, Hungary made some provocative troop movements and threatened to go to war if Slovakia opened the dams. Direct negotiations between these two countries and then mediation by the European Union failed to avert or resolve the potentially violent conflict. Arbitration conducted by the International Court in The Hague finally defused the dispute (Fitzmaurice 1996).

In central Asia, the Kyrgyz Republic ran its hydroelectric dams all winter long to heat its cities; as a result, Uzbekistan and Kazakhstan were deprived of water for cotton planting in the spring (Marcus and Brauchli 1997). With the mediative assistance of the U.S. Agency for International Development, the three countries found a potential solution—the Uzbeks and Kazakhs promised to give Kyrgyz gas and coal in the winter if Kyrgyz agreed to accumulate water for the spring. However, this agreement has not been ratified by any of the parties, and tensions are still running high.

Many other shared water situations threaten to produce conflict and instability because of competition for limited resources or disputes over ownership (the Jordan, Litani, and Euphrates Rivers), because of the pollution of shared water by upstream nations (the Rhine and Mekong Rivers), and because of multiple competing interests in the use of river resources (the Mekong and Niger Rivers).

In the Ganges-Brahmaputra-Barak River basin, there are still no long-term, basinwide agreements among the five riparian states—Bangladesh, Bhutan, China, India, and Nepal—despite the continuous mediative efforts of the South Asian Association for Regional Cooperation (SAARC) (Elhance 1996b; Gyawali 2000). As a result of these failures, contentiousness persists among these countries, stemming from upstream/downstream tensions, flooding, drought, and population migration.

In the Nile River basin, no basinwide agreement has yet been devised among the ten riparian countries (Burundi, Ethiopia, Egypt, Eritrea, Kenya, Rwanda, Sudan, Tanzania, Uganda, and Zaire), despite decades of negotiation and mediation efforts (Elhance 1996b; Waterbury 1979). This has resulted in an extremely unstable situation in the region—unresolved territorial disputes, ideological and military rivalries, proxy wars during the Cold War era, growing ethnic conflicts that have burst into full-scale genocides, and the rise of religious fundamentalism.

Any negotiation process is driven toward outcomes through change—changes in the stakes and interests, attitudes and perceptions, and tactics of the negotiators. The environmental stakes and interests of the negotiating parties can be viewed from the perspective of how norms are created or modified. A review of the cases presented here shows an interesting pattern in this regard. New regimes and norms were developed successfully for the Aral basin, the Zambezi basin, the Indus River, the Beagle Channel, and the de la Plata River. The norms in these cases involved sharing and coordinating national efforts to ensure that the limited resource would be available to all parties according to some justice principle. Existing norms were appealed to or modified to deal successfully with emerging disputes over fisheries (the Canada-Spain incident, the UK-Iceland incident, and the U.S.-Mexico incident); these norms were reinforced or adjusted to change the way regime rules were monitored and applied. By contrast, norms were lacking in all of the failed or troubled cases (south Asia, central Asia, and the Nile basin).

It is not that the parties in the successful cases considered the stakes any less valuable. Perhaps the complexity deriving from the larger number of actors and issues involved in the failed cases has made it more difficult to resolve these disputes and to find a common set of norms (although some of the successful cases were similarly complex). Both imminent threats and overwhelming incentives helped to motivate movement in perceived stakes across many of the cases. In some, the environmental threats were well understood and alarming to the protagonists—the growing desertification of the Aral basin, the threat posed to dolphins by Mexican fishing practices, the flooding resulting from the Gabicikovo-Nagymaros Dams. And the likely costs of doing nothing or failing in preventive negotiations pushed the parties off their initial positions and moved them toward agreement.

It seems that the major rewards that could be accrued from successful negotiations were an even more powerful motive. Indeed, the promise of large-scale economic cooperation, technology transfer, and financial investment and assistance has proven to be highly motivating for many developing countries. Again, in the Aral basin, in the Zambezi basin, and for the Indus River riparians, large international and national donor programs helped reorient the protagonists' stakes in the conflict and pushed the process toward successful results. These incentives helped to achieve positive-sum outcomes and prevent crisis.

Environmental resources are things that can be owned. When such resources are in short supply, decreasing in number, or being degraded, disputes can be perceived as conflicts over the fixed stakes of those resources, fostering a distributive mind-set among the parties and a win-lose framework for negotiations. However, if the conflict can be reframed from one focusing on resource *ownership* to one highlighting resource *usage*, the pie of possible solutions is expanded. Integrative, win-win solutions become feasible within this reframing of the problem, as was demonstrated by the fishing disputes (via an increase in the catch quotas) and the de la Plata River case (via a clear distribution of the land territory but joint use and economic exploitation).

Changing Attitudes

Countries change their attitudes and perceptions in response to negotiation initiatives on environmental security threats because they want to be thought of as responsible partners in the family of nations. In such cases, countries may be willing to subsume sovereignty claims to achieve a common regional good in the hope of reaping certain specific rewards, such as foreign investment or foreign aid, that serve their self-interests. Such is certainly the case in the Aral and Zambezi basins.

In most of the cases, the protagonists recognize their vital interdependency. When there is a critical sharing of common environmental resources, nations come to recognize that only by appreciating their interdependency and releasing aspects of traditional sovereignty will a rational and sustainable availability of environmental resources be achieved. This both requires and inspires a modification of attitudes. The need to share scarce, degraded, or maldistributed resources is common to all the cases; a mutually accepted redistribution of the resources and a coordination of efforts are required to successfully deal with the problem at hand.

In each of the cases, the environmental trigger for the potential conflict has anthropogenic sources. Technological or redistributive solutions seem to be prominent and require coordinative and interdependent thinking and action. Parties in the cases seem to recognize that conflictual responses would not rid them of their common environmental problems; therefore, appeals to their interdependencies have a better chance of addressing the technological or redistributive options.

How can we identify the ripe moments for resolving these transboundary environmental conflicts? Timing is ripe when environmental security threats are dealt with early and at a local level and when those threats are directed against the initiating conditions of environmental change. A readiness to negotiate is also present when the affected countries possess the institutional capacity to overcome environmental stress, when a strong civil society exists to implement necessary changes, and when the required technology or substitutable resources are available to compensate for the unavailable ones. The large number of water resource cases that have been successfully negotiated suggests that finding the ripe moment for negotiation is not difficult, especially if rewards for negotiation are offered to the major parties.

Although interstate conflicts may arise as a result of transboundary environmental problems, some of the more prominent solutions involve domestic policy reform. Many such conflicts can be reduced, mitigated, or prevented if countries unilaterally develop and enforce reasonable measures to stem polluting emissions, remediate industrial plants, or put constraints on development activities that are unsustainable, for instance. The fisheries cases required changes to national regulations on fishing practices and agreed fishing areas. The Aral and Zambezi basin regimes required the riparian countries to modify their domestic use of water and the production of transboundary pollution.

Emerging environmental problems and disputes have often resulted in the establishment and growth of nongovernmental organizations that can serve as pressure groups, lobbyists, educators, and implementers of new standards and regulations. Such NGOs, including the media, often play an important catalytic role in reshaping patterns of compliance with existing environmental regulations and keeping the problems before the public eye, forcing action and possibly conflict resolution. Businesses often seek to participate in the domestic policy-making arena, as new regulations are designed. The growing participation and influence of NGOs was evident in the Aral and Zambezi basin cases, as well as the fisheries cases.

Because of the scientific and technological issues that must be addressed in transboundary environmental disputes, scientists are increasingly involved in roles usually reserved for diplomats. There is some belief that their involvement may result in a change in the direction and tenor of the negotiations. But in regard to a case dealing with negotiating environmental issues within the Baltic Sea environmental regime (the Helsinki Convention), Matthew Auer (1998) asserted that the many scientists who participated quickly assumed the traditional role of country diplomats, suggesting the predominating effect of the situation over professional socialization.

The cases in this chapter also demonstrate various creative ways in which regimes are employed. The Zambezi case shows how already established regional organizations can offer a useful cooperative structure within which a new package of environmental norms can be interpolated. And in the U.S.-Mexican tuna incident, GATT's mission was expanded to include environmental concerns in addition to traditional trade functions.

Conclusion

What are some of the barriers to preventive diplomacy in transboundary environmental conflicts? Preventive environmental diplomacy seems to fail in situations involving multiple actors and issues; complexity appears to confound the ability of negotiators to reach effective outcomes, at least in the short run. Direct bilateral negotiations seem more likely to succeed.

Other principal difficulties arise from a lack of early recognition or willingness to accept that dealing with low-level, latent disputes can fend off more serious conflicts that might arise in the future. Another factor inhibiting preventive diplomacy in such conflicts is power asymmetry. Dominance breeds disdain for negotiation and reluctance to compromise. Leveling the playing field and creating the capacity to negotiate—a readiness to negotiate—is essential. Finally, an inability to pinpoint meaningful superordinate goals and reasonable interdependent roles for the disputants can raise barriers to effective preventive diplomacy efforts.

When a threat to environmental security exists, perhaps the most difficult problem for preventive diplomacy is determining whether negotiations should target the environmental trigger, the political, economic, and social secondary effects, or the tertiary effects—the security threat or conflict itself. Practical experimentation, as well as research on the subject, is still required.

In each of the cases presented in this chapter, preventive negotiations began at a different stage in the conflict. Some of the negotiations might be better characterized as crisis-management negotiations rather than preventive negotiations (as in the fisheries disputes). It is likely that if talks had occurred at earlier stages and if the eventual problems had been recognized when still emergent, negotiations would have been more effective in preventing security threats. First, however, parties must be able to recognize and diagnose potential threats early enough to know that negotiations are, in fact, necessary. Ultimately, recognizing the existence of a problem that requires solution is the principal confounding factor in initiating preventive diplomacy on transboundary environmental threats. If that recognition is forthcoming, then the first major hurdle toward conflict prevention will have been surmounted. And if early and successful preventive diplomacy is to become the norm in transboundary situations, stronger links must be forged between the scientific monitoring of environmental problems and the policy formulation and decision processes.

Notes

This chapter was written, in part, under a grant from the United States National Defense University (Contract no. DADW49-97-M-0321). I also gratefully acknowledge the support of the U.S. Office of the Deputy Under Secretary of Defense (Environmental Security) and the NATO CCMS (Committee on the Challenges of Modern Society) pilot study on environment and security in the international context, of which I am a participant. The opinions, conclusions, and recommendations expressed or implied within this chapter are solely my own. They do not necessarily represent the views of the National Defense University, the Department of Defense, the U.S. government, or the North Atlantic Treaty Organization.

1. The NATO CCMS pilot study is entitled "Environment and Security in the International Context." NATO and Partnership for Peace countries are participants in this study, and I am a major contributor to it. The final report is Lietzmann and Vest 1999.

2. This section draws heavily on Spector 1995.

3. One of the major criticisms of the research to date in the environmental security field is the assumption of a singular outcome—violent conflict (Dabelko 1997). An alternative and perhaps more reasonable hypothesis examined by the NATO CCMS study is that environmental change may produce instability or cooperation, depending on the level of technological capacity and infrastructure, negotiation readiness, and other political-social factors. Other critiques of the existing research (see Gleditsch 1998) find problems of definition, excessive theoretical complexity, lack of control groups, and reverse causality.

4. The differences and similarities between norm-seeking negotiations and other types of negotiation have been explored in Spector, Sjöstedt, and Zartman (1994a, 1994b).

5. Sjöstedt (1993) presented several excellent in-depth case studies of negotiations that were conducted to resolve worsening environmental problems between nations when armed conflict or interstate instability was not at risk—for example, marine pollution in the Mediterranean, acid rain in Europe and North America, and industrial pollution along the Rhine River.

References

Auer, Matthew. 1998. "Colleagues or Combatants? Experts as Environmental Diplomats." *International Negotiation* 3, no. 2: 267–87.

Clawson, Patrick. 1992. "The Limited Scope for Economic Cooperation in the Contemporary Levant." In *The Arab-Israeli Search for Peace*, ed. S. Spiegel. Boulder: Lynne Rienner.

Dabelko, Geoffrey D. 1997. "Report on the Proceedings." In *Conflict and the Environment*, ed. N. P. Gleditsch. Dordrecht: Kluwer.

Elhance, Arun P. 1996a. "Conflict and Cooperation over Water in the Aral Sea Basin." Social Science Research Council, New York.

———. 1996b. "Hydropolitics: Conflict and Cooperation in International River Basins." In *Contested Grounds: Conflict and Security in the New Environmental Politics*, ed. Daniel Deudney and Richard Matthews. Albany: State University of New York Press.

Fisher, Franklin. 1994. "The Harvard Middle East Water Project: Overview, Results and Conclusions." Cambridge, Mass.: Harvard Institute for Social and Economic Policy in the Middle East (December).

Fitzmaurice, John. 1996. *Damming the Danube*. Boulder: Westview.

Gleditsch, Nils P. 1998. "Armed Conflict and the Environment: A Critique of the Literature." *Journal of Peace Research* 35, no. 3 (May): 381–400.

Gleick, Peter. 1992. "Water and Conflict." Occasional Paper no. 1, series on the Project on Environmental Change and Acute Conflict. University of Toronto, September.

———. 1996. "Basic Water Requirements for Human Activities: Meeting Basic Needs." *Water International* 21: 83–92.

Goodrich, Jill W., and Peter Brecke. forthcoming. "The Paths from Environmental Change to Violent Conflict." *Journal of Environment and Development*.

Gyawali, Dipak. 2000. "Nepal–India Water Resource Relations." In *Power and Negotiation*, eds. I. William Zartman and Jeffrey Z. Rubin. Ann Arbor: University of Michigan Press.

Hammond, Allen, A. Adriaanse, E. Rodenburg, D. Bryant, and R. Woodward. 1995. *Environmental Indicators: A Systematic Approach to Measuring and Reporting on Environmental Policy Performance in the Context of Sustainable Development*. Washington, D.C.: World Resources Institute.

Homer-Dixon, Thomas. 1994. "Environmental Scarcities and Violent Conflict: Evidence from Cases." *International Security* 19, no. 1 (Summer): 5–40.

Homer-Dixon, Thomas, and Valerie Percival. 1996. *Environmental Scarcity and Violent Conflict: Briefing Book*. Toronto: University College, University of Toronto, Project on Environment, Population and Security.

Lietzmann, Kurt, and Gary Vest. 1999. *Environment and Security in an International Context*. Report no. 232. Brussels: North Atlantic Treaty Organization, Committee on the Challenges of Modern Society, Report, March.

Lonergan, Steve, Ken Gustavson, and Mark Harrower. 1997. "Mapping Human Insecurity." Research report. University of Victoria, British Columbia.

Marcus, Amy, and Marcus Brauchli. 1997. "Greenpolitik: Threats to Environment Provoke a New Security Agenda." *Wall Street Journal*, November 20, p. A19.

McCaffrey, Stephen C. 1993. "Water, Politics and International Law." In *Water in Crisis: A Guide to the World's Fresh Water Resources*, ed. Peter H. Gleick. New York: Oxford University Press, pp. 92–116.

McDonald, Alan. 1988. "International River Basin Negotiations: Building a Database of Illustrative Successes." Working paper WP-88-096, International Institute for Applied Systems Analysis, Laxenburg, Austria, October.

Naff, Thomas, and Ruth Matson, eds. 1984. *Water in the Middle East: Conflict or Cooperation?* Boulder: Westview.

Porter, Gareth, and Janet Welsh Brown. 1996. *Global Environmental Politics*, 2nd ed. Boulder: Westview.

Shaw, Brian, et al. 1997. "Framework for Identifying and Managing Environmental Problems." Paper presented at a meeting of the NATO/CCMS pilot study committee, Pacific Northwest National Laboratories, Washington, D.C.

Sherif, Muzafer. 1967. *Social Interaction: Process and Products*. Chicago: Aldine.

Sjöstedt, Gunnar, ed. 1993. *International Environmental Negotiation*. Newbury Park, Calif.: Sage.

Sloep, Peter, and Andrew Blowers. 1996. *Environmental Policy in an International Context: Conflicts*. London: Arnold.

Spector, Bertram. 1995. "Fostering Resolution of Water Resources Disputes Project, Technical Proposal." Report prepared for Management Systems International, Washington, D.C., July.

Spector, Bertram, Gunnar Sjöstedt, and I. William Zartman. 1994a. "Getting It Done: Post-Agreement Negotiation and International Regimes." Final report submitted to the United States Institute of Peace, Washington, D.C., July.

———. 1994b. *Negotiating International Regimes: Lessons Learned from the United Nations Conference on Environment and Development (UNCED)*. London: Graham & Trotman.

Spector, Bertram, L. MacNamara, R. Hayes, and K. Kaizer. 1996. "Strategies and Coalition Building in International Environmental Security: Alternative Definitions and Approaches." Paper presented at a workshop on environment and security, National Defense University, Washington, D.C., August.

Trolldalen, Jon Martin. 1992. *International Environmental Conflict Resolution: The Role of the United Nations.* New York: UNITAR.

Tunstall, Dan. 1992. "The Growing Importance of Scientific Rules of Thumb in Developing Indicators of Resource Sustainability." Paper prepared for the International Conference on Earth Rights and Responsibilities, World Resources Institute, Washington, D.C.

Tunstall, Dan, Allen Hammond, and Norbert Henninger. 1994. *Developing Environmental Indicators.* Washington, D.C.: World Resources Institute.

United Nations Commission on Sustainable Development. 1996. *Indicators of Sustainable Development: Framework and Methodologies.* New York: United Nations, August.

Waterbury, John. 1979. *Hydropolitics of the Nile Valley.* New York: Syracuse University Press.

Wilkenfeld, Jonathan, ed. 1973. *Conflict Behavior and Linkage Politics.* New York: David McKay.

Wolf, Aaron, and John Ross. 1992. "The Impact of Scarce Water Resources on the Arab-Israeli Conflict." *Natural Resources Journal* 32, no. 4: 919–58.

Woodrow Wilson Center. 1995, 1996. *Environmental Change and Security Report,* no. 1 and 2.

World Bank. 1993. *A Strategy for Managing Water in the Middle East and North Africa.* Washington, D.C.: World Bank.

———. 1995. *Monitoring Environmental Progress.* Washington, D.C.: World Bank.

Zartman, I. William, Daniel Druckman, Lloyd Jensen, Dean Pruitt, and H. Peyton Young. 1996. "Negotiation as a Search for Justice." *International Negotiation* 1, no. 1: 79–98.

10

Global Natural Disasters: Securing Freedom from Damage

Winfried Lang

Preventive Diplomacy and Environmental Negotiations

Since the end of the Cold War, concepts such as "preventive diplomacy" or "preventive defense" have figured high on the international agenda. In respect to both notions, the debate is much more about means than about goals. Goals were broadened as soon as "security" went well beyond armed conflict, encompassing, among other things, migration, organized crime, and the degradation of the environment (Albin 1995; Thomas 1992; Lynn-Jones and Miller 1995; Timoshenko 1992; Fischer 1993). Such threats had existed well before the end of the Cold War, but given the global tensions of that era, these so-called new risks were relegated to a secondary position.

Diplomacy has always been about a search for peaceful means, about employing measures short of war, about crafting laws that regulate and make predictable the behavior of governments. Diplomacy was and still is about negotiations that either prevent or settle disputes. In terms of global disasters, diplomacy deals not only with conflicts or disputes but also with risks and damages, with responsibility for damages, and with questions of compensation. Such diplomacy can focus either on ad hoc measures or on regime building, the latter having a much more far-reaching dimension both in scope and in time (Krasner 1983; Young 1989).

Preventive diplomacy in general is oriented toward a wide range of options. It addresses events that should not occur at all and should therefore be prevented or avoided, events that should be prevented from escalating (conflict damage control), and the consequences of events that cannot be prevented but should be mitigated. In the case of global disasters, the option of full prevention or avoidance should be the top priority, but because this objective

may not be achieved with the means available, the second and third options—
no escalation, mitigation—are valid alternatives.

In this context, it should be noted that preventive diplomacy as such depends to a large extent on a *cost-benefit analysis*: Is there a balance between
costs and benefits in the short-term and long-term perspectives? Are these
costs and benefits equally shared by all actors involved? Zero-sum games are
probably the least likely possibility because among those who lose and those
who gain may be the global commons or humankind, entities that are rarely
counted among the players in international relations. Some new kind of calculation may be necessary: a solution that benefits humankind as a whole but
whose costs are borne only by a small group of actors.

Preventive diplomacy in general implies *early awareness* and early action or
reaction. Sounding an early warning means looking further ahead into the future than is common practice; in the case of environmental degradation, this
requires improving scientific certainty. It also requires technological, legal,
economic, and political creativity in order to ensure timely and adequate reaction or adequate preventive action. The big challenge that follows from this
fact is how to translate early warning into early action because it is tempting
to delay action until things clarify, and by then, the best opportunities for influencing events may have passed.

Those engaged in preventive diplomacy in the specific context of global disasters have much to learn from environmental diplomacy in general. Its attributes have been summarized elsewhere (Lang 1994, 1991), but it may be
helpful to recapitulate the lessons of this discipline before moving to the
various cases.

Because environmental problems usually affect a plurality of actors—on
neighborhood, regional, and global levels—environmental negotiations frequently involve a considerable number of governments and/or regional integration organizations. Such a plurality of actors implies that many environmental negotiations take place in the context or under the auspices of
competent international organizations. These institutions serve as conveners
and forums and as advisers and catalysts whenever serious conflicts of interest emerge between governments. Science and scientists constituting an epis-
temic community have become a crucial factor in environmental negotiations; they frequently discover the threat, they may suggest remedies, and they
may facilitate compliance and control once governments have entered into
binding commitments. Nongovernmental organizations (NGOs), which represent green or business interests, also play crucial roles in environmental negotiations; they try to influence governments in respect to the need for and
feasibility of countermeasures. These organizations mainly act through the
media, which have an impact on environmental negotiations because many
people feel directly concerned by events and risks related to the environment.

Other factors that have an impact on environmental negotiations are the following:

- Time: Short-term costs may have to be balanced against long-term benefits (both possibly affecting different actors differently).
- Exposure: Some regions may be more affected than others by similar risks (differences in vulnerability).
- Open-ended nature: Most environmental negotiations follow a step-by-step pattern (framework agreements, protocols to be periodically amended). Thus, in many instances, no final close of negotiations can be determined; a process of continuously refining countermeasures is a more likely result.
- Sovereignty and national borders: Because of the transboundary nature of many environmental threats, traditional notions of sovereignty and national borders are likely to be abandoned; solidarity and joint commitments are the new criteria.
- Vested interests: Economic interests are linked to the competitiveness of businesses in world markets; goals such as establishing an even playing field may serve as major incentives for businesses to support restrictions on the production and consumption of hazardous substances in order to cut the competitive edge of other producers.

Environmental diplomacy, with its traditional precepts and insights, plays an important role in preventing global disasters (Sjöstedt 1993a; Susskind 1994, esp. 124–41). But "urgency" as a specific requirement has to be added, and the distance between early warning and early action has to be shortened as much as possible. If total prevention is unlikely to be attained, actors should envisage ways to avoid the escalation of damage or mitigate negative outcomes. Natural and environmental disasters will only be managed by incorporating the utmost concern for humankind and nature and by applying a preventive approach, which is about to become a constituent element of international environmental law.

The Preventive Approach in Natural and Environmental Disasters

In environmental matters, the preventive approach aims at averting disaster in two fundamental forms: damage and conflict. First, environmental disasters have to be prevented to avoid serious damage to the environment as a whole irrespective of the location of that environment or the source of pollution, be it within or outside the national jurisdiction of another state. Damage occurring beyond national borders can affect the so-called global commons, including the ozone layer, the global climate, and the high seas. Second, environmental disasters have to be prevented because they may trigger or escalate interstate conflict. This can occur if one state considers itself the victim of some kind of environmental aggression perpetrated by another state (or states), as in the Iraq-Kuwait case, or if it believes it has been affected by accidental pollution caused by activities taking place under the jurisdiction of another state.

From the perspective of preventive diplomacy, it may sometimes be difficult to distinguish between these two types of threats, but they reflect two distinct challenges. In the case of conflict, actors clearly aim at the traditional goal of maintaining or re-establishing peace among states. The case of damage is less political, that is, less linked to a power struggle or to a conflict of immediate national interests because the environment as such, mainly that beyond national borders, is the main concern. Damage generally transcends national borders, and humankind as a whole is the focus of attention.

But even in this scenario, the national dimension cannot be totally ignored. Some countries with high levels of economic development contribute far more to the depletion of the ozone layer than others because they produce and export or consume many more ozone-depleting substances. In addition, some countries disproportionately affect the global climate because they emit far more carbon dioxide into the atmosphere and absorb much less of the greenhouse gases than others. Thus, countries relying on nuclear power for the major part of their energy needs cause less damage to the global climate than those that mainly depend on coal or oil. Similarly, countries that earn much of their national income by exporting coal and oil indirectly contribute more to global warming than others with different sources of income.

Why does the preventive approach have such relevance for environmental policy in general? Traditionally, if one state causes damage to the interests of another—its property, its nationals, and so on—international laws require that the perpetrator, usually an agent of that state, be punished and that the victim state be compensated for its losses in respect to goods or persons. If the culprit state abides by these rules, a political conflict is avoided. If, however, there is no agreement on the origins of the damage or on the causality between actions or omissions in one state and loss or damage in another, the usual procedures of dispute settlement may have to be triggered.

If damage is not caused directly to another state but to the environment as a whole, the main question is whether it can be compensated at all, given its scope and nature. Can any monetary value be assigned to the losses? (Damage done to the ozone layer or the global climate, for example, cannot be expressed in dollars and cents.) As a consequence, avoidance and prevention of damage have become the hallmarks of environmental policy, for to prevent is almost always better than to repair. Certainly, prevention is the best option for the environment, and it is also the appropriate approach in regard to environmental problems that could cross national borders and spark conflict among nations (Sands 1995; Hohmann 1994).

Global Natural Disasters to Be Prevented

Environmental problems that go beyond national borders may inflict damage at three levels—local, regional, and global. Local damage may affect neighboring states and trigger interstate conflicts. Transboundary water pollution, for instance, can harm multiple countries, just as the chemical accident that occurred in Basel in 1986 heavily affected the riparian states of the Rhine River (Dupont 1993).

Regional damage affects a broader area, as in the case of long-range air pollution: Emissions of sulfur dioxides can travel across several borders (e.g., from Central Europe to Scandinavia), and acid rain may cause significant damage to faraway forests and rivers. The Chernobyl accident of 1986, despite all the excitement it caused, was only regional in scope (Sjöstedt 1993b). In most of the cases mentioned thus far, the main response strategy was largely preventive: to reduce emissions, which are likely to cause damage, and to give early warning in cases of accidental pollution. But such strategies were not implemented solely through national actions. In each case, preventive diplomacy was used to harmonize the states' efforts and to develop legal instruments and regimes upon which further cooperation between states could be built (Lang 1992). The Chernobyl accident, in particular, greatly strengthened the concern for early warning and notification in order to minimize damage as far as possible or to allow for early protective measures.

Although disasters causing global damage are relatively rare events, they cannot be neglected because the damage they cause is likely to be of a size no one can manage. Rather than being accidental or momentary events, such disasters are more likely to have a "creeping" nature. The main areas in which such disasters are about to occur are the stratospheric ozone layer and the global climate. In both areas, preventive multilateral diplomacy has taken up the challenge, primarily to prevent or at least mitigate damage but also to prevent damage-triggered interstate conflicts from occurring or escalating.

The threat to the stratospheric ozone layer, which is primarily caused by emissions of chlorofluorocarbons, was discovered in the late 1970s. Response strategies were developed at national levels (mainly in the United States) in the early 1980s. Legal instruments designed to frame coordinated international action were approved in 1985 (the Vienna Convention on the Protection of the Ozone Layer) and in 1987 (the Montreal Protocol on Substances That Deplete the Ozone Layer). Hence, a full-fledged ozone-depletion regime has emerged (Gering 1994, 195–320). Reduction commitments have become more stringent, new substances have been added to the list of prohibited or controlled chemicals, trade in such substances has been restricted (especially with regard to nonparties), a highly sophisticated system of compliance and control ("peer review") has been established, and incentives have been devised to encourage noncomplying countries to abide by their obligations. If all parties fulfill their obligations, science tells us, the depletion of the ozone layer is likely to be mitigated by the middle of the twenty-first century.

The issue of ozone depletion is considered a typical case of successful preventive diplomacy: When states agreed on the key instrument to combat the threat by means of reductions and prohibitions (the Montreal Protocol), full scientific proof that there was a serious danger to humankind was not yet available. Thus, ozone depletion as a scientific and political challenge has contributed considerably to the establishment of the so-called precautionary principle: We must not wait for full scientific certainty if the threat is extremely serious to all humanity, for if we wait too long, it may be too late for remedial action (Makhijani and Gurney 1995).

The threat to the global climate, namely, global warming, is mainly caused by energy policies that rely on the burning of fossil fuels (coal and oil) (Goudie 1996, esp. 302-11). Public awareness concerning this issue emerged by the late 1980s, and the problem became a subject of preventive diplomacy by the early 1990s. The 1992 Rio Summit (also known as the UN Conference on Environment and Development [UNCED]) approved the Framework Convention on Climate Change, a treaty that did not contain clear and binding obligations on reducing emissions of carbon dioxide and other gases (Spector, Sjöstedt, and Zartman 1994). But this legal instrument did serve as the basis for further negotiations aimed at establishing a protocol that provides for clear-cut commitments involving at least the industrialized states. Again, preventive diplomacy took a first step. Progress at Rio and thereafter was limited because conflicts of interests arose, both between and within industrialized states and developing countries. Furthermore, scientific certainty on global warming was even less developed than in the case of ozone depletion; full scientific consensus had yet to emerge on the consequences of global warming (such as changes in agriculture and rising sea levels) (Nordhaus 1994). In the meantime, agreement was achieved in late 1997 via the so-called Kyoto Protocol.

These two examples of preventive diplomacy in respect to potential global disasters are analyzed in some detail later in this chapter. The analysis is largely based on the lessons I have learned during my personal involvement in some of the respective negotiations.

Problems That Can Give Rise to Escalating Conflict

In discussing the problems of ozone depletion and climate change, it should be made clear that conflict and damage do not necessarily coincide or coexist;

that is, there can be conflict without damage and damage without conflict. Interstate conflicts may arise out of a perpetrator-victim relationship or out of different or even opposite approaches used to combat or mitigate damage to the global commons.

In the case of ozone depletion, escalation of both damage and conflict may occur soon after the year 2000 as a result of the following developments:

- Industrialized states are not abiding or are insufficiently abiding by their commitments to reduce production, consumption, and exportation of ozone-depleting substances;
- Developing countries, having enjoyed a ten-year grace period before their reduction duties went into effect, are failing to comply with those obligations and are even increasing their emissions;
- In addition, both developing and industrialized countries are not eliminating illegal trade in controlled substances.

Conflict—and, indirectly, damage—may also arise out of the simple fact that certain regions are more exposed than others to ultraviolet (UV) radiation, the main consequence of ozone depletion. Therefore, countries outside areas of high vulnerability have a much lower incentive to reduce their emissions; global solidarity still remains a rare good. Another major obstacle to preventive action may be the significant costs entailed in switching from ozone-depleting chemicals to substances that deplete less ozone or do not deplete ozone at all: Some countries are unable or unwilling to bear such costs. And if a low vulnerability to the consequences of ozone depletion coincides with a high financial burden to be borne when switching to less hazardous chemicals, a country is unlikely to take concrete and verifiable action against ozone depletion.

In regard to global climate change, damage and conflict tend to be more separate. If global warming is not restrained or at least mitigated, damage could well result from the rise of ocean levels, which would destroy low-lying countries and numerous islands. Such disasters would again trigger a broad flow of so-called environmental refugees. If global warming continues at its present pace, agriculture will suffer in certain already arid regions, but it will benefit in others. As a result, production patterns are likely to shift on a large scale. Conflicts may arise for countries whose national incomes rely heavily on the export of fossil fuels such as coal and oil; they will object to any compulsory switch away from these energy sources because that would put their natural wealth in jeopardy. At a minimum, these countries will invoke their sovereignty over their natural resources, even if their opposition to countermeasures conflicts with the moral duties of solidarity. Finally, an imposed switch in energy policy—a switch largely justified in order to mitigate global warming—may require current consumers of fossil fuel energy to rely on other and more expensive energy resources. If such a modification in energy policy goes beyond countries' respective economic capabilities, resistance and noncompliance are the most likely outcomes.

Has Negotiation Been Used to Prevent Escalation and Conflict?

In regard to the ozone-depletion problem, negotiations have succeeded in convincing most industrialized states to reduce emissions of substances that damage the ozone layer. But that stratospheric layer had suffered considerable harm well before the danger was discovered by science and before counter-measures went into full operation. Moreover, it is possible that the entire effort will fail if new emissions from developing countries outstrip any progress achieved by reductions and phase-outs in industrialized states. To help developing countries switch from the use of ozone-depleting substances to the use of less dangerous chemicals, a transfer of technology from North to South is required, a transfer that again must be financed by industrialized states through a multilateral fund. Developing countries will modify their consumption patterns in respect to ozone-depleting substances if they themselves feel vulnerable to increased UV radiation and if they believe such a switch is economically feasible.

In regard to climate change, only a framework instrument has entered into force. As a first step, negotiations on concrete measures that would help to reduce if not reverse the process of global warming led to the Kyoto Protocol, which obliges industrialized states to limit their emissions. But this treaty does not yet have the force of law. Past negotiations have revealed a serious conflict of interests between two groups of countries. On one side are those directly threatened by a probable rise in sea levels, as well as countries with enlightened environmental policies. On the other side are oil- and coal-producing countries, which are dependent for their economic development on fossil fuels, and countries that reject stringent commitments that would force them to abandon their luxurious lifestyles, which depend on a high consumption of fossil fuels. Thus, negotiations that aim to prevent harm to the global climate have produced new conflicts, and the threat of a global disaster has failed to deter a large number of countries from continuing their traditional energy policies. For many, such a threat appears too abstract and too distant, and preventive action appears too costly.

How Did Perceptions of Stakes Change?

Negotiations on ozone depletion began as a purely government-to-government exercise supported by some concerned scientists and low-profile activity on the part of certain NGOs. Once the ozone hole was discovered and its significance impacted on public opinion, pressure grew on governments that had been lukewarm on the matter of ozone depletion. These governments abandoned their reluctance, especially because a cost-benefit analysis had clearly demonstrated that environmental benefits prevailed over economic sacrifice. In addition, another stakeholder—business—perceived the issue of the ozone hole and ozone depletion in general as an opportunity to develop and sell substitute chemicals that could replace ozone-depleting substances; companies that had such substitutes already at their disposal were the first to enter the newly framed market. The stakes for those who were not part of the new regime changed when they realized they might suffer from the trade bans called for in the protocol and thereby lose important market opportunities. Therefore, they, too, joined the protocol. Again, the North-South divide played an important role in changing perceptions of the stakes involved: Developing countries that perceived themselves as seriously threatened by ozone depletion and that were also sufficiently supported by the North to carry out the switch declared themselves willing to abide by their obligations to reduce the production and use of chemicals that deplete the ozone layer.

Thus, stakes changed because (1) an external shock (the discovery of the ozone hole) mobilized public opinion, (2) the business sector had alternative substances that could be marketed either directly or through patents and licenses, (3) developing countries were given special treatment (grace periods, technological and financial support), and (4) nonmembers of the regime were afraid of losses caused by trade bans.

Preventive diplomacy in respect to climate change has been less successful because the stakes have not yet fully changed in the eyes of many participants in the negotiation. A great number of parties have realized that they would be seriously affected by concrete measures to combat global warming because such measures would mean either losing a major source of national income or making a very expensive change in their energy policies. Furthermore, no external shock has impacted on public opinion to mobilize governments to combat this threat, and perceptions related to the urgency of countermeasures are slow to change because scientific certainty is not developed to the same degree as it was in the case of ozone depletion (Foster, Bernstein, and Huber 1993). Only those countries that already had progressive environmental policies and that were potential victims of a rising ocean level were ready to acknowledge the threat and to signal their willingness to act accordingly. Clearly, the prevention of global disasters requires that the threat be adequately perceived *and* that benefits and costs be adequately balanced within the context of the countries' respective economic capacities.

How Did Attitudes Change?

Regarding both ozone depletion and climate change, the attitudes of the chief players—countries, groups of countries, businesses, and NGOs—shifted to the same extent that perceptions of the dangers and of the benefits and costs of countermeasures shifted. Attitudinal changes were closely linked to the immediate interests of the participants in the negotiation process. They occurred relatively quickly, for example, when external events such as the discovery of the ozone hole had a strong impact on public opinion. Attitudes also changed when science could predict the imminence and broad scope of the danger with a high degree of certainty. When full scientific consensus was not available early enough, as in the case of climate change, participants were not confronted with the need to take some sort of emergency action: Unless the sense of urgency was strong, no concrete countermeasures were likely to be triggered. Beyond that, attitudinal change was resisted by many developing countries, especially in the case of global warming, because for the last two hundred years, industrialized states had been building their economies on the basis of exactly those energy resources whose use was now to be limited. As the developing countries saw it, the North was mainly responsible for the deterioration in the global climate. Therefore, they felt it was primarily the responsibility of industrialized states to undertake repair work and to prevent further deterioration. The clear-cut division of attitudes in respect to the issue of responsibility for harm caused to the global commons makes united action against global disasters highly difficult and hampers preventive diplomacy.

What Tactics Were Used to Promote Negotiation as a Means of Preventing Damage, Conflict, and Escalation?

On the basis of scientific advice and with some support from the media, a core group of industrialized countries launched a campaign to raise awareness of the ozone-depletion problem. They also initiated a legislative process at both the domestic and international levels. This process gained momentum and broadened when the business sector had alternative substances at its disposal. A further accelerating and broadening factor was the special treatment to be granted to developing countries (financial and technological assistance as an incentive, trade bans as a disincentive). Another element of success was the significant role played by the competent international organization, the United Nations Environmental Program (UNEP). Because this organization was led by a dynamic personality from a developing country, secretary-general Mohammed Tolba, many developing nations were confident they would not be betrayed by the early promoters of the negotiation, mainly countries in the North. In terms of the specific tactics used in promoting negotiation, the main device was the tailor-made treatment given each and every group of stakeholders.

In the area of climate change, dominating individuals were far less available, and no well-established international organization could support the problem-solving process. Furthermore, the economic stakes were much higher, but the scientific evidence was a great deal weaker than in the case of ozone depletion. In addition, North and South were divided in their own approaches, a division that continued throughout the negotiations. The internal division in the North (pitting the United States against other countries in the Organization for Economic Cooperation and Development [OECD]) especially weakened the leading role played for the most part by European countries in calling for countermeasures and promoting negotiations. Tailor-made solutions were also envisaged in this context, but they were far less effective in dealing with stakeholder groups' interests.

In regard to negotiating tactics and legal techniques, it should be noted that a step-by-step approach was used in both cases. After a minimum of political consensus was built up by means of declarations and other actions, the first generation of legal instruments to be adopted provided only a relatively vague framework. These instruments contained nothing more than general obligations to cooperate closely. In the ozone regime, a second step was taken by means of the Montreal Protocol, which stipulated specific reduction targets, and during the follow-up process, these targets were broadened and tightened. Negotiations on climate change followed the same pattern, with the Kyoto Protocol negotiated on the basis of the framework convention of 1992. From a tactical perspective, this amounts to a "bottom-up" approach: First, the parties agree on the self-evident or least controversial issues, and from there on, negotiations move to the more difficult problems, which require that certain countries make substantial sacrifices. But as these countries have become increasingly familiar with the process as such, their resistance to real commitments is likely to weaken.

The other tactical device used in both instances was to customize some of the important obligations to the specific circumstances of the contracting parties. By granting temporary or permanent exceptions to several groups of countries, the goal of getting everybody on board was more attainable. The special treatment accorded developing countries or economies in transition in both instances has already been mentioned. Economies in transition were also to enjoy special advantages, and the Montreal Protocol even contained advantages for the members of the European Economic Community. But a word of caution is necessary here: Although a temporary or permanent differentiation of duties, which had special significance in the context of the Montreal Protocol, may be of great help in achieving agreement in the short term, it entails an equivalent number of loopholes that may jeopardize the effectiveness of a regime in the long term. Thus, a tactical short-term advantage may turn into a longer-term disadvantage because in both instances, the effort of preventive diplomacy to avoid or mitigate a specific global disaster is weakened, delayed, or both. Therefore, in every case, short-term benefits have to be balanced against long-term costs. This point highlights the importance of the time factor in negotiations in general and in environmental regime building in particular.

Conclusion

Two cases of potential global disasters were investigated in this chapter in order to determine whether diplomatic means have succeeded in totally preventing such disasters, in preventing escalation toward unbearable damage, or in at least mitigating the consequences of global catastrophes (Benedick 1997). In both instances, negotiations were the key instrument of preventive diplomacy. A regime that functions relatively well has been established to address ozone depletion; a regime has also been built to deal with climate change, but it still requires functioning institutions and clearly binding commitments. This experience tells us that although regime building is important, it is just the beginning of a comprehensive program to prevent a global disaster. Regimes are mainly composed of rules, institutions, and procedures—rules that must be adequate to the task and complied with by the relevant actors; institutions that must be accepted by all stakeholders; and procedures that should be followed by those who share the same goal, namely, preventing a certain disaster.

What are the similarities between the two global disasters discussed in this chapter? In both cases, the immense scope of the challenge—with humankind as a whole threatened and with a plurality of actors at the origin of the threat—has required multilateral negotiations, which should have led to effective response strategies. In both cases, the global commons—an environmental area that belongs not to one or a few states but to everybody—is at risk, although the likelihood of damage is greater in one case than in the other. In both cases, there are losers and winners. Among the winners are the environment, future generations, and humankind itself. Among the losers are certain chemical industries ("sunset industries") and the producers and consumers of certain energy resources. And in both instances, regimes have been built in order to give a firm ground to preventive diplomacy. But preventive diplomacy does not end with the establishment of regimes; instead, it requires that regimes be improved whenever the need arises. They need to grow as living organisms.

What are the differences between the two cases? One of the most visible differences is the much weaker leadership in the issue of climate change. Neither a fully committed international organization nor a group of progressive countries, sufficiently strong and willing to bear the majority of the costs, was available. Short-term considerations prevailed over long-term perspectives. Scientific certainty was another key issue: Although it was available or became available to a large extent in the area of ozone depletion, it was much less developed in the area of climate change. Here again, a major difference is revealed—the difference in the size of the stakes. Whereas ozone depletion only affects a limited sector of chemical industries, climate change remains a challenge to traditional energy policies, to lifestyles, and to the revenues of major countries. This introduces still another factor—the ripeness of the situation for preventive action. Action on the problem of climate change was long delayed because the situation was not yet ripe for concrete measures. Public opinion may, to some extent, be a reliable indicator of ripeness in this area; to date, it has not been sufficiently shocked by an event similar to the discovery of the ozone hole.

In considering these two cases, one being highly successful and the other much less so thus far, two concluding questions may be posed: What ingredients are required for successful preventive diplomacy? And can the success of preventive diplomacy be defined and measured?

There is one basic dilemma inherent in diplomacy involving issues that affect the global commons: The global commons is not sitting at the negotiation table, and nobody is acting on its behalf. Certainly, some traditional actors are likely to benefit from a successful outcome—the vulnerable countries that lie under direct sun and are exposed to a high degree of UV radiation caused by ozone depletion or that lie low and will be affected by rising sea levels caused by global warming. But such countries only benefit in an indirect way; that is, they gain only through the preservation of the global commons. But since the principal stakeholder, global commons, has no voice in the negotiations, preventive diplomacy in the environmental arena is different from some other cases of preventive diplomacy.

As to the ingredients of success, it should be noted that no single factor dominates. It is the appropriate mix that matters—the proper combination of costs and benefits fairly spread across countries, sufficiently advanced scientific evidence, a well-informed but not necessarily excited public opinion led by responsible NGOs, and a broad consensus on choosing the right moment to take action. This mix can lead to success in preventive diplomacy, although the ultimate yardstick is difficult to identify. Even the Montreal Protocol is not yet a real success because the full compliance of developing countries cannot be foreseen; but clearly, the protocol was a major step in the right direction. Only by the middle of the twenty-first century will humankind know whether the depletion of the ozone layer has been stopped and a global disaster thus averted. In regard to climate change, the time frame is much longer, and the conditions for successful preventive diplomacy must still be met.

A final question relates to the very essence of preventive diplomacy. Should it address conflicts between countries *and* damage caused by large-scale events? The reply should be positive because global disasters are likely to affect many more people than local disputes about territories or borders. In addition, response strategies used to combat global threats may trigger political conflicts, as demonstrated in the cases discussed in this chapter. Thus, preventive diplomacy is primarily about peace, but it is also about security and freedom, including freedom from large-scale environmental damage.

References

Albin, Cecilia, ed. 1995. "Negotiation and Global Security—New Approaches to Contemporary Issues." *American Behavioral Scientist* 38, no. 6 (May).

Benedick, Richard E. 1991. *Ozone Diplomacy: New Directions in Safeguarding the Planet.* Cambridge, Mass.: Harvard University Press.

———. 1997. "Protecting the Ozone Layer: New Directions in Diplomacy." In *Preserving the Global Environment,* ed. Jessica Tuchman Matthews. New York: Norton.

Dupont, Christophe. 1993. "The Rhine." In *International Environmental Negotiation,* ed. Gunnar Sjöstedt. Newbury Park, Calif.: Sage.

Fischer, Dietrich. 1993. *Nonmilitary Aspects of Security.* Geneva: UNIDIR and Aldershot, England: Dartmouth.

Foster, Kenneth, David Bernstein, and Peter Huber, eds. 1993. *Phantom Risk—Scientific Interference and Law.* Cambridge, Mass.: MIT Press.

Gering, Thomas. 1994. *Dynamic International Regimes: Institutions for International Environmental Governance.* Frankfurt: P. Lang.

Goudie, Andrew. 1996. *The Human Impact on the Natural Environment.* Cambridge, Mass.: MIT Press.

Hohmann, Harald. 1994. *Precautionary Legal Duties and Principles of Modern International Environmental Law.* London: Graham & Trotman.

Krasner, Stephen, ed. 1983. *International Regimes.* Ithaca: Cornell University Press.

Lang, Winfried. 1991. "Negotiations on the Environment." In *International Negotiation—Analysis, Approaches, Issues,* ed. V. Kremenyuk. San Francisco: Jossey-Bass.

———. 1992. "Diplomacy and International Environmental Law-Making: Some Observations." In *Yearbook of International Environmental Law,* ed. Gunther Handl. London: Graham & Trotman.

———. 1994. "Environmental Treatymaking: Lessons Learned for Controlling Pollution of Outer Space." In *Preservation of New Earth Space for Future Generations,* ed. J. A. Simpson. Cambridge: Cambridge University Press.

———. "Regimes and Organizations in the Labyrinth of International Institutions." In *Völkerrecht zwischen normativem Anspruch und politischer Realität,* ed. K. Ginther et al. Berlin: Dunker und Humbolt.

Lynn-Jones, Sean, and Steven Miller, eds. 1995. *Global Dangers: Changing Dimensions of International Security.* Cambridge, Mass.: MIT Press.

Makhijani, Aryus, and Kevin Gurney. 1995. *Mending the Ozone Hole.* Cambridge, Mass.: MIT Press.

Nordhaus, William. 1994. *Managing the Global Commons: The Economics of Climate Change.* Cambridge, Mass.: MIT Press.

Sands, Philippe. 1995. *Principles of International Environmental Law,* vol. 1, *Frameworks, Standards, Implementation.* Manchester: Manchester University Press.

Sjöstedt, Gunnar. 1993a. *International Environmental Negotiation.* Newbury Park, Calif.: Sage.

———. 1993b. "Negotiations on Nuclear Pollution." In *International Environmental Negotiation,* ed. Gunnar Sjöstedt. Newbury Park, Calif.: Sage.

Spector, Bertram I., Gunnar Sjöstedt, and I. William Zartman, eds. 1994. *Negotiating International Regimes: Lessons Learned from UNCED.* Boston: Graham & Trotman.

Susskind, Lawrence S. 1994. *Environmental Diplomacy—Negotiating More Effective Global Agreements.* New York: Oxford University Press.

Szell, Patrick. 1993. "Negotiations on the Ozone Layer." In *International Environmental Negotiation,* ed. G. Sjöstedt. Newbury Park, Calif.: Sage.

Thomas, Caroline. 1992. *The Environment in International Relations.* London: Royal Institute of International Affairs.

Timoshenko, Alexander. 1992. "Ecological Security: Response to Global Challenges." In *Environmental Change and International Law: New Challenges and Dimensions,* ed. E. Brown. Tokyo: UN University Press.

Young, Oran. 1989. *International Cooperation—Building Regimes for Natural Resources and the Environment.* Ithaca: Cornell University Press.

11

Global Security Conflicts I: Controlling Arms Races

James Goodby

The notion that weapons are not the causes of tensions but rather that tensions generate a need for weapons is an idea that precedes the nuclear era. It has long since become a slogan for those who doubt the value of negotiating with adversaries about weapons. But it is a false dichotomy. Tensions do, of course, give rise to arms races. It is also true that arms and arms races give rise to tensions. On January 7, 1912, First Lord of the Admiralty Winston Churchill wrote that "until Germany dropped the Naval challenge her policy here would be continually viewed with deepening suspicions and apprehension" (Massie 1991, 820). World War I began two years later. Nikita Khrushchev (1970, 494), recalling his reasons for placing Soviet missiles in Cuba, said that they "would have equalized what the West likes to call 'the balance of power.' The Americans had surrounded our country with military bases and threatened us with nuclear weapons, and now they would learn just what it feels like to have enemy missiles pointing at you." Commenting on the new elements that nuclear weapons had introduced into international relations, Henry Kissinger (1979, 202) wrote that "arms buildups, historically, were more often a reflection rather than a cause of political conflicts and distrust. But I substantially agreed that what marked our time as a period of revolutionary change was the high state of readiness of strategic weapons and their destructiveness." His point was that fear of an enemy's first nuclear strike generated instabilities.

That arms could be the source of misunderstandings, if not tensions, is illustrated by the well-known "security dilemma": A nation preoccupied with strengthening its own military forces purely for defensive purposes may unintentionally trigger a military buildup in another country. And yet, as Jean-Jacques Rousseau vividly illustrated in his story of the stag hunt, the hope of gaining material benefits through cooperation is often destroyed by the expectation of reaping a sure reward through noncooperation. In fact, experience has shown that arms control, a special type of cooperation, is difficult to achieve between two military adversaries. This has led to yet another dubious aphorism: Arms control is possible only when it is not needed. Put another way, two friendly nations have no need for this type of cooperation, and adversaries, almost by definition, cannot cooperate. This notion needs to be evaluated in the context of past and current relations between the United States and Russia and with an understanding of the various purposes that preventive diplomacy through arms control and arms control negotiations have served.

Peace has several definitions. Between two states at peace, at least three forms can be distinguished: a *precarious* peace, in which war may be imminent; a *conditional* peace, in which war may be unlikely but is not excluded as a policy option under certain conditions; and a *stable* peace, in which war is simply not considered as a method of resolving disputes and deterrence by military means is not a part of the bilateral relationship.[1] Arms control has little relevance when a stable peace exists between two countries, since there is no cause for an arms race in such a situation. And it is true that arms control is next to impossible in a situation of precarious peace—as the case of the Korean Peninsula illustrates. But under a conditional peace, such as that which prevailed between the United States and the Soviet Union throughout most of the Cold War and still exists today between the United States and Russia, arms control can be a key element of the relationship, not only in constraining an arms race but also in filling a broader preventive diplomacy role. Those critics who have dismissed the relevance of arms control have failed to consider the various forms of peaceful relations and ignored the contributions that arms control negotiations can make to political relationships or a regime between two states. The common understanding of arms control is that it should address the instruments of war that could cause a potential global security disaster. But this is not its only purpose. Arms control also can indirectly define a cooperative political relationship between two rivals; this was what it did during much of the Cold War in relations between the United States and the Soviet Union (for the building of a Cold War bipolarity security regime, see Kanet and Kolodziej 1991). The use of arms control negotiations in this sense was one method of heading off a global security disaster.

Arms Control and the U.S.-Soviet Relationship

The arms control process during the Cold War involved the use of symbols. Nuclear arms talks helped to define superpower status. The Soviet Union's claim to a position in the world equal to that of the United States was symbolized and validated by Moscow's bilateral negotiations with Washington.

Negotiating was a less dangerous way of dramatizing that claim than other techniques that were occasionally used, such as missile rattling. Negotiations also served as a genuine tension-leaching measure. During the Vietnam War, Secretary of State Dean Rusk talked repeatedly with Andrei Gromyko about a common interest—nuclear nonproliferation. It was one of the few areas in which they could discuss cooperation instead of confrontation, and it reminded the two governments of their shared interests.

Arms control during the Cold War was not exclusively a bilateral U.S.-Soviet preserve. Washington and Moscow actually managed a degree of teamwork in some of the multilateral talks. Proliferation of nuclear weapons to additional states, for example, was seen as a potentially destabilizing factor in big-power relationships, as well as inherently dangerous just in regional terms. Therefore, considerable effort was invested by the United States and the Soviet Union in building a regime to prevent this from happening. They did this not only through the formal mechanism of the Treaty on the Non-Proliferation of Nuclear Weapons (NPT), which entered into force on March 5, 1970, but also through security assurances and agreement on guidelines for nuclear-related exports.

Another example of U.S.-Soviet cooperation in multilateral negotiations concerned military operations such as exercises and maneuvers. The West thought that secrecy in these matters contributed to miscalculations and accidents, as well as to heightened tensions. Transparency and predictability were the antidotes for these problems, and the negotiating process focused on implementing these safeguards. Although Moscow and Washington did not share a common view on these matters, they were able to negotiate a series of confidence-building measures, including on-site inspection, as will be further discussed.

Arms control negotiations aimed at reductions or limitations in conventional force levels, even when they produced no agreements, had the effect of stabilizing the multilateral NATO-Warsaw Pact confrontation in Central Europe. The process of negotiations lessened political pressure for U.S. troop reductions on the part of the U.S. Congress, which was seemingly the intent of Soviet general secretary Leonid Brezhnev when he offered to begin talks on mutual troop reductions in Europe.

Irrelevance of Third-Party Mediation

Because arms control was the main item on the U.S.-Soviet agenda through most of the Cold War years and served to reinforce the special character of the relationship between the two superpowers, there was no need, desire, or room for a third-party mediator in U.S.-Soviet bilateral talks. Even though the United Kingdom was a partner in the negotiation of the first U.S.-Soviet arms agreement, the Treaty Banning Nuclear Weapons Tests in the Atmosphere, Outer Space, and Under Water, essential decisions were made by U.S. and Soviet leaders, with London playing, at best, a facilitator role. Whether seen as an asset in building a cooperative relationship or an aid to stabilizing a competitive relationship, arms control served larger political purposes for the governments of the two countries.[2] Other countries and their concerns had to be considered seriously in Washington, and allies were constantly consulted, but, as they themselves complained, "consultations" often turned out to be briefings.

Success in Preventing World War III

Preventive diplomacy failed to prevent World War I and World War II, but it was successful in preventing a World War III from exploding out of the confrontation between the Soviet Union and the West. It has been said that "the only thing the Germans did not know in 1914 was that they were going to lose the war" (Seaman 1955, 158). Vladimir Lenin (n.d., vol. 21, pt. 1, p. 68) exhorted his followers to believe that "at the decisive moment and in the decisive place, you must prove the stronger, you must be victorious." E. H. Carr (1964, 93) commented that Lenin's statement could equally well have been said by such a believer in the power of the human will as Benito Mussolini. And, of course, Adolf Hitler believed that he would lead the German nation to victory in World War II. As Raymond Aron (1955, 165) remarked, "The wars of the first half of the twentieth century have ripened a catastrophe that would be to the catastrophes of the past what the atomic bomb is to Big Bertha [World War I long-range artillery]." And yet, the catastrophe did not happen—mainly because it was widely understood by those who possessed the ultimate weapon that victory in a total war was no longer possible.

"What deterred the Americans ... was the simple dilemma of disproportion: how does one actually use means that are clearly incommensurate with the ends one has in view." John Lewis Gaddis came to this conclusion after asking why the U.S. leaders never used nuclear weapons again after Nagasaki, even when they had a monopoly. "For the Russians," he wrote, "it made sense from the beginning not to initiate the use of nuclear weapons because the prospect of American retaliation was always present" (Gaddis 1987, 146). Of all the factors that contributed to the "long peace," the most critical was the emergence after World War II of the U.S.-Soviet bipolar regime for managing conflict (Gaddis 1987, 221–23). The viability of that regime depended on the rules put into place by the two superpowers in recognition of the fact that "a nuclear war cannot be won and should never be fought" (Goodby 1988). All of the arms control negotiations during the Cold War period were essentially aimed at reinforcing those rules and, therefore, upholding the bipolar order. They were, in effect, a part of an order-building diplomacy.

Conceptual Approaches to Arms Control
and Their Functions in Preventive Diplomacy

The conceptual underpinnings of arms control changed and broadened in the United States as official thinking evolved about exactly what was to be prevented through arms control and as new circumstances arose. The first serious nuclear arms control effort in the post–World War II period resulted from the Acheson–Lillienthal Report, commissioned by President Harry Truman. It was a utopian plan for the complete international control of atomic energy in all its aspects, after which atomic bombs would be banned and destroyed. The theory was that only international ownership of all nuclear facilities could prevent a nuclear arms race. The Soviet government, determined to have its own atomic bomb, rejected the offer, and the nuclear arms race ensued. Preventive diplomacy had over-reached and had failed in the attempt, but the effort had begun to imprint the idea that atomic bombs were wholly different from what had gone before.

Thinking in the United States in the 1950s and 1960s moved away from the idea of eliminating armaments and toward making the U.S.-Soviet competition more predictable and stable. Khrushchev's nuclear diplomacy of 1957–62 was not repeated by his successors in Moscow, and, despite the tensions of the Vietnam War, the Soviets were ready for U.S.-Soviet negotiations on strategic nuclear systems by the late 1960s. With this, arms control moved from the periphery to the center of the bipolar relationship. Strategic nuclear arms control was aimed, first, at stabilizing the U.S.-Soviet bilateral nuclear relationship through agreements designed to de-emphasize first-strike forces and, second, at restraining the arms race through imposing ceilings on the numbers of delivery vehicles that could be deployed.

U.S. and Soviet nuclear forces did not evolve in a completely symmetrical way, and, therefore, differences existed concerning just what constituted a stable force balance. That there were many problems in translating "stability" into actual practice was vividly demonstrated in Brezhnev's heated rejection of President Jimmy Carter's March 1977 nuclear arms proposals, which departed from President Gerald Ford's solution (reached at Vladivostok in 1974) by giving more emphasis to the destabilizing character of multiple independently targeted re-entry vehicles (MIRVs). President Ronald Reagan switched the U.S. approach to arms control back in the direction of disarmament. Reagan was viscerally antinuclear and had accepted the argument that merely limiting nuclear weapons was an insufficient response to the threat they posed. He championed ballistic missile defenses for the same reason, launching the U.S. Strategic Defense Initiative (SDI) in March 1983. Eliminating some ballistic missiles rather than simply limiting them became a goal both in the intermediate-range nuclear forces treaty (INF Treaty) and in the Strategic Arms Reduction Talks (START I) treaty.

Arms control aimed at the nonproliferation/counterproliferation of weapons of mass or indiscriminate destruction has depended on

- Global treaty regimes,
- Security assurances given by the United States and others to compensate certain nations for their forbearance in renouncing nuclear weapons,
- Pressure tactics of various types to influence waverers,
- Denial of materials and technology, and
- Self-restraint imposed either by bilateral treaties with the Soviet Union/Russia or unilaterally.

The McMahon Act of 1947, the first U.S. legislation governing atomic energy activities after World War II, was based on the assumption that the U.S. lead could be protected through a ban on transferring atomic energy information. It prohibited any cooperation with third countries in the nuclear field, even requiring Truman to cut off communications with the British, who had helped the United States develop the atomic bomb. The proliferation of nuclear weapons capabilities into the hands of any other nation, as this experience shows, was viewed as a threat to U.S. national security from the very beginning of the nuclear age. The nuclear non-proliferation treaty signed by the United States, the Soviet Union, and others in 1968 was the codification, at the international level, of this view. Similar conclusions were reached by the United States regarding other weapons of indiscriminate destruction in the biological weapons convention of 1975 and the chemical weapons convention, ratified by the U.S. Senate in 1997.

A mix of carrots, sticks, and mutually understood rules served to contain the proliferation of weapons of mass destruction (chemical, biological, and nuclear) during the Cold War. But the disciplines and incentives created by the bipolar structure of the Cold War world were critical elements in the success of the effort.

Arms control reasoning based on the idea of a stable balance underlaid the U.S./NATO proposals on mutual and balanced force reductions (MBFRs) introduced in 1973, which sought to create equality in manpower between NATO and Warsaw Pact forces in a zone in Central Europe. The successful negotiations between 1984 and 1986 on conventional forces in Europe (CFE), which superseded the MBFR talks, focused on eliminating and limiting major pieces of equipment over a much wider area (up to the Urals) (Goodby 1988; Borawzki 1992). Tanks and artillery, for example, were units of account. The CFE treaty, which has been adapted to fit the new circumstances arising from the end of the Cold War, still serves to underwrite stable force relations among the nations of Europe. Despite the changed environment, therefore, conventional arms control remains an important factor in European security matters.

Arms control in the 1960s and 1970s was the handmaiden of defense planning in the sense that both sought to create force postures that would give military commanders and political leaders options for action and time for decisions. Essentially the same reasoning led to the idea of "confidence-building measures" (CBMs). This is a class of intergovernmental arrangements designed to clarify the intentions of certain military operations, such as field exercises. The idea is to reduce the risk of inadvertent conflict and to complicate the task of military planners who might see some advantage in a surprise military attack. Confidence-building measures rest on the premise that parties to such arrangements wish to avoid a war and that they will cooperate, while that premise holds, in the interest of preventing a war that no one wants.

Confidence-building measures promote transparency about designated types of military operations, enhance communications between the parties, and establish guidelines concerning operations of military forces that might be most susceptible to misunderstanding. Restraints on such operations may also play a role in a confidence-building regime. Europe has been the home of the most fully developed program of CBMs in conjunction with the Conference on Security and Cooperation in Europe (CSCE), now known as the Organization for Security and Cooperation in Europe (OSCE). (In the OSCE context, confidence-building measures [CBMs] have been called confidence- and security-building measures [CSBMs].) In Europe, CBMs in new garb are being developed in the framework of NATO's Partnership for Peace. Many of the conditions for CSBMs are met by sharing information on defense budgets and on military doctrine and tactics and by exercising together for peacekeeping operations. NATO expansion may also create new requirements for special forms of CSBMs (see chapter 12 by Victor Kremenyuk).

Crises and Arms Control

The use of a single nuclear weapon by either side during the Cold War easily could have led to a global security disaster. Soviet and U.S. leaders were working from the same set of assumptions about the effects of a thermonuclear war. Khrushchev's futile attempts at nuclear coercion from 1957 through 1962 reflected a miscalculation about the limits of psychodrama, not a denial of the consequences of a hostile use of nuclear weapons. It was not entirely a coincidence that the first U.S.-Soviet nuclear arms agreement of the Cold War period—the limited nuclear test ban treaty—was successfully negotiated soon after Khrushchev caught a glimpse of an imminent nuclear catastrophe during the Cuban missile crisis. But this was the only occasion when it can be said that going to the brink of war provided the shock needed to conclude an agreement. And even in this case, the poor state of Soviet-Chinese relations seems to have been a major factor in Khrushchev's thinking. Bedrock reasons for nuclear arms control other than a momentary crisis motivated U.S. leaders and all Soviet leaders after Khrushchev.

It is fair and necessary, however, to ask why arms control failed to head off crises in U.S.-Soviet relations; for example, only a year after the 1972 strategic nuclear agreements signed by Richard Nixon and Brezhnev, the United States and the Soviet Union found themselves in a major crisis over the Middle East in which U.S. nuclear forces went on heightened alert. One answer is that the arms control agreements did what they were intended to do—they worked to prevent nuclear weapons from being used, and they reinforced the idea that U.S. and Soviet forces should not come into direct combat. To ask more of arms control in the preventive diplomacy sense would have been unrealistic, especially considering the inability of Moscow and Washington to control the actions of third parties. Another answer was given by President Nixon in the wake of the 1973 crisis. In his answer, he spoke more generally of détente, rather than of arms control specifically, but arms control was a key part of the U.S.-Soviet détente. His view was that "without détente, we might have had a major conflict in the Middle East. With détente, we avoided it."[3] Under either analysis, it is a fact that with growing numbers of arms control agreements, there were fewer U.S.-Soviet crises. The deployment of NATO nuclear forces in Europe in 1983 generated a crisis of sorts, but arms control negotiations brought an end to it.

Stakes, Attitudes, and Tactics in Evolution

At times when arms control agreements were concluded, two major factors and a trend seem to have come into play, especially on the Soviet side—all of which changed Soviet and U.S. perceptions of what was at stake. One was a realization that the political relationship between the two superpowers was important enough to over-ride other hesitations. This was the case with the first serious arms treaty, the limited nuclear test ban treaty of 1963. The agreement was concluded less than a year after the trauma of the Cuban missile crisis. And it was concluded just as the Soviets were moving toward a major break with China, a fact that made good relations with the United States more important to Moscow. The desire for a changed political relationship also came to the fore in the signing of the INF Treaty. Mikhail Gorbachev had become convinced that the Soviet Union needed a new relationship with the West. The INF Treaty was one of the ways in which this could be accomplished.

The other major factor was a realization that unilateral policies and programs would not yield a military advantage and might even worsen the security situation. This was probably the case with the Anti-Ballistic Missile Treaty (ABM Treaty) and the Strategic Arms Limitation Talks (SALT I) agreement on strategic offensive forces, the first agreements limiting strategic nuclear forces. Treaties of the Gorbachev era—for example, the treaty on limiting conventional forces in Europe and the START I treaty—probably were made possible by a combination of a desire for political change and a conclusion that security could best be attained by cooperation rather than confrontation.

A long-term secular trend that developed in U.S.-Soviet relations encouraged changed perceptions of the stakes that each side had in mutual cooperation. At the onset of the Cold War, U.S. and Soviet leaders thought that their mutual interests were extremely limited, and, in any case, each party doubted that a will for cooperation existed on the other side. The *feasibility* of cooperation, therefore, was heavily discounted by both nations.[4] War, rather than mutual cooperation, was in the air from 1948 through 1956. Soviet overtures to the West led to improvements in Finland and Austria during the latter part of this period, following Joseph Stalin's death in 1953. There was no lasting change for the better, however. Khrushchev's nuclear diplomacy from 1957 to 1962 led to crises over Berlin and finally over missiles in Cuba. John Kennedy's 1961 decision to build 1,000 Minuteman intercontinental ballistic missiles (ICBMs) raised the ante in the nuclear arms race. Nevertheless, in Dwight D. Eisenhower's second term, 1957–61, mainly through his interest in and support for a nuclear test ban, seeds were planted that later grew into an appreciation on both sides that limited cooperation was, indeed, feasible.[5]

Negotiations on a comprehensive nuclear test ban began in 1958, and a mutual moratorium on all nuclear testing was in effect from then until August 1961. Other ideas advanced by the United States during that time clearly went well beyond the level of confidence that existed in Moscow. The "Open Skies" proposal, advanced by Eisenhower in 1955 and pushed vigorously by his administration through most of his second term, was unacceptable to the Soviets. His proposal for talks on preventing a surprise attack led to a multilateral conference in 1958, but it collapsed after a few weeks. Eisenhower's proposal to establish the International Atomic Energy Agency, however, was accepted by the Soviet Union after several exchanges of views between Moscow and Washington. In the light of this experience, it was obvious that the first steps in U.S.-Soviet cooperation would have to be quite limited because Moscow's obsession with tight secrecy and total control over events in its territory would not permit a more expansive approach.

Arms control negotiations during the Cold War succeeded in producing agreements from time to time, frequently because of the stakes that Moscow and Washington saw in a special relationship between the two countries—a factor that was strong enough to supersede other concerns. This was the case with the first serious arms treaty, the limited nuclear test ban treaty of 1963. The Treaty on Intermediate-Range Nuclear Forces of 1987 is a more important reflection of the stakes that Moscow perceived in the late 1980s, promoting a radically different relationship with the United States. The fundamental element of Gorbachev's "new thinking" at that time was that security could be attained better through cooperation than through confrontation. He consciously used arms control to achieve this goal.

Between the modest step of 1963 and the bold move of 1987 was the long incumbency of Brezhnev—a period during which the Soviet leaders saw arms control as a means of consolidating U.S.-Soviet détente and advertising their superpower status in agreement with the United States. The perspective that both sides shared was that they could cooperate when doing so would prevent their military postures from suffering a disadvantage relative to the other side. This perspective yielded agreements but only rather slowly and aimed more at predictability than at dramatic changes in the balance of forces. An exception to this was the Anti-Ballistic Missile Treaty of 1972, which was a major achievement of the period. Secretary of Defense Robert McNamara often spoke of the action-reaction cycle that drove the arms race, and he saw an ABM deployment as an act that would fuel an all-out arms race. President Nixon also understood the phenomenon well and shared that view of ABM deployment.

Presidential leadership was a key factor in changing U.S. public attitudes. Eisenhower's reputation as a military leader in World War II gave him total credibility when he spoke of the need for cooperation with the Soviet Union. Without him, attitudes in the United States likely would have changed more slowly. To a large degree, he legitimized the quest for a test ban treaty during his second term. President Kennedy spoke favorably of a comprehensive nuclear test ban many times, and his great speech of 1963 at the American University resonated very well with the public. Kennedy's leadership in securing the nuclear test ban treaty despite a series of crises in U.S.-Soviet relations was a model for his successors, Lyndon Johnson and Richard Nixon, who consciously emulated his example and built on the foundations he had laid.

By 1968, experience had proved that common interests existed and that cooperation was, indeed, feasible. As they invested more heavily in the process of détente, both the United States and the Soviet Union accepted the fact they had a larger stake in cooperation. The next big question was whether cooperation could be extended to the very center of the U.S.-Soviet nuclear relationship—strategic nuclear forces. Verification had become possible through the mutual acceptance of satellite reconnaissance, and nuclear deterrence was not essentially affected by capping the number of missiles and bombers. Nixon and Brezhnev each saw that his country's interests were served by a stable relationship based on the status quo. And so problem solving, rather than confrontation, became a dominant feature, with some notable exceptions, during the Nixon-Kissinger-Brezhnev era.

But the problem-solving mode did not extend to agreement on what constituted a stable nuclear posture, nor could it overcome residual distrust and suspicion. The constructive working relationship between the two nations, with arms control as its centerpiece and shared perceptions on the stakes involved, suffered a setback during the Carter administration when President Carter's effort to deal with the destabilizing effects of MIRVed ICBMs was bluntly rejected by the Soviet Union. Problems cropped up over the U.S. "neutron bomb" and the Soviet SS-20. Carter decided to proceed with a new MIRVed ICBM—the MX missile. His administration ended with a monumental and unrealized plan for basing the new missile and with a nuclear doctrine that included planning for protracted nuclear war. His SALT II treaty was withdrawn from the U.S. Senate as U.S.-Soviet relations deteriorated in 1979–80 over, among other things, a misunderstanding about a Soviet brigade in Cuba, Cuban and Soviet troops in Africa, and the Soviet invasion of Afghanistan.

The problem-solving mode was revived on a more dramatic scale during the 1986–92 period as a result of the rise to power of Reagan and Gorbachev and Gorbachev's decision to use arms control to change the Soviet Union's relations with the West. His decision was probably based, in part, on prior successful U.S.-Soviet experiences in arms control, but his major motivation clearly was rooted in his "new thinking" paradigm.[6] President Reagan's attitude, as noted, was motivated by a strong desire to rid the world of the nuclear threat.

The Balance Sheet

In some instances, arms control actually did what arms control theorists thought it should do: solve serious security problems and moderate the arms race. In other cases, failure to use the arms control instrument of policy effectively led to an escalation in the tempo of the arms competition and to heightened tensions.

One of the most important illustrations of successful arms control is the U.S.-USSR antiballistic missile treaty of 1972, in which the two nations defined an envelope within which U.S. and Soviet nuclear forces could be built. Excluded from the permissible areas was competition in building defenses. The technology of the time could not have provided an effective defense, but the effort would have stimulated an offensive buildup to overcome the other side's defense effort. But the failure to use arms control effectively contributed to an arms race in one area even while it was restraining an offense-defense arms race. Part of the price that Nixon and Kissinger paid for the acquiescence of Congress and the Joint Chiefs of Staff to the ABM Treaty was to permit the testing and deployment of MIRVs. This development conferred advantages on striking first against an adversary, since one ballistic missile armed with MIRVs could, in principle, destroy more than one of the adversary's ballistic missiles. This situation gave rise to an arms race in MIRVed missiles, resulting in tens of thousands of warheads on each side and policies characterized by the United States as "protracted nuclear war." Considerable effort was expended to deal with the problem through elaborate basing schemes that were never actually carried out. In the end, an arms control treaty (START II) was negotiated to eliminate all land-based MIRVed missiles.

An even more complex instance of the failure and then success of preventive diplomacy in arms control involved the Soviet deployment of the SS-20, a highly accurate, three-warhead ballistic missile targeted on Western Europe. Despite receiving repeated warnings that the deployment would be seen as a destabilizing move, the Soviets went ahead with it. This led to a NATO decision in 1979 to deploy ballistic missiles and ground-launched cruise missiles in Western Europe and to offer negotiations regarding limits on these and on Soviet SS-20s—an offer extended, in part, to make deployment of the missiles politically acceptable in Western Europe. In this case, therefore, the arms control process facilitated a difficult decision for the Western democracies. The subsequent deployment of the NATO weapons in 1983 led to one of the lowest points in U.S.-Soviet relations in the late Cold War period. This problem was solved only when a radical Soviet leader, Mikhail Gorbachev, accepted the radical idea of President Ronald Reagan that all missiles in this category on both sides should be eliminated. The resulting treaty on intermediate-range nuclear forces was the first arms control treaty to eliminate a whole class of nuclear weapons.

Preventive diplomacy in arms control has also had side effects as important as military security itself. An environmental disaster was in the making during the 1950s and early 1960s when both the United States and the Soviet Union were extensively testing nuclear weapons in the atmosphere. The resulting increase in radioactivity levels, particularly in areas downwind of the nuclear explosions, was creating a hazardous situation for large populations. Today, it is estimated that thousands of people have been affected by the radiation released by the explosive testing of nuclear weapons in the earth's atmosphere. After years of effort, the limited nuclear test ban treaty (LTBT) of 1963 put an end to U.S. and Soviet atmospheric nuclear explosions. The other states with nuclear weapons followed suit later. Here, the process limited an environmental hazard—an unusual effect of an arms control agreement—and also served two important political purposes: helping Khrushchev at a difficult time for him in Moscow's relations with China and establishing the precedent that U.S.-Soviet security cooperation was truly possible.

One of the most successful exercises in preventive diplomacy is the nuclear nonproliferation treaty of 1970. One can argue about the extent to which this treaty, as opposed to other factors, was responsible for limiting the spread of nuclear weapons capabilities. There can be little doubt, however, that the regime created and encouraged by the treaty has succeeded in influencing national decisions in an antinuclear direction. The process worked by assuring potential proliferators that their neighbors were bound by the same agreement that they were, an assurance that placed a damper on regional arms races. The regime held for nearly thirty years, until the Indian and Pakistani nuclear tests of 1998 and events of this type elsewhere (North Korea, Iran, Iraq) raised new challenges for further efforts of preventive diplomacy.

The Changed Nature of U.S.-Russian Arms Control Diplomacy in the Post–Cold War Period

Arms control as preventive diplomacy, in the sense of two or more states in an adversarial relationship seeking to prevent a nuclear catastrophe, is no longer the centerpiece of U.S.-Russian relations.[7] Other issues have come to the fore. Today, economic and political issues are more often at the top of the agenda than nuclear arms control. START III negotiations will deal with some of the traditional issues of strategic nuclear arms control, for the same mix of political and military elements is present, in a somewhat attenuated form. But a special relationship still exists between Russia and the United States, and START III will demonstrate that. It still matters how the shrinking strategic forces of Russia and the United States are configured, and the emphasis on secure basing remains. A relatively new issue relates to rapid-launch procedures for ICBMs and cooperation in early warning of missile launches as ways of relieving stress on command and control systems.

These issues are not really different, as technical matters, from corresponding issues in Cold War days. As in the past, negotiations will be required to resolve differences and to create a legally binding basis for implementing the results. But the context and style of these negotiations will be different. They will be less adversarial and more cooperative, aimed less at the danger of a U.S.-Russian nuclear war and more at reducing the salience of nuclear weapons in the evolving relations of the two countries. In addition, negotiators will pay more attention to the connection of other countries to the nuclear arms control process, and, no doubt, they will also consider financial costs far more than they ever did in the past. Nonetheless, the resemblance to arms control negotiations of the past is strong, and preventive diplomacy is an accurate description of the START III negotiating process. But that type of negotiation and agreement cannot be a complete answer to the issues that have arisen since the collapse of the Soviet Union.

The four main goals of preventive diplomacy in the post–Cold War nuclear area are

- Preventing mutual nuclear deterrence from generating tensions in the U.S.-Russian relations,
- Preventing nuclear materials from falling into the hands of terrorists or international criminal organizations,
- Preventing a global nuclear arms race, and
- Preventing conditions that might be conducive to an unauthorized launch of nuclear-armed missiles.

The familiar methodologies of nuclear arms control negotiations during the Cold War do not fit the changed circumstances. Preventive action is badly needed, but traditional diplomatic approaches will not suffice. Perhaps the most threatening of these new developments stems not from the ambitions or fears of states contending in an international system but from the changing character of substate units and the possibility that they may acquire weapons of mass destruction. How governments can mobilize their resources to confront this new situation has become a central problem for preventive diplomacy. It all comes down to the question of how joint action by governments can combat the rise of what, a quarter of a century ago, the late Hedley Bull (1995) called "the new medievalism."

Bull cited five features of world politics that provided evidence that inroads were being made on the supremacy of the state over its territory and citizens. These were (1) the regional integration of states, (2) the disintegration of states, (3) the restoration of private international violence, (4) transnational organizations, and (5) the technological unification of the world. He asked whether these trends suggested that the state system may be giving way to a secular reincarnation of the system of overlapping authority and multiple loyalty that was the central characteristic of medieval Europe. He thought not, partly because all the actors in these trends were "intellectually imprisoned by the theory of the states system." Bull argued that private international violence was nothing new and that the substate groups then engaged in violence appeared, in every case, to be aiming at the establishment of new states and calibrating their use of violence to build support for their aims.

Yet Bull's description of the aims of terrorists—valid a quarter century ago—is no longer an apt depiction of what terrorist groups are after. The World Trade Center bombing, the Oklahoma City bombing, and the Aum Shinrikyo's nerve gas attack in Tokyo do not fit the patterns of the past. Some observers of these events have suggested that they represent a new kind of terrorism, one aimed at retribution or eradication of what alienated groups define as evil. Such groups are not constrained by concerns about losing popular sympathy for their causes, so the use of weapons of indiscriminate destruction—chemical, biological, and nuclear weapons—may become more attractive to groups interested in mass violence.

The shape of preventive diplomacy today is very different from its Cold War manifestation. Here are some illustrations:

- To prevent a brain drain of former Soviet nuclear scientists to aspiring nuclear powers such as North Korea, the United States and other countries funded the International Scientific and Technology Center in Moscow and a similar center in Kiev. These centers provide grants to scientists who were involved in the Soviet nuclear weapons program, enabling them to work on civilian projects. No scientists are known to have left for work in the nuclear programs of other countries.

- To tighten controls at major Russian nuclear research centers, especially those in open cities (that is, cities to which access is not controlled by the Russian government), the United States entered into agreements with the Russian government to improve the methods and equipment available to the centers. The Luch Production Association, where fissile material was stolen in the past, is now one of the many places in Russia where physical protection systems and material control and accounting have been up-graded because of U.S.-Russian cooperation.
- To tighten controls at other research centers, U.S. and Russian laboratories and institutes—including Los Alamos, Livermore, and Sandia and Arzamas 16, Chelyabinsk 70, and the Kurchatov Institute—have entered into direct laboratory-to-laboratory agreements. Six U.S. laboratories and eight Russian laboratories participate in the program. These agreements have significantly upgraded access controls at many laboratories, thus responding to the "insider threat," and a culture of material control and accounting is taking root.
- To enhance security at nuclear weapons sites controlled by the Russian Ministry of Defense, the United States and Russia are cooperating in programs designed to install physical security equipment and train rapid-reaction forces.
- To increase the security of nuclear weapons in transit, the United States and the Russian Ministry of Defense have cooperated in modifying Russian railcars. Supercontainers to protect nuclear weapons while in transit also are being provided, as is mobile emergency response equipment to deal with the consequences of accidents.
- To improve Russia's ability to account for and track nuclear warheads in transit or in storage, the United States and the Russian Ministry of Defense are cooperating in establishing an automated inventory control and management system.
- To strengthen Russia's national regulations and standards for material protection, control, and accountability, close cooperation has been established between Russia's national regulatory agency (Gosatomnadzor) and the U.S. Department of Energy and the U.S. Nuclear Regulatory Commission.

In April 1996, Russia and the United States also agreed to cooperate within the framework of the Group of Seven industrialized nations in dealing with nuclear smuggling. Two key elements of the agreement were (1) the sharing of information on nuclear theft and smuggling incidents and establishment of national points of contact for this purpose, and (2) the enhancement of cooperation among national intelligence, customs, and law enforcement agencies.

Still left unfinished is an immense amount of work connected with

- Storing, for decades to come, large numbers of dismantled Russian nuclear warheads in a facility jointly monitored by the United States and Russia and by the International Atomic Energy Agency;

- Building mutual confidence in the accurate knowledge of each other's holdings of nuclear weapons and fissile material and gaining assurance that nuclear weapons are being dismantled;
- Converting highly enriched uranium and plutonium from dismantled warheads into forms difficult for substate entities or even many governments to exploit for weapons purposes.

Measures of the types just outlined involve a high degree of technical content, and much of the implementation must be conducted directly by engineers and military people. In nearly every case, however, negotiations were a necessary precursor. Some negotiated agreements laid the basic legal foundation for U.S.-Russian cooperation; others simply spelled out the contractual arrangements for specific actions.

The common link between all of these agreements is the idea that how well a government safeguards its holdings of fissile materials and its technological expertise is a matter of international concern. The adversary is no longer another state. The goal, in fact, has become to work with other governments in a common struggle against nuclear theft, nuclear smuggling, and nuclear terrorism. In the age of globalization, preventive diplomacy may increasingly deal with a very new problem—that states no longer have a monopoly over the use of force on a devastating scale. If the states are to win this fight, they will have to cooperate more fully in areas that are still thought of as sovereign prerogatives and primarily matters of internal concern.

Conclusion

Summing up the Cold War experiences with arms control as preventive diplomacy, it can be said, first, that the agreements that were achieved, even though quite limited in the early years, provided both safety nets and ratchets. Even when U.S.-Soviet relations went through rough patches, the arms control agreements and even the negotiations in themselves saved the superpowers' relationship from being damaged beyond repair. Successive agreements and the experience in cooperation ratcheted up the belief in the possibility and feasibility of cooperation, so that the relationship never went back to the place where it had started. Even the difficult relationship in late 1983, after the Soviets shot down a Korean airliner, was on its way to improvement by early 1984 as the dialogue returned to nuclear arms control.

The fundamental reason for the phenomenon of adversarial cooperation was a recognition of interdependence or mutual dependency, stemming mainly from a mutual vulnerability to nuclear weapons. This concept has been noted by many scholars for many years, among them Alexander George, Robert Keohane and Joseph Nye, and Thomas Schelling. But it also has been acknowledged that a recognition of mutual dependency is not enough to generate cooperation in sensitive security matters. Tactical considerations and the personalities of arms control negotiators have played important roles, of course, in bringing arms control agreements into being. Leadership at the top of the U.S. and Soviet governments was the critical factor, driven, in large part, by internal politics and by hopes for achieving a favorable position in the history of the age.

An important secondary factor was the creation of institutions that hardened the regime and perpetuated the ideas and the mechanisms of arms control. The arms control experience built up an infrastructure that facilitated cooperation. The channels, negotiating forums, personal contacts, procedures, and implementing arrangements amounted to a form of institutionalized cooperation. This tended to make purely autonomous decisions less likely by enhancing the chances that in making decisions, each party would take the other's views into account.

The success of arms control during the Cold War in physically eliminating the threat posed by the existence of nuclear weapons admittedly was limited. But through most of that period, this was not the objective of arms control. The objective was to make war less likely; arms control agreements, for the most part, were aimed at reassurance.[8] Raymond Garthoff has pointed out, correctly, that the nuclear arms race could not be ended until the ideological foundations of the Cold War had been removed.[9] But the possibility of war and the use of nuclear weapons could be made less likely through the arms control form of preventive diplomacy, as well as through prudent force planning.

A basic problem that arms control has sought to address is the use, whether deliberate or otherwise, of nuclear weapons. McGeorge Bundy (1988, 587) observed that "the 'tradition' of nonuse is the most important single legacy of the first half century of fission." Many factors in the U.S.-Soviet relationship contributed to that outcome, among them being arms control negotiations and arms control agreements. This process of preventive diplomacy during the Cold War concerned, to a large degree, enhancing predictability by creating tacit or explicit rules of behavior.[10] It was not necessary to pass through dangerous crises to prevent a global security disaster. In the mid-1950s, Raymond Aron (1955, 149) pointed out the remarkable fact that "for the first time, the contemporaries of an invention believe themselves to be endowed with foreknowledge."

The central focus of U.S.-Soviet nuclear arms control, therefore, was to underwrite mutual nuclear deterrence but not to eliminate or transform it. For example, the negotiating process focused heavily on threats to vulnerable, land-based missiles that could become incentives for first, disarming strikes, underscoring Kissinger's point, cited earlier, about the special destabilizing properties of nuclear weapons. In addition, each side gained some sense of the other's strategic thinking through the process of negotiations and some reassurance that unleashing nuclear war was not a realistic policy option for the other superpower.

A great lesson of the Cold War was that decision-making that was truly autonomous generally misjudged the interests of the other superpower and led to results that no one liked. The Cuban missile crisis was a perfect example of this. So was the Soviet decision to deploy large numbers of SS-20 nuclear ballistic missiles targeted on Western Europe. Khrushchev's reckless attempts to change the status quo in his favor, especially after acquiring thermonuclear weapons and an intercontinental ballistic missile capability in 1957, led to several major crises.[11] He personified the threat to peace and stability that could result from decisions divorced from the tacit rules that had emerged in the aftermath of World War II. He highlighted the risks of truly autonomous decision-making.

Especially after the Khrushchev interlude, Moscow and Washington came to believe strongly in the value of predictability and stability, above all in Europe. Their rivalry was strong and frequently bitter, but the elements of restraint and cooperation in it offered political advantages for both sides. Cooperation achieved under the threat of annihilation and under conditions of bipolar rivalry is difficult to accept as a regime built around norms and rules. Hard-edged competition and the constant evocation of the nuclear threat naturally concealed the restraint that was, in fact, practiced and expected.

Notes

1. I am indebted to Professor Alexander George of Stanford University for these terms and distinctions.

2. For further discussion of the political side of arms control, see Talbott 1979, 48.

3. From President Nixon's press conference of October 26, 1973, as quoted in Garthoff 1994a, 439.

4. A very useful description and analysis of the experience of U.S.-Soviet security cooperation can be found in George, Farley, and Dallin 1988. In his analysis, Professor George described the problem of feasibility this way: "U.S. leaders must have reason to believe that the Soviet Union is capable of, and willing, to enter into or to accept the kind of relationship Washington would like to develop. Soviet leaders must arrive at a similar judgment regarding U.S. acceptance of the type of superpower relationship they wish to create" (p. 667).

5. Raymond Garthoff believes that from 1953 on, leaders on both sides favored détente over confrontation even though periods of confrontation repeatedly succeeded periods of détente. My judgment is that the periods of confrontation never returned the relationship to what it had been before the latest period of détente.

6. Alexander George (George, Farley, and Dallin 1988, 697) identified linkage with the overall U.S.-Soviet relationship as one of the key elements in strategies facilitating security cooperation. I believe that this factor was very important in each of the major U.S.-Soviet/Russian negotiations.

7. This section draws on a lecture I gave on April 10, 1997, at Stanford University. It was subsequently published by the university under the title Loose Nukes: Security Issues on the U.S.-Russian Agenda (Goodby 1997).

8. For a valuable discussion of this point, see Sims 1990. The author identified five objectives for arms control policy as seen by U.S. specialists in the 1950s and 1960s: Reaffirmation of the conventional-nuclear threshold, reaffirmation of the nuclear-conventional firebreak, pursuit of arms race stability, pursuit of crisis stability, and the attainment of a long-term relaxation of tension (p. 35).

9. See Garthoff, 1994b, 752–53. This book contains an excellent description of the uses of arms control in ending the Cold War. Garthoff 1994a contains a detailed account and analysis of the politics of arms control during the 1970s. In this book, Garthoff showed that parity in strategic nuclear weapons, as codified in nuclear arms control agreements, was seen in Moscow as a means of achieving political parity with the United States.

10. Michael Lund, for example, viewed preventive diplomacy as necessary under conditions "where existing international relations or national politics appear unable to manage tensions without violence erupting" (see Lund 1995). In my view, preventive diplomacy should come into play long before the appearance of tensions that threaten to erupt into violence. I also use the term order-building diplomacy to distinguish this type of diplomacy from the crisis prevention category of preventive diplomacy.

11. A useful account of this period is Beschloss 1991.

References

Aron, Raymond. 1955. *The Century of Total War.* Boston: Beacon.

Beschloss, Michael R. 1991. *The Crisis Years—Kennedy and Khrushchev, 1960–1963.* New York: HarperCollins.

Borawzki, J. 1992. *From the Atlantic to the Urals.* New York: Pergamon.

Bull, Hedley. 1995. *The Anarchical Society: A Study of Order in World Politics,* 2nd ed. New York: Columbia University Press.

Bundy, McGeorge. 1988. *Danger and Survival: Choices About the Bomb in the First Fifty Years.* New York: Random House.

Carr, E. H. 1964. *The Twenty Years' Crisis, 1919–1939.* New York: HarperTorchbooks.

Gaddis, John Lewis. 1987. *The Long Peace: Inquiries into the History of the Cold War.* Oxford: Oxford University Press.

Garthoff, Raymond L. 1994a. *Détente and Confrontation: American-Soviet Relations from Nixon to Reagan,* rev. ed. Washington, D.C.: Brookings.

———. 1994b. *The Great Transition: American-Soviet Relations and the End of the Cold War.* Washington, D.C.: Brookings.

George, Alexander L., P. J. Farley, and A. Dallin, eds. 1988. *U.S.-Soviet Security Cooperation: Achievements, Failures, Lessons.* New York: Oxford University Press.

Goodby, James. 1988. "Stockholm Conference." In *US-Soviet Security Cooperation,* ed. Alexander George, P. Farley, and Alexander Dallin. Boulder: Westview.

———. 1997. "Loose Nukes: Security Issues on the U.S.-Russian Agenda." Lecture, April 10, 1997. Stanford, Calif.: Stanford University.

———. In press. *Europe Undivided.* Washington, D.C.: U.S. Institute of Peace, chapter 1.

Kanet, Roger, and Eduard Kolodziej, eds. 1991. *The Cold War as Cooperation: Superpower Cooperation in Regional Conflict Management.* London: Macmillan.

Keohane, Robert, and Joseph Nye. 1977. *Power and Independence: World Politics in Transition.* Boston: Little, Brown.

Khrushchev, Nikita. 1970. *Khrushchev Remembers.* Boston: Little, Brown.

Kissinger, Henry. 1979. *White House Years.* Boston: Little, Brown.

Lenin, V., ed. *Collected Works* (English translation). Moscow: International Publishers.

Lund, Michael. 1995. "Underrating Preventive Diplomacy," *Foreign Affairs* 74, no. 4 (July–August): 161.

Massie, Robert K. 1991. *Dreadnought: Britain, Germany, and the Coming of the Great War.* New York: Random House.

Schelling, Thomas. 1960. *The Strategy of Conflict.* Cambridge, Mass.: Harvard University Press.

Seaman, L.C.B. 1955. *From Vienna to Versailles.* London: Methuen.

Sims, Jennifer E. 1990. *Icarus Restrained: An Intellectual History of Nuclear Arms Control, 1945–1960.* Boulder: Westview.

Talbott, Strobe. 1979. *Endgame: The Inside Story of SALT II.* New York: Harper & Row.

12

Global Security Conflicts II: Controlling Alliance Crisis

Victor Kremenyuk

Negotiation to prevent conflict or the escalation of conflict has acquired an urgent dimension. In current international practices, such negotiation is regarded as both a necessary and a standard approach that should be promoted, supported, and perfected. Alliance spirals, like arms races, have been identified as one of the major causes of war, through their contribution to states' security dilemmas (Jervis 1978; Snyder 1984). However, these operations need to be kept under control, and the security of the opposing—as well as the initiating—side must be assured by parallel negotiations to prevent escalation and confrontation. Alliances, like arms, are critical elements in the balance of power, itself the product of security negotiations (Walt 1985; Haas 1953). The negotiations between the North Atlantic Treaty Organization (NATO) and Russia that ended in May 1997 with the conclusion of the Founding Act and established some ground rules between the two sides is an example of such an approach.

The Conflict Between Russia and NATO

Russia and NATO are the two major military entities in Europe. In the years of the Cold War, there was a rough military balance between the two dominant military blocs—NATO, led by the United States, and the Warsaw Treaty Organization (WTO), led by the Soviet Union. After the Cold War ended and the Soviet Union collapsed, Russia emerged as the largest successor of the Soviet Union, as measured by military strength and other capabilities. The ratio in arms and military personnel between the two sides has changed significantly, however: In some areas, it has become 3 to 1, and in others, it is 4 to 1 in favor of NATO (Bertram 1995). Yet even with that unequal ratio, the possibility of war between the two sides cannot be excluded completely ("Kontseptsia" 1997).

Both Russia and NATO have frequently indicated that they do not regard each other as enemies (Solana 1997). Indeed, in both declarations and concrete actions, they have acted as partners (if not allies), as peacekeeping operations in Bosnia, Kosovo, and other parts of the former Yugoslavia demonstrate. Furthermore, the two sides cooperate closely within the North Atlantic Cooperation Council, and they have signed an agreement on cooperation within the Partnership for Peace program and established some embryonic organs for managing bilateral cooperation.

But these developments do not present the complete picture. Attempts on both sides to emphasize their desire to live in peace and cooperation are counterbalanced by rather widespread hard feelings and bitter memories. For the majority of Russians, NATO is not simply a strong residue of the Cold War; it is also considered a current threat because of its military capabilities, because it is oriented toward the use of military force, and because its deployment and structure are essentially directed to the east. Russians do not yet feel that they have become an integral part of Europe, and they understand that the West has turned a cool cheek to almost all their initiatives. Consequently, they regard NATO as essentially anti-Russian (because there is no other similarly strong argument for the continuation of the alliance), and they do not accept the assurances of the Western leaders that NATO is not a threat.

This feeling is paralleled by a rather widespread anti-Russian sentiment in the West, shared by the majority of the Western military, some prominent political writers (Zbigniew Brzezinski, Henry Kissinger), and significant elements of the public. In any case, NATO's military doctrine and its nuclear planning still address the possibility of a military conflict with Russia (Angelakis 1997).

This quasi symmetry of views was significantly strengthened by the whole process of rhetoric surrounding the problems of NATO's enlargement. It is clear that the three Central European nations that opted for membership in NATO in 1993 did so because of their fears of Russia. The dominant feelings in the Czech Republic, Hungary, and Poland were and still are essentially anti-Russian. These nations suffered from Soviet forays in the 1950s and 1960s; they have accepted the end of the Cold War and of the Soviet Union as a good opportunity to change sides; and they regard the current developments in Russia with concern and suspicion because they do not think that democracy will prevail in that country.

There is little reason to believe that all NATO countries and leaders of transnational mechanisms shared the same anti-Russian views in the early 1990s. On the contrary, many of them were ready to give serious consideration to the idea of a "New World Order" in which U.S.-Soviet/Russian cooperation might have played a central role (Zartman and Kremenyuk 1995). But with the fading of these ideas because of the collapse of the Soviet Union, the major interest in some Western quarters has been to save NATO despite the fact that the danger of a new war in Europe has ceased to exist. In this regard, the concerns of the Central European nations about Russia and the anxieties of those in the West who want to preserve NATO have merged and have changed the whole political climate in Europe to a significant degree.

The Russian attitude toward NATO has also changed. As of the early 1990s, Russia was ready to agree with NATO's stabilizing role in Europe, and it was looking ahead toward rapprochement, with the goal of establishing close military cooperation under the aegis of the Organization for Security and Cooperation in Europe (OSCE). But one of the conditions for such a relationship was that NATO not take advantage of the period when Russian (formerly Soviet) troops were leaving their bases in East Germany, Poland, Hungary, the Czech Republic, and the Baltic states. The void was not to be filled with the NATO structure in order to avoid giving the impression that the Soviet (Russian) troops were withdrawing involuntarily, forced out in the way Iraqi troops were driven from Kuwait during the Desert Storm war. This principle, laid down as one of the cornerstones of the Soviets' agreement to German reunification in 1989 (as discussed in chapter 5 by Sukyong Choi), was unequivocally accepted at the time by the West and solemnly endorsed both in the German State Treaty and in NATO's pledge in its Copenhagen statement following the NATO summit of 1990 (Konovalov, Kortunov, and Oznobishchev 1996).

Russians assumed that security arrangements for the Eastern European countries, both former WTO members and former Soviet republics, would be negotiated under the OSCE umbrella and that, until then, the situation had to be frozen. From this point of view, the pursuit of NATO enlargement has simply exploded the vision of future European security and raised the prospect of a new division in Europe, pitting NATO nations against non-NATO nations. The new arrangement has destroyed the backbone of the Yalta-Postdam agreements, which, for better or worse, have served as the only negotiated legal basis for the European settlement since 1945. In short, the Russian government believed it had valid reasons to feel that its security and other legitimate interests were impaired and that, as a consequence, it had to prepare for a new, sharp confrontation in Europe.

Possible Responses

From any point of view, Russia had to regard NATO's actions with a high degree of concern and as an indication of imminent danger. The major threat, although perhaps not the immediate one, was the growing possibility of a new war with the West. It is deeply entrenched in the Russian mind that the West can and will be a source of mortal danger. Several times in its history, Russia was attacked from the West; whether in Napoleon Bonaparte's era or Adolph Hitler's time, a coalition of European powers invaded Russian territory. And in every instance, recovery took tremendous effort and great sacrifice. Given this historical background, NATO is simply considered the acronym for another European coalition against Russia. So, even though NATO cannot be regarded as an immediate military threat in the current context, the Russian collective memory suggests that the advancement of a strong military alliance to its borders may one day turn into an open risk of yet another surprise attack.

The other risk to Russian security seen in NATO enlargement is the sense that this alliance, like a malignant growth, is gradually spreading over Europe, reducing Russia's chances of playing an active European role. Russia has lost all the former Soviet allies in Europe and has not acquired new ones. More than that, it has lost control over strategically important Baltic states and the Crimean peninsula in the Black Sea. Its capacity to project power in the immediate vicinity has thus been limited, and the strong anti-Russian sentiment in the Baltic states and in the Ukraine (which, by the way, was strongly supported in the West) can be used against it. As a result, Russia's ability to pursue its interests in Europe has been impaired, as has its power to develop its economic ties freely and to participate as an equal in European politics (Rogov 1997).

The conclusion open to any Russian ruler or government is that the nation must prepare for a long and radical confrontation, perhaps another war, on its western borders. This becomes a shared goal for Russian politicians, not because of a possibility that a new dictatorship will emerge in Moscow or that some aggressive parties and groups will rise to power but because the notion has widespread resonance in a country that has lost its superpower status but retained its historical memory. In the event of an authoritarian turn in domestic politics, which this perception feeds, the conclusion that a confrontation must be anticipated will be forced on Russia. But even if democracy prevails, Russia's normal interest in development—economic, social, cultural, and technological—and its legitimate desire to have assured and unlimited access to European markets and spiritual treasures will inevitably lead it to demand and fight for another "window," just as Peter the Great did in the early eighteenth century. When the current period of transformation in Russia comes to an end and when the need for economic and social advancement becomes dominant in its foreign and security policies (as has happened with all developed nations), the Russian government will have to consider the issue of revising all the European arrangements, and it will have to be ready to use force if its legitimate demands are not recognized. This is one of the possible scenarios for the future due to NATO's expansion to the east. And it adds much to the attempts at building a national consensus in Russia for its future development.

Currently, Russia cannot meet the challenge presented by NATO enlargement as it might have done when it was in a better shape. Any attempt to re-

spond with force now would be suicidal, given its weakened state, and no reciprocal enlargement of any alliance of its own is possible. This understanding is widespread in the Russian policy-making community, though a significant group of individuals would prefer to risk another confrontation even
now. But the majority of people in Russia do not regard a new showdown with
the West as appropriate and desirable today. On the contrary, the far more
prevalent and popular view is that there is nothing to do but to swallow this
humiliation and prepare for revenge at some point in the future.

Strong and heated public debate in Russia over NATO enlargement and the
Russian response ended in a consensus that a conflict was not in the nation's
interest and should be avoided. This encouraged those in the government and
especially in the Foreign Ministry who contemplated the need for a compromise with NATO, disregarding the fact that the leaders of the alliance completely ignored Russian pleas to either reconsider or delay enlargement. Thus,
a consistent and productive process of negotiation between Russia and NATO
to prevent a confrontation and to craft some alternative to hostility or sub-
mission became possible (Angelakis 1997).

The Process of Russia-NATO Negotiation

It is hard to establish exactly when this negotiation started. The first contacts
between the two sides took place as early as 1992 during a European trip by
Russia's state secretary at the time, Gennady Burbulis. Since then, Russia has
supported a permanent dialogue with NATO, although this dialogue can
hardly be labeled "negotiation" and has been aimed at various subjects. It was
only in late 1994—when a consensus clearly emerged among the members of
the alliance to expand to the east, incorporating the Czech Republic, Hungary,
and Poland, and when strong Russian opposition to that plan was made apparent—that the idea of special Russia-NATO negotiations was formulated as
a policy goal. Inside Russia, only a few minor political figures risked speaking
about the necessity of this negotiation at that time. In the West, one of the
strongest partisans of the idea was William Perry, who was then the U.S. secretary of defense. Strange as it may seem, a number of important military
leaders in the West were either strongly against the idea of enlargement or insistent that enlargement should be coupled with negotiations with Russia,
while diplomats usually were much more "hawkish."

The first stage of Russia-NATO negotiations over whether to have a special
agreement between the parties took place on two levels: direct official negotiation and indirect diplomatic exchanges via public statements issued by each
side. By the end of 1994, the ball was in Russia's court because the West publicly admitted the importance of some kind of NATO-Russia treaty and indicated its willingness to start discussing the agreement without specifying the

type of treaty it sought or the specific items that should be included. This lack of clarity in purpose permitted those in the Russian leadership who were against immediate talks (but supported the idea of talks in general) to insist that Moscow's response to the proposal should be delayed. In the meantime, Russian leaders continued their harsh, propagandistic campaign against the prospect of NATO enlargement, threatening "countermeasures" and other retaliatory moves if the decision to expand the alliance was taken.

The essence of the bargaining in the first stage was clear: Western nations hoped that Moscow would buy a deal by which Russia would give its blessing to the idea of enlargement and NATO would pay for it by a treaty. This would, first, give Russia a completely unique status as NATO's only strategic partner in Europe and, second, establish working mechanisms between the two sides. Russia, in turn, hoped that its opposition would eventually force the West to dismiss the idea of enlargement and agree to a treaty that would guarantee Russian participation in NATO's decision-making. This period of indirect exchanges continued into late 1996, when Russian president Boris Yeltsin decided to replace pro-Western Andrey Kozyrev with middle-of-the-road Yevgeny Primakov as foreign minister.

By the end of 1996, it became clear to Moscow that its strategy, largely authored by Kozyrev, did not work. The West was firm in its intention to go ahead with enlargement, and there was no way to reverse its intent. The change of personalities in the Russian Foreign Ministry was part of a more sweeping change, connected with the general revision of Russian foreign policy. Moscow was not going to open hostilities with the West immediately, but the idea of a "strategic partnership" was definitely replaced by an approach in which Russia would keep its distance from the West and question all the elements of cooperation with the West that had been achieved until then.

The broad change was also reflected in the Russian attitude toward negotiations with NATO. It was not considered appropriate to start direct talks immediately, although indirect exchanges were still considered useful and relevant. But the essence of the dialogue had changed: Russian leaders understood that the decision on enlargement was imminent and that there was no sense in insisting again on its dismissal or delay. The official attitude had not changed. Publicly, Russia continued to protest. But in reality, the focus of discussion had shifted toward the conditions under which Russia would agree not to retaliate against this decision.

A unilateral pledge by NATO not to deploy nuclear forces and foreign troops on the territories of new members, another pledge to limit the decision on enlargement to the three previously mentioned Central European nations, and a promise to make Russian participation an indispensable part of NATO's decision-making on issues of European security were the major items sought by Moscow. Russia also wanted to get Western promises on these topics before official negotiations between the two sides started. NATO's position was both resolute and cautious: It would stand firm on enlargement but agree to discuss other Russian demands at the negotiations without making any preliminary commitments.

The second period of negotiations ended in early 1997. At the U.S.-Russian summit in Helsinki in March 1997, NATO enlargement was finally discussed between the Russian and U.S. presidents. President Bill Clinton did not accept the idea that Russia needed compensation for the NATO enlargement in the form of preliminary guarantees and a NATO-Russia agreement. He simply re-iterated his administration's position that a decision on enlargement would be taken in Madrid at the summit meeting of the alliance. He disregarded Russia's anxieties and expressed the hope that the NATO-Russia dialogue, which by that time was elevated to the level of NATO secretary-general Javier Solana and Russian minister Yevgeny Primakov, would produce an "acceptable" agreement. Unhappy with the results of these talks, Yeltsin addressed his friends in the West, German chancellor Helmut Kohl and French president Jacques Chirac, in order to push the negotiation to a decisive stage. Their response revealed a much better understanding of the Russian position, and they used their influence to bring the NATO side to a far more conciliatory and cooperative position. The French president even announced the deadline by which the negotiation had to be ended—May 27, 1997.

The third stage of negotiation was direct and decisive. During this stage, conducted within a short period between March and May 1997, a last effort was made to reach an agreement. Both sides acknowledged that a treaty orchestrating NATO-Russia relations had to be concluded and that it should be signed before the Madrid summit of NATO leaders; otherwise, there would be no need for an agreement at all. They also agreed that it would be somewhere between a full-size, detailed agreement and a brief, symbolic charter. The two negotiating teams would meet directly to discuss both the final format of the agreement (the Russian proposal of a "founding act" was accepted) and the major items of its content: relationship, institutions, mutual guarantees, and so forth. This was the most intensive stage of the negotiations, with both teams working almost day and night under strict supervision. The controversial issues that arose from time to time were immediately discussed and solved by Solana and Primakov, who were urging all parties to press forward with negotiations in order to meet the officially accepted date of signature. Finally, by May 27, 1997, the treaty was negotiated, and the Founding Act was signed on that day (published in *NATO Review,* vol. 45, no. 4, pp. 7–11).

It is unnecessary to give a detailed analysis of the document here because it is the process that is important. Suffice it to say that those who wanted an agreement, both in Russia and in the West, considered it a success. At least it accomplished the main task—preventing a possible crisis in NATO-Russia relations when a final decision to enlarge NATO was made at the NATO summit in Madrid in early July. In that sense, negotiations between Russia and NATO proved fruitful and relevant. What is left to analyze is how this outcome was made possible and what processes worked to bring it about.

Avoidance of Crisis: Changing Stakes

When the first signs of a possible crisis between Russia and NATO became visible, the issue of stakes acquired ominous significance. The issue seems of no great strategic importance: Whether or not Poland, Hungary, and the Czech Republic became members of NATO will not have any decisive impact either on the future of the alliance or on the security of Russia. The change, it appears, will not be of a strategic magnitude. Indeed, even some in the West think that inclusion of these three nations into the NATO structure may lead to its growing weakness. If making the three Central European nations members of the alliance only symbolically increases the power of the West, that cannot be regarded as a major threat to Russia.

But the issue, from the very beginning, was never approached in realistic terms. It acquired symbolic value, particularly in regard to such sensitive problems as post–Cold War policy and its rules, East-West relations, concepts of European security, alliance politics, partnership, national interest, and national ambition. Beneath what, on the surface, seemed a rather simple question of two overlapping desires—the desire of the three Central European nations to join NATO and the desire of the alliance to invite them as members—there was a complicated web of mutually irreconcilable interests that has produced real sources of international conflict of potentially global dimension.

To begin with, Poland, Hungary, and the Czech Republic worked out a policy to join NATO with a double purpose: first, to change sides in a typically dissident manner, reminiscent of Cold War times, and thus punish Russia for past Soviet misdeeds and, second, to get closer to Europe proper and to identify themselves as a part of the West. This, as was argued, would strengthen democracy in these countries and direct their drift toward a liberal economy. In a way, the move was a political response to certain failures in economic reforms in those countries that have seen a real or imagined specter of a Communist comeback. But the foreign policy dimensions of this intention had a value in themselves: By initiating the prospect of joining NATO, the Central Europeans managed not simply to attract the attention of the major powers to their needs but also to contribute to the new situation that emerged in the early 1990s from the ruins of the Cold War—a unified Germany, a collapsed WTO, a disintegrated Soviet Union, a divorced Yugoslavia, and so forth.

In Russia, the pleas of the Central European governments were largely underestimated. The Russian government was engaged in a lively dialogue with the West, experiencing something of a honeymoon at the time. Leaders in Moscow hoped that the magic formula of a strategic partnership would help them to freeze the situation on the continent and give them adequate time to complete negotiations on troop withdrawals from the Baltic states and work out a blueprint for a new European security structure. These aspirations were largely supported by certain Western powers, the United States and Germany first of all, who were eager to see Russian troops leave all the "foreign" territories and Russia itself join the West in controlling the conflict in the former Yugoslavia. The impression was that the desires of the Central Europeans would be largely ignored and that the development of security schemes would basically proceed along the lines of Russia-NATO cooperation, not NATO's unilateral expansion.

In this sense, the shift in NATO's position after the Brussels summit in January 1994, where the Partnership for Peace and direct U.S. involvement in Bosnia were proclaimed, played a crucial role in pricing the stakes. For the West, the shift marked a serious change in policy priorities in which Russia's role was moved to a secondary, "regional" level, and for Russia, it was a signal that the West was ready to revise its position on European security and turn NATO into its major security mechanism. This change was vital in raising the stakes in the relationship and bringing them to the level of principles. Having changed its policy, the West could not avoid being caught in its own contradiction—paradoxically insisting that although NATO's expansion was something not to be discussed with Russia, it should not be regarded as anti-Russian (*NATO Review* 1997). Every time Russian diplomats legitimately asked, "If it is not directed against Russia, then what is the reason for enlargement?" they were brushed aside with an arrogant assertion that "this is no business of yours." Almost overnight, the stakes reached the ceiling of a zero-sum game.

For Russia, any change in Europe connected with NATO expansion seemed like a loss in a war, like a policy of diktat from the West, or like an unacceptable shift in the European balance. Both official statements and policy analyses in Russia were filled with harsh rhetoric and efforts to work out an appropriate response—including changes in strategic and conventional arms control policies and new alliances with former Soviet republics, China, and Iran. The Russians indicated their readiness to go rather far in retaliating for NATO's expansion. A host of measures were suggested, such as a reversal of tactical and intermediate nuclear weapons deployment, abrogation of conventional arms limits, harassment of the Baltic states, and a complete review of the Balkans policies, including strong support to Serbia and to Serb nationalists in Bosnia. The credibility of these threats was heightened by the rhetoric of the Russian president, who considered U.S. policy on NATO enlargement "treacherous" and "challenging," bringing a "Cold Peace" (Kennan 1997).

The West, for its part, also heightened the stakes, indicating that Russia wanted too much (veto on NATO's decisions), that there should be no great power diktat, that European nations were free to opt for alliances, and that the West would defend that freedom.

As a result, a prospect of imminent crisis became evident. Strong second thoughts had to be applied before the sides went too far in escalating their rhetoric and then their actions. The West came to realize that while aiming at a more secure objective, it might, by its clumsiness and arrogance, undermine its own security and provoke a crisis. Russia, as has been already mentioned, came to understand that the poor state of its economy and the shaky position of the new regime both in the center and in the regions, coupled with growing opposition from the Communists and the nationalists, could bring an end to President Yeltsin's rule. Comparing real risks of enlargement with possible risks of a new confrontation, both sides agreed that a compromise should be sought. This was immediately reflected at the negotiations. Thus, a joint effort in crisis avoidance was brought about by a reevaluation of the stakes and a desire to create new ones.

Changing Attitudes

Clearly, the distance between changing stakes and changing attitudes is long. One may cite, as an example, the lengthy period during the Vietnam War between the moment when the U.S. administration changed its stakes in the conflict (President Johnson's speech in March 1968) and the moment when the change of attitudes permitted negotiations to start (under President Nixon's administration in February 1969). In the Vietnam case, the warring parties first had to avoid a further escalation of war, and only after that could they stop it. This example sheds additional light on the fact that there is no automatic and guaranteed transition from changing stakes to changing attitudes in the negotiation process of crisis prevention. Changing stakes is the necessary element to begin the process, and changing attitudes is the next necessary step, but it may or may not lead to success.

Changing stakes is often a unilateral process that develops within the thinking of one or both sides under the influence of primarily domestic, internal considerations. Changing attitudes combines internal and external—domestic and foreign—considerations. Once decision-makers on one side conclude that it is in their interest to take a course toward conflict prevention or crisis avoidance and then try to probe the other side on this subject, they need to reconsider their attitude both toward the other side and toward the subject of the conflict but this time with other actors taking the necessary parallel steps. This is not negotiation proper on the subject of prevention but a part of the whole negotiation process, mainly covering the prenegotiation stage.

All this was part of the Russia-NATO preventive negotiation process. Perhaps in this case, the issue of changing attitudes was not as painful and dramatic as in some other cases because contacts between the two parties, as mentioned, started long before NATO enlargement became a focus of debate. Generally, the contacts between Russia and NATO that have developed since 1992 have involved other issues: confidence building, mutual learning, joint and individual studies of possibilities for cooperation, identification of joint interests and areas for cooperation, and the building of the first fragile elements of infrastructure (communications, liaison officers, personnel training). Tangible elements of discord first appeared when, instead of being treated as a privileged partner of NATO, Russia was invited with others to join the Partnership for Peace program. Moscow's unhappiness was translated into a delayed and slow process of Russian adherence to the program activities. But the news on enlargement played a decisive role in changing the attitudes for the worse.

The first phase in changing attitudes had a rather dramatic nature. From the Russian side, attitudes changed profoundly. The period between 1992 (with the appearance of Russia as an independent state) and 1994 was filled with a deep euphoria, largely similar to that in the West, and the most promising and fantastic schemes of cooperation and partnership were widespread among policymakers and observers alike. It was assumed that the end of the Cold War not only brought a full stop to ideological hostilities but also opened a totally new era of cooperation based on common values, shared interests, and joint goals. Western support for President Yeltsin and Russian reciprocity embodied in Kozyrev's foreign policy seemed to have opened a direct way into an alliance relationship between the East and the West.

News on NATO's enlargement, regarded as a policy goal of the West, had the effect of a cold shower. It was a shock, followed by political disaster for the Russian "pro-Westerners." It gave a major boost to Russian nationalists, and it greatly helped to resurrect the Communists after several years of political lethargy. All in all, it contributed to deep emotional stress throughout the foreign policy community and almost overnight changed attitudes toward the West. But then, a second reversal of attitudes began. Strange as it may seem, the reversal started while the propagandistic campaign against NATO enlargement continued. With the change of leadership in the Foreign Ministry, it became possible to soften the impact of the Western "stab in the back" decision by changing priorities. Now, the West's decision to enlarge NATO was not seen as a breakup of the ongoing process of partnership formation but as a more or less natural and egoistic move that freed Russia from many of the commitments that Kozyrev had made previously. Besides, the imminence of the decision on enlargement buried all hopes that the decision would be reversed and encouraged those who formulated Russian foreign policy to look for a realistic solution. Finally, it was understood that without some sort of cooperation with NATO, it would be difficult for Russia to save face if the decision on enlargement was finally taken despite Moscow's protests and threats.

Something similar happened on the other side. It is hard, at this point, to give a grounded evaluation of the Western views on Russia prior to the developments of 1994. Of course, there were friendly feelings and attitudes magnified by the desire to help the Russian people overcome the consequences of Communist rule. Some Western political leaders and writers also shared a conviction that sometime in the future, Russia would grow, as a democratic nation with a market economy, into an acceptable partner and ally of the West. But the majority were cautious and restrained. Quick transformations rarely deserve confidence, and the transformation of Russia, yesterday's headquarters of communism where many former Communists were still in power or playing a central role in changes, was regarded as an opportunity but not as a fact. Consequently, the U.S. administration and the governments of some other NATO countries agreed that a strategic partnership with Russia outside of NATO might be a good goal for the future but definitely was not a part of the current reality.

After early 1994, it was assumed that while Russia was completely engaged in its domestic quarrels and could not play a significant and sustainable foreign role, NATO could afford to listen favorably to the pleas of the Central Europeans and to agree to make them members of the alliance. Understanding that this would infuriate Russia, the West still considered inclusion of the three Central European nations into the alliance as a necessary step in (1) consolidating NATO under the "no war" conditions in Europe, and (2) expanding the area of NATO's responsibility, which, by that time, included not only traditional spheres but also the former Yugoslavia. Russia's concerns could be largely ignored. Besides, there was a strong hope that President Yeltsin, surrounded on one side by Kozyrev and on the other side by pro-Western Anatoly Chubais, would finally surrender and agree to NATO's policy.

When it became clear that Yeltsin, for all his pro-Western sympathies, had changed his foreign policy priorities and was in no way inclined to accept what was viewed in Russian society as a matter of ultimate danger, Western attitudes also changed. It was apparent that the whole matter of NATO enlargement could become counterproductive. The West realized that forging an alliance with Poland, Hungary, and the Czech Republic at the expense of provoking the hostility of a Russia that, though weak, was still overarmed with nuclear weapons—and capable of stirring up problems for the West in Europe (Balkans, Baltic area, Transcaucasia) and in such sensitive areas as the Persian Gulf and the Korean Peninsula—was more than a mistake; it could be labeled a "fateful error" (Kennan 1997). Something had to be done in this area to avoid hard and grounded domestic criticism, if not a crisis.

Somewhere toward the end of the first phrase of the negotiation in 1996 (the prenegotiation, in formal terms), attitudes changed, perhaps at the moment when both sides agreed that negotiations to conclude a NATO-Russia treaty were needed and when the focus of the debates shifted to the exact contents of this treaty, points of future agreements, and other technical details. This transition did not take long, but it was important because it incorporated changes in the attitudes of both sides—attitudes toward the idea of enlargement and, as a result, toward the idea of a treaty that could help both parties avoid a crisis and continue to live together after the decision on enlargement was made.

Working Out Relevant Tactics

As studies of the Arab-Israeli conflict and other disputes demonstrate, even when actors reassess their stakes and manage to change attitudes, the success of negotiations to prevent conflict or avoid crisis is not guaranteed (Pruitt 1997). The heart of the problem here is that although both sides may rather painlessly conclude that stakes and attitudes need to change, questions of appropriate conduct, of mutual restraint, and of mutually acceptable rules sometimes acquire crucial importance once real negotiation begins, especially if it is being closely observed by outside parties. Even when negotiation is carried out between close friends or allies, as analyzed by Fen Osler Hampson in chapter 7, or when the issue discussed bears no conflict in itself, inadequacies in the conduct of the parties or an underestimation of important but less visible elements may still completely block the path to agreement. In other words, a change of stakes and a change of attitudes need to be crowned with appropriate tactics in order to bring negotiation to success.

In cases such as the NATO-Russia negotiation, the issue of appropriate tactics and conduct acquires special significance. In any negotiation on crisis prevention, a certain vulnerability to criticism from radical groups is an inevitable element. The parties to such a negotiation want to demonstrate flexibility, restraint, and understanding of the need to ease tensions. But at the same time, they want to show that they are not "selling out," and they do not want to appear to negotiate because of weakness or indecision. That makes them good targets for demagoguery and propagandistic attacks. Thus, in each case, they have to devise a way to protect the process of negotiation from undesirable interference and public debate while also helping all parties save face and arrange something like a common propagandistic cover for the negotiation.

This was the case in the NATO-Russia negotiations. In the West, some critics accused the governments of capitulating to Russian demands and of being inconsistent in policy matter by enlarging the alliance and yet sweetening the deal for Moscow. Those who were against enlargement accused the governments of hypocrisy and of having double standards, and they labeled the incorporation of Poland, Hungary, and the Czech Republic as propagandistic gains that the NATO governments wanted to sell to the public as a realistic achievement by means of negotiations with Russia. In Russia, the public attacks came mainly from the nationalist and Communist extremists who accused the government of surrendering and being incapable of standing firm against Western provocations. But the partisans of NATO in Russia were equally unhappy. They considered that, instead of openly supporting the idea of enlargement, the government was doing too little too late and doing it too clumsily. The process of negotiation had to be conducted on both a public and a private track, each of which had its own purpose: Public speeches and statements issued to large audiences were designed to demonstrate the toughness and ruggedness of the policy, and the actual negotiation was concentrated on a search for realistic solutions. Taking this two-track approach was highly risky, and it was possible that the negotiators would get the tracks crossed and undermine the negotiation. So, it was important for both parties to see to it that the two tracks remained separate and did not interfere with one another.

The other important tactic employed by both sides was to avoid formal, direct negotiation (this was primarily the Russian position, but it was understood and agreed upon by the West) until the time was ripe for an agreement. Emphasis on public debate in the first two stages of exchanges helped to clear the air and facilitate agreement in several major areas: (1) A direct NATO-Russia agreement should precede NATO's decision on enlargement; (2) the conditions were not ready for negotiations over a full-size, detailed treaty that would put all the issues in their appropriate places; (3) at the same time, there should be no empty declarations that would produce only an appearance of agreement, leaving behind unsettled issues that could later blow up the accord; (4) the treaty agreed to by both sides should only set some ground rules of their relationship, opening a way for a series of further agreements and understandings; and (5) both sides would conduct themselves in a way that would not put either of them into a difficult and confusing position. Only after all these necessary initial steps were completed could direct talks between closed groups of experts take place.

Conclusion

Too often, crisis-avoidance negotiation is regarded as a one-shot, self-fulfilling act. Once the crisis is avoided by a negotiated agreement, the situation is considered ended. This happens because this type of negotiation has a highly specific and identifiable purpose. But to give a balanced judgment, a much larger accounting should be made.

It is well known among those who study international relations that a relationship between a pair of states is a certain combination of "conflict-cooperation" attitudes (Saunders 1999). Depending on the type and nature of the parties' relationship, elements of conflict or elements of cooperation may prevail, thus creating allied or adversarial relations. The real difference between alliance and hostile relations is not that in one case (alliance) elements of conflict do not exist while on the other (hostility) they prevail. The difference is in existing mechanisms and regimes of conflict resolution, which are an integral part of the alliance relationship and designed to help actors jointly identify possible conflicts, work out means to deal with them, and then agree on solutions. Understandably, in case of hostile relations, there is no such mechanism.

In this respect, partnership of the type defined in the Founding Act may be regarded as both an intermediate stage between alliance and hostility and as a process of evolution, moving hostile relations in the direction of an alliance regime. In both capacities, such a partnership means that a certain mechanism of conflict resolution is being built in relations between former adversaries. And here lies the significance of crisis-avoidance negotiation, which usually becomes a first step in creating a durable and long-standing conflict-resolution regime.

The NATO-Russia Founding Act may be viewed as the first step, in which both sides agreed that conflict still may happen in their relationship even though they have decided that they are no longer adversaries. Still, even after an ideological split has ceased to exist, both entities may very easily be drawn into conflicts of potentially high risk. The fact that they have found much in common in trying to avoid crisis is extremely important in and of itself. But having signed the act, they may well feel that the worst is behind them and that they can look more enthusiastically into the future. These aspirations may be justified only if there is a mutual understanding that both sides should go ahead in developing a conflict-resolution mechanism that will help them to deal adequately with new crises when and if they come up as a result of their activities. If not—if the effort from both sides stops at this stage—then the parties will have to prepare for new conflicts in the future, and there is no guarantee that they all will be settled peacefully.

References

Angelakis, T. 1997. "Russian Elite's Perceptions of NATO Expansion: The Military, Foreign Ministry, and Duma." Briefing paper no. 11. International Security Information Service, Brussels, May.

Bertram, C. 1995. *Europe in the Balance: Securing the Peace Won in the Cold War.* Washington, D.C.: Carnegie Endowment for International Peace.

Haas, Ernest. 1953. "The Balance of Power: Prescription, Concept or Propaganda?" *World Politics* 5, no. 4 (July): 442–77.

Jervis, Robert. 1978. "Cooperation Under the Security Dilemma." *World Politics* 30, no. 2 (January): 167–214.

Kennan, G. 1997. "A Fateful Error." *New York Times,* April 15.

Konovalov, A., S. Kortunov, and S. Oznobishchev. 1996. "Rossia i NATO: Vremia diskussiy konchilos" (Russia and NATO: The Time for Debate Is Ended). *Nezavisimaya gazeta,* September 27.

"Kontseptsia natsionalnoy bezopasnosti rossii" (The Concept of Russian National Security). 1997. *Rossiyskaya gazeta,* December 26.

NATO Review. 1997. Vol. 45, no. 5 (September-October).

Pruitt, Dean, ed. 1997. *Negotiations Between Israel and Palestine.* Special issue of *International Negotiation* 2, no. 2 (April).

Rogov, S. 1997. "Nas vytalkivayut iz Yevropy" (We Are Pushed Out from Europe). *Vek,* October 25–31.

Saunders, Harold. 1999. *A Public Peace Process.* New York: St. Martin's.

Snyder, Glenn. 1984. "The Security Dilemma in Alliance Politics." *World Politics* 36, no. 4.

Solana, Javier. 1997. "The NATO-Russia Relations: A Key Feature of European Security." *NATO Review* 45, no. 3 (May-June).

Walt, Stephen. 1985. "Alliance Formation and the Balance of Power." *International Security* 9, no. 4: 3–43.

Zartman, I. William, and Victor Kremenyuk, eds. 1995. *Cooperative Security: Reducing Third World Wars.* Syracuse, N.Y.: Syracuse University Press.

13

Labor Disputes:
Making Use of Regimes

Mark Anstey

Preventive diplomacy has been defined as "action to prevent disputes arising between parties, to prevent existing disputes from escalating into conflicts and to limit the spread of the latter when they occur" (Boutros-Ghali 1992, 45). It is "employed to forestall policies that create social and political tension. These policies include human rights violations (such as denial of individual's freedom of expression, or right to a fair trial) or discrimination against people on grounds of ethnic, linguistic or religious identity or political belief. [It is] by definition low key, undramatic, invisible, but it is cheaper than peacekeeping or war" (Glover 1995, 2).

Claims that preventive diplomacy is an inexpensive, effective, and relatively risk-free means of reducing conflict have been challenged as simplistic and exaggerated (Lund 1995; Stedman 1995), but the concept of conflict prevention nonetheless remains attractive to many. Recent contributions make a distinction between prevention in the sense of conflict containment through dispute settlement and conflict resolution and provention directed at removing causes of conflict and promoting conditions in which collaborative and valued relationships control behaviors (Burton 1990). Efforts are aimed at replacing exchanges of short-term political expediency with long-term policy development founded on informed analysis. Prevention of this type involves tackling problems before they become conflicts.

Viable preventive diplomacy or conflict prevention is concealed precisely because of its effectiveness, for that which does not occur leaves no traces, and it resides in the processes and institutions of stability. Modern systems theories suggest, however, that such states of stability are but temporary in the life of evolving systems, which progress through periods of disorder and order. Early systems theories viewed fluctuations and disturbances in functioning as symptoms of trouble, but today, such periods are increasingly seen as triggers for organizational renewal. Far from perceiving the "normal state" of systems as one of stability, modern theories depict cycles of instability as part of the coherence of larger systemic or organizational adaptation and survival. M. J. Wheatly (1994) argued that equilibrium is neither the goal nor the fate of living systems. They need nonequilibrium for their survival and growth and to develop responses to new internal and external conditions. Adaptive social systems and organizations are resilient rather than stable in character and are driven by purpose. Structures are only manifestations of what is required to achieve goals at any given time—they are functional to purpose. Social systems are the products of interaction between environmental conditions and strategic choices made by their stakeholders as they seek to protect and advance their interests. As a consequence, they must be understood as malleable and having the capacity to assume many forms.

Within cycles of equilibrium and disequilibrium, stakeholders make choices regarding the organization of their system. The scope of such decision-making includes the choices such parties make regarding how they will deal with current and future conflicts. Decision-making in the labor relations arena plays an important role in shaping larger social systems, not least of all in the manner parties choose to deal with inherent conflicts of interest under diverse conditions. It is suggested here that interest in regulating, containing, and preventing conflict may only be shared among system stakeholders under certain conditions; in others, one or more may have an active interest in escalating rather than preventing or regulating conflict. As such, interest in designing and sustaining conflict prevention systems cannot be assumed to be automatic for stakeholders who somehow find themselves in conflicts that they wish they could end if only they could see a way to do so. Indeed, as much as conflict may emerge as a consequence of changing conditions, so may it be actively engineered and its energy utilized by one or more parties to reconfigure relations.

Labor Relations Systems as Conflict Prevention

J. T. Dunlop (1958) made an early (and often ignored) distinction between conflicts played out within systems and those associated with tensions over the shape of such systems. In the post–World War II period, labor relations in many developed countries have been expressed through the medium of collective bargaining arrangements that have the appearance of regular, set-piece exchanges with well-defined boundaries and rules of play. These characteristics have tended to conceal the conditions and levels of confrontation in which such systems took root. It is argued here that such labor systems represent examples of relatively successful conflict prevention, in which key societal stakeholders took steps not only to contain and regulate deep societal conflict but also to forestall and reduce conflict through multitiered exchanges in the engine rooms of national economies. They represent the transformation of conflicts *over* systems into conflicts *within* systems.

Communist and developing nations have reflected different configurations of development, strategic capacities, power relativities, and choices between the key stakeholders associated with labor relations systems (state, business, and labor). Largely, the configuration has been one in which the state has been the key powerholder and the most influential party in shaping the wider society and the labor relations system within it (Siddique 1989; Henley 1989). However, in many such nations, conditions have shifted sufficiently in recent decades for unitarist systems to be challenged and a search for more democratic systems of governance obliged. In other words, these nations are involved in struggles *over* systems design. Exchanges in the labor relations arena reflect such struggles and are often vital to their outcomes. In recent times, labor has played a significant role in struggles for the restructuring of social and political systems—South Africa and Poland are salient examples, but experiences in many countries in South America, Eastern and Southern Europe, Asia, and Africa are also illustrative (Anstey 1997; ILO 1994; Shadur 1994; Valenzuela 1989). In designing new labor dispensations congruent with the values, structures, and systems of democracy, such countries have looked to the systems of developed economies and the guidelines provided by the conventions and recommendations of the International Labor Organization (ILO).

Even as new democracies attempt to install the systems that have served the developed economies so well for conflict-management purposes since 1945, however, there are signs that the viability and usefulness of those systems are under revision. Some argue that the conditions that spawned and sustained their characteristic institutions and compromises are in a process of rapid and fundamental change and that new arrangements recognizing this reality are required.

Internationally, then, labor relations systems have reached an important juncture. In many nations that have never enjoyed the freedoms and collective bargaining institutions associated with democracy, there are strong drives to this end; in those nations that have enjoyed such freedoms and institutions, conditions that sustained them for decades have been eroded. In both instances, it may be argued that there is a rise in processes of conflict *over* the shape of systems rather than the management of conflict *within* systems. This global reality is recognized in Sarosh Kuruvilla and Christopher Erickson's (1995) punctuated equilibrium theory, which proposes that after their introduction, labor relations systems within nations tend to hold for long periods until conditions arise that demand rapid and fundamental change. During such periods, the system is up for grabs, as it were, offering opportunities for governments, labor, and business to reshape systems rather than simply play out existing ones—indeed, they have to design a new system because the old is redundant in the face of new conditions.

The exploration of preventive diplomacy in this book is concerned with its process elements in different issue areas. Under consideration are the manner in which parties' vision of the *stakes* is shifted from a zero- to a positive-sum situation, the way in which *attitudes* are shifted from conflictual to accommodative, and the *tactics* used to bring about these changes. Cycles of stability and instability characterize systems as key stakeholders make strategic decisions to protect or further their interests under changing conditions. All parties may have strategic interests in preventing, containing, or regulating conflict under certain conditions, but all may equally well see advantage in escalating tensions under other conditions. When all parties perceive their interests to be served best through system maintenance, then conflicts tend to be of a "within-system" character. However, changing conditions or perceptions of strategic opportunity may prompt any one of the stakeholders to pursue its interests in a manner that disrupts the balance of relations, and this may require a fundamental revision of the system as a whole. Relations are transformed into a conflict *over* the system.

Within the cycle of relations from equilibrium to disequilibrium, parties' perceptions of the stakes, their attitudes toward one another, and their strategic and tactical capacities and proclivities are in constant change. Stability in a system may be measured by the extent to which all its stakeholders perceive their interests to be best served through the maintenance of that system and the institutions and processes that they introduce to preserve it. These would represent, to an extent, the institutions of effective conflict prevention. The desire to create such institutions, however, is rooted in periods of intense conflict: It is the joint recognition of the realities of destructive conflict that prompts recognition of the need for effective conflict management, prevention, and reduction. Any investigation into conflict prevention must therefore span periods of stability and instability in a system's life and consider the durability of arrangements under changing conditions.

The labor relations of developed economies provide useful insights into the design of effective conflict-prevention systems, the rationale and compromises on which they are founded, and the conditions under which they have proven sustainable. Such systems emerged from a period of fundamental conflict between stakeholders and stabilized effectively for several decades, but in the context of changing conditions, they are currently in a process of revision. In developing countries, conditions that have facilitated unitarist or state-dominated systems have changed in many instances to oblige a shift from authoritarianism to democracy. The manner in which the tensions inherent in such transformations are managed is key to the evolution and consolidation of conflict prevention and management in emerging democracies.

Labor Relations Systems in Developed Economies

The Origins of Labor Relations Systems in Developed Economies

Toward the end of the nineteenth century, the world moved into a period of turmoil. The decline of monarchies and the emergence of the nation-state strengthened nationalist sentiments; powerful forces of imperialism expanded nation-state tensions into global conflicts; and gaps between productive, distributive, and consumption capacities facilitated successive economic depressions. New mass-production technologies underpinned the emergence of factories, which brought together thousands of people in places of work for the first time, giving rise not only to a major dislocation of traditional societal structures and problems associated with rapid urbanization but also to new points of ideological mobilization around concepts of class. Within and between nations, major and often very violent conflict erupted in this period, which E. J. Hobsbawm (1994) has termed the "age of catastrophe." The evolution of modern labor relations systems occurred within this context. Trade unions, often mobilizing around visions of a radical restructuring of capitalist economies, emerged as a powerful force for change, acting in concert with socialist and communist parties and posing a serious threat to traditional modes of political and economic governance.

The origins of modern labor relations systems in developed economies lie in compromises reached in the early part of the twentieth century between (1) owners of capital seeking to entrench ownership and control of the means of production and anxious to reduce disruption of manufacturing processes in the new mass-production factories, (2) militant labor movements resistant to exploitation and capable of stopping production processes through collective action, and (3) governments anxious to promote economic growth and conditions conducive to social and political stability. Within this context, the evolution of collective bargaining and various forms of employee participation can be understood as a form of national pact between key parties in economies, by which they agreed to limit their powers for mutual harm in both their own and each other's interests. Strong ideological stances gave way to social compromise, and maximalist demands were muted through institutionalized collective bargaining. The question of relevance here is why the parties should make such choices. What factors facilitated a muting of demands and positions and the transformation of conflicts over systems into conflicts within systems?

First, the parties' vision of the stakes shifted largely because both sides realized how interdependent they were. Much as employers resented intrusions by organized labor and resisted socialist ideologies, they needed predictability in the production process—and, to this end, a reliable labor input. And much as early trade unions were committed to a vision of radical restructuring in which capitalist exploitation would be eradicated, workers needed ongoing employment and wages. Pragmatism prevailed. Emerging labor relations systems were almost universally characterized by a compromise: Trade unions achieved recognition, access to workplaces for organizing and representation purposes, the right to periodic bargaining over terms and conditions of employment, and, in many instances, the right to strike over such matters; employers were relieved of constant wage demands, given a degree of predictability in production, and protected from wildcat action on matters falling within agreements; and the state achieved a level of regulated stability in the economy, securing viable production processes and revenues. Collective bargaining offered two basic means of joint control—market control (removal of wages from competition) and managerial control (regulation of behavior in workplaces through negotiated procedural agreements) (Flanders 1975).

Second, in growth economies, the prospects and benefits of regulated conflict through collective bargaining were perceived to be larger than those offered by unilateralism or radical restructuring through confrontation. The change in perceptions of the stakes was enabled, in no small measure, by the prolonged postwar growth of the economies of Europe and the United States, allowing rising standards of living, increasing wages, and full employment (pie enlargement with benefits for all). Confrontational attitudes were softened through a process that acknowledged the inherent conflict of interests in labor relations but regulated them through jointly agreed upon rules in a manner that offered mutual benefits. Unilateralism gave way to management by consent; rigid free-market and socialist ideologies found a compromise in concepts of social democracy, welfare capitalism, and active labor-market policies.

Collective bargaining systems assumed multiple forms internationally, finding a "fit" with social, economic, and political conditions across countries. In Europe, multiemployer collective bargaining emerged as the predominant form. Employers already had a long tradition of cooperation as a consequence of mutual efforts to cope with volatile markets (bulk buys, joint warehousing, cartels), and in the face of powerful centralized labor movements, this cooperation was simply extended into the formation of employer organizations. Centralized bargaining offered employers and unions the best opportunities to remove wages from competition and achieve economies of scale in bargaining, training, and benefit funds. In addition, small and medium employers saw centralized bargaining as the means of neutralizing the workplace from a direct union presence. In the United States, joint employer activity was constrained by antitrust laws. To smooth markets and control business conditions, mergers and buyouts replaced European cartels and employer bodies, giving rise to the huge corporations at the center of the national economy. In addition, the emerging U.S. labor movement, unlike its counterpart in Europe, was fragmented, and local unions jealously guarded their autonomy. Indeed, the American Federation of Labor (AFL) could only establish itself on the basis of union autonomy and decentralized policies (Sisson 1987; Dulles and Dubofsky 1993).

In whatever forms they took, the core purposes and processes of collective bargaining remained the same. The process represented the formalized means of regulating conflictual relations in the engine rooms of national economies within a jointly recognized interdependence and commitment to the national economy. The systems that developed represented strategic choices on the part of key actors to limit confrontation, recognizing that it was in their own interests to secure the interests of the others in a form of "national bargain" (Reich 1992; Sisson 1987). The rules of the game having been established, the parties played within them for decades, prompting perspectives of labor relations as a form of regulated adversarialism for purposes of system maintenance rather than as a vehicle for societal transformation. Indeed, collective bargaining systems had some success in translating conflicts over social systems into conflicts within social systems, given legitimacy through compromise. The effectiveness of collective bargaining as an institution of conflict management in many systems was enhanced by the introduction of specialized agencies of conciliation, mediation, and arbitration to facilitate relations, promote settlement searches, and determine outcomes in dispute situations. The Federal Mediation and Conciliation Service (FMCS) in the United States and the Advisory, Conciliation and Arbitration Service (ACAS) of Britain are examples. Within systems of collective bargaining, then, stakeholders tend to center their energies less in the legitimacy of the market system and more in the concept of an equitable distribution of its fruits. Across Europe and the United States, this was facilitated and strengthened through a postwar period of plenty—rising employment, wages, and standards of living.

The systems that have been configured around institutionalized negotiation are a reflection of facilitative conditions and strategic choices made by key stakeholders, whereby they recognized their interdependence and perceived the returns on regulated conflict to be greater than those offered through struggles over the system. Although some adopted a minimalist approach in this regard (British voluntarism), others actively built systems of articulated conflict management designed to limit disputes through extensive negotiation at all levels of society (Swedish centralized self-management). The idea of a "negotiated economy" was to forestall policies and actions that create social and political tension, to prevent disputes from arising, and to limit the escalation and spread of those that did.

Tripartism and Participation as Conflict Prevention

Many European countries went a good deal further than relying on the regulated adversarialism of collective bargaining. Institutionalized forms of tripartism were introduced as an alternative to robustly open pluralism, which was perceived as too conflictual, costly, and destabilizing, allowing governments to consult employers and unions on social and economic policy and to coordinate collective bargaining at other levels in the economy (Treu 1992; Slomp 1992). Neocorporatist arrangements reflected a desire to reduce the costs of looser pluralist systems through joint management of national resources in the national interest. Participation at a national level allows peak organizations to regulate or coordinate relations in accordance with a country's needs. Such arrangements represent efforts to bring key stakeholders together into national consensus-building processes for purposes of conflict reduction and containment.

This was the shape of arrangements in the "centralized self-management" model of Sweden until the 1990s, which continues to prevail in a social corporatist system such as Austria's. Research indicates that during the 1970s and early 1980s, economic performance was strongest at both ends of the spectrum: in neocorporatist systems (the Scandinavian countries and Austria) and decentralized labor systems (the United States and Canada). It was worse in those countries (Britain and Italy) whose labor systems were of an intermediate character, reflecting interest organizations strong enough to impose conditions on bargaining but not internally disciplined enough to sustain delivery to the conditions of national bargains. However, in a changing global economy with increased pressures for cost reduction and flexibility in business practices, the neocorporatist systems have been outperformed by decentralized systems, which allow greater room for enterprise-level trade-offs and flexibilities at the point of production and are sensitive to specific business conditions (Dell' Aringa and Lodovici 1992).

In Germany, a system of institutionalized codetermination and consultation was introduced at the level of the enterprise. Again, its roots of representative dualism lie in compromises achieved between the state, capital, and organized labor at the turn of the twentieth century. Collective bargaining is largely centralized at sectoral levels and is the domain of trade unions, which enjoy a right to strike over collective bargaining matters. At the level of the enterprise, however, collective bargaining is supplemented by an extensive system of employee representation on the supervisory boards of companies and, in regard to daily operational matters, through works councils with wide-ranging rights to information and consultation. No rights to strike exist at this level, but alternative forms of dispute resolution are provided for in the form of binding and nonbinding arbitration. The ethos is one in which the management accepts limitations on its right to manage unilaterally and the employees accept limitations on their right to use weapons of "industrial warfare" (Weiss 1989; Streeck 1994; Anstey 1997). The system represents a joint recognition that, although there may be tensions over the distribution of wealth created through corporations, it is in the parties' joint interests that wealth *is* generated—a notion that is captured in a German observation that "the cow must be fed before it can be milked."

Labor Relations Systems in Developing Economies

In recognizing the significance of collective bargaining, tripartism, and employee participation as forms of societal conflict regulation (prevention, containment, reduction), it must also be recognized that these traditions have not been experienced by the majority of nations. In most communist and developing nations, state-dominated systems have prevailed with patterns of tight controls over trade unions and restrictions or prohibitions on collective bargaining. Authoritarian governments have tended to argue that economic growth is paramount and has priority over the extension of political or civil liberties—which might be granted when society "is ready for them and can afford them." Indeed, it has been argued in the context of development programs that workers' interests are best secured through state controls rather than the activities of trade unions, which tend to be both too small and too sectional to be effective. In seeking the necessary balance between growth and equity, the state is perceived as better placed to shape the economy in the interests of the population as a whole (Shadur 1994).

In such contexts, organized labor has often been interested not only in achieving the freedoms and rights of trade unions in developed economies but also in promoting fundamental political change, and where it has managed to gain a foothold in such countries, it has often played an important role in the transition to democracy. Labor movements in these countries have been and continue to be vitally involved in conflicts over the shape of social systems; they have not simply played within established and accepted rules of the game. In such contexts, conflict-prevention or conflict-regulation measures may be seen as inappropriate or premature, muting disputes whose energy is necessary for larger societal transformation. Here, labor is engaged in struggles beyond which trade unions in developed economies had moved decades ago but under quite different economic and political conditions.

Conditions in developing countries have tended to limit the range of strategic choices. Weak industrial development has given rise to dual economies characterized by high levels of subsistence agriculture, low levels of manufacturing employment, and economies centered in state activity—factors unconducive to the emergence of a strong civil society. Scarce resource economies make it difficult to deliver to the spread of key stakeholders and their constituencies. In such systems, there has historically been a tendency on the part of stronger powerholders to impose an order rather than negotiate one and to limit negotiations within its operations (Moore 1966). Such systems have delivered political stability and economic growth in many nations for periods of time (South Africa, Brazil, South Korea, and Taiwan, for example), but they are founded on the capacity of a single dominant actor rather than societal legitimation. Under certain conditions, such systems become unsustainable in the face of pressures for legitimacy—other stakeholders become powerful enough to make demands for system change. One of these conditions is industrial growth, which strengthens both the middle and the working classes and contributes to a rise in class conflict. In such configurations, organized labor may become an important actor in reshaping power relations within nations.

Transforming Conflicts from *Over* Systems to *Within* Systems

Recent decades have witnessed a thrust away from authoritarian rule to democracy in many countries in Eastern Europe, South America, Asia, and Africa. A broad pattern of negotiated political transitions has emerged, typically involving shifts through phases of softening within an authoritarian regime, liberalization, and pacting before fully democratic founding elections are held. Following elections, interest is centered in consolidating democracy, often in difficult economic and social conditions (O'Donnell and Schmitter 1986; Stepan 1986; Ethier 1990; de Villiers 1993).

Typically, a nexus of economic, political, and social conditions alerts a governing regime to the reality that authoritarian rule is becoming increasingly untenable. Internal divisions emerge between soft-liners and hard-liners, the former recognizing the boundaries of authoritarian rule and the need for popular legitimation at some future point. When the soft-liners achieve dominance within government, reforms may be initiated in the shape of liberalization steps that do not go as far as full democratization but do offer citizens civil freedoms and protections from the state (O'Donnell and Schmitter 1986). The labor arena may assume center stage in the change process for a number of reasons.

First, sufficient development has often occurred to permit the mobilization of a working-class movement with meaningful strategic influence in the engine room of the economy. Second, in closed political systems, labor is often the only arena allowing room for mobilization, even though tough restrictions may exist over trade unions and collective bargaining. Activism in the form of strikes demands a response beyond simple repression. Employers require stable, motivated workforces to ensure uninterrupted production, an interest shared by governments seeking growth economies. Unlike political activity, work cannot be banned, and workforces cannot be collectively arrested or removed. The removal of leaders may quell resistance for a period, but it often simply incites further disruption. In the absence of political space, then, labor movements frequently offer opposition groups an important vehicle for mobilization, and tight links often emerge between trade unions and political interests (Valenzuela 1989).

Early reforms instituted by an authoritarian regime tend to soften an oppressive system but leave power in the hands of the current leadership. Their intent is not to relinquish power but to change the perceptions of citizens regarding those who wield it. The regime seeks to take the heat out of a situation without a fundamental reconfiguration of power relations between stakeholders. In Poland, the Gdansk Accords in 1980 conceded the right to form trade unions outside the official state structures as well as the right to strike, and they extended civil liberties. In South Africa, early reforms in the 1980s involved a softening of petty apartheid and pass laws, the extension of labor rights to all employees, and the introduction of a tricameral system of parliament with "common" and "own" affairs to be handled jointly or separately by the chambers, respectively. The formula still excluded the black population, but it sought to co-opt colored and Asian people. In both cases, the intent of the government was to ease repression in the hope that it might defuse opposition and reframe relations on its own terms. Not surprisingly, opposition groups have an interest in mobilizing against or exploiting rather than applauding such reforms. Indeed, they are seen as dangerously co-optive and as having the potential to divide and mute opposition with cosmetic changes that do not address fundamental injustices.

The moment is important strategically in a struggle for control over attitudinal elements of the exchange—a government seeking to convince citizens of its commitment to meaningful reform and opposition groups resisting reforms as co-optive and seeking to obstruct powerholders' efforts to translate perceptions of the conflict into a positive-sum game. The moment is a reminder that achievement of a shift from zero to positive sum may be elusive, residing as much in parties' perceptions of each other's intentions as in substantive compromises of position. Accommodative moves may have or be perceived to have adversarial or co-optive motives. Similarly, even if offers of movement are understood to have merit, they may be rejected if one or more parties see a strategic advantage in escalating the conflict rather than joining in a search for settlement. Thus, opposition groups may retain a strategic interest in discrediting change initiatives and hardening attitudes even as genuine reforms are under way. The key for reformers is less what represents significant change from their own perspectives and more what will be sufficient to tempt opponents into joining a process of systems redesign, at what time, and under what conditions. Stakes must be defined and understood in this light.

Although partial change may be rejected as co-optive and insufficient to transform the conflict into a positive-sum game, it does offer openings for exerting further pressure on the regime. Opposition groups may see tactical opportunities and greater rewards in hanging tough, increasing pressures, and discrediting reform initiatives. Powerholders may, in turn, respond by aborting reform processes. It is a delicate moment. Somehow, opposition groups must discredit reforms in a manner that forces improvements rather than withdrawal; they must somehow reward reformist elements even as their offers are rejected. At the same time, powerholders have an interest in securing control over the process even if they are committed to change. Consequently, repression may often accompany reform, with the transition process reflecting an oddly disjointed dance between progress and regression and between negotiation and insurrection rather than a smooth trajectory.

In Poland, the rise of Solidarity represented a "social movement" unionism that pushed beyond labor reform into political change, escalating strike action to a point at which the state banned it and reverted to martial law in 1981. Solidarity was obliged to pursue its interests underground, and it was only later in the decade that it re-entered formal negotiation forums on the basis of leverage provided by widespread strike action and international pressure. In South Africa, a succession of labor and political reform initiatives was met with strike action by a fast-growing trade union movement representing disenfranchised black workers. Even as reforms continued and collective bargaining increased, the state persisted in detaining labor leaders and suppressing union activities. In many other countries' transitions (in South Korea, Taiwan, Argentina, Brazil, and Chile, for example), sharp increases in labor unrest, accompanied by student and other protest action, were salient as the countries moved toward democracy. The effectiveness of such mobilization, as J. S. Valenzuela (1989) pointed out, is based on the strength of the union movement, the degree of centralization of the labor system and the labor movement, and the extent of the freedoms labor enjoys. In other words, the capacity to raise the stakes must be present. Beyond this, however, much depends on the strategic choices labor makes as the transition progresses.

Pre-Election Pacting

As G. O'Donnell and P. C. Schmitter (1986) observed, even as militance obliges a transition forward, it may also put transition at risk, discrediting reformists, reinforcing the fears of conservative elements, raising the potential of a right-wing coup, disrupting the economy, and evoking a flight of capital. Quite often, the process is stabilized through to full democratization via short-term pacting arrangements at political, military, and social and economic levels. Such pacts represent mutual guarantees on the part of powerholders that they will temporarily restrain their capacity for inflicting damage on each other in their own and other interests and to foster progress in the transition. The pacts represent the moment of interaction at which all stakeholders realize they are at risk—there is no returning to the previous system, and power needs to be carefully used in order to secure a future in which their interests are secured. This may require accepting old enemies as partners in a negotiated system rather than simply seeking their elimination.

Thus, perceptions of stakes are centered in a mutual recognition that unless the situation is carefully managed, a lose-lose scenario might easily eventuate. A jointly recognized potential for a no-win situation precipitates a win-win solution search—a search for mutual gains founded in self-interest. In tactical terms, some key judgment calls are required regarding toughness, terms, and timing. The existing shape of any given society has an important influence on such choices. South Africa's trade unions escalated strike action and hung tough on participation with the apartheid government until meaningful progress had been achieved in political negotiations. However, bilateral pacting took place with organized business a good two years before political reforms were enacted, signaling a willingness to entertain relations "on terms." This was an interesting contrast to the Polish experience. The Gdansk Accords were achieved between Solidarity and the state: The absence of a private sector made this the only option. However, in South Africa, the existence of a strong business sector provided opportunities for pacting at the level of civil society before participation with the government. The foundations for such an arrangement were laid through the experience of collective bargaining, adversarial though it had been. The bilateral accord not only provided a base for an economic pacting process but also facilitated further pacting—business and organized labor, together with the churches, crafted a comprehensive nonaggression agreement in the form of the National Peace Accord, which assisted in attenuating violence in the political change process. Once political reform was meaningfully under way, organized labor used its strength to bolster political opposition groups in the political negotiation process and to strengthen its own position in a future democracy; it entered an alliance with the African National Congress and the South African Communist Party but also secured participation in the National Economic Forum, where it, rather than its political partners, held sway in economic and social policy development. These tactical choices secured and strengthened both the labor movement and civil society through and beyond the political transition process. Organized labor may spearhead popular upsurges in political transitions, but strategically, it has an interest in surviving the wider change process and locating a position of influence in a viable democracy. This reality of organizational conservatism makes organized labor a potentially useful partner in conflict-prevention initiatives.

The emergence of a vibrant, multitiered labor relations system was a key component of South Africa's political transition process in both the liberalization/upsurge and pacting phases. In the face of strategic labor initiatives, business had to organize itself more effectively, locate a meaningful political role for itself, and iron out clear labor relations values and positions—a further contribution to strengthening civil society. Steadily, South Africa's labor movement shifted from hanging tough in conflicts over the shape of South

Africa to hanging tough on issues within its emerging system. Although mass action was used to reject government and its reforms in the 1980s, current action is directed not at the legitimacy of the legislature but at influencing the laws it passes. There has been a strong shift from nonparticipation to active participation.

The labor movement in South Africa actively laid a base to preserve its own strength and independence after the elections, and it sank the foundations for long-term influence at a social policy level. It did not wait to be invited to do so by a new government but proactively generated forums and processes prior to full democratization as it ceded leadership of the country's transformation to political parties. In this process of "strategic participation," labor was able to pressure and then reward progress toward a democracy, open options for itself and the wider society, and then entrench a multitiered system of participation through which it could exert influence from the social policy-making level to the shop floor level. Business, anxious to reduce the potential for state interference and to counter labor's influence with the government, became a willing partner in the process. With these choices, the dangers of simply repeating a state corporatist system in new form were averted to some extent. A struggle *over* a system was reframed to one *within* a system.

Old and New Democracies in Continuing Change: Implications for Conflict Prevention

It has been argued to this point that social systems are best understood as being in a process of ongoing change, passing through periods of stability and disequilibrium caused by changing environmental conditions and the strategic choices made by key stakeholders. The review of conditions, compromises, and processes associated with the emergence of labor relations systems in both developed and developing economies indicates that, at certain points, key stakeholders made choices that translated conflicts over a social system into conflicts within a social system. There is evidence across developed countries that profound conflict existed between labor, business, and the state in the early part of the twentieth century. By midcentury, however, most had transformed intense conflicts into national bargains founded in collective bargaining and increasingly sophisticated systems of participation, extending from social policy-making to the factories. Equally in the case of many developing nations, there is more recent experience of the transformation of conflicts over systems to conflicts within systems in a succession of transitions away from authoritarian rule and toward democracy. In both, it is argued that conditions arose that eroded the capacity of existing powerholders to govern unilaterally in political and economic spheres. As organized labor acquired strength, it forced accommodation within the decision-making systems of companies and countries. Tactically, it used its strength initially to disrupt existing systems, but at certain points, it saw greater advantage in participating in the design of structures and processes for purposes of conflict regulation and prevention. This shift in perception was reciprocated by business and the state to facilitate the shaping of national bargains in various forms.

The compromises associated with the design of labor relations systems have had an important role in embedding old democracies and in assisting in transitions to new democracies. However, just as developing nations have reached the point of industrial democracy achieved decades earlier in developed nations, there are signs that these systems are under revision. It is not simply a matter of achieving a milestone in democratic development. Conditions have changed to the extent that a new search is under way for viable labor systems. Old democracies face a crisis in redesigning systems with which they had become comfortable over decades and are now cited as obstacles to competitiveness. New democracies face crises of consolidation—transitions are not simply or uniformly shifts to democracy. History is littered with examples of weak democracies collapsing to authoritarian rule—the experiences of Germany, Spain, Italy, Chile, and Venezuela at various times all speak to this point. The last section of this chapter considers the factors giving rise to a revision of modern labor systems and the prospects of systems of conflict prevention and regulation within them.

Changes in the Balance of Labor Relations

Across Europe and in the United States, there is evidence of a change in the balance of national bargains and the organizations, structures, and processes that underpinned them. There has been a decline in union densities, a decentralization of collective bargaining, and a drop in strike activity (Anstey 1997; van Ruysseveldt and Visser 1996; Ferner and Hyman 1992; Kochan, Katz, and McKersie 1986; Jackson, Leopold, and Tuck 1993; ILO 1989). Wages have increased by steadily falling amounts in European collective agreements since the 1970s, as they have in the United States. Unemployment is rising, and, increasingly, collective bargaining agendas are as much concerned with job security and benefit retention issues as they were with wage increases a few decades ago. With Sweden's vaunted social accord in the lead, the social accords of Europe are under revision and even in decline (Treu 1992; Slomp 1992; Kjellberg 1992; Pestoff 1992).

Since the 1970s, conditions have arisen that profoundly alter the balance of the national bargains in developed economies (Reich 1992). Economic growth has slowed. Manufacturing has given way to service-based economies. Regional economies are being organized to replace nation-state arrangements. Transnational corporations have disrupted the balance of interdependence between national workforces and national corporations; new technology is reconfiguring needs for and dependence on certain forms of labor; flexible employment practices and outsourcing continue to erode the traditional base of union mobilization; lean production systems reduce workforces and place increased pressure on those who remain; organizational restructuring and re-engineering processes have cut across decades of traditional structures and grading systems, sweeping away the foundations for "job unionism." After decades of secure employment and rising wages in developed nations, many employees face a future of declining employment standards and job security. The collective agreements and arrangements with employers thrashed out through decades of collective bargaining in an effort to secure employment standards have been cited as a core obstacle to achieving the flexibilities needed to compete with Asian manufacturers and to secure jobs. The trade unions that had negotiated these deals face problems of identity and declining memberships. Serious questions have been raised as to the sustainability of labor standards in a global economy. (Anstey 1997; Sengenberger 1994; Sengenberger and Campbell 1994; Reich 1992; Heckscher 1988; Dicken 1992).

Simply put, the conditions that underpinned the balance of collective bargaining have been eroded. The new conditions are *conflict-generative*: job insecurity, falling terms and conditions of employment, raised work pressures, tougher management. However, the traditional means of expressing collective dissatisfaction have become dangerous to implement. In a global economy, a strike that removes national manufacturers from the market for a period may simply compel customers to buy imported products. New technology may see a permanent replacement of jobs. Owners of capital may close factories and invest in other countries offering attractive incentives. There is an emerging recognition on the part of labor that the strategic power of the strike has narrowed considerably, and its usage has become far more circumspect. In a global context, labor's strategic strength increasingly may lie in its capacity to offer skilled and uninterrupted work rather than in its capacity to stop work. Capital is internationally mobile, labor (apart from very skilled labor) is not. Employers have achieved a new dominance in labor relations systems even as they themselves are in a crisis of competitiveness (Anstey 1997; Kochan, Katz, and McKersie 1986; Reich 1992; Kester and Pinaud 1996).

Implications for Conflict Prevention and Regulation

Traditional collective bargaining played out in the context of national corporations and national economies is being rendered dysfunctional in a global economy for purposes of market control. Wages have re-entered the employment equation on an international scale, and in a context of global economic dualism, labor solidarity is an unlikely achievement—and certainly not at the standards achieved by organized labor in developed nations. Although it may no longer offer the same substantive securities, however, collective bargaining as a process does offer important societal options for conflict reduction and management purposes. The question is whether existing relations and processes might be effectively utilized to respond to the challenges associated with new forces for change. The international trend to decentralize bargaining arrangements has assumed many forms, but it reflects an employer desire and capacity to push wage determination to the point of production in the context of a global economy in which individual enterprises must achieve competitive strength in an international rather than a nation-state context. European unions have traditionally located their influence at centralized levels within national economies (national or sectoral) and wielded collective power most effectively from this vantage point. The reshaping of bargaining systems does not suit traditional union interests in centralizing collective power in national economies, and it reflects a loss of influence in the design and implementation of collective bargaining systems.

In addition, collective bargaining has traditionally been centered in issues of distribution through institutionalized, regulated adversarialism. This was functional during periods of growth when a seemingly ever enlarging pie could be apportioned in a manner in which all stakeholders' interests were met. However, slowed growth has limited redistributive capacities. Labor's satisfaction with the fruits of collective bargaining has been tempered, and the capacity of the system to deal with matters of production (pie enlargement) is in question. Here, the participative systems of countries such as Germany may prove more useful. Whichever way it is turned, the mix is a difficult one for organized labor. It requires a redefinition of goals and roles precisely at the moment that labor's strengths are declining and traditional forums of influence are being eroded.

Earlier discussion indicated the extensive use of tripartite arrangements as a means of conflict prevention internationally. Such arrangements became institutionalized in diverse forms in many European nations and have been salient in the efforts of many developing nations to introduce and consolidate new democracies (Anstey 1997; Slomp 1992; Alvarez 1994; Trebilcock 1994; Treu 1992). In all forms, they represent preventive thinking in regard to societal conflict. However, several researchers argue strongly that their effectiveness is premised on particular economic and social conditions (Sheahan 1986; Ducatenzeiler 1990; Morgado 1992; Alvarez 1994; Trebilcock 1994). Unraveled, these conditions represent a specific mix of beliefs, interorganizational arrangements, internal organizational qualities and capacities, and economic conditions. The institutionalization of tripartite arrangements in Europe was facilitated through national commitments to rebuild postwar economies that bridged traditional labor-management divides, boosted by prolonged economic growth that provided a context for full employment and rising wages. Powerful centralized organizations of employers and labor accorded each other legitimacy and were given high status by governments as social partners in a process of national compromise on ideological and substantive levels. However, the conditions and belief systems that favored social concertation on the part of government, labor, and business are changing.

First, the balance of interdependence in the labor-management relationship has been realigned in favor of employers. A global labor surplus, new technologies, and new forms of work organization have, in many senses, reduced a dependence on labor for production purposes. Second, the products of the system of institutionalized conflict regulation in the developed economies (detailed collective agreements applying across sectors and enterprises, rigid procedures, high wages) have been identified as obstacles to competitiveness—yesterday's means of competitive advantage have been cited as barriers to today's. Third, one of the consequences of societal reshaping is that in a reconfiguring work scenario, trade unions cannot deliver to pacts with the discipline of previous eras. In such a context, the need for pacts and their value to employers have dissipated. Several examples are illustrative.

Some countries have never managed to achieve a viable system of tripartism. In Britain, the income policies of "labor friendly" governments proved unsustainable in the face of ongoing economic crises and an undisciplined but militant labor movement that insisted on pushing demands at enterprise levels beyond those achieved at centralized levels. Unlike the multitiered, disciplined, and strong Swedish labor movement, the British labor movement has found itself progressively sidelined on both political and collective bargaining fronts. Italian pacts have foundered on similar grounds, as have those of developing countries with labor movements that are powerful enough to stamp a presence on the national economy but not so powerful or internally coherent as to be able to deliver to any national deals.

In other nations, long traditions of concertation are under challenge. The Swedish system of centralized self-management that prevailed from 1938 has been seriously eroded as a consequence of, inter alia, slowed economic growth and increased pressures for competitiveness; a shift from manufacturing to service employment, with consequent divisions in the labor movement; an inability on the part of labor to deliver to a solidaristic wage position because of these emerging divisions; loss of commitment on the part of employers to centralized agreements in the face of pressures for competitiveness and flexibility at enterprise levels, in conjunction with labor's inability to deliver to a centralized deal; and the election to power of conservative governments. In short, the shape of institutionalized social concertation lost its fit with emerging national and international conditions. In Australia, a long tradition of tripartism was expanded considerably under Labor Party governance between 1983 and 1996. The government sought to minimize the conflict and costs of unilateral restructuring through a series of accords with organized labor. This strengthened the trade unions and steadied levels of strike action. However, the overall results of the accords were equivocal, and by 1994, some commentators warned that the arrangement might have run its course in terms of positive results (Isaacs 1994). Already, there was evidence in the accords of an awareness that wage determination would have to become decentralized. In 1996, a conservative government won election, heralding the end of pacting arrangements.

Problems in sustaining tripartism are not only evident in developed economies. It was argued earlier that pacting processes have value in stabilizing negotiated transitions to democracy. Some contend that new democracies are best consolidated through grand coalitions and national consensus building rather than through the adversarialist politics associated with developed nations in the West. Advocates of this thinking suggest that the test for a consolidated democracy should be evidence of open and accountable government rather than alternations of power through election. The links between government and civil society become critical as a check and balance on government unilateralism and abuses of power. The liberal democracies and market economies promoted in structural adjustment programs are perceived as inappropriate to the conditions that prevail in many developing nations. A shift to market economies and accountable and lean government may be required for growth purposes, but such a shift might also create conditions of greater inequality, social hardship, and political instability, at least in the short term (Friedman 1994; Sandbrook 1993).

Social pacting initiatives have had some limited success in South America (Alvarez 1994; Morgado 1992) and Spain (Martinez Lucio 1992; de Villiers and Anstey in press). The paradox of many new democracies is that the conditions that indicate the greatest need for national consensus through social accords are those that are least conducive to their success. Underdevelopment spawns weak business and labor institutions, prolonged repression often fragments their organization, and stressed economies limit their capacity to deliver to the stakeholders. Pre-electoral pacts are different from postelection ones. Whereas the former serve to hold interest groups in place during the final stages of relinquishing authoritarian rule, the latter are expected to deliver more substantively to their stakeholders.

Labor conflict was attenuated for a period in a newly democratic Spain through pacting arrangements. The General Workers Union (UGT) aligned with the ruling Spanish Socialist and Workers Party (PSOE) at first supported pacting initiatives, perceiving them as serving to consolidate a new democracy and affording the union influence at the highest levels of decision-making on social, economic, and labor matters, with the promise of substantive benefits. The communist unions resisted participation, eroding the viability of pacts by making demands beyond those agreed upon with UGT and striking in pursuit of these demands. Steadily, the substantive benefits hoped for by UGT failed to materialize. Indeed, unemployment rose even as requests for wage restraint were made by government and employers. In the face of these conditions, it became untenable for UGT to continue supporting tripartite pacts, and it moved closer to the communist unions, participating in industrial action to pursue its demands.

Ad hoc efforts to achieve social pacts in Argentina and Brazil in the 1970s and 1980s were short-lived, and in both countries, newly democratic governments eschewed pacting after early flirtations with the idea, preferring the option of government-driven structural adjustment programs. In both cases, organized labor rejected demands for wage restraint and privatization. Labor unrest greeted Argentina's Austral Plan and Brazil's Cruzado Plan in the 1980s. The new democratic governments perceived that greater economic benefits resided in pursuit of structural adjustment programs, despite labor's resistance, rather than in seeking a compromise with trade unions. The trade unions saw dangers of co-option and few deliverables in the pacting option. However, there is evidence that despite its resistance to government policy, organized labor did not challenge the democratic system as such. In Argentina, organized labor backed Raul Alfonsin in facing down a coup threat, despite his unpopular economic policy. In this sense, it can be argued that conflict had been successfully shifted from an over-system mode to a within-system mode (de Villiers 1993; Munck 1989).

In Venezuela, a broad tripartism founded in the historical alliance between the governing party (Acción Democratica) and the Venezuelan Labor Confederation (Confederación de Trabajadores del Venezuela, CTV) proved reasonably successful in attenuating conflict from 1958 until a slowdown in the economy in the 1980s. However, the 1981 tripartite National Costs, Prices and Salaries Council formed to concert prices and incomes failed in its task, with both organized labor and business leaving its ranks. In 1989, the tripartite National Agreement: Concertation was founded with broadly the same mandate, but it had equally little success in an increasingly unstable political and economic environment.

In South Africa, pre-election pacting was carried forward and entrenched as a cornerstone for the development of a social democracy in the establishment of a statutory tripartite body, the National Economic Development and Labor Council (NEDLAC), in which business, labor, and the state seek a consensus on all economic and social policy issues. The body has managed to achieve agreement over several new labor relations laws but not without difficulty; tensions between the parties have been reflected particularly on substantive matters and in the use of mass-action tactics by organized labor at various points. All stakeholders have voiced concern over the viability of NEDLAC at various times, and its future is under constant scrutiny in the media.

Systems of Conflict Regulation and Prevention under Review

The first part of this chapter argued that, as a consequence of changing environmental conditions and strategic choices made by stakeholders, social systems are in a constant process of transformation, punctuated by periods of stability and instability, order and disequilibrium. Periods of apparent stability are those in which stakeholders perceive that the benefits of mutual accommodation outweigh those of confrontation and in which they participate in structures and processes designed for purposes of conflict prevention and regulation. Within pluralist systems, inherent conflicts of interest are recognized as normal, but there is a shared desire to regulate the expression of differences and to prevent and limit the consequences of conflicts. Labor relations systems in most developed economies have been premised on pluralist principles, values, and institutions. The origins of systems designed to limit and manage conflict, then, lie in decisions made by key stakeholders during periods of intense conflict, when their interests are jeopardized by its escalation.

Usually, the conflict is a consequence of changing conditions that see the rise of interest groups powerful enough to challenge existing power relations. To the extent that they are excluded from the mainstream of societal decision-making, these groups have an interest in disrupting its functioning, and to the extent that they have power, they are capable of ensuring that this happens. Often, they mobilize under visions of total systemic reorganization. However, to the extent that other parties have power, they may realize not only that such objectives are unobtainable in pure form but also that, if pursued, they will have major negative consequences. Powerholders recognize concurrently that blunt repression will not secure their interests. In the ensuing interactional crisis, the risks and benefits of accommodation are evaluated against those of ongoing confrontation. To the extent that accommodation outweighs escalated conflict, confrontation may be transformed into a search to secure the parties' own interests by securing those of their opponents. Further, there may be a strong drive to design a system jointly that actively seeks to prevent, reduce, contain, and regulate conflict expression. These are the goals of collective bargaining and employee relations systems traditionally associated with the developed economies of Europe and the United States and, to an extent, in the new democracies of the developing world.

Changing environmental conditions may have an impact on one or more of the stakeholders, eroding their capacity or willingness to influence or contribute to conflict-reduction or conflict-regulation mechanisms. The interdependence of the actors is reduced, and some may even begin to see others—or negotiated arrangements with others—as obstructive to their efforts to pursue or protect their interests. At this point, some parties may begin to see greater advantage in terminating relations, redesigning negotiation forums, ignoring such forums, or merely paying lip service to them. This would seem to be the current global reality within labor relations systems. The reshaping of businesses in response to pressures for competitiveness has seen a rise in transnationalism, a shift to a global economy, and the introduction of new technologies and forms of work organization, all of which have combined to weaken the strength of trade unions and reduce dependence on labor. The reshaping of the parties has caused the old national bargains to lose their fit with conditions and even to be identified as the obstacle to effective system adaptation. Increasingly, employers have found that they do not need labor's consent to pursue their interests, and labor has found it increasingly dangerous to use the strike weapon. Even as conditions have become more conflict-generative in many senses, it has become more dangerous to express such conflict through traditional mediums such as the strike. Arguably, then, strikes are not in decline internationally because of the success of conflict-prevention mechanisms founded in a joint commitment to preserve relations; they are in decline simply because one stakeholder (business) has reduced its dependence on another (labor) and because there is no means by which the latter can respond with hostility without incurring further damage to itself. Therefore, the drop in manifest conflict does not mean a reduction in latent conflict. Tensions are likely to find expression in other areas—such as rising crime and social and political unrest. We may be witnessing an era in which the centrality of the labor pact in securing national stability is being sidelined. Its value potential for conflict prevention has been eroded even as related social tensions are in evidence.

Conclusion

In closing, it is important to recognize that although there is evidence of a systemic shake-up under way in the labor relations arena, this hardly indicates the end of work or employment relations or interdependence between major stakeholders. The openings created by shifts in power relativities may, for instance, tempt employers to believe that their best interests might be pursued outside deals with organized labor. Trade unions' slow response to new conditions and reluctance to proactively reshape bargaining and participation options with employers and the state may have fostered such perceptions. Rather than simply discarding systems of collective bargaining, tripartism, and enterprise participation as outmoded or obstructive, we might consider using existing systems and relationships as a basis for renewal and strategic redirection. If the institutions of conflict prevention that have taken so much effort to build are cast aside, what will take their place? Might it not be wiser to seek their regeneration and empowerment in the larger social interest?

To the extent that all stakeholders are unable to find common cause or capacity on this front, however, such potentials may be lost in a return to system redesign founded on adversarial rather than accommodative tactics. The question is not whether some useful systems of conflict prevention are losing their fit with changing conditions or whether a period of system stability is ending; it is whether existing arrangements might not be more effectively used as a foundation for designing and building new societal mechanisms for managing the transition process. If they can, there is a prospect for discussion about building conflict-prevention systems to manage periods of conflict over as well as within systems. If not, then conflict prevention remains the product of choices made during escalated conflicts that carry a system through a period of stability before losing their usefulness in an emerging new conflict configuration that itself throws up new stakeholders, introduces new power relations, and awaits negotiation into a new but temporary period of stability.

The appendix (p. 319) provides a summary of key propositions emerging from considerations of conflict prevention and labor relations systems.

References

Alvarez, O. H. 1994. "Latin America." In *Towards Social Dialogue,* ed. A. Trebilcock. Geneva: ILO, pp. 335–71.

Anstey, M. 1990. *Worker Participation: South African Options and Experiences.* Cape Town: Juta.

———. 1991. *Negotiating Conflict.* Cape Town: Juta.

———. 1992. "Mediation in the South African Transition: A Critical Review of Developments, Problems and Potentials." *Geneve-Afrique* 30, no. 2: 141–63.

———. 1993. *Practical Peacemaking.* Cape Town: Juta.

———. 1997. "Corporatism, Collective Bargaining and Enterprise Participation: A Comparative Analysis of Change in the South African Labour System." Ph.D. diss., University of Port Elizabeth, South Africa.

Bergquist, C. 1986. *Labor in Latin America.* Stanford, Calif.: Stanford University Press.

Boutros-Ghali, Boutros. 1992. *An Agenda for Peace, Preventive Diplomacy, Peacemaking, and Peacekeeping.* New York: United Nations.

Burton, J. 1990. *Conflict: Resolution and Prevention.* New York: St. Martin's.

Clegg, H. 1975. "Pluralism in Industrial Relations." *British Journal of Industrial Relations* 13, no. 3: 309–16.

Dell' Aringa, C., and M. S. Lodovici. 1992. "Industrial Relations and Economic Performance." In *Participation in Public Policymaking,* ed. T. Treu. Berlin: de Gruyter.

de Villiers, D. 1993. "Transition by Transaction: A Theoretical and Comparative Analysis of Negotiated Transitions with Special Reference to South Africa, 1989–1992." Ph.D. diss., University of Port Elizabeth, South Africa.

de Villiers, D., and M. Anstey. in press. "A Comparative Analysis of the Role of Trade Unions in Transitions to Democracy in South Africa, Spain and Brazil." In *Trade Unions in Transition,* ed. E. Webster and G. Adler.

Dicken, P. 1992. *Global Shift.* London: Chapman.

Ducatenzeiler, G. 1990. "Social Concertation and Democracy in Argentina." In *Democratic Transition and Consolidation in Southern Europe, Latin America, and South East Asia,* ed. D. Ethier. London: Macmillan.

Dulles, Foster Rhea, and Melvyn Dubofsky. 1993. *Labor in America.* Arlington Heights, Ill.: Harlan Davidson.

Dunlop, J. T. 1958. *Industrial Relations Systems.* New York: Holt.

Mark Anstey

Ethier, D., ed. 1990. *Democratic Transition and Consolidation in Southern Europe, Latin America, and South East Asia.* London: Macmillan.

Ferner, Anthony, and Richard Hyman, eds. 1992. *Industrial Relations in the New Europe.* Cambridge: Blackwell.

Flanders, Allan D. 1975. *Management and Unions.* London: Faber.

Fox, A. 1975. "Industrial Relations: A Social Critique of Pluralist Ideology." In *Industrial Relations and the Wider Society,* ed. B. Barrett, E. Rhodes, and J. Beishon. London: Collier Macmillan.

Friedman, E., ed. 1994. *The Politics of Democratization: Generalizing East Asian Experiences.* Boulder: Westview.

Friedman, S. 1986. *Building Tomorrow Today: African Workers in Trade Unions, 1970–1984.* Johannesburg: Ravan.

Glover, A. 1995. *A Tool for Human Rights and Preventive Diplomacy.* London: Foreign and Commonwealth Office.

Heckscher, Charles. 1988. *The New Unionism.* New York: Basic Books.

Henley, J. S. 1989. "African Employment Relationships and the Future of Trade Unions." *British Journal of Industrial Relations* 27, no. 3: 289–309.

Hobsbawm, E. J. 1994. *The Age of Extremes.* New York: Pantheon.

Hyman, R. 1975. *Industrial Relations—A Marxist Approach.* Hong Kong: Macmillan.

Hyman, R., and A. Ferner. 1994. *New Frontiers in European Industrial Relations.* Oxford: Basil Blackwell.

ILO (International Labor Organization). 1989. *Current Approaches to Collective Bargaining.* Geneva: ILO.

———. 1994. *World Labor Report 1994.* Geneva: ILO.

Isaacs, J. E. 1994. "Australia." In *Towards Social Dialogue: Tripartite Cooperation in National Economic and Social Policy Making,* ed. A. Trebilcock. Geneva: ILO.

Jackson, M. P., J. W. Leopold, and K. Tuck. 1993. *Decentralization of Collective Bargaining.* London: Macmillan.

Kester, G., and H. Pinaud. 1996a. "The Decline, Consolidation or Growth of Participation." In *Trade Unions and Democratic Participation—A Scenario for the 21st Century,* ed. G. Kester and H. Pinaud. Aldershot, England: Avebury.

———. 1996b. "Democratic Participation: A Challenge for Democracy." In *Trade Unions and Democratic Participation—A Scenario for the 21st Century,* ed. G. Kester and H. Pinaud. Aldershot, England: Avebury.

Kjellberg, A. 1992. "Sweden: Can the Model Survive?" In *Industrial Relations in the New Europe,* ed. A. Ferner and R. Hyman. Oxford: Blackwell.

Kochan, T. A., H. C. Katz, and R. B. McKersie. 1986. *The Transformation of American Industrial Relations.* New York: Basic.

Kuruvilla, Sarosh, and Christopher Erickson. 1995. "Labor Cost Incentives for Capital Mobility in the European Community." In *The Workers of Nations,* ed. Sanford Jacoby. New York: Oxford University Press.

Lund, M. S. 1995. "Underrating Preventive Diplomacy." *Foreign Affairs* 74, no. 4 (July–August): 160–63.

Martinez Lucio, M. 1992. "Spain: Constructing Institutions and Actors in a Context of Change." In *Industrial Relations in the New Europe,* ed. A. Ferner and R. Hyman. Oxford: Blackwell.

Moore, Barrington. 1966. *Social Origins of Dictatorship and Democracy.* Boston: Beacon.

Morawski, W. 1992. "Industrial Democracy and Power Structuration in the Polish Economy." In *Labour Relations in Transition in Eastern Europe,* ed. G. Szell. Berlin: de Gruyter.

Morgado, E. 1992. "Social Concertation in Latin America." In *Participation in Public Policy-Making,* ed. T. Treu. Berlin: de Gruyter.

Munck, R. 1989. *Latin America: The Transition to Democracy.* London: Zed.

O'Donnell, G., and P. C. Schmitter. 1986. *Transitions from Authoritarian Rule.* Baltimore: Johns Hopkins University Press.

Pestoff, V. A. 1992. "The Demise of Concerted Practices and the Negotiated Economy in Sweden." In *Participation in Public Policy-Making,* ed. T. Treu. Berlin: de Gruyter.

Reich, R. B. 1992. *The Work of Nations.* New York: First Vintage.

Ryan, S. 1992. "Peacebuilding in Violent Intercommunal Conflicts." Paper presented at the meeting of the International Peace Research Association, Kyoto, July 27–31.

Sandberg, A. 1996. "Participation and Co-Determination in Sweden." In *Trade Unions and Democratic Participation in Europe: A Scenario for the 21st Century,* ed. G. Kester and H. Pinaud. Aldershot, England: Avebury.

Sandbrook, R. 1993. *The Politics of Africa's Economic Recovery.* Cambridge: Cambridge University Press.

Sengenberger, Werner. 1994. *Creating Economic Opportunities.* Geneva: Institute for Labor Studies.

Sengenberger, Werner, and Duncan Campbell, eds. 1994. *International Labor Standards and Economic Interdependence.* Geneva: International Institute for Labor Studies.

Shadur, M. 1994. *Labour Relations in a Developing Country: A Case Study on Zimbabwe.* Aldershot, England: Avebury.

Sheahan, J. 1986. "Economic Policies and the Prospects of Successful Transition from Authoritarian Rule in South America." In *Transitions from Authoritarian Rule: Comparative Perspectives,* ed. G. O'Donnell, P. C. Schmitter, and L. Whitehead. Baltimore: Johns Hopkins University Press.

Siddique, S. A. 1989. "Industrial Relations in a Third World Setting: A Possible Model." *Journal of Industrial Relations* (September): 385–401.

Sisson, K. 1987. *Management of Collective Bargaining: An International Comparison.* Oxford: Basil Blackwell.

Slomp, H. 1992. "European Labor Relations and the Prospects of Tripartism." In *Participation in Public Policy-Making,* ed. T. Treu. Berlin: de Gruyter.

Stedman, S. J. 1995. "Alchemy for a New World Order: Overselling Preventive Diplomacy." *Foreign Affairs* 74, no. 3 (May–June): 14–20.

Stepan, A. 1986. "Paths Toward Redemocratisation: Theoretical and Comparative Considerations." In *Transitions from Authoritarian Rule,* ed. G. O'Donnell, P. C. Schmitter, and L. Whitehead. Baltimore: Johns Hopkins University Press.

Streeck, W. 1994. "Codetermination and Trade Unions." *South African Labour Bulletin* 18, no. 5: 87–95.

Trebilcock, A., ed. 1994. *Towards Social Dialogue: Tripartite Cooperation in National Economic and Social Policy Making.* Geneva: ILO.

Treu, T., ed. 1992. *Participation in Public Policy-Making.* Berlin: de Gruyter.

Valenzuela, J. S. 1989. "Labor Movements in Transitions to Democracy: A Framework for Analysis." *Comparative Politics* 21, no. 4 (July): 445–73.

Vally, B. 1992. *A Social Contract—The Way Forward?* Johannesburg: Phambili.

van Ruysseveldt, J., and J. Visser, eds. 1996. *Industrial Relations in Europe: Traditions and Transitions*. London: Sage.

Wang, J.C.F. 1994. *Comparative Asian Politics*. Englewood Cliffs, N.J.: Prentice-Hall.

Weiss, M. 1989. *Labor Law and Industrial Relations in the Federal Republic of Germany*. The Hague: Kluwer.

Wheatly, M. J. 1994. *Leadership and the New Science*. San Francisco: Berret-Koehler.

Young-bum Park. 1994. "State Regulation, the Labor Market and Economic Development in the Republic of Korea." In *Workers, Institutions and Economic Growth in Asia*, ed. G. Rodgers. Geneva: ILO.

Yudelman, D. 1984. *The Emergence of Modern South Africa: State, Capital and the Incorporation of Organised Labour on the South African Gold Fields, 1902–1939*. Cape Town: David Phillip.

14

Conclusion:
Discounting the Cost

I. William Zartman

Preventive diplomacy begins at home. Whether in dealing with divided or disintegrating or neighboring states or with commercial or environmental or security relations, the anticipation and prevention of conflict by negotiation, rather than pursuing current conflicts from given positions, is always an available policy option. It involves replacing an approach of winning (prevailing) over other parties with one of winning over (persuading) other parties, and it calls for future-based cost-benefit calculations and for reframing the conflict to allow for a positive-sum formula for agreement. These are the three basic elements of preventive diplomacy—cooperation, calculation, and reformulation. In a sense, the discussion stops there: When the parties are moved by the prospects of future costs to adopt a reconciling rather than a confronting mentality toward each other and a problem-solving attitude toward their conflict, the rest is detail and tactics. Indeed, many of this volume's issue-area analyses—on divided and disintegrating states, on territorial and boundary disputes, on interethnic negotiations and cooperative conflicts, and on transboundary and global environmental disputes—have emphasized these elements as the key to successful preventive diplomacy in their area. The preceding chapters have brought out the special characteristics of preventive negotiations in each issue area; it is the common elements to the practice and underlying mentality of preventive diplomacy drawn from disparate issue areas that this final chapter addresses.

A preventive diplomacy policy is not merely an ideological choice. It does not depend on a party's "believing in" peaceful relations or disaster avoidance or conflict prevention or other idealisms. It is a policy for realists, made in the name of efficiency and effectiveness. Parties find that they can increase their chances of attaining their goals and of doing so at a lower cost by making allies out of their opponents and by making collaborators out of fellow targets of impending disasters. This involves buying the other party's cooperation with a consideration of its own goals, as in any negotiation, but with a particularly forward focus achieved through an emphasis on the avoidance of future conflict rather than the ending of present conflict. It involves not a renunciation of goals in conflict but a recasting—a reduction or expansion—of goals to make them fit into the same frame and be attainable in cooperation with the other party. The choice is made under the impulsion of an awareness of future versus present costs and of present versus future achievabilities.

The requirements of preventive action go beyond early warning and reach into early awareness, before any warnings are sounded. The parties calculate that unless actions are taken in the present, at some cost, the future costs will be significantly higher and future actions significantly more difficult. They reckon that there is a greater chance of achieving a greater part of the goals now than later (and that holding out, in turn, will raise future costs). More lives will be saved by waterproofing the hull now than by subsequently fishing survivors out of the open sea. Unless something is done now, things will get doubly worse—worse not only in terms of costs but also in terms of chances of gain. This is not like normal negotiation calculations, which tend to compare alternative current outcomes, nor does it emerge from usual cost calculations, which tend to respond to the pressure of current costs.

Nor are such future calculations usual in the policy-making business. Cost-benefit considerations are common enough and are the usual basis of decision-making (Raiffa 1968; Sfez 1973). But preemptive decision-making to avoid future costs sets statesmanship apart from merely minding the store and putting out fires. Yet this is what "normal diplomacy" should be. Preventive policy-making is associated with terms such as *farsightedness* and *vision*, underlying the fact that its success depends on a clear identification of future uncertainties that will—if the policy is successful—never materialize to confirm its wisdom. It is the need for action against uncertainty that has kept preventive diplomacy from being commonplace. Even when one party has adopted a preventive diplomacy stance, it usually has to overcome different calculations from the other party or parties to the conflict. And when neither of two parties has thought in preventive terms, a third party is needed to create new perceptions and calculations.

So preventive diplomacy, in fact, begins not at home but in the need to convince others—domestic as well as foreign, to be sure—of the need to think ahead. Yet if the nub of the preventive diplomacy challenge appears to be not how to practice it but how to get other parties to practice it, the ways of doing both are actually identical. The main arguments available to a first or third party to convince a second of the need to join preventive diplomacy negotiations lie in the looming costs of inaction, the prospects of a positive-sum outcome, and the attraction of a reconciling attitude from the other party. These defining characteristics of preventive negotiation are also its main incentives—a situation that has its coherence and benefits but also its drawbacks. When conflicting parties find the costs of inaction distant and bearable, the prospects of joint gains irrelevant to their current zero-sum aims, and offers of reconciliation either untrustworthy or a sign of weakness to be exploited, then preventive negotiation is not yet on the table, and the very basis for the attractiveness of the policy is absent.

Conditions

Behind the choice of preventive diplomacy over confrontation or neglect lie objective criteria for efficiency and effectiveness, not just an ideological choice or a philosophical predilection for a liberal rather than a realist approach in international relations. Since that choice is made by human beings, that objective basis is filtered by subjectivities, a matter of awareness if not of philosophy, concerning at least the ability to perceive the components of cost and benefit calculations. But the objective basis for that awareness involves real costs and opportunities that provide the structural conditions for preventive negotiating and that can be presented as six conditions, in ascending order of specificity.

The most basic requirement is a *problem* to be solved. Preventive diplomacy is a problem-solving effort. It is impelled by a felt need for some order in interdependencies and interactions, where the cost of disorder, inefficiencies, and uncertainties impedes the achievement of the purposes for which the transactions were instituted. Although this may appear so basic as to be banal, it is important to recognize that preventive efforts begin their justification in response to the challenge, "What's the problem?" Impending dangers are a collective social "bad" that diminishes some aspect of the security of affected parties. But parties must be convinced that the danger is indeed impending, a worsening situation that makes relations or transactions costly, and that their security is indeed at stake. In other words, the free-spectator stake-related (equivalent to the solution-related free-rider) phenomenon must be avoided, by avoiding the perception that it is someone else's problem that will pass us by. Whether it is an undefined status causing boundary or territorial disputes, the instability inherent in divided or dividing states, the disruption brought on by runaway competition in trade or other cooperative relationships, or the uncertainties endemic to competition in superpower or labor-management relations, the problem is an unregulated relationship that is turning costly to the parties who are part of it.

The second component is *preventability*, a problem that is removable and not just something pasted on the horizon about which nothing can be done. If the problem is to be understood as an opportunity, the preventable element must appear as a possibility if preventive negotiations are to take place. Although, as has been noted, the major challenge of preventive diplomacy is to make the parties understand the likelihood of the impending cost, prevention fits very well in the current emphasis, expressed in prospect theory, on the protection against loss as a motivator over the accession of gain (Kahneman and Tversky 1979, 1995). The clearer the evidence of a worsening situation, the more appropriate the situation is for prevention, but "clear evidence" has a subjective dimension large enough to allow for many shades of gray. This, of course, is what makes preventive diplomacy so rare and so difficult: By the time the evidence is incontrovertible, it is often too late for prevention.

Awareness of a worsening and preventable situation posed no difficulty to diplomats focusing on the global security dangers of the nuclear arms spiral. They saw the possibility that competitive nuclear armament would run out of control, and they worked to introduce predictability, stability, and transparency into the relationship. In other issue areas, the awareness has been less clear-cut, with some perceptions of worsening situations providing an impetus to preventive negotiations and other situations generating awareness only too late, when things had already worsened beyond prevention.

Thus, some countries' boundary disputes have been forestalled by demarcation, and others' uncertainty has led to war; some countries' ethnic grievances have been handled before they became irremediable, whereas others' experience has shown that grievances can only be handled when the aggrieved come in control of their own affairs; and when violence threatens to derail negotiations to end ethnic violence, the crucial element in keeping talks on track is the motivation to avoid a worse outcome; divided Germany was able to avoid the danger of war through constraint and then unification, contrasting with Yemen's experience with war in both division and unification and learning from Korea's experience in both constraint and war; in some cases, disintegrating states have sensed the specter of disaster sharply enough to part ways peacefully, but others have proven the specter real; and in the case of ozone depletion, clear awareness of the impending danger brought negotiations to stave it off, but in the case of climate change, diplomats waffled before clouded awareness. The difference between prevented and unprevented cases on each issue must therefore be found in further contextual elements, as well as appropriate policy responses.

The third objective element is a *cost-sharing* opportunity. If parties are to be involved in efforts to head off impending cataclysms, they need to be assured of the participation of others in bearing the burdens of the effort. Preventive negotiations always involve several parties, whether they are the parties to a conflict or problem or third parties intervening between first and second parties to a dispute. Preventive diplomacy always involves costs incurred in heading off worse costs, and it is the costs of current action, not of avoided catastrophe, that enter first into the calculations of the preventing negotiators.

Involved parties therefore need to be awakened to the need to share current costs, so as to diminish them for any one party, as well as to the need to avoid future costs for all.

Demarcation and autonomy policies impose restrictions on parties on both sides of the borders and both sides of the governance relationship. Unification efforts of divided states were not surrenders but bailouts, political or economic. Conflicts in normally cooperative relations, including trade, are averted when the costs of cooperation can be shared rather than allocated unevenly. Much of the debate over preventive environmental measures against global natural disasters has centered on the way costs can be distributed equitably, without which preventive measures cannot find support; the debate mirrors, mutatis mutandis, the same concerns in preventing global security disasters. In building nonproliferation and chemical weapons regimes, the nuclear powers imposed self-restraint as an inducement to the restraint of nonnuclear powers, and when they did not, the regime-building efforts faltered.

The fourth condition is an opportunity for *new benefits* through prevention. Despite the strength of the prospect theory literature, already referred to, prevention of losses has not proved to be enough to motivate preventive negotiations on numerous issues; there must be an alternate pull factor, an opportunity to benefit from the outcome of prevention. Preventive diplomacy can create prosperity, not just avoid losses. Such benefits impel action, although as prospect theory does indicate, they must have a higher level of certainty than protection against losses. Preventive action is most likely to be mobilized by special interests who see a chance to make a profit from the new situation.

Preventive action is motivated by a change in stakes, when parties see an occasion for beneficial cooperation instead of zero-sum conflict. Thus, awareness of the ozone threat and measures to prevent it sharpened most notably when chemical companies saw in the threat an opportunity to sell replacement chemicals, where before they had seen preventive measures as a threat to their current sales. Divided states united when either incumbent leaders, as in Yemen, or alternative leaders, as in Germany, saw an opportunity for better fortunes in unity as their divided base faced collapse; they saw a chance not just to jump from a sinking ship but to board a seaworthy one. Long-festering boundary disputes come to settlement not only when the danger of ongoing disruption becomes evident to the parties but also when some new good— such as mineral deposits or grazing areas or simply regional development—is discovered whose exploitation is not possible as long as the dispute hangs over the parties, as occurred in the Peru-Ecuador, Mali-Mauritania, and Egypt-Sudan border disputes.

The fifth condition is supportive *domestic pressure*. The domestic base of preventive diplomacy is involved in both the challenge and the response. The relevant public has to join in—or even precede—official awareness of the coming cost and has to support the current costs of preventing it. If the public is not convinced that a danger is looming, it will not condone the efforts necessary to stave it off. There are a number of side implications of this awareness. The public must be convinced that it is implicated in the danger to be prevented, that, in cause or effect, the danger is not someone else's problem. Usually, the supportive reaction comes not from a broadly undifferentiated public but from a "lumpy" public composed of ideologically motivated consciousness-raising groups and payoff-motivated interest groups, the latter particularly susceptible to the opportunity for benefit in a preventive solution. Public interest and private interest groups make strange bedfellows, but support from both is needed to face future, not-yet-occurring dangers. Their marriage is facilitated when the worsening situation and therefore the required cost sharing has larger implications beyond the case at hand, so that generalized measures need to be undertaken and negotiations need to deal with causes and consequences in generic terms.

The need for public support also relates to the composition of the leadership group. Many studies have emphasized—as in any kind of conflict management—the need for a "centrist moderate coalition," broadly based in the various interest groups, open to the attitudes and calculations involved in preventive action, and committed to sidelining hard-liners who could use confrontation to reinforce their position. In many types of dangers, an additional motivation to prevention is to avoid giving extremists an issue that could be used as a distraction in internal politics. Rather than leaving perceptions and awareness on a subjective level, the matter of internal support coalitions places preventive diplomacy on the more objective level of interelite politics. Polarized extremist groups make war or eventually peace but rarely undertake farsighted preventive action.

These elements of public and elite support are evident in the experience of various issue areas. Public support has been a crucial ingredient that has paced the negotiations to prevent both security and natural disasters; it was courted and generated when flagging, and it sometimes got ahead of official actions to lead the efforts. Leaders seeking to make long-range accommodations in their own disputes over territorial or population aspects of sovereignty or third parties seeking involvement in others' sovereignty disputes have been reined in when they got too far ahead of popular support for their action. The existence of a moderate centrist coalition has been the crucial variable in highly distributive situations revolving around sovereignty issues such as state disintegration and unification and ethnic and territorial conflicts. To be sure, leaders involved in preventive démarches need to pull popular and leadership support around them, but they also need to some extent to be pushed by a rising popular demand for action, as a precondition, in a very interactive relationship between leaders and followers.

The final condition is a *galvanizing event,* positive or negative, that can work up the ladder to improve the other broader objective elements. Like Oscar

Wilde's hanging, galvanizing events focus the mind marvelously, bringing costs and problems into perspective and building public support for leaders' action. Often, however, they run perilously close to a crisis itself, coming too late to prevent. A boundary and ethnic incident, a violent outbreak between divided or within disintegrating states, or a close brush with a global security or natural disaster are often last-minute warnings of sustained conflict if the problem is not handled, the last cry for attention before the situation turns irrevocably worse. Confirming scientific evidence, near accidents, unexpected crop failure or wildcat confrontations, and even warning declarations can all be triggers to the early awareness required to start the other conditions climbing up the ladder to preventive action.

Parties cannot deal with a future problem until it presents itself. The near-assassination of President Ronald Reagan and the permanent disablement of Jim Brady, the subway attacks of the sect in Tokyo, the terrorist assassination of Israeli athletes in Munich, the bomb in the World Trade Center, the Chernobyl or Torrey Canyon or Exxon *Valdez* disasters, and the Cuban missile crisis all brought the future dangers of uncontrolled guns, uncontrolled chemical weapons, environmental hazards, and superpower nuclear relations home in the present and sparked efforts to deal with them. Consumers enjoying their condition are unlikely to mobilize against a future threat to it until the rumble of the impending stampede is clearly heard.

Processes

Given these six structural conditions, corresponding processes can be employed by either a first party or a third party to promote preventive diplomacy negotiations. These processes are designed to bring about changes in both attitudes and the stakes themselves in order to provide early awareness of both the impending dangers to be prevented and the alternative opportunities deriving from effective prevention. A sequence of six steps emerges from the record across issue areas.

The basic step is a cultivation of *early awareness.* The term is used as a more meaningful alternative to *early warning,* which has become a popular but misleading road sign on the path to prevention (George and Holl 1997). Early warnings abound in any issue area where prevention could be involved (Jentleson 2000). The problem is not the scarcity of timely indicators but the lack of looking, the absence of a political culture that favors pre-emptive, proactive analysis and problem-solving. Early awareness therefore means a combination of "looking" and "seeing," a willingness to look ahead for distant problems and an ability to identify the warning signals that are available. Early awareness also involves an analytical understanding of the possibility of prevention, an awareness that not only is a problem looming but also that something can be done about it. As in any negotiation, diagnosis is the beginning of action (Zartman and Berman 1982).

Ultimately, awareness and prevention may well be a cultural matter, with some societies more apt to look to the future and more open to the notion that something can be done about it than others. U.S. society is torn between the two notions but is more prepared to take on the future than are more traditional societies imbued with fatalism. In popular culture, maxims such as "an ounce of prevention is worth a pound of cure," "a stitch in time saves nine," "better safe than sorry," "forewarned is forearmed," and "plan ahead" vie with "never trouble 'til trouble troubles you," "don't go looking for trouble," "sufficient unto the day is the evil thereof," "let sleeping dogs lie," and a recent addition, "if it ain't broke, don't fix it."[1] It is this ambivalence that is probably the most basic expression of the difficulties that preventive action runs into.

The next step is the elimination or at least reduction of *uncertainties*. Awareness is encouraged by a shift from certainty of no-danger to uncertainty; preventive negotiation solutions need to convert that uncertainty back again to certainty of no-danger under newly preventive conditions (Kahneman and Tversky 1995). The first shift is accomplished by gaining information on the current and impending situation and analyzing the dangers inherent in it, as discussed. The second is created by taking adequate measures to deal with the problem of conflict, removing its causes, allaying its effects, limiting the chance of accidents or motivated incidents, and replacing its dangerous dynamic with a more beneficial one. The need to reduce uncertainties underscores the importance of regime building, as James Goodby and Mark Anstey have noted, enhancing predictability through rules.

The third step in prevention is the *reframing* of the problem in such a way that those involved can see a positive-sum outcome to the preventive efforts. This means removing or softening the distributive nature or perception of the problem and converting it into an integrative problem. Or, if the problem is indeed basically distributive, it means seeking an accepted notion of justice to govern the allocation of outcomes. These are the standard components of reframing an integrative perception of a conflict (Tversky and Kahneman 1981; Zartman and Berman 1982; Bazerman and Neale 1992; Pruitt and Carnevale 1993; Spector 1994), but they are of special importance when costs and trade-offs take place over time, as in preventive negotiations. Thus, reframing is the key to the continuing process and a natural extension of the first step, awareness of the problem-solving possibilities. Indeed, it is also the key to the supportive mood that is crucial in underlying the subsequent efforts, one that continually keeps hope alive for a peaceful and beneficial solution.

At the same time and in the same process, as a fourth step, first and third parties need to build home *constituencies* within their target partners and nourish the home support that must already exist within their own polities. This cannot be an effort separate from the other steps, since, as noted, it is interdependent with the sorts of solutions being worked out in the preventive negotiations. If the issue is large enough, it may even involve efforts to keep a moderate centrist coalition in place, by providing benefits and addressing appeals to the support groups of the coalition and helping isolate the extremist opposition. The use of information across national boundaries becomes an important aspect of preventive activity.

The fifth step involves the development of an attractive and balanced *package* of costs and opportunities, across several dimensions. As the objective characteristics have indicated, present costs need to be lower than discounted future costs, and they need to be equitably distributed. In addition, there should be up-front opportunities for benefits to outweigh both present and future costs and to attract clusters of support among public and leadership groups. The same reasoning extends to the control elements of the agreement, by building in sanctions for noncompliance and benefits for compliance with its future provisions (Victor, Raustiala, and Skolnikoff 1998). The distribution of costs and opportunities needs to discriminate between adhering and nonadhering members of the affected community, so that free riding is discouraged and, equally explicitly, participation is rewarded. This may even mean that already convinced first or third parties may need to provide side payments or sweeteners in addition to the otherwise available benefits for second-party participation so that the initiators may be able to enjoy the benefits of a preventive agreement. Awareness and participation need their reward, and, as coalition theory indicates (Riker 1962; Dupont 1994; Brams, Dougherty, and Weidner 1994), late awareness may require greater encouragement from the early joiners.

The final step is the creation or refinement of an appropriate *regime* to provide continuing prevention of the problem. Farsighted policy-making can deal preemptively with conflict in two ways, anticipating the consequences either of a specific situation or of a general type of situation. The first involves specific calculations and specific solutions, negotiating to prevent a particular conflict from breaking out or escalating; the second involves generic solutions and mechanisms to remove uncertainties, both in cost-benefit calculations and in solutions, negotiating to set up regimes to handle difficulties inherent in a category of problems that could lead them into conflict and violence. Each seeks to replace the current, dangerous course of events with an assured, alternative outcome, attaching negative payoffs to the former to make it less inviting and positive payoffs and certainties to the alternative to make it more attractive.

But the first course is not effective as prevention until it has been generalized to handle the possibility of other such problems occurring in the future (Hasenclever, Mayer, and Rittberger 1997). In some issue areas, the number of cases is small and idiosyncratic enough that regimes will take the shape of informal learning rather than formal instruments; such is the case in regard to the three divided states discussed in chapter 5. Even where the number of cases is larger, the regime may remain on the level of implicit understandings on norms, practices, experiences, and expectations rather than rules and conventions; such is the case in regard to boundary, territorial, ethnic, or disintegration conflicts, where the limitations of sovereignty work strongly against broad codified agreements. But in most cases, the problem is not prevented until formal regimes have been established through conventions, which are then continually reviewed and revised to make sure that they cover the problem (Spector, Sjöstedt, and Zartman in press). In the light of the previous discussion, regimes are important not only in terms of preventing future recurrences but also as mechanisms for formalizing the balance of costs and benefits for prevention and compliance that make the negotiated agreement possible. There is no need here to repeat the literature of regime formation; I would merely emphasize that preventive negotiations necessarily join that process in their ongoing effort to handle their problem.

Negotiation

Lots of conflicts have been prevented, more than can ever be counted (because there is no methodology for counting things that have not happened). Many of these have been prevented specifically by negotiation, in a number of issue areas. Their lessons can be played back to the practice of negotiation, in order to improve its exercise. Although each issue area has its own characteristics, there are common threads that can be useful across issues.

Preventive negotiations focus on restructuring *stakes*, since it is easier to change stakes than to change attitudes and since a change in stakes facilitates a change in attitudes. The key to bringing parties to a preventive outcome— either by one of the parties in a conflict with another, by one among many parties in a conflict against nature, or by a third party—is the ability to bring them to revise their view of what is involved in the conflict. There is no a priori basis to indicate whether side payments, reframing, or trade-offs are preferable or appropriate as a means of stake handling, although, as Fen Osler Hampson suggests, it might be useful to look first at trade-offs and side payments for coordination disputes (where there are multiple equilibriums), trade-offs and reframing for public goods and externality (public bads) disputes, and any of the above for distributional disputes.

Conceiving of power as an added value (negative or positive) joined to available outcomes allows the negotiator to think of ways to make alternatives more or less attractive (Zartman and Rubin 2000). Both attractive incentives and dissuasive consequences can be highlighted as adjuncts or alternatives to either ending or continuing the conflict, respectively. For example, if parties see that jointly achieved prosperity or economic development is preferable to a boundary, territorial, or state-division conflict or that continued progress in talks to end ethnic conflict is the alternative to avoiding a worse outcome, preventive negotiations can move ahead. In many negotiations, one party often breaks and gesticulates or worse in order to test the alternative or brandish it before the other party (Druckman 1986; Zartman 1995). Unfortunately, there is no way to brandish favorable alternatives, at least with the same effectiveness. That would seem to support the lesson of prospect theory that parties tend to avoid losses rather than to assure gains. However, issue-area experience shows that incentives are indeed more frequently effective but that they take a longer time to sink in. Parties are less often threatened than promised into cooperation, and even in the case of conflicts with nature—as in environmental prevention—it is the prospect of new benefits that clinches cooperation to avoid the impending worst.

Stake handling also involves reframing. When the present elements of the dispute can be redefined in other terms, even without new elements as incentives, negotiations to prevent conflict are facilitated. Thus, when parties can see the issue as one of usufruct rather than ownership, autonomy rather than secession, or mutual notification rather than prohibition of military exercises, the stakes are moved from being sharply distributive to only mildly distributive and possibly even integrative.

Finally, stake handling can also involve trade-offs among differently valued items, either by dividing the current stakes into two piles of different worth or by introducing new tradable stakes. Trading off environment against development to head off climate change effects, compliance against incentives to head off global warming, access against demarcation to avoid boundary problems, consultation against enlargement to prevent security alliance confrontation, and security and then aid against unification to remove divided-state tensions were all the keys to deals that prevented conflict and escalation.

Preventive negotiation fundamentally and necessarily involves *attitude* change. As noted, parties must change their views about cooperation, with their adversaries to prevent conflict between them and/or with others in the same boat to prevent conflicts with nature. No matter how the stakes are altered objectively, unless attitudes about cooperation are changed, the conflict will go on. One branch of attitude change goes back to the way stakes are viewed; the other leads to the way the other party or parties are viewed. It is striking that parties locked in the demonizing demagoguery of global security conflicts in the end (or along the way) have less trouble in seeing each other as potential cooperators in preventing global security disasters than do nonadversaries faced with global natural disasters. Obviously, the difference is the degree of certainty of the impending disaster; actors are more readily galvanized by the prospects of being fried by an atomic exchange than by an ozone deficiency.

Finally, the process of preventive diplomacy has its special nature among the *tactics* of negotiation. Preventive negotiations are integrative negotiations par excellence. The absence of this characteristic is the key to failure. Unlike other negotiations, preventive diplomacy does not respond to ripeness. By its nature, it is action before the problem calls for it. As a result, in the absence of urgency, it has to create its own motivation. It must build a disposition to negotiate out of the push factor of early awareness and the pull factor of future gain. Both are difficult to achieve, which in itself explains the rarity of effective prevention. Early awareness requires a receptivity to warnings and a willingness to make a place among present fires for future smoke. But allaying and redistributing future costs is not enough. Measures to do so must also carry with them an opportunity for gain to offset present and opportunity costs. Future trade-offs under uncertainty are among the hardest to make, yet in the end, preventive diplomacy must depend on the provision of early gains if it is to galvanize action to avoid later costs.

Notes

1. Note that in the latter list, the first three expressions come from fatalistic or traditionalistic strands in U.S. culture, Negro spirituals, and Judaic tradition.

References

Baker, Pauline, and A. Weller. 1998. *An Analytical Model of Internal Conflict and State Collapse.* Washington, D.C.: Fund for Peace.

Bartos, Otomar. 1987. "How Predictable Are Negotiations?" In *The 50% Solution,* ed. I. William Zartman. New Haven: Yale University Press.

Bauwens, W., and L. Reychler, eds. 1994. *The Art of Conflict Prevention.* London: Brassey's.

Bazerman, Max, and M. Neale. 1992. *Negotiating Rationally.* New York: Free Press.

Boutros-Ghali, Boutros. 1992. *An Agenda for Peace.* New York: United Nations.

———. 1995. *An Agenda for Peace,* rev. ed. New York: United Nations.

Brams, Steven, Ann Dougherty, and Matthew Weidner. 1994. "Game Theory." In *International Multilateral Negotiation,* ed. I. William Zartman. San Francisco: Jossey-Bass.

Chasek, Pamela. 2000. *Environmental Negotiations.* Boulder: Westview.

Clavel, Jean-Janiel. 1991. *De la négociation multilatérale.* Brussels: Bruylant.

Conybeare, J. 1987. *Trade Wars.* New York: Columbia University Press.

Cross, John. 1969. *The Economics of Bargaining.* New York: Basic.

Davies, John, and Ted Gurr, eds. 1999. *Preventive Measures: Building Risk Assessment and Early Warning Systems.* Boulder: Westview.

Deng, Francis, et al. 1997. *Sovereignty as Responsibility.* Washington, D.C.: Brookings.

Druckman, Daniel. 1986. "Stages, Turning Points and Crises." *Journal of Conflict Resolution* 30, no. 2: 327–60.

Dupont, Christophe. 1994. "Coalition Theory." In *International Multilateral Negotiation,* ed. I. William Zartman. San Francisco: Jossey-Bass.

George, Alexander, and Jane Holl. 1997. *The Warning-Response Problem and Missed Opportunities in Preventive Diplomacy.* New York: Carnegie Commission on Preventing Conflict.

Gurr, Ted, et al. 1994. "Special Issue on State Collapse and Early Warning." *Journal of Ethno-Development* 4, no. 1.

Hasenclever, Claus, Peter Mayer, and Volker Rittberger. 1997. *International Regimes.* New York: Cambridge University Press.

Hopmann, P. Terrence. 1996. *The Negotiation Process and the Resolution of International Conflicts.* Columbia: University of South Carolina Press.

Jentleson, Bruce. 2000. *Opportunities Seized, Opportunities Missed.* Lanham, Md.: Rowman & Littlefield.

Kahneman, Daniel, and Amos Tversky. 1979. "Prospect Theory: An Analysis of Decisions Under Risk." *Econometrics* 47, no. 2: 263–91.

———. 1995. "Conflict Resolution: Cognitive Perspective." In *Barriers to Conflict Resolution,* ed. Robert Mnookian and Kenneth Arrow. New York: Norton.

Kahneman, Daniel, Paul Slovic, and Amos Tversky, eds. 1982. *Judgment Under Uncertainty.* New York: Cambridge University Press.

Karrass, Chester. 1970. *The Negotiating Game.* New York: World.

Keohane, Robert, and Joseph Nye. 1989. *Interdependence and International Politics.* Boston: Little, Brown.

Kressel, Kenneth, and Dean G. Pruitt, eds. 1989. *Mediation Research.* San Francisco: Jossey-Bass.

Lax, David, and James Sebenius. 1986. *The Manager as Negotiator.* New York: Free Press.

Nierenberg, Gerard. 1973. *Fundamentals of Negotiating.* New York: Hawthorne.

Petty, R. E., and J. T. Cacioppo. 1981. *Attitudes and Persuasion.* Dubuque, Iowa: Brown.

Pruitt, Dean G., and Peter J. Carnevale. 1993. *Negotiation in Social Conflict.* Pacific Grove, Calif.: Brooks/Cole.

Raiffa, Howard. 1968. *Decision Analysis.* Reading, Mass.: Addison-Wesley.

Riker, William. 1962. *The Theory of Political Coalitions.* New Haven: Yale University Press.

Rubin, Jeffrey Z., Dean G. Pruitt, and Sunghee Kim. 1994. *Social Conflict.* New York: Mc-Graw-Hill.

Rupesinghe, Jumar, and M. Kuroda, eds. 1992. *Early Warning and Conflict Resolution.* New York: St. Martin's.

Sfez, Lucien. 1973. *Critique de la décision.* Paris: Colin.

Smoke, Paul. 1977. *War.* Cambridge, Mass.: Harvard University Press.

Snyder, Glenn, and Paul Diesing. 1977. *Conflict Among Nations.* Princeton: Princeton University Press.

Spector, Bertram I. 1994. "Decision Analysis." In *International Multilateral Negotiations,* ed. I. William Zartman. San Francisco: Jossey-Bass.

Spector, Bertram, Gunnar Sjöstedt, and I. William Zartman, eds. In press. *Negotiating Regimes.*

Stein, Janice, and Louis Pauly, eds. 1993. *Choosing to Cooperate.* Baltimore: Johns Hopkins University Press.

Taylor, Michael. 1987. *The Possibility of Cooperation.* New York: Cambridge University Press.

Touval, Saadia, and I. William Zartman, eds. 1985. *International Mediation in Theory and Practice.* Boulder: Westview.

Tversky, Amos, and Daniel Kahneman. 1981. "The Framing of Decisions and the Rationality of Choice." *Science* 211: 453–58.

Verstegen, Suzanne. 1999. *Conflict Prognostication.* The Hague: Netherlands Institute for International Relations Clingendael.

Victor, David, Kal Raustiala, and Eugene Skolnikoff, eds. 1998. *The Implementation and Effectiveness of International Environmental Commitments.* Cambridge, Mass.: MIT Press.

Walton, Richard, and Robert McKersie. 1965. *A Behavioral Theory of Labor Negotiations.* New York: McGraw-Hill.

Zartman, I. William. 1983. "The Strategy of Preventive Diplomacy in Third World Conflicts." In *Managing US-Soviet Rivalry,* ed. Alexander George. Boulder: Westview.

———. 1989. *Ripe for Resolution.* New York: Oxford University Press.

———. 1995. "Negotiating the South African Conflict." In *Elusive Peace: Negotiating an End to Internal Wars,* ed. I. William Zartman. Washington, D.C.: Brookings.

———. 1997. "The Structuralist Dilemma in Negotiation." In *Research on Negotiation in Organizations,* vol. 6, ed. Roy Lewicki et al. Greenwich, Conn.: JAI Press.

———. 1998. "The Toughness Dilemma." Report to the International Studies Association annual meeting.

———. 1999. "Ripeness Revisited." In *Conflict Resolution,* ed. Alexander George and Paul Stern. Washington, D.C.: National Academy of Sciences.

Zartman, I. William, and Maureen Berman. 1982. *The Practical Negotiator.* New Haven: Yale University Press.

Zartman, I. William, and Saadia Touval. 1996. "International Mediation in the Post–Cold War Era." In *Managing Global Chaos,* ed. Chester Crocker, Fen Hampson, and Pamela Aall. Washington, D.C.: U.S. Institute of Peace.

Zartman, I. William, ed. 1978. *The Negotiation Process.* Newbury Park, Calif.: Sage.

Zartman, I. William, and Guy Olivier Faure, eds. 2000. *Escalation and Negotiation.* Laxenburg, Austria: International Institute for Applied Systems Analysis.

Zartman, I. William, and Jeffrey Z. Rubin, eds. 2000. *Power and Negotiation.* Ann Arbor: University of Michigan Press.

Appendix

A Summary of Key Propositions Emerging from
Considerations of Conflict Prevention and Labor Relations Systems

Phase 1: Changing Conditions: Systemic Conflict and Instability

- Changing conditions give rise to new stakeholders and *shifts in stakeholder strengths* within societies.
- If a stakeholder's interests are not met within the existing frame of a system and if the stakeholder has no participative influence within the system, the stakeholder's energies are likely to be directed at *disrupting the status quo*, quite often with stated objectives of radically restructuring the entire system.
- *Existing powerholders resist* such objectives through a mix of coercive and co-optive tactics, expressed through reforms designed to change but not fundamentally reconfigure relations (i.e., to change perceptions of the system but to retain control).
- At this point, the *conflict is* over *the design or shape of the system itself:*

  —Parties perceive greater potential benefits in eliminating others' claims than in accommodating them;
  —Perceptions of others' intentions of elimination foster hostile attitudes;
  —Coercive tactics are employed to eliminate claims of others to participate in system design or control.

- To the extent that powerholders or claimants perceive that a straight "win" in the contest is possible or that defeat is preferable to compromise (matters of honor), *conflict can be expected to continue and to escalate.*

Phase 2: Conditions and Choices Underpinning the Design of Conflict-Regulation and Conflict-Prevention Structures and Process

- Even when such perceptions and attitudes exist, *pragmatism* founded in building, strengthening, and sustaining parties' own organizational capacities to meet primary goals and needs is likely to be evident among all parties—translating into short-term pacting or accommodation even as long-term goals of mutual elimination are adhered to.
- Steadily or suddenly, parties *jointly recognize power relativities* in the conflict are such that:

  —Although they cannot be entirely defeated, neither can they defeat the other party,
  —Continuation of the conflict in a confrontation mode will be costly and inhibit achievement of own primary objectives and needs,
  —Own interests might be best secured by accommodating the interests of other stakeholders,
  —Others' interests must be secured sufficiently to transform a desire to eliminate parties' own interests into a willingness to participate in and preserve a system.

- Parties *extend participative legitimacy* to each other in the realm of system redesign directed at accommodation of interests—the first step in transforming conflicts over systems into conflicts within systems.
- Parties actively design and participate in forums and processes centered in preventing, limiting, containing, and regulating conflict, often involving ongoing negotiation and problem-solving processes rather than ad hoc exchanges—*negotiation is institutionalized.*
- Parties *limit demands* on each other in order to preserve the functionality of the wider system (national versus sectional interests).
- Parties *limit use of pressure tactics* in order to pursue demands to test the boundaries of possibility and commitment to positions rather than eliminate others.
- Self-constraint is rooted in a perception that own interests are best served through *system maintenance* rather than system destruction.
- Parties not only share such perceptions and beliefs but also have the organizational *capacity* to deliver to system maintenance.
- Steadily, *relations become transformed* from winning issues to securing relationships.
- The transformation of perceptions and attitudes is *premised on conditions* that are conducive to all stakeholders that perceive the rewards of conflict prevention, reduction, and containment as more rewarding than conflict escalation.
- The conflict is now *within the system rather than over the system.*

Phase 3: Conditions and Choices Recycling Conflicts *Within* Systems into Conflicts *Over* Systems:

- *Shifts in conditions* are such that:

    —One or more parties perceive that meeting others' needs will jeopardize their own interests or survival,

    —One or more parties perceive that there is a greater advantage in obstructing others' interests than in accommodating them,

    —One or more parties' capacity for leverage in pursuing its interests is weakened,

    —One or more parties' capacity to deliver to arrangements designed for joint-benefit purposes is weakened.

- *Perceived values of institutions of conflict prevention and regulation are diminished* and may even translate into perceptions that escalated conflicts are necessary to terminate relations or redesign the system as a whole, as well as participation and influence within it.
- At this point, there is a potential return to *conflict over a system*, but options are open for using established relations of joint endeavor as a *platform for managing a way* through a period of new systemic uncertainty.

Index

About the Contributors

Mark Anstey is a professor and the director of the Labor Institute at the University of Port Elizabeth in South Africa.

Anatole Ayissi is a professor and director of at the International Relations Institute of Cameroon.

Sukyong Choi is a professor of political science at Chungnam National University in Taejon, Korea.

James Goodby was the former U.S. ambassador serving in arms control negotiations and is a visiting professor at Stanford University.

Fen Osler Hampson is a professor of international affairs at the Norman Patterson School of International Affairs at Carleton University in Canada.

P. Terrence Hopmann is a professor of political science and a member of the Watson Institute for International Studies at Brown University.

Victor Kremenyuk is the deputy director of the U.S.-Canada Institute of the Russian Academy of Sciences and a member of the Steering Committee of the Processes of the International Negotiation (PIN) Program of the International Institute for Applied Systems Analysis (IIASA).

The late *Winfried Lang* was a professor of international law at the University of Vienna and the Austrian ambassador to Belgium.

Kjell-Åke Nordquist is a professor in the Peace Studies Program at the University of Uppsala.

Timothy Sisk is an associate professor at the Graduate School of International Studies at the University of Denver.

Gunnar Sjöstedt is a research associate at the Swedish Institute for International Affairs and a member of the Steering Committee of the Processes of the International Negotiation (PIN) Program of the International Institute for Applied Systems Analysis (IIASA).

Bertram Spector is the director of the Center for Negotiation Analysis in Washington and the former project leader for the Processes of International Negotiation (PIN) Program at the International Institute for Applied Systems Analysis (IIASA) in Laxenburg, Austria.

I. William Zartman is the director of the Conflict Management Program at the Nitze School of Advanced International Studies of the Johns Hopkins University in Washington and the author of a number of books on negotiation and conflict management. He is a member of the advisory group to the Carnegie Commission on Preventing Deadly Conflict and a member of the Steering Committee of the Processes of the International Negotiation (PIN) Program of the International Institute for Applied Systems Analysis (IIASA).